ANTIGONE, INT.

Sophocles' *Antigone* is a touchstone in der.
theory, possibly the most commented-up
philosophy and political theory. From Hei   ᵒⁿ ᵗᵒ
Jacques Derrida, Judith Butler, Peter Euben   ᴍᴏnhouse, Lee
Edelman, Joan Copjec, Slavoj Žižek, and many more, interpreters
turn to the play for instruction regarding issues such as civil disobedience, the clash between public and private, the hubris of sovereignty,
and the politics of psychoanalysis, gender, sexuality, and mourning.
Bonnie Honig's rereading of the play thus intervenes in a host of
literatures and unsettles many of their governing assumptions.

References to the play and its heroine also circulate in contemporary
political culture, featuring in discussions of Argentina's Madres of the
Plaza, West Germany's response to the Baader-Meinhof group as
depicted in the 1978 film *Germany in Autumn*, Butler's theorization
of "precarious life," and recent work by others following 9/11 in
political theory and cultural studies on mourning as a resource for a
politics that rejects sovereignty. Analyzing the power of Antigone in
these political, cultural, and theoretical contexts, Honig explores what
she calls the "Antigone-effect," which moves those who enlist the play
from an activist politics that quests for sovereign power into a lamentational politics that bemoans the excesses of sovereign power.

However, Honig argues, this effect can be overcome by way of a
new reading of the *Antigone*. Read in historical context, and in
dialogue with contemporary political, literary, feminist, and queer
theory, Sophocles' great tragedy offers something more than a model
for resistance politics or a mortalist humanism of "equal dignity in
death." Instead, Honig writes on behalf of an agonistic humanism: a
politics of counter-sovereignty and solidarity which emphasizes
equality in life.

BONNIE HONIG is Nancy Duke Lewis Professor of Modern Culture
and Media and Political Science at Brown University. She was
formerly Sarah Rebecca Roland Professor in Political Science at
Northwestern University and Research Professor at the American
Bar Foundation, Chicago. She is an award-winning author whose
work has been translated into numerous languages and is read by a
wide interdisciplinary audience composed of scholars and researchers
in political theory, philosophy, classics, gender studies, cultural studies, American studies, comparative literature, critical theory, media
studies, law, and international relations.

ANTIGONE, INTERRUPTED

BONNIE HONIG

There are dangers, after Stalin, in 'identifying Creon as a democratic ~~tyrant~~ ~~type~~ ~~sort~~ of tyrant, and indeed Honig occasionally tends towards Soviet-era programmatic positivism, ~~esp.~~ when she refers to the "so-called fact of mortality", and esp. when she gives us the example of —

— if only the grief-stricken would keep their political wits about them'.* Only a critic determined to make Greek literature fit-in with their own preformed agenda would tell us that Achilles" mourns too long" for Patroclus. Who is can reason the need? What is the correct length of time allowable for grief? These questions are central to Honig's reading of Antigone, and she feels she must answer them firmly.

CAMBRIDGE
UNIVERSITY PRESS

* These are the moments that Honig sounds most like Brecht — and it should be noted that, half a century after his death, Brecht's theories aren't doing nearly as well as his plays.

CAMBRIDGE UNIVERSITY PRESS

Cambridge, New York, Melbourne, Madrid, Cape Town, Singapore,
São Paulo, Delhi, Mexico City

Cambridge University Press
The Edinburgh Building, Cambridge CB2 8RU, UK

Published in the United States of America by Cambridge University Press, New York

www.cambridge.org
Information on this title: www.cambridge.org/9781107668157

First published 2013

Printed and bound in the United Kingdom by the MPG Books Group

A catalogue record for this publication is available from the British Library

Library of Congress Cataloguing-in-Publication data
Honig, Bonnie.
Antigone, interrupted / Bonnie Honig.
pages   cm
ISBN 978-1-107-03697-0 (Hardback) – ISBN 978-1-107-66815-7 (Paperback)
1. Political science.   2. Political science–Philosophy.   I. Title.
JA71.H619 2013
320.01–dc23
2012038176

ISBN 978-1-107-03697-0 Hardback
ISBN 978-1-107-66815-7 Paperback

For Naomi, whose interruptions have taught me more than I can say . . .

If we wish to do justice to the conflicts that surround us and lead to one tragedy after another, we can do *no better* than to keep the example of *Antigone* constantly in mind.

James Tully

[W]e are, in our ethical situation, more like human beings in antiquity than any Western people have been in the meantime.

Bernard Williams

It is not a good time for *Antigone*.

German television executive in *Germany in Autumn*

Contents

Preface

It is always possible to give up the search for a meaning [and] . . . say
that established facts need no further explanation.

Nicole Loraux

At my grandmother's funeral, I noticed that my grandmother and my
grandfather who predeceased her were buried in plots located in the
Socialist Bünd section of the Jewish cemetery in Montreal.

"Grandpa's buried in the Bünd section?" I asked my mother.

"No, he isn't," she replied.

"But look; there's the sign," I showed her. "It says the Bünd on it."

"Oh, that. That's nothing."

"What do you mean 'That's nothing'? If he is buried in the Bünd
section that must mean something. Was Grandpa a member of the Bünd?"
(My questions bore the mark of yearning. If my grandfather had been in
the Bünd then perhaps I was a member of some oppositional leftist family
and not in fact the child of middle-class, upwardly mobile post-war
European immigrants to Canada.)

My mother would have none of it. "No, Grandpa was *not* a member of
the Bünd. Don't be silly."

"Then *why* is he buried in the Bünd section? There must be a reason,"
I asked.

"There *is* no reason. He just bought the plots from them, that's all."

"But why? Why would he buy from them if he was not a member?"
I persisted. "That doesn't make any sense."

"Yes, it does. They were cheaper," she said. "The Bünd sold them all
together, and could make them available at a good price. Grandpa had just
come to Canada and he did not have a lot of money so he bought from
them. That's all."

And then, as I began again to press her further, my mother voiced a
complaint I had heard before in a voice fatigued by the need to reprise it

yet again: "It doesn't *mean* anything, Bonnie. You always think there is more to things than there is."

A fascination with an excess or dearth of meaning may be a sign of madness. Susanna Kaysen notes in her memoir, *Girl, Interrupted* (1993), that one early sign that all was not well with her was her sense of being overtaken by patterns (*patterns?* but maybe she means, in scrambled form, her parents/paternals): "all patterns seemed to contain potential representations, which in a dizzying array would flicker to life. That could be . . . a forest, a flock of birds, my second grade class picture. Well, it wasn't – it was a rug, or whatever it was, but my glimpses of other things it might be were exhausting. Reality was getting too dense" (1993: 41). At the same time, for the same reason in effect, reality was losing some of its density: "When I looked at someone's face, I often did not maintain an unbroken connection to the concept of a face. Once you start parsing a face, it's a peculiar item: squishy, pointy, with lots of air vents and wet spots. This was the reverse of my problem with patterns. Instead of seeing too much meaning, I didn't see any meaning" (1993: 41).

Buried in detail, Kaysen saw too much or too little: unable to see the forest for the trees, and unable to see the trees for the forest.[1] Gripped by the patterns of a rug yet unable to discern the face of the other, Kaysen seems to confuse two different economies, as well: that of singularity (of the face) with that of goods (carpets). Kaysen was out of order.

Finding meaning in the right place and in the right amount is as good a definition of sanity as any. The same goes for lamentation and mourning. These are supposed to manifest just the right amount of attachment to the lost loved one: not too much lest we slide into melancholy, not too little or we risk infidelity to those we loved and lost.

Of course poetry, art, religion, philosophy, and political theory all turn on getting this balance wrong, on resetting it somehow. These arts and disciplines all seek to unbalance us because, out of balance, we might find deeper truths than those we live by every day.[2] Through hyperbole, fable, repetition, metaphor, parable, and more, the scales of the familiar are reset. Art may invite us to lament more than religion or convention tell us we should. Song may enable us to experience sadness more profoundly than mere weeping. A fable may reorient us to see a rug not as a mere floor covering nor even as a unique Persian handicraft but rather as a magic carpet.[3] With the guidance of critical theory, an animal can move from being a bearer of weight for man, to a source of meat in an industrial agricultural economy, to a sign of sacredness, to a creature indifferent to human needs and vulnerable to pain. A person possessed of dignity and individuality can become a type for the social scientist, a number for a store clerk, an abject thing for a prison guard, a precious source of inspiration for the poet, a loved one for anyone at all.

Resetting the balance is not the same as becoming unbalanced, however, and the latter is what happens to Kaysen; her story is one of sliding from surfeits of meaning into madness, it is a tale of balance lost, but then regained. Two years after (un)wittingly committing herself to an institution for the mentally ill, Kaysen decides to marry and is released from institutional care.[4] In the film version of the book, release comes by way of a different dramatic device, not marriage but intervention. An uncharacteristically kind nurse takes Kaysen aside and talks some sense into the teenage girl, suggesting she is not really sick but rather self-indulgent. The nurse urges the girl to pick herself up, stop playing with madness, and go home to live her life, a life that is, the nurse emphasizes, worth living.[5] Kaysen is called back to herself by this intervention into what is cast as her faux-suffering (but this is from the perspective of her later "recovery"). Through an apparent act of will, Kaysen decides to be well. Released from the lure of madness, her madness interrupted just as it had earlier interrupted her, Kaysen leaves the institution. In the book version of *Girl, Interrupted* it is clear that her departure is aided by a fortuitous shift of circumstances: only a year or two after her institutionalization in the 1960s, Kaysen's resistance to responsible subjectivity, expressed by her teenage disinterest in school and her numerous boyfriends, are de-medicalized. What were once problematic alienation and promiscuity are now more accepted for a girl as adolescent underachievement and sexual liberation. Furthermore, Kaysen is vindicated when it turns out that bypassing college and supporting herself as a writer are viable life choices.[6]

If I begin *Antigone, Interrupted* with some discussion of Kaysen's book, it is not only to acknowledge this book's titular debt to hers, but also to note one reason for that debt: a slight and strange affinity between Kaysen's self-portrait and the subject of this book, another young teen who also makes unconventional choices and is said by some to flirt with madness – Sophocles' Antigone. In the case of Antigone, there will be no last minute sensible talking-to to rescue her from her path; and no saving marriage will pull her back from the brink. But, notwithstanding this significant difference, for many commentators over the centuries the one central question about Antigone is the one that precipitated the filmic Kaysen's return to normal life: if the girl's actions were mad, was she truly mad or merely self-indulgent?

Creon, Thebes' ruler, thinks the girl is mad *and* self-indulgent. His governor's perspective in this as in other matters governs receptions of the play to this day, or so I shall argue here as part of a broader effort to unsettle his lingering framing power. For Creon, Antigone's madness in defying his ban consists in unqualified attachments to the underworld and to her incestuous, destructive clan. Apparently unmoved by the prospect of marriage to Creon's son, Haemon, Antigone is overly devoted to her dead brother, Polynices, to the point where she seems indifferent to everything else including even the stability of the always vulnerable polis. Beyond reason, seemingly incapable of acknowledging and balancing plural goods, she is, as we say, unbalanced.

For Jacques Lacan, one of Antigone's many admirers, the heroine's lack of balance is striking. Her uncompromising stance is a sign of her passion, which has nothing to do with her brother, as such. The brother is simply the occasion for her expression of desire which ennobles Antigone and makes her a creature of monstrous beauty. For others, her lack of balance is a kind of self-indulgence. Most notably Jean Anouilh (1946) and more recently Jeremy Menekseoglu (2008) interpret the heroine through a chiasmus: in their versions of the play, she is not driven mad by too much love (for family or underworld). She is, rather, driven to exorbitant love by being mad.[7] In Menekseoglu's adaptation, Antigone is cast as a sort of late-modern celebrity and the Chorus are her paparazzi. Finding herself followed by a Chorus, she is delighted. Effect replaces cause as she comically infers that if she has a Chorus she must be a heroine whose story will someday be told, and she resolves to act accordingly. In both Menekseoglu's and Anouilh's adaptations of the play, the heroine is motivated less by substantive commitment or principle than by the sheer thrill of conflict and the reward of renown.[8] She is self-regarding, self-absorbed. It is not insignificant that both feature Antigone, in one scene, quite taken with her own image as she combs her hair in a mirror.

It is my aim in this book to move Antigone beyond the mirror stage.[9] I treat Antigone as a complex political actor engaged in struggle with Creon and others about the terms and sites of sovereignty in Thebes.[10] The focus is neither on her madness nor on her self-indulgence but on the political frames of reception that press us to see her that way. The focus here is on her speech acts, her historical context, and her signifying power in circulation in the twentieth and twenty-first centuries, which has no small impact on how we receive and interpret all sorts of political conflicts today. The aim is to show how the various received Antigones, whether mad, self-indulgent, passionate, or principled, fail fully to prize this protagonist's abundant political promise. The aspiration is to re-politicize this political actor or to understand her politicization differently and to do so in part by showing how she traffics in surfeits of meaning, in double and triple entendres, counter-sovereignties, lamentations that are also calls to vengeance, and raging rejections that are full of intimacy. These are her stock in trade. Attentive to them, I work through the *Antigone*'s ongoing impact on political thinking, and look for ways to rework it, in Part I, Interruption. In Part II, Conspiracy, I develop new readings of Sophocles' play. The hope is to inspire democratic theorists today seeking to theorize politics as a meaning-making practice, as action in concert on behalf of collective life, rather than as the sorts of solitary, heroic performances that may sometimes shift the plates of tectonic politics but also seem fated to rock undecidably on the border of self-indulgence and madness.

Acknowledgments

Henry Bienen got me started on this project by asking me in 2007 to contribute an essay to a special issue of *TriQuarterly Review* that he planned to edit on the topic, *The Other.* I had to say yes. He was not only a friend, he was at the time President of Northwestern University. I had a lecture on the *Antigone* I had been giving to undergraduates at Harvard and Northwestern for years and thought I might find something in that to contribute. Drafting my speculative classroom thoughts, I realized I had to do more research. There followed more than four years of reading in the political and legal history and archaeology of ancient Greece and *Antigone* scholarship in classics, political, feminist, and queer theory. The paper for Henry became two papers, then three, and before I knew it I was writing a book on *Antigone* or rather, as I often said: it was writing me.

At Northwestern, my exploration of new disciplines opened new conversations for me. Colleagues in classics and comparative literature were kind enough to respond to my new work and patient with my early errors. I began attending classics colloquia; I was even invited to participate in some. I want to thank the Classics Department for its hospitality, and also Sara Monoson, my colleague in political theory, who chaired the Classics Department for most of this time period.

Northwestern colleagues who shared work with me or generously responded to mine include: Kate Bosher, Héctor Carrillo, Nick Davis, Penny Deutscher, Mary Dietz, Steve Epstein, Peter Fenves, Jay Grossman, Marianne Hopmann, Andy Koppelman, Richard Kraut, Jeffrey Masten, Sara Monoson, Martin Mueller, Anna Parkinson, Ken Seeskin, Laurie Shannon, Viv Soni, Julia Stern, Jackie Stevens, Lars Tønder, Bob Wallace, Sam Weber, Reg Gibbons, and Will West. Cynthia Nazarian read the whole thing in penultimate draft just as I turned to the final revisions and gave me fabulous comments. I am grateful to the graduate students in political theory, and the undergraduates in my Antigone seminars, for working through the play and its contexts with me in a variety of seminars from 2008 to 2010. I also taught parts of this book as a seminar at the School of Criticism and Theory in the summer of 2010 at Cornell University. This book owes a great deal to that incomparable experience. I want to thank especially Amanda Anderson, who makes the School an intellectually demanding and fun place, and who suggested I read *Middlemarch* (promising Antigone connections, the only explicit one of which came on the second to last page of that very long and fabulous novel).

I published parts of some chapters in *Political Theory* (Chapter 4), *New Literary History* (Chapters 1 and 5), and *Arethusa* (Chapter 6). All have been radically rewritten, reconsidered, and revised for this book. I thank those journals, the Johns Hopkins University Press Sage Press, for permission to use those materials here. I presented early versions of parts of this book at places too numerous to list, in the US, Canada, the UK, Sweden, and the Netherlands, as keynotes at graduate student conferences, as memorial lectures (for Linda Singer and Ferdie Schoeman), in Philosophy Departments and political theory colloquia, at conferences in political science, classics, and the humanities, at colleges, universities, and law schools. The University of Nottingham group, CONCEPT, hosted a conference on themes related to my work in April 2011 at which I presented the final pieces of this project. I am grateful to all my audiences and hosts for their questions, archives, and film recommendations. Colleagues at other institutions who supported, inspired, and helped improve this work with comments, criticisms, and the benefit of their own research include: Seyla Benhabib, Jane Bennett, Anna Bialek, Peg Birmingham, Tina Chanter, Bill Connolly, Davina Cooper, Page duBois, Peter Euben, Rita Felski, Chris Finlay, Alan Finlayson, Jason Frank, Jill Frank, Marcie Frank, Alexander Hirsch, Steven Johnston, George Kateb, Vassilis Lambropoulous, Julia Lupton, Lida Maxwell, David McIvor, Dana Mills, Stewart Motha (who always has relevant films to recommend), Josiah Ober, David Owen, Yopi Prins, Bruce Robbins, Diego Rossello, Elizabeth Rottenberg, Eric Santner, Arlene Saxonhouse, Andrew Schaap, George Shulman, James Tully, Stephen White, and especially John Seery and Christina Tarnopolsky, who read several drafts of several chapters and gave me encouragement early and often. Conspiring at the last minute with James Martel was a pleasure. James Porter, Adam Sitze, Elizabeth Wingrove, Simon Stow, Brooke Holmes, and one or two anonymous others read the penultimate manuscript for the presses and the book is much improved as a result of their reports.

The Chicago Legal History Seminar hosted my first public presentation of work from this book at the American Bar Foundation, where I am a half-time Research Professor. At the ABF, Bob Nelson supports an environment conducive to rigorous research on law-related topics defined broadly enough to include this book. Allison Lynch and then Katy Harris provided superb staff support for this project. The ABF funds research assistance, for which I must thank, in particular, Doug Thompson, Rachel Ricci, Demetra Kasimis, Diego Rossello, Nick Dorzweiler, and Lexi Neame. Javier Burdman, Anna Terwiel, and Ella Haselswerdt worked on the project at the very end and provided fabulous support. At the ABF, Bob Nelson, Laura Beth Nielsen, Susan Shapiro, Traci Burch, Vicki Woeste, John Hagan, Terry Halliday, Carol Heimer, Jim Heckman, until recently Bryant Garth, Chris Tomlins, John Comaroff, and many others constitute a great interdisciplinary intellectual community.

In the process of writing and researching this project, I sent drafts to people whose work I was reading but whom I did not know at the time. In response to emails from a stranger, Adam Sitze, Paul Allen Miller, Richard Seaford, Yannis Stavrakakis, and Robert Fowler entered into spirited conversation with me. My contact with Fowler was enabled by Chris Brooke, who with characteristic zeal followed up a casual question in an Oxford taxi and set in motion an email chain of inquiry about Wilamowitz's time at Oxford, the answers to which Bob Fowler knew. Late in the day, Jim Porter became another important email interlocutor. I cannot overstate the pleasure of just out of the blue finding someone fun to think with and I am always grateful when it happens. Miriam Leonard was a discussant of a very early version of Chapter 4 and has since become a cherished colleague. She read several drafts of this manuscript and illuminated problems I might not otherwise have seen. This book has benefitted greatly from our conversations over the years.

One of my interests in this book is how economies – of signs or money – work or fail to and by way of what powers they are (re)instituted and maintained. Related to that theme, I owe a debt to Richard Dunn and the American Philosophical Society, which helped fund a year of leave for me in 2008–2009 in support of my last book, *Emergency Politics*. I finished that book early in the year and spent most of my leave writing this one. I think of it as the dividend, a term with which I was reacquainted over dinner with Mary Dunn at the APS Sabbatical Fellows conference in the spring of 2008.

The American Bar Foundation and Northwestern University provided matching funds to support the year of leave during which I wrote the first draft of this book. I spent that year at Oxford University's Nuffield College and the Centre for Political Ideology (CPI). Marc Stears organized a one-day conference on a very early version of this book (supported by the CPI, University College, and the Department of Politics and International Relations) and did a great deal more as well to make me feel welcome. At the conference, Marc along with Miriam Leonard, Melissa Lane, Simon Goldhill, Robin Osborne, and Lois McNay offered prepared responses to the manuscript. Throughout that year at Oxford, Mark Philp, Sunetra Gupta, Michael Freeden, Stephen Mulhall, Chris Brooke, and Josephine Quinn responded to bits of the manuscript with comments that prodded me further. I was fortunate that year as well to attend several Oxford student productions of Greek myths and tragedies.

For sharing that sabbatical year with me and supporting this book project throughout, I owe thanks as well to my family, Michael Whinston, Noah Whinston, and Naomi Honig. Noah's interest in ancient Greece preceded mine. Early on, he was so soaked in ancient Greek mythology that when his sister was born he wanted to name her "Athena." Michael, Noah, and Naomi started off a year of tragic theater (*Romeo and Juliet*, *Othello, Andromaque, Hippolytus, The Song of the Nightingale, The Bacchae* [performed in a summer-sunsetted Port Meadow], and others) when they came with me to see *The Burial at Thebes* performed as an opera at the Globe Theatre in London in the fall of 2008. Soon after, we traveled to Athens, and Noah and Naomi helped me find the Memorial to the Unknown Soldier. As I wrote, Noah reminded me – often! – of Greek myth details that eluded me. Michael watched, without complaint, all the films I rented, remarking only late in the year that all the films we had been watching seemed to be about death and burial. And Naomi saw other movies with me including, our favorite that year, the fabulous *Coraline*. Watching it in the dark of an Oxford cinema on a sunny Sunday afternoon, I laughed when out of the film suddenly burst several direct references to Greek tragedy and *Antigone* (one in a sung celebration of theatrical imagination: "You simply say / I'm in Hawaii /And you're there / You can be Antigone / Or Cher!"). Naomi came up with her own great readings of the films we saw together, while also asking often, but not too often, how the book, which she calls "my" book, was going.

This book is dedicated to Naomi.

I wrote my original lecture on *Antigone* before Naomi was born but this book would not have been what it is without my knowing her. Her family nickname is "born-without-volume-control" and it is an apt one. From her I have learned about the power and longing of sound.

Her vital force reminds me of a character in one of my favorite childhood books, John Wyndham's *The Chrysalids*. The character's name is Petra and she is born into the family of a puritanical minister whose oppressive community vigorously regulates physical normality in a post-apocalyptic world. Disfigured babies, people, animals are put to death or banished. Some children in the community discover they have telepathic powers which put them at risk because of their abnormality but these also provide the children with an undetectable alternative community they need to survive. Petra's arrival changes everything. She too has telepathic powers it turns out, but hers are an uncontrolled, blinding force that interrupts the older children's secret conversations, leaving them reeling and vulnerable to discovery (i.e., I only just now realize, Petra is *born without volume control* . . .).

As a child, reading this book over and over, I did not see what I cannot fail to see now: that Petra's *baby-sister-power* was like the semiotic breaking through the symbolic order, interrupting it to open the way to something more promising than the corrupt, cowed, or just limited everyday life to which Petra's fellow telepathic communicators resign themselves. In their dystopic context, they can only clutch at mere life, but Petra seeks more; or better, she never recognizes that dystopic world as her world. Unacquainted with resignation, she is receptive to calls from afar that sound like mere noise to her fellows, if they sound at all. Responding to sounds undetected, unresigned to what others call "reality," she is available to enter into conspiracy with others far and near – these are key elements of what I call in this book: agonistic humanism.

Introduction

The *inter* of a political *interesse* is that of an interruption or an interval. The political community is a community of interruptions, fractures, irregular and local ...

Jacques Rancière

The lifespan of man running towards death would inevitably carry everything human to ruin and destruction if it were not for the faculty of interrupting it and beginning something new, a faculty which is inherent in action like an ever-present reminder that men, though they may die, are not born in order to die but in order to begin.

Hannah Arendt

Interruption is one of the fundamental procedures constitutive of form. It extends far beyond the orbit of art. It lies at the root – to take only one example – of citation. To cite a text means to interrupt its context.

Walter Benjamin

This book is divided into two parts. In Part I, Interruption, I look at the role of Sophocles' play and its heroine in contemporary debates about agency, power, sovereignty, and sexuality. I suggest that the turn to Antigone in the latter half of the twentieth century and the first years of the twenty-first is best seen in the context of a series of turns to ethics, humanism, or maternalism, each aimed at countering certain forms of sovereignty or rationality (identified often with Oedipus). Lamenting sovereignty's excesses and the disappointments of rationalism, theorists and critics then seem to find in that very lamentation a new universalism that might take the place of these discredited contenders: whatever our differences, we are all mortal and we all lament our finitude, since the time of Antigone.[1] Thus, for them, lamentation also reassures as it steps in to take the place of the very thing whose loss we lament: universalism.

I go on to ask whether feminist and democratic theorists might rethink the rejection of sovereignty and consider devoting themselves instead to its cultivation. We might be critical of sovereignty's operations in particular contexts while still seeking to enlist the powers of sovereignty in others, for our own democratic or redistributive agendas. Analyzing some turns to Antigone, I ask whether the conventional figure of Antigone herself, much admired for her principled dissidence but also for her self-sacrifice, ultimately presses a certain impotence and resignation on her admirers as she leads them to embrace, as they think she once did, a politics of *lamentation.*

Part I's interruption of Antigone's reception history – in political theory, philosophy, feminist theory, and cultural politics – prepares the ground for a new reception, and stages my turn in Part II to an alternative reading of Sophocles' *Antigone* that might better inform and guide feminist and democratic theory. The aim is to break many theorists' fascination with rupture over the everyday, powerlessness over sovereignty, and heroic martyrdom over the seemingly dull work of maintenance, repair, and planning for possible futures.[2] My alternative reading identifies an Antigone who engages in a politics of counter-sovereignty. In place of the currently seductive politics of *lamentation*, I find in the play, read in fifth-century context and with twentieth- and twenty-first-century theory, a more robust *politics* of lamentation, in which lamentation is not "human," ethical, or maternal – tethered to the fact of finitude – but an essentially contested practice, part of an *agon* among fractious and divided systems of signification and power.[3] The issue posed by the *Antigone* (as opposed to by Antigone, the character) is not whether to lament the dead but rather how to do so, and what undergirds that question, broached repeatedly in the play, is the knowledge that lamentation stands for certain forms of life, social orders, ontologies, and histories.

The work of decaptivation and, ultimately, recaptivation to which this book is dedicated requires an immanent counter-reading of *Antigone.* This I proceed to offer in Part II, Conspiracy. Although Parts I and II can be read independently of each other and in either order, Part I's interruptions are meant to prepare the way for Part II's conspiracies, and to show why such conspiracies are important now. From the politics of *lamentation,* the focus in Part I, I turn in Part II to the *politics* of lamentation, tracking the ways in which various elites in the play can be seen to conspire with or against the new fifth-century democracy which is not the play's dramatic setting but is the context of the play's performance. Moreover, I argue that Antigone herself is a figure of conspiracy. She begins plotting in the dark with her sister and moves gradually into more open and then into more veiled confrontations with Creon. Her open confrontations, tragic, doomed, courageous, have been the focus of scholarship until now. Attending to her other mode of engagement, though, and approaching Antigone as a conspirator, we see something else, in particular, her nuanced facility with language or, as we will see, language's conspiracy with her: she whispers, nudges, and puns her way through to communicate things on stage and to her audience that go right over Creon's head. On this reading, then, she is a heroine not only of resistance and frank speech (though she tries these too) but also of the open secret, that conspiratorial form of communication whose figure is *adianoeta*.

Interruption – there are several in the play – is the other important speech act, attention to which opens the play up in new ways. Although interruption is itself a speech act (even if J. L. Austin does not discuss it), it is the one kind of speech act to which the *Antigone*'s philosophical readers have been inattentive. Why? Perhaps because interruption is an odd sort of doing, not always a sort of doing, in fact. Interruption, which aborts another's speech, may be a deliberate speech act – "stop!" or "I object!" – but sometimes interruption just happens as a side effect or by-product of other doings. Thus, it seems different from the performatives to which J. L. Austin (1962) and Jacques Derrida (1988) call our attention and it is harder to track. Is interruption any speech act that precedes or causes the cessation of another? If so, it might be entirely perlocutionary – exhausted by that trait, unlike Austin's other performatives, which carry other forces as well.

The speech act of interruption has even less content, as it were, than Eve Sedgwick's "periperformatives," which broach or dance around speech acts but are never quite uttered and in this reticence find their power (2003: chapter 2). Like periperformatives, interruption is rarely straightforward. It does not take the form of the conjugal "I promise" or "I do" (whose centrality to speech act theory Sedgwick rightly decries), though it could of course take the form of another iconic performative solicited at weddings – the rarely uttered response to: "If there is anyone who believes there is a reason why these two should not be wed, speak now or forever hold your peace."[4] That is, interruption can take the form of saying or doing almost anything at all, if the effect is that of stopping the current speaker or redirecting unfolding events, or even just trying to do so (interruption may itself be interrupted, after all; and it may, like all speech acts, succeed or fail). Interruption is, then, often a *side* effect of other kinds of speech, whereas Austin's other, exemplary speech acts generally have effects that are understood to be quite direct (indirect side effects are not ruled out but neither are they exemplary in Austin's speech act theory). This means we may miss the speech act of interruption unless we look out for it and this requires that we approach the texts we study dramaturgically. Those who approach Sophocles' play looking to identify its arguments or endorse certain of its characters' stances may miss the interruptions on which I will focus here. When political and feminist theorists approach the *Antigone* dramaturgically, we also interrupt many elements of its canonical reception history and open up new interpretative possibilities.

Set in a time and place distant from fifth-century Athens, Sophocles' *Antigone* provided a way for Athenians to work through issues that might have been too close to home to be worked out safely in an Athenian setting.[5] The play's distant setting might have allowed Sophocles to broach for public consideration issues that would otherwise be dangerous to consider. It may be for this reason that, as Jean-Pierre Vernant (1988) points out, the hero of Greek tragedy is almost always alien and from a distant past.[6]

The play begins in the aftermath of near civil war. The conflict occurs in the wake of the rule of Oedipus who ruled Thebes wisely and well but who also, with his acts of parricide and incest – unintended, unknowing, but still his acts – polluted the polity and brought it to near ruin. Oedipus' reign ends with his wife's/mother's suicide and his own exile and death. Left behind are the four children of his incestuous marriage to Jocasta: Eteocles, Polynices, Antigone, and Ismene. The sons, Eteocles and Polynices, both claim the throne after their father leaves. Some versions of the story suggest they agree to rule by turns. Eteocles takes power first but when the time comes to pass the throne to Polynices, Eteocles refuses to do so. Polynices (whose name means *many quarrels*) marries a daughter of the Argives, raises an army at Argos, and besieges his native city to claim what is his. The brothers do battle and each dies by the other's hand.

The play opens with Antigone telling her sister Ismene awful news. Ismene has not yet heard it. Their brother Eteocles has been buried with full honors by Thebes' new leader, their uncle Creon. Antigone participated in this ritual. But Creon has decreed that Polynices, their other brother, is "to be left," as Antigone puts it, "unwept, unburied, a lovely treasure for birds that scan the field and feast to their hearts' content" (28–30 [35–36]).[7] Creon, Antigone rightly perceives, has "graced one with all the rites and disgraced the other" (21–22 [27–28]).

Antigone cannot permit her brother's body to lie exposed. She feels compelled to bury him and assumes her sister will feel the same way. Thus when Ismene demurs, Antigone is shocked and angry. She insists she will act alone and that she is willing to die for her cause – eager, even, to win glory. She leaves, resolute, and in the next scene a sentry, who has been guarding the body of Polynices to prevent its burial, appears before Creon to let him know someone has violated his edict. It happened at night and so quietly that none of the guards witnessed it. Creon sends the guard back to the scene with threats of dire consequences if he and his fellows do not guard the body better and catch the culprit who violated his edict.

The sentry soon returns with Antigone who this time has been caught in the act, dusting the body in broad daylight. Creon resolves to punish her along with her sister, whom he assumes was complicit. But, queried by the Chorus, he releases Ismene. Antigone is taken away. Haemon, Creon's son and Antigone's betrothed, enters and tries to persuade his father to a more moderate course. Haemon argues that the people of Thebes support Antigone though they dare not speak up for fear of Creon. Creon rejects his son's arguments and the son leaves furious at his father's recalcitrance.

Although Creon had announced that anyone who violated his edict would be stoned to death, he now commands that Antigone be immured in a cave with enough rations to last a few days. It seems he is distancing himself from her death and is asking the gods to decide it. She is taken to the cave, outside the city, and along the way she sings her own dirge, lamenting her losses and her fate but not her actions.

Creon is then visited by the blind seer Tiresias who warns him he has gone too far in leaving a dead body unburied and putting a live person underground. Creon remains recalcitrant but, increasingly concerned after Tiresias' departure, Creon seeks the counsel of his elders, then rushes to undo his actions. He goes to bury Polynices and then to release Antigone. When he gets to the cave in which she is immured, he hears the sound of Haemon wailing inside. Antigone has hanged herself and Haemon has found her corpse. Creon enters the cave, calling his son out. Haemon tries to kill his father, fails, and then kills himself with his sword. His body spurting blood on Antigone's, he dies in her arms in an iconic marriage-to-death scene. Creon carries Haemon's body home in his arms, lamenting the loss of his son, only to find when he arrives that his wife Eurydice has also killed herself, having already heard from a messenger the news of her son's death. The play ends with Creon lamenting all his losses, begging someone to kill him, to put him out of his misery. But, as with most of his other orders, no one seems to obey and he is led away.

This brief summary of the play passes over the Chorus' role and many other important details, some of which I address in the chapters that follow. For now I want to call attention to one theme that is significant for my purposes: the several scenes in which Antigone is interrupted.

- *When Antigone tends to the body of her dead brother, Polynices, in violation of an edict against doing so, she is interrupted by her uncle Creon's guards and arrested.*
- *Later, when she sings her own dirge en route to her death, she is interrupted by Creon who mocks her and tells his guards to take her away.*
- *When the guards fail to act on Creon's orders, Antigone goes on with her dirge, but Creon interrupts her again. This time, he threatens the guards – if they do not act quickly they will be punished – and so the guards interrupt her and seal her in the cave that will be her tomb.*
- *Antigone is interrupted yet one more time when her final act, virginal suicide, scripted by her as a return to her natal family, is redirected by her betrothed and Creon's son, Haemon. When the grieving Haemon commits suicide on Antigone's corpse, he marries her in death (the messenger says: "he has won his bride at last poor boy" [1240–1241 (1370)]), and reclaims her for the conjugal family form she rejected in life.*[8]

Sophocles' *Antigone* may be the most commented-upon drama in the history of philosophy, feminism, and political theory. But the interruptions listed here play no role at all in most readings of the play. Theorists and philosophers neglect the play's *dramaturgy* to attend to the play's role in the history of philosophy and to focus on what they see as the play's *arguments* about burial, obedience, authority, sovereignty, religion, gender, and more.[9] Other elements of the play, like gesture, tone, music, voice, rhetoric, and speech act for the most part go unremarked.[10] But approaching the play with its dramaturgy in mind has, paradoxically, more to offer political theory than any "arguments" we may cull from the play. A dramaturgical approach treats the text as a performance that may succeed or fail rather than as an argument that may be true or false, right or wrong.[11] It attends to shifting contexts in the play, noting for example the significance of how information circulates, which things are said directly by one character to another, which are said within another's hearing and are overheard, which are uttered in someone's absence, and which are said over another's head. In addition, a dramaturgical approach calls attention to double entendres, puns, and jokes, most of which have escaped the notice of critics until now. Such an approach is attentive to the asymmetrical powers of different speakers, the errancy of utterance which may end up in the wrong place, the pace and trajectory of textual and historical events, the possibility of conspiracy, coded communication, irony, sarcasm, and hyperbole. All of these, as we shall see, play important roles in Sophocles' great tragedy. And through them we are shaped into certain fundamental assumptions about humanity, universality, loyalty, and more. They carry the force of argument.

Looking, in Part I, at the reception of Sophocles' play and its protagonist in contemporary feminist and queer theory, cultural politics, and political theory, and then, in Part II, reading the play in historical and contemporary contexts, I tack back and forth between classics and philosophy, feminist and political theory, reception studies, and historical, contextual approaches. I approach these literatures critically, sensitive not only to the history of philosophers' reception of the arguments in the play but also to the fact that even interpreters oriented to arguments and utterances are affected, though unavowedly so, by genred expectations. Throughout, I look at how the genred expectations of philosophers, literary critics, and theater-goers have shaped receptions of text or performance until now.

Reading *Antigone* in part through the trope of interruption, this book stages yet one more interruption: that of the received "Antigone." Since G. W. F. Hegel first canonized the play for modern philosophy in the early nineteenth century, admiring the heroine who would go on to haunt his modern state as its eternal irony, the various contending readings of Antigone that have filled the pages of political theory and philosophy books tend to identify Antigone with one of three roles:

(i)   heroic conscientious objector who on political grounds violates an unjust law, challenges a powerful sovereign, and all by herself dares speak truth to power. This is the legalists' Antigone, invariably paired, whether or not to her advantage, with Socrates, that other famous civil disobedient.

(ii) humanist lamenter of the dead, grieving sister/mother/daughter, whose cries for her brother accentuate a sense of loss said to be familiar to all humans, instancing a universal that is pointedly poised against time-bound, divisive, and merely political distinctions between friend and enemy.

(iii) monstrous creature of desire unbound by the ordinary satisfactions of everyday life and therefore willing, even passionately eager, to die for her cause.

To these I add another; or better, against these I posit another.

The Antigone that emerges here is heroic but not isolated. She is pointedly political not transcendently universal but she can still speak to us, centuries later, nonetheless. She laments, but she does so in a way that is also partisan, vengeful, not just mournful or humanist. And she is willing to die, yes, but not only for the divinely approved cause of equal burial rites nor because she exemplifies desire that, as followers of Jacques Lacan argue, appears as a monstrous attraction to death. She dies for her *atê*, her family *atê*, as classicists and Lacanians, in their different ways, have long argued. But she also, in a way perhaps less alien to contemporary readers, dies for her living sister. Antigone is impatient with Ismene and seems to scorn her, as virtually every commentator on the play has noted for centuries, but, as we shall see here, a close dramaturgical reading of the play shows that Antigone is also deeply loyal to the sister most critics think she only disdains.

This new Antigone may inspire those who see no path to action in times of confinement, constraint, or catastrophe. Herself faced with catastrophe (most of her family dead, her way of life criminalized by Creon), Antigone nonetheless *acts* politically in conditions of impossibility. When she laments, she does not only lament; she not only buries her brother against her uncle's edict, she also calls for vengeance against those who desecrated his body. She does not only resist sovereign power and martyr herself to an impossible cause, she makes a claim for sovereignty, both for herself and the form of life to which she belongs. She enters into political conspiracy against Creon, she conspires with language, and it with her (to borrow a phrase from James Martel [2011]), to solicit a public that may see things her way. These traits, I will argue here, rather than her resistance and martyrdom per se, are what democratic theorists now should be positing as exemplary. And we should be noting how Antigone does not act alone, though she is repeatedly isolated by devotees who celebrate her (or her act's) singularity. A close reading of the play shows that her actions are embedded in and enacted on behalf of forces, structures, and networks larger than the autonomous individual that modern liberals, humanists, and even radical democratic theorists tend to both love (as courageous, heroic) and berate (as anarchic or irresponsible).

The conventional Antigone – isolated and heroically transgressive, even monstrous – is also instructive. The new readings of the play developed over the course of this book show how selective were the canonical interpretations that generated the iconic tragic heroine and how symptomatic these insistent receptions were of her readers' needs, over time, for a certain kind of heroine: Christian martyr, Romantic suicide, idealized sister, heroic individual, maternal lamenter. That said, it must be owned that the new Antigone developed here may be a product of *its* moment as well. She is surely made possible by recent work in classics on women's laments and the politics of burial in the fifth century. And she is surely enabled by over forty years of feminist work which has interrogated again and again received depictions of women in the history of philosophy and politics. New habits of reading, developed during that time, question every received gendered assumption and follow the injunction always to look again and take nothing for granted. These habits play no small part in generating the new readings offered here.[12]

There is also in these pages a not insubstantial engagement with queer theory, a relatively recently developed branch of political and cultural analysis rich with implications for *Antigone* interpretation. Some queer theorists are drawn to this heroine; most are not. Those who do turn to her differ in their judgments of her. Peggy Phelan (1997) rejects Antigone as a bad model for queer politics, while Lee Edelman (2004) and Judith Butler (2000) both endorse her, albeit for diametrically different reasons. Butler, who says that Antigone is a "not quite queer heroine," sees in her a generative example of political resignification – of language and kinship done otherwise – as well as a potent symbol of human equality in death (2000: 72).[13] Edelman sees Antigone as personifying forms of adamant refusal that queer theory ought to endorse and cultivate. Finally, queer theory, in particular, has emerged in part out of a politics of contested death, mourning, and lamentation practices, dealing with the impact of AIDS on the gay community since the 1980s. In the context of AIDS and AIDS activism, we find more polarized, politicized death practices than those we get from the ethical, mortalist, or maternalist humanisms with which Antigone these days is so often affiliated. My turn to queer theory, like my turn to Antigone, is on behalf of democratic theory, the branch of political theory devoted to enhancing or rethinking equality, and to investigating the subtle and explicit workings of power, enabling and inequitable. Queer theory shares those commitments and is, like the great tragedians, also interested in exploring the possibilities of action in conditions of seeming impossibility. Queer theorists more than others attend to how the politics of lamentation slides all too easily into the lamentation of politics. Critical democratic theorists do well to enlist feminist and queer theory along with cultural critique, psychoanalysis, film and literary theory, in their quest to identify and overcome obstacles to equality.

But, some will object, most of these obstacles are material and, in current contexts of inegalitarian, neo-liberal capitalism and globalization, the reinterpretation of classical texts hardly seems the most pressing task. There is something undeniable in this. And yet, as I write this, Sophocles'

Antigone is being staged in London's National Theatre, has just finished a run in Perth, Australia, and plans for its staging are under way in Ramallah, where it will be the first play performed in a new theater school.[14] The play's various restagings are not this book's object of inquiry. When I talk about "receptions" in this book I mean for the most part to refer to theoretical and philosophical receptions, not theatrical ones. But such restagings are surely part of its occasion. For the play, still alive, is working on us, framing our views of dissidence, martyrdom, and democratic politics, the politics of burial and lamentation, the clash between public and private, and the promise and politics of a pre-, post-, and ongoingly Christian humanism, often now secularized as a mortalist humanism. As I note here, those seeking to advance the cause of equality often turn to Antigone as a model of civil disobedience or alternative equality (of the dead) and are drawn, in part by received interpretations of this iconic figure, into mere resistance politics, reflexive anti-statism, or an extra-political humanism of equal dignity in death. There is another option: an agonistic humanism whose politics of counter-sovereignty, conspiracy, and solidarity is more promising for them and, arguably, more true to the richness of Sophocles' play and its complex reception history. The extra-political universalism of grief with which this classical heroine is increasingly identified in feminist and critical theory emphasizes equality in death; a politics of counter-sovereignty emphasizes equality in life. The latter is more properly the focus for democratic theory and is actually better, if still imperfectly, promoted by the divisive, vengeful, and politically partisan Antigone I find reason to promote from beneath centuries of distinct but overlapping Christian and Romantic interpretations caught up in an ardor for martyrdom that goes on to pervade the humanisms to which they give rise.[15]

PART I

Interruption

Introduction to Part I

I am one of those people who finishes other people's sentences. Some people see such interruption as impolite and resent the intrusion. Others appreciate it and see it as a part of a kind of conversational co-stewardship. You can tell pretty quickly which are which. With those who resent the intrusion, I hold back and try not to let them hear my foot tapping as I wait for them to finish making their point in their own way.

Although often offered in the spirit of mutuality, interruption can be a sign of power. In the parental injunction "please do not interrupt me; let me finish my sentence" which I have had occasion to utter from time to time, I hear the power I disavow elsewhere. And to my kids' response "but you interrupt *us* all the time!" I can only laugh and shut up. (I think everyone should have a kid in their life – you don't have to *have* one, just have one in your life – so you too can learn to laugh and shut up.)

As a social practice, then, interruption postulates both equality, as when two people interrupt each other to knit together a conversation in tandem, and inequality, as when one party must yield the floor, as it were, to the other. Posing as an interruption, this book traffics in both. It is a hybrid that seeks agonistically to engage with prior operations of this powerful text, and to overcome some of them. Approaching Sophocles and his legacy agonistically could hardly be more appropriate since the *agon* between his Antigone and Creon is probably for most political theorists the template for what is meant by agonism. I will seek here to alter that template by adjusting our understanding of the play, noting not just the elements of conflict, plotting, and struggle in agonism but also its commitments to mutuality, conspiracy, and intimacy, evident in Sophocles' drama, as well as in politics more generally. For this to emerge out of the play, it will be necessary to look at Antigone not only in dialogue with Creon but also at Antigone in agonistic engagement with Ismene, with the Chorus, and with the audience. This will be the work of Part II of the book: Conspiracy.

First, the three chapters that make up Part I look at receptions of Antigone in political, feminist, and queer theory, and film. In each chapter, I track a "turn to Antigone," looking at how particular theorists, philosophers, critics or directors cast some problem of culture or politics as Oedipal and then propose some solution, labeled Antigonean. I note the limits of these turns to Antigone: in each case, lamentation, ethics, and/or resistance turn out just to feed rather than break cycles of violence and, more often than not, they just recirculate gender stereotypes rather than interrupt them. In each case, what starts out as a politics of lamentation soon slides into something more like a lamentation of politics (and a turn to ethics or humanism). Because of these limitations, I turn in Part II to Sophocles' text in quest of a different Antigone who might interrupt the received ones. She is discernible in Sophocles' text and thus one pressing question posed for us by this work is necessarily: why have we managed until now to read past Antigone as she is read here?

One of the things that emerges from Part I's three chapters together is a sense of the power of maternalism in political thinking: moving from Cindy Sheehan in Chapter 1 to Jean Bethke Elshtain's Madres of the Plaza in Chapter 2 and to the AIDS quilt in that same chapter, a maternal object if there ever was one, Part I ends with an analysis, in Chapter 3, of *Germany in Autumn*, an omnibus film in which Rainer Werner Fassbinder reperforms the role of Antigone in dialogues with his lover and with his mother; his father, in the film as in life, is absent. Fassbinder's gay male Antigone ends collapsed in a heap on the floor and exercises no apparent political agency. How should we interpret such a collapse? Is it mere resignation? Surrender? James Martel points out that Walter Benjamin invites us to see something else in collapses like this when he finds something worthwhile in the drunkenness that Marx castigates as politically retrograde.[1] Thomas Elsaesser works in Benjamin's wake when he finds in Fassbinder's performance of vulnerability a valuable interruption of post-war West Germany's dominant narratives of fathers and sons. But, I will argue, Fassbinder raises for us the question of genre, as well: in the end it is not so much his plot or his images but his emplotment of the events of the day as melodrama that undoes the father–son script that has a genre of its own: tragedy.

Chapter 1 looks at how the mourning mother in American political culture becomes the site of a new universalism or humanism that promises redemption for suffering but not without some political-cultural costs. Classicization – as when we compare our mourning to that of ancient tragic heroines – is one device by way of which a sense of the universal and extra-political character of lamentation is secured. But might it be the maternalism rather than the classicization that does the real work of universalism here? And is there only power in this promotion of extra-political powerlessness as a kind of admirable female power and political chasteness? In Chapter 2, I look at how Elshtain leashes Antigone to an ideology of chaste maternal politics that is rejected by critics of kinship like Judith Butler. But, I argue there, chasteness and maternalism return when Butler embraces the AIDS Names Project quilt. Butler does not attend to the complex politics of the quilt, indeed she obscures them, even though the quilt may not only enable grief for ungrievable life (which is what Butler admires about it), it may also reabsorb such grievability into the fabric of American sentimentalism. I end Chapter 2 with some discussion of Douglas Crimp's ambivalence about the quilt, focusing in particular on his adamant insistence on natality and pleasure, not mortality and grief, as the bases of queer politics.[2]

One of the devastations of the AIDS epidemic was its destruction of generational order. As young men died in droves, the lines connecting past and future were also attenuated. In the years since the height of the epidemic's destruction in the US, queer theorists and activists have diagnosed the politics of loss and erasure that ensued, trying to restore past and future, and recreate the memory links that might have been embodied by the generation nearly lost.[3] The politics of generational norm transmission are at the center of Chapter 3, as well, where the legacy of the fathers, as it were, is not too little, but too much. In the film *Germany in Autumn*, made and set in 1970s West Germany, former Nazis are everywhere and the task for democratic activists and radicals is to find ways to *dis*connect from the past, not reconnect to it. The democratic need is to break the bonds of generational time, not restore them.[4] Seeking to relax the Oedipal binds of generational guilt transmission and male sibling rivalry, the film gestures at the end to sororal ties as an alternative and potentially promising kinship resource. This is a theme to which I find myself returned, again, in the third chapter of Part II: in Chapter 6, I reconsider Ismene's role in the play and strive further to conjure an Antigone whose political import exceeds grief and combativeness. On close reading, a conversation of knitted-together interruptions emerges between the two sisters in Sophocles' play, contrasting sharply with Creon's powerful interruptions of Antigone.

Can sorority displace maternalism? Should it? Here we must be cautious. The historic alliance of mothering with mourning does not just maternalize lamentation, it also naturalizes motherhood and invests it with ideological power. No less than maternalism, sorority too must be seen as the basis or product of an ideology (sororalism?), not an idealized, extra-political relationship but an always already politicized construct or artifice. Still, a focus on sorority, licensed by the play and hinted at in *Germany in Autumn*, may help to undo maternalism's extra-political spell by decentering maternalism and pluralizing kinship. But the problem here is not finally maternalism, nor any other kin-based ideology: at stake always in maternalism, sorority, and (the more usually invoked) fraternity is humanism, to which I now turn.

CHAPTER I

Tragedy, maternalism, ethics: toward an agonistic humanism

> By insisting on a "common" corporeal vulnerability, I may seem to be positing a new basis for humanism.
>
> Judith Butler[1]

> Certain great themes, such as humanism, can be used to any end whatsoever.
>
> James Tully[2]

> Only tragedy can deal adequately with humanism on its high horse.
>
> Laurence Michel

Humanism has in recent years been making a comeback; not the rationalist universalist variety discredited by post-structuralism and the horrific events of the twentieth century, but a newer variant. This humanism asserts that what is common to humans is not rationality but the ontological fact of mortality, not the capacity to reason but vulnerability to suffering. This *mortalist* humanism is connected to what has been dubbed recently, "the turn to ethics" or "the ethical turn."[3] Finitude is said to soften us up for the call of the other, to open us up to the solicitations of ethics and to bypass the intractable divisions of politics. I argue here that even this humanism is implicated in political divisions it claims to transcend and, moreover, that an ethics of mortality and suffering is no adequate replacement for a (post)humanist politics with agonistic intent.[4] Humanists have long found in Greek tragedy an illustration of their ideal but tragedy seems a strange genre on which to pin the celebration of the human. In tragedy, after all, "[e]verything humanistically worthwhile is blighted, then irretrievably cracked; men are made mad, and then destroyed," says Laurence Michel.[5] Rather than depict a "Human Spirit" that is "autonomous and transcendent," tragedy debunks such "pretensions" (1961: 634). Humanist critics miss this, Michel argues, because they focus in Aristotelian fashion on the spectators' assumed pity for tragedy's victims

("the heart of the beholder") rather than on the play's disposal of them
("the heart of the play") (1961: 636).

This split between text and reception, recently revived by classics' turn
to reception studies, is not necessary to explain humanism's appropriation
of this difficult genre, however, for where Michel sees only death and
defeat, others find inspiring self-sacrifice and redemption. (Is Michel's
approach secularist and that of many humanist critics providential?) If
humanists promote tragedy as their genre of choice, it is because they think
tragedy is redemptive: it renders clear the human spirit. It exhibits a
human willingness to sacrifice on behalf of a principle, commitment, or
desire; or knowingly to accept one's implication in unchosen acts; or
defiantly to march to one's death with head held high; or to refuse
vengeance or even justice on behalf of love for another or perhaps even
an ideal of self.[6] Tragic characters die but their principles live on. They
suffer but something beautiful is made of their suffering.[7]

For other humanists, it is not the tragic protagonists' martyrdom but
rather their *vulnerability* that is attractive. Enduring unspeakable pain,
tragedy's protagonists are reduced often to wordless suffering before they
die or shamble off stage. Stripped of their civilizational trappings, they
seem bare but not abject. There are exceptions: Lear is too abject, for
some; *Persians'* laments are unbearable for others. But as a rule, the
protagonists of tragic theater are said to dignify, universalize, and
humanize suffering. For Dorothea Krook (1969), such tragic heroes make
suffering intelligible, redeem it, and reconcile us to it. Terry Eagleton calls
hers "a square-jawed masculinist ideal of tragedy, replete with pugnacious,
public-spirited heroes who take their punishment like a man even when
they are not guilty" (2003: 76). Nevertheless, many humanists share
Krook's view. They may stop short of redemption but they do see promise
in identification with suffering: a certain human commonality is furthered
by tragedy's tendency to depict with sympathy the suffering on all sides of
a conflict. Just as the "cry" of suffering gets under language's surface to
access a common humanity said to underlie our linguistic divisions, so
tragedy gets under the skin of divisive politics to scratch the essence of our
common humanity. *Phonê* is universal and can subtend the divisions of
logos. Here tragedy's power is not that it redeems suffering, but that it
exemplifies it in ways that highlight what many think to be the human's
most basic common denominator – the capacity to feel pain and suffer.[8]

Of the various tragic heroes, Sophocles' Antigone is taken best to
exemplify universal suffering and the ethical turn, both by those who favor
the turn to ethics (Butler) and by those who oppose it (Rancière). Keening

over her brother's body, Antigone is compared by the sentry to a "bird" at an "empty nest" (424–425 [472]). For humanists, her suffering cries mark an extra-linguistic, universal experience of human grief or the isolating solitude of deep human pain recognizable to all. For anti-humanists, they are signs of a dehumanizing, monstrous animality that limns the limits of human meaning. The former emphasize the maternalism of the "empty nest," the latter the "bird" to which Antigone is likened. Humanists anthropomorphize the bereaved bird when they see it as a mourning mother; anti-humanists also universalize maternal mourning but they do so by naturalizing and dehumanizing grieving mothers, likening them to birds.

Are these the only options? A humanism of universal or principled suffering versus an anti-humanism of death-driven, desiring monstrosity? In reading after reading, staging after staging, Antigone represents grief for ungrievable life or solitary conscience rising up against arrogant power, though she could – and sometimes with better textual exegesis *should* – represent the dissident quest for sovereignty or sororal solidarity, or the autonomy of aristocratic life opposed to appropriation by or complicity with the new democratic polis. The aim here, then, is to foreground the politicality of lamentation all the way down, as it were, in the hope that this may help release us from the spellbinding assumption that suffering or lamentation get beyond politics to the stark "human." Thus, we might draw from Antigone inspiration for an agonistic humanism that sees in mortality, suffering, sound, and vulnerability resources for some form of enacted if contestable universality, while also recognizing these resources are various and opaque in their significations, just like language. In quest of a politics that is not reducible to an ethics nor founded on finitude, agonistic humanists draw not only nor even primarily on mortality and suffering, but also on natality and pleasure, power (not just powerlessness), desire (not just principle), and *thumos* (not just *penthos*). As Eve Sedgwick says, it is "reifying and, indeed, coercive to have only one, totalizing model of positive affect always in the same featured position" (2003: 146).[9] The agonism in this humanism means it even insists on attenuating, rather than re-securing, the human/animal distinction on which other human-isms are founded or on behalf of which they are promoted.

This alternative, agonistic humanism grows out of my reading of Sophocles' *Antigone*, detailed in Part II, in which Antigone is not just a figure of resistance or a lamenter. Or better, what it means to lament turns out to have not only something to do with shared human finitude but also something to do with vengeance, politics, and the quest for sovereignty.

This book offers, in part, a historical reading of the play in which Antigone is not merely the lamenting sister Hegel admired nor the political martyr appropriated by dissidents all over the modern world. She *is* a lamenting sister and she *does* die for her cause but she is, more fundamentally, a political actor embroiled in burial, kinship, and polis politics, one who plots, conspires, and maneuvers her way in and out of trouble on behalf of the sovereign form that she considers to be hers by right.

This reading of the play, in turn, grows out of critical engagement, in each of the three chapters in Part I, with some recent efforts to develop a new humanism based on finitude and vulnerability. Such efforts are roundly rejected by Jacques Rancière when they are connected to catastrophe, but they win a qualified endorsement from him when he approves of artistic practices of commemoration that focus on naming the dead (while avoiding what he casts as the idolatry of images). Naming combats indifference. The victims of the mass murder in Rwanda, Rancière says, speaking of a memorial to them, "had to be given their names, an inscription in the order of discourse and memorial, because indifference to all these deaths in fact prolongs a certain invisibility, the feeling that these lives are external to the world of discourse" (2008: 8).

This of course is what Judith Butler too will identify as cause for concern when she calls on US citizens to cross the lines of friend and enemy to grieve ungrievable life. She too will refer to naming, singling out in particular the need to learn to say and identify with alien-sounding names that find no ready grooves of familiarity in our lexicons of lament. She too will claim that such learnings, sayings, and recordings are important. But whereas she identifies her project with Antigone and with an ethics derived from Lévinas, Rancière identifies his with Oedipus against Antigone and against various strands of ethics, including that identified with Lévinas.[10] The latter are all part of philosophy's unhappy turn to catastrophe since the Holocaust, Rancière says, which results in a replacement of conflict with fusion. The divisions that generate politics give way to a new focus on a miasmic evil that destroys everything and just generates paralysis or violence in response. The impact on philosophy is serious. Rancière says: "Ethics . . . takes on as its own mourning the mourning of politics" (1999: 136). Ethics, that is, is philosophy's atonement for its "old pretension of philosophical mastery" (1999: 135). In short, when Antigone laments, or when philosophy laments with her, politics disappears.

Still, Rancière does at one point here indulge his own inner Antigone (we all have one). When he and Butler, their diverging judgments of ethics notwithstanding, intervene to protect the dead from disappearing without remark, they bind themselves to one of humanism's most fundamental commitments – to memorialize and bury the human and prevent its degradation and erasure.[11] This commitment is thematized by Hegel in a passage of the *Phenomenology* usually read as a commentary on Sophocles' *Antigone*. For Hegel, the function of burial, the purpose of interment (from *in terra*, literally "in the ground"), is to inter-rupt the natural processes by way of which the dead become organic parts of nature. With the word and deed of ritual, materiality, and speech act, with the stone marker, the cemetery plot, and the coffin, with the prayers, eulogies, and rituals for the dead, the family inserts itself into nature's processes, inter-rupts them, and claims even the dead for human community. In Hegel, these so-called universals underwrite a contested kinship structure in which it is the sister's duty to bury the brother. It may also be that burial as a humanist obligation is what makes a sister of the woman.

When Butler privileges mourning, or grief for ungrievable life, as the centerpiece of an ethical practice that reproaches sovereignty for its aggression and violence and reaches across its dividing lines, she reorients the practice that, for Hegel, served both to support the state's aims and to give order to the family by reconciling the family to its loss of sons in war. But Butler also innovates in another way: she seeks to mobilize the mourning without the kinship on behalf of a new kinship, sensing perhaps that it is the universal mourning that generates the kinship, rather than kinship, with its supposedly natural close ties, that motivates the mourning. But doesn't conventional kinship then reassert itself in the mourning structure that also underwrites it? What are the promises and risks of appropriating the very apparatus that once privileged, as in Hegel, the family as heir and the sister as chief mourner on behalf of a new post-kinship, non-partisan consensus on rights, non-violence, mutuality, and commemoration?[12]

Notably, the practice of mourning is, in Hegel, already an appropriation. Though Hegel does not note it, the mourning family as he describes it takes on the role of the gods in ancient Greece, who stopped the abuse and disfigurement of dead heroes to vouchsafe for them a "beautiful death." As Jean-Pierre Vernant explains,

The gods miraculously save the hero from the shame of abuse that – by disfiguring, denaturing his body until it is no longer recognizable as his own, or even as a human body, or even as a body at all – would reduce him to a state of nonbeing. To preserve him as he was, the gods perform the human rituals of cleansing and beautification but use divine unguents: these elixirs of immortality preserve "intact," despite all the abuse [as in Achilles' destruction of Hector], that youth and beauty which can only fade on the body of a living man . . . [D]eath in battle fixes forever on the hero's form [his youth and beauty], just as a stele remains erect forever to mark a tomb. (1991: 74)[13]

Preserving the name, treating the body with dignity (remaining forever erect?): these seem to be universal and uncontroversial goods – the stuff of an inoffensive humanism, drawn from ancient gods and their heroes, taken over by modern families and their members who receive it in transmuted form from the monotheistic religions which introduce the need for certain kinds of after-death care to secure the soul's safety for eternity or to safeguard the body's return to its maker.

A more agonistic orientation to commemoration and memory is invited by Jacques Derrida, who sees how politics intrudes even in this ostensibly apolitical realm. In his *The Work of Mourning*, he warns about "what in this century has come to replace the funeral oration ... the corpus of declarations in newspapers, on radio and television ... the rhetorical constraints, the political perspectives, the exploitation by individuals and groups, the pretexts for taking a stand, for threatening, intimidation, reconciling" (2001).[14] When Derrida here contrasts modern eulogizing, which is politicized, with the Oration it replaces, he may seem to be saying that the Oration was a pure origin corrupted by present bad faith practices of eulogy. But as his critique of Aristotle in *Politics of Friendship* (1997) suggests, such bad faith efforts are better seen as *part* of the practice in question, not as external to it, nor as corruptions of it. Where Aristotle distinguishes among virtue, pleasure, and use as distinct bases of distinct kinds of friendship, Derrida highlights their points of contact and contamination in Aristotle's writings, and insists that this is where politics and friendship are situated: in the moments of undecidability, where we cannot distinguish for certain among virtue, pleasure, use, where they supplement and infiltrate each other, even though they are opposed.[15] Already in the Funeral Oration, such contaminations are evident; indeed, the *Antigone* can be seen as an effort to expose or expunge them (a case I make in Part II). And even the steles on which Vernant thinks we can rely "forever" to memorialize the dead were once, Alison Renteln says, not signs of loving memorialization designed to rescue the dead from nature's obliteration but rather evidence of their surviving family's or comrades' desire never to re-encounter the dead on earth (2004: 179).[16] Putting heavy stones on the graves, survivors hoped to prevent the dead from rising up again. Our current practices may be different, more sentimental and more sanitized of conflicting passions, but surely they carry traces of this earlier ambivalence? The stones are still heavy. Perhaps this is a sign of the "cannibalism" in relations among the living and the dead, to which Derrida sometimes refers.[17]

In sum, just as in our relations with the living, so too with the dead, we find our relations with them are suffused with hybrid combinations of virtue, pleasure, use. But these combinations are obscured in contemporary theory by a kind of purity in relation to the dead, often purchased by way of Antigone herself, represented as pure – as classical icon, virginal beauty, loving sister, or principled burial zealot. Some of those who deploy her turn to her in quest of a post-political universal position; others soon end up in such a position, unwittingly.

A NEW HUMANISM?

As Mark Griffith notes, renewed interest in Antigone since the 1970s may be attributed to the rise of feminist theory in classics as well as to the influence of Jacques Lacan's famous seminar on the play (2005: 91). But there may also be another factor. The turn to Antigone has taken place as scholars reworking humanism have shifted from an enlightened humanism whose exemplary figure is Oedipus, the much-admired albeit ultimately thwarted, self-knowing, puzzle-solving sovereign of Thebes, to a post-Enlightenment humanism of lament and finitude whose model is Antigone, the woman who keens and cries and demands death rites for her brother in resistance to sovereign power. This is different from the Holocaust-centered catastrophic thinking that Rancière criticizes in certain French philosophers. Or at least its genealogy is different. In contrast to the "universality fathered by Oedipus," Victoria Wohl argues, "there might be a different humanist tradition" (2005: 158–159). This alternative humanism is "mothered by Antigone" and it "exposes the limits and limitations of the masculine universal" (2005: 159). For Wohl, "critique" stands out as the trait Antigone brings to humanism. Other Antigonean humanists replace humanism's focus on knowing with dying, reason with lamentation, sovereignty with finitude.[18]

This humanism, which finds compelling universals in the cry of pain and in the fact of mortality, is instanced in statements such as Lord Eames' (co-chair of the Consultative Group on Irish Reconciliation in 2008), defending a proposal to provide recognition payments to survivors on both sides of the Northern Irish conflict: *"there is no difference in a mother's tears"* (Montague and Stourton 2009).[19] Antigone is not a mother: she refuses to be one and laments the fact that she will never be one. (Wohl is just the most recent in a long line to turn to Antigone to mother something.) But her insistence on lamenting equally both her brothers, one who attacked the city and the other who defended it, stands for many as a statement of the pure equality to which we are solicited by finitude, but which eludes our grasp in almost every other domain of life.

For Nicole Loraux, this shift from reason to finitude is reason to turn to tragedy. For her, tragedy as performance speaks particularly powerfully to our ontologically tragic condition. The disappointment of Enlightenment promise in a world "convulsed by history" leaves us particularly needful of tragedy's "meditation on the aporias" of such a world (2002a: 13). For Gloria Fisk, this history repeats itself: "[I]t makes sense that tragedy works during the periods before and after modernity because our age resembles the ancients' to the degree that the limits of our political communities are in flux" (2008: 895). For David Scott, this history is irresistible: "the hoped-for futures that inspired and gave shape to the expectation of the coming emancipation are now themselves in ruin . . . they are futures past. And this is why a tragic sensibility is a timely one" (2008: 201). Other students of tragedy, like Bernard Williams (1993), Olga Taxidou (2004), Dennis Schmidt (2001), and Rita Felski (2008), see such worldly convulsions together with "the growing self-doubt of philosophy and the questioning of reason, analytical method, and conceptual knowledge" as solicitations to tragedy (Felski 2008: 1).[20] For Schmidt, today's worldly convulsions seem to reprise philosophy's earlier ones, as in Schelling's call to return to tragedy because tragedy showed how "thinking can endure rather than shirk the most extreme contradiction, namely the contradiction between freedom and necessity" made unavoidable by Kant's antimony of reason (2001: 76).

Loraux suggests, however, that if we turn to tragedy now it is not just because tragedy stages irresolvable conflicts in a way that might well inform an irredeemably conflicted and never entirely free world. If tragedy speaks to late-modern crises and self-doubt, it does so specifically as oratorio which interpellates us as mortals defined by finitude. Oratorio accesses a world in which such finitude is managed by way of sound, song, dance, and dirge. When performed on stage outside of Athens, Loraux says, tragedy's sung laments were particularly effective in bringing together diverse spectators. From the particularities and partisanships of diverse polis memberships, audience members were moved to experience their commonality as mortals. In other words, for Loraux, tragedy does not just mirror or even explore the divisions of the political world. It offers an "anti-politics" that points beyond them. Her anti-politics of grief is an example of what I call here mortalist humanism.

Mortalist humanists commonly take Antigone, the great lamenter, as their representative, but Loraux prefers Cassandra, in whom Loraux finds a particularly compelling "tragic configuration of the mingling of voices" (2002a: 74–75). Presumably this is because Cassandra, who cannot be understood, is farther than Antigone from the pellucid polis discourse Loraux wants to resist. Antigone keens and laments but she also reasons in a way that is compatible with the polis' *logos*. And Antigone participates in the official permitted burial of her brother, Eteocles, while of Cassandra "the inspired seer," Loraux says: "Elegiac lament is not for her" (1998: 61). However, in *The Birth of Tragedy*, a key text in Loraux's construction of an extra-political humanism of song and cry, Nietzsche does not choose between these two. Noting "how 'the Dionysian and the Apollonian, in new births ever following and mutually augmenting one another, controlled the Hellenic genius,'" he says "the child of this long combat or union," tragedy, is "'at once Antigone and Cassandra'" (1967: 47; cited in Loraux 2002b: 74).[21] Thus, Nietzsche resignifies as natal two women normally associated with lamentation and death. Loraux, who does not miss much, misses the significance of this move away from mortality to natality and she also neglects Nietzsche's "at once." Ironically, aiming to rescue Nietzsche from a century-long misreading claiming he opposes Apollonian versus Dionysian, Loraux herself reads binarily when she homes in on Cassandra, not Antigone.

In *The Invention of Athens*, her early work on tragedy, Loraux saw tragedy as operating in the service of the city (1986: 50). She argued that fifth-century Athenians watching Aeschylus' tragedy, *Persians*, would have been reconstituted as Athenians by the shared joy they felt watching their enemies, the Persians, grieve and lament. Almost twenty years later, in *The Mourning Voice*, she is not so sure. Focusing on the fifth-century ban on lamentation, which constrained and marginalized the loud and showy lamentations then identified with women and elites, she wonders whether tragedy with its own loud, showy laments might not have been perhaps subversive rather than complicit. Where earlier Loraux thought the city of forgetting's ban on laments was upheld by staging banned laments safely away from the city in the circumscribed space and time of the theater, now she wonders whether maybe the opposite is taking place: what if tragedy did not interpellate citizens into polis ideology, as she earlier argued, but instead interpellated spectators into membership in an extra-political community? Rather than impress citizens into polis identification, tragedy may overcome political divisions by way of non-discursive sound, inciting spectators into a mortalist humanism of universal voice, cry, or suffering.[22]

This is the alternative to the divisive and political city: a humanism that threatens the polis' narrow citizenship ideology. With its diverse, pan-Hellenic audience and its appeal to human finitude, the theater, Loraux now argues, was not a civic but a humanist institution that solicited spectators "less as members of the political body than as members of that entirely apolitical body known as the human race or, to give it its tragic name, 'the race of mortals.'" The effect was powerful: "it may be that that experience abolished the boundaries so carefully drawn in ancient Greece to define the communal and the individual spheres" (2002a: 88–89). Once tethered to the city's purpose, tragedy takes flight.[23]

Stephen White finds intimations of a similar mortalist humanism in ancient Greece. In *The Ethos of a Late-Modern Citizen* (2009), White comments on what happens in Homer's *Iliad* when Priam visits Achilles to ransom Hector's body. White sees unity in grief as the two enemies, Priam and Achilles, weep together and then go on to eat and drink in each other's company that night. White concedes that Priam leaves quickly, anxious perhaps that Achilles' hospitality may not last long. But, White insists, when Achilles suspends Greek hostilities against Troy so as to allow Trojans a mourning period for Hector, Achilles goes beyond what the gods require him to do and it is the spirit of shared finitude that enables him to do this. White focuses on the two men's shared mourning because he seeks to identify the minimal bases out of which ethical conduct may arise. Ontologically, White argues, mortality is a more minimal condition than most others on offer in political theory, such as autonomy or individuality.[24]

The mortalist humanist idea that we should dwell longer in grief or forge in grief new solidarities, or find in grievability a new social ontology of equality, informs the recent move away from a justice of accountability in (post)conflictual politics and toward truth and reconciliation commissions that focus, rather, on forgiveness for or acceptance of those who confess their crimes and recount what happened to their victims. Shared suffering, publicly acknowledged, provides the basis of a new order.[25] The mortalist humanist option may also seem attractive now given contemporary democracies' tendency to suppress or instrumentalize grief on behalf of national, often violent, aims but the focus on mourning and the claim of minimalism are problematic: lamentation and the so-called fact of mortality are always also wrapped up in – inseparable from – their meaning, which varies (as Judith Butler notes, most recently, in *Frames of War*:

"There is no life and no death without relation to some frame" [2009: 25]). Just as Butler in her earlier *Gender Trouble* (1990a) and *Bodies That Matter* (1993) argued against a sex-gender distinction in which sex was the natural, univocal, material ground of gender, which was plural, culturally constructed, and behavioral, so too here, we might say, we need to deconstruct the binary of death and burial in which death is seen as the natural, univocal, material fact that undergirds burial, which varies by culture and is constructed.[26] (This does not mean death is not a fact; it means simply that as a fact it is wrapped up in its meaning.)

Mortalist humanism leads White to focus on the shared mourning of Priam and Achilles and not also on their shared feast. Loraux and Butler turn to mortalism, too, to animate the sorts of sharedness on which they think political action depends. But, although we may all be mortals (with varying deaths and varying attitudes toward and experiences of death), we are, as Hannah Arendt insists along with Nietzsche, natals as well. And a focus on natality – which is no less minimal than mortality, ontologically speaking – may generate new commonalities while orienting humanism differently than mortality does. In Sophocles' *Antigone* the Chorus' response to divisions of civil war and conflict is to issue an invitation in the play's fifth *stasimon* to go to the feast of Dionysus and forget their strife, in dance. No one takes up their invitation. But its issuance is enough to indicate an alternative that mortalist humanists do not consider as fully as needed: not a dwelling deeper in grief (as in White's *Iliad*, Butler's ethics of grievable life, and Loraux's late reading of *Persians*) nor its displacement or suppression (as in Creon's ban on burying Polynices), but a natalist's pleasure-based counter to grief.[27]

Faced with the undeniability of death and decomposition, inconsolable at the loss of his friend, his brother, Patroclus, Achilles mourns. He mourns too long, and his quest for vengeance is excessive. When he ravages Hector's body, Achilles goes too far and stops only when he is interrupted . . . not, like Antigone, by Creon, but by the gods or by his mother, Thetis, sent by the gods. But that is not the only interruption.

Achilles' appetites press themselves upon him and call him back to the realm of the living. As Henry Staten (1995) points out: for Achilles, the loss of Patroclus is irreparable and incomparable – "there will come no second sorrow like this to my heart again" (*Iliad*, 23.46–47) – yet eventually, Achilles returns to life, even if only briefly before his own heroic demise.[28] When Priam visits to ransom Hector's body, the men eat and drink together and Achilles sleeps with Briseis, so the episode invites a different ontological conclusion than that drawn by mortalist humanists, suggesting the importance of both feast and finitude, appetite and hunger, abundance and lack, pleasure and lamentation, violence and truce, to the cessation of political conflict. If we attend as well to the Chorus' invitation in the play's fifth *stasimon* to go to the feast of Dionysus and forget, in dance, we may see yet further that Sophocles' play, too, points to a pleasure-based counter to grief attuned to the limitations of solidarity forged in sorrow.[29]

Such a third option is raised by Freud, who argues that mourning is a process that *begins* with the ego wanting to die along with the "lost object," but it does not end there. In the end, as Staten also points out, the ego "is 'persuaded' [as it were] by the sum of the narcissistic satisfactions it derives from being alive to sever its attachment to the object that has been abolished" (Freud 1963: 255). (Note that Freud juxtaposes narcissistic satis-faction to mourning here, though for Achilles, in the night with Priam, narcissistic satisfaction is derived from mourning: Achilles mourns as he imagines his father mourning his, Achilles', own death.) Without desire's "persuasion" or interruption, mourning would be ceaseless, like melan-choly, like Antigone's dirge before Creon's interruptions. Thus, for Freud, in this essay anyway, it is not, as we usually think, mourning done well that enables us to "move on."[30] It is rather mourning interrupted that recasts us into life. It is the *interruption of mourning* by bodily wants and desires, by hunger for food or sex. Faced with a choice between fidelity to the lost object (expressed as sharing its fate, wanting to die) and severing its attachment (to go on living without it) on behalf of its narcissistic desires, the ego is "persuaded" to do the latter. The ego is "persuaded" by a force we least identify with persuasion as such – hunger. We are moved out of need not by reasons but by need. The focus on the body's decomposition in death is combated by the body's claim to recomposition in life, by pleasure or hunger. Narcissistic satisfactions exert a certain counter-pressure. Instead of a claim to reason against passion we get a displacement of pain by pleasure, or of one pain (loss) by another (hunger).

The dance of lament and hunger, pain and pleasure, maps onto the two great Homeric epics, argues Pietro Pucci in his intertextual reading of the *Odyssey* and the *Iliad* (1987: 147): the *Iliad* turns on *thumos* or heart, meaning courage, manliness and the heroic code, while the *Odyssey* centers on *gastêr*.[31] The word *gastêr* appears only once with this valence in the *Iliad*, the epic of lament, when Odysseus urges Achilles to leave off mourning Patroclus. An army cannot fight on an empty stomach, Odysseus says (*Iliad* 19.225). The truth of the two epic characters is captured in this exchange. In the *Odyssey*, "Odysseus grieves only a few hours – even after the loss of all his friends – then eats and faces life again [but in the *Iliad*] Achilles knows that because Patroclus is dead, he cannot remain among the living." From this Pucci concludes that Odysseus and Achilles "represent two opposite economies of life" (1987: 169). They are opposed, but they also intersect, as Henry Staten points out. When "Achilles urges Priam to leave off mourning for Hector and join him in eating" (*Iliad* 29.602–620), does not Achilles himself, then, submit to the "wisdom of the belly?" Staten asks (though Staten admits the word used here is more elevated than Odysseus' *gastêr*, which is a low diction) (1995: 45). Also, when Achilles hosts the games by way of which Patroclus is memorialized, mourning survivors remember the dead and are also returned to life by the play of the races, their wins, losses, and prizes.[32]

Does our analysis of grief in relation to appetite take us away from Sophocles' *Antigone*, in which *eros* is invoked but no characters sate their appetites? In Pucci's terms, after all, Sophocles' play is (like all tragedies) all Achilles, no Odysseus. Indeed, we might see Sophocles' Antigone as what is left of Achilles in the domesticated democratic polis (and this, I will suggest in Part II, all by itself may be a comment on the post-heroic form of life of fifth-century Athens/Thebes). Both Achilles and Antigone, in love with Patroclus and Polynices, their brother-like lovers or lover-like brothers, cannot stop grieving without being forcibly interrupted. But it is surely important that the interruptions differ: the dance of lament and hunger, pain and pleasure, central to Homeric Greece, is replaced in Sophocles' Thebes, as in the democratic Athens it mirrors distortedly, by sovereign power. As we shall see in detail in Chapter 4, in fifth-century Athens, lament is cut short by new regulations, and displaced by the Oration.

Sophocles' use of the theatrical device of interruption (what Freud also relies on but refers to, perhaps jokingly, as "persuasion") calls attention to the costs of the polis' interruption of the heroic form of life: its effort to displace appetite with reason, desire with wants, and bodies with words. This is no rejection of reason but rather a way to highlight its work. This is one of Sophocles' contributions, still underexplored, to (post)modernity's critique of reason, to which I attend in Chapter 5. It may be worth noting, further, that the larger context of tragedies like *Antigone*, which were after all performed at the feast of Dionysus and staged alongside comedies and satyr plays, may find or establish the balance between *gastêr* and *thumos*, hunger and heart, desire and lament, whose division by the fifth-century polis Sophocles' *Antigone* invites us to explore.

Antigone is almost always interpreted as death-identified, a willing martyr whose self-sacrifice evidences her orientation toward death. She

tells her sister she does not mind dying for her cause, that she is dead
already anyway, and that if she dies for this just cause, her death will be
glorious. She longs for death, is obsessed with it, some say with admiration
and others more critically. Heidegger, Lacan, and Žižek admire her
because she is not moved by the all-too-human attachment to mere life
that grips most of the rest of us today. But Antigone's death identification
does not mean she is just self-destructive. In Sophocles' play she also longs
for vengeance against those who have wronged her brother. She is violent,
full of rage. And she is not, in any case, only death-identified. She also acts
in ways that promote life, though this facet of her is rarely noticed. We will
see it in Chapter 6: the text gives us reason to think that Antigone sacrifices
herself not only for her dead brother, but also for her living sister who is
also the object of Creon's wrath.

Interestingly, those who do see Antigone in more vital terms tend to ally
her not with natalism but with maternalism, casting her (like Wohl, above)
as mother to a different future in one way or another, or as expressing
mother-like dedication to Polynices. But natality should not be so quickly
collapsed into maternity. My several readings of the play in Part II develop
a natal but not maternal Antigone, with textual and contextual support.
The play promotes through the Chorus a celebration of the miracle of
human existence, yoking together, we might say, the natal and mortal
elements of the human condition. This combination of mortality and
natality does not just position us better to comprehend Sophocles' play;
it may also generate a different humanism – an agonistic humanism – that
might better inspire progressive democratic imaginations than common
receptions of this ancient heroine as mortal (death-identified) or maternal
(and mournful).

The task of an agonistic humanism is laid out for it: it is difficult indeed
right now to carve out room in late-modern Western democracies for
protest or politics that do not slide into lamentation of singular loss or
sovereign excess. The problem with lamentational varieties of protest
politics is that they seem to fall into Hegel's trap of putting the (now
private) sorrow of suffering survivors above *raisons d'état*. Protesting or
lamenting state violence is a limited and limiting politics, as the examples
of some modern figures of lamentation make clear. Classicizing them, as so
many do, is limiting as well, at least so long as such classicizations work to
(re)produce Antigone simply as a mourning mother or sister, leaving
behind the rivalry, violence, vengeance, promising, forgiveness, plotting,
and conspiracy that may invite us to engage anew with the complexities of
political life lived in connection with others. If grievability, and the

precariousness it postulates, secure equality, they do not only secure equality. They position us also in a sentimental ontology of fragility, not resilience. Judith Butler says "Precariousness has to be grasped not simply as a condition of this or that life . . . the injunction to think precariousness in terms of equality emerges precisely from the irrefutable generalizability of the condition" (2009: 22). But there are other irrefutable generalizabilities that could be ontologized and on which we could build a politics as well: humans all eat, for example, and this too could ground an equality – a less minimal one – of social rights to food; perhaps even to healthy, non-cancerous food that truly nourishes us in sustainable ways.[33] Humans also all seek pleasure, rebirth, and more. A focus on these ontological traits might generate orientations to different equalities and powers that define not just human but also creaturely life.[34]

FOUR WOMEN AND A FUNERAL: THE COSTS OF CLASSICIZATION

[T]he sensibility of classicism . . . goes beyond a musealizing admiration and involves a sense of vividness and presence in the face of what is definitively past. (James Porter)

If we want to ask after the potential costs of classicization, we need look no further than Cindy Sheehan, the bereaved mother and anti-war activist who protested the US' second war on Iraq. So-called "peace mom," Cindy Sheehan has been likened many times to Antigone in the popular and scholarly press. When Donald Pease (2009), for example, calls Sheehan "Antigone's kin," his aim is political, to ennoble certain dissidents by classicizing them, underlining commonalities between contemporary actors and classical ones. But that aim is to some extent also undone by such classicization, which gives the impression that the pain to which mourning mothers appeal now is the same pain as that experienced by spectators at the tragic theater in the fifth century. Thus, maternal pain is universalized as both wide and deep: it is one unitary thing with which we are all familiar and it reaches all the way back to the fifth century.

The problem is that this move, made in the name of politicization, works to distill our potentially powerful politics into the mortalist human-ism criticized here for enacting the ethical turn away from politics. Jacques Rancière resists such moves when he says that "the ethical turn is not an historical necessity" (2006a: 18). Given the ahistorical nature of classiciza-tion, it is surely just as important to say that the ethical turn is not an ahistorical necessity, either, and that some attention to historical and political specificity can help us resist the lure of mourning-centered humanism that Sophocles' play actually contests and politicizes, as we shall see. If we read Sophocles' *Antigone*, as I do, as an intervention into a fraught, divisive, and classed politics of lamentation, and if we read lamentation itself as a fraught, divisive, and classed intervention into politics, as such, then we can see how the play is depoliticized by a classicism that universalizes (finding, postulating, or enacting human universals in pain, mourning, maternalism, or even, as we will see in Chapter 3, Oedipal father–son rivalries that work to depoliticize the play and its reception contexts).

Classicization is not quite the same thing as classicism.[35] Classicism, as James Porter (2006b) argues, consists in aesthetic claims to universality, as evidenced in the classical object (tragedy, statuary, lyric) said to possess the power to capture the human as such and to appeal to diverse audiences across vast stretches of time and space. Such classicism aims to ennoble the human as eternal but it is caught by this quest in such circularities that it reduces its devotees to mere stammering tautology, as in Schadewalt: "[W]e remain who we are in the face of that form," or "classical is what – for us – counts as classical" (cited in Porter 2006b: 8).[36] Classicization, by contrast, is focused on the present and turns for understanding to ancient circumstances, scripts, or images for analogies that might illuminate our condition or even mirror our circumstances. Thus tragedy is said to help us navigate past the shoals of the tragic and drama is said to address existential needs. At the same time, and this is no small part of the aspirations of classicization, we dignify and ennoble the meaner present by assimilating it to a grander past. If our mourning is just like theirs, if we suffer as they did, if our father–son rivalries echo back to those of antiquity and repeat them, then we gain some redemption from our mere temporality and the indignities of our situation are dignified.[37] Of course, as we will see Diana Taylor (1997a) argue in Chapter 2, the costs of positing this eternal return of the same may be the subversion of our sense of freedom and possibility, the very sense of freedom and possibility that we admire and attribute to the classical age to which we seek, for that very reason, to liken ourselves.

But not all classicization necessarily likens. Some classicize in order to invoke more fractious comparisons of past and present, and to underline the differences between them. And, as I will suggest throughout this book, classicization that treats the classical past as alien and resistant to appropriation may produce more instructive insights than the sort that seeks and finds our stammering selves in its mirror.

Those who classicize Cindy Sheehan underline the commonalities and name Antigone as her forebear. Other mourning mothers, however, may help us confront the power and the limits of classicization and the mortalist humanism it underwrites. Lila Lipscomb, for example, is never named an American Antigone. Perhaps that is because, unlike Cindy Sheehan, who is depicted in the popular media as a mother whose political agency is ignited by loss, Lila Lipscomb is depicted in Michael Moore's film, *Fahrenheit 9/11* (2004), as a mourning mother whose agency is undone by loss. After her son dies in the US' second Iraq war, Lipscomb is devastated, and then decides to go to the White House. She seeks a place to put her anger, not an opportunity for political activism.[38] But en route to the White House something happens and through this incident we see the power and limitations of mortalist humanism.

In Lafayette Park, across the way from the White House, Lipscomb has an unlikely encounter with a woman, a stall-protestor whose cardboard shelter is festooned with pictures of dead babies and who blames Bush for lives lost in Spain.[39] While the woman makes her charges, Lipscomb nods in shared vulnerability and murmurs "yes, my son [too]."[40] Stephen White might note with approval how shared finitude brings these women together, reprising the improbable connections between Achilles and Priam, mourners whose truce instances the power of mortalist humanism. But, as in that scene from Homer, the parties here are also easily driven apart. They are soon interrupted by a third, conservative-looking woman who stumbles on the scene and questions its authenticity. "This is staged," she says for the camera's sake, a comment that is not untrue: Moore is filming the women's encounter, after all. Truer still, their encounter is staged in another sense too: it takes place in the reception context of Greek tragedy, which joins women together across political divisions to lament their losses. It is not, however, true that the losses lamented here are false, though this seems to be the real objection.

The interrupting woman contradicts the stall-protestor and rejects Lipscomb's lament for her son, first, with disbelief ("Oh, yeah? Where did he die?"), and then by cruelly countering her authenticating facts ("Karballah, April 24th") with cold equality: "There are a lot of other people too." This not untrue (but not only true) effacement of her singular loss silences Lipscomb and drives her away from this scene of potential political awakening. By contrast, the stall-woman and the conservative one are both politicized and both focused on equality: the stall-protestor speaks on behalf of equal, ungrievable life and, appropriately, her voice is shrill and hard to take – more *phonê* than *logos*. Meanwhile, the conservative woman – whose voice is also hard to take, it must be said, but her words are clear to North American audiences – rejects Lipscomb's focus on her son above all the other US soldiers already lost or still in the fight. And so Lipscomb leaves behind this conflict, gives up her fledgling solidarity with the stall-woman, and turns to the White House. Alone and away from the two politicized, equality-centered women in Lafayette Park, Lipscomb returns to her focus on her singular son: "I need my son. God, it's tougher than I thought it was gonna be ... to be here. But it's freeing also ... because I finally have a place ... to put all my pain and all my anger ... and to release it."

In Moore's film, Lila Lipscomb is a woman brought down by grief and incapable of political engagement, more Ismene than Antigone, we might think. Moore may see that loss of agency as itself a compelling call to agency.[41] In real life, however, Lila Lipscomb does far more: she joins Cindy Sheehan in political activism, founding Gold Star Families for Peace. Yet it is Sheehan, not Lipscomb, who is depicted in the popular media as a mourning mother radicalized into activism by her son's death. Resisting the regime's effort to instrumentalize all military deaths on behalf of the ongoing Iraq war, it is perhaps unsurprising that Sheehan is classicized more than once. True, she does not stand up for the right to bury her son; his burial is not forbidden. But publicizing it is. When Sheehan takes a stand on behalf of a dead loved one against the unapologetic sovereign power of the state, she calls to mind none other than Antigone.

The comparison may enrich our (not unqualified) appreciation of Sheehan, who does not keen; she makes demands. First, she speaks in ways that are unlicensed, writing an open letter to Bush in which she demands democratic accountability for the war, and enacts equality with the president when she refers to him as "George."[42] Second, rather than take up the "Gold Star Mother" identity offered to those who have lost children in the military, Sheehan helps found (along with Lila Lipscomb and others) Gold Star Families for Peace in 2005, a pacifist parody of the official organization of maternal mourning. Gold Star Families prizes peace over sacrifice and includes all self-identified family members, not just "mothers." And third, Sheehan allows her loss of her son to press her into an encounter not just with mortal finitude but with *political* loss, which dawns on her when police fingerprint her after an arrest: "That's when the enormity of my loss hit me. I have lost my son. I have lost my First Amendment rights. I have lost the country that I love. Where did America go? I started crying in pain" (2006). As we will see, similar strategies – of enacting equality, performing parody, and moving from mortalism into politics – are also discernible in Sophocles' text and they plot the path of his protagonist.

Sheehan also embraces the media's label "peace mom" (so titling her memoir), however, and so fails to attend to the label's reinstatement of contested heteronormative identities. Is "peace mom" a new subject position or is Sheehan just folded by that term into a very old one? In the end, it seems that rather than rework contested identities, Sheehan's maternal pacifism is underwritten by and further underwrites the most conventional roles on offer. And this is aided and abetted by her classicization as an "American Antigone." Perhaps (to anticipate a theme fundamental to this book) there is no avoiding the to-ing and fro-ing whereby parodic reiteration succumbs to mere repetition before it may take flight again.[43]

But the most important critical question is surely not whether Sheehan is worthy of comparison with classical figures like Antigone but rather: what are we doing when we classicize her in that way? We support her mobilization of maternity for peace which (no less than Lord Eames') redeploys the iconic mourning mother to ground a universalism built undecidably on mourning and/or motherhood. (In other words, it is not clear here what is doing the work, what is really the universal: mourning or maternity? Or does each require the other to stand as the universal we would like each, on its own, to be?) That universalism is further evidenced and advanced when we turn to Antigone to ground the figure of the universal mourning mother, even though she – as political icon – is surely an effect of that very figure. I turn now to look at the mourning figure in more detail, in the work of Jean Bethke Elshtain and Judith Butler. Both turn to Antigone in quest of resources for an anti-authoritarian politics. As we shall see, the classical text in its reception contexts itself exerts a certain pressure on its interpreters to turn from an agonistic politics of mutuality and conflict to a mortalist humanism or sentimental ethics of loss and lament.[44]

CHAPTER 2

"Antigone versus Oedipus," I: feminist theory and the turn to Antigone

We only smoke the *Lamentations*.

Hunger, dir. Steve McQueen[1]

"Even if you are not aware of it, the latent fundamental image of Antigone forms part of your morality," says Jacques Lacan and so, Lacan suggests, working through the trope (if not the play) of Antigone is necessary to establish a critical relationship to morality (1992: 284). Sophocles' heroine forms latently part of our *politics* as well. It is now a mainstay of political and cultural theory to diagnose certain political problems as "Oedipal" and to recommend a solution that is, somehow, "Antigonean." What is meant by Oedipal and Antigonean varies, however, so much so that it sometimes seems as if these terms might be empty signifiers. I argue here, however, that the "Antigone versus Oedipus" frame is itself generative, it resists instrumentalization, and its unintended political-cultural effects are not always positive.

As we saw in Chapter 1, those who turn to Antigone now do so in the hope she might break the spell of the father's legacy of rationalism (Oedipus, the puzzle solver), rule, or governmentality (Oedipus, the king), or hierarchical, naturalized patriarchal power (Oedipus, the incest and parricide). Against these, political and feminist theorists have variously embraced Antigone as a bearer of true feeling possessed of a true ethical compass, powerful disobedient to tyrannical, tone-deaf, or impositional law, anti-patriarchal devotee of the natal over conjugal family form, or great lamenter and lover of the equal brother whom she grieves and buries at no small risk to herself.

For those who worry that invocations of "Antigone versus Oedipus" do not always have a salutary effect on democratic theory and politics, one response to her recent omnipresence might be to dispense with this figure entirely and turn elsewhere for inspiration. But, as Lacan's observation suggests, and as our contemporary political culture's ubiquitous classicization of mourning mothers also shows, abandoning Antigone is not something we are simply free to do. This classical heroine is everywhere. The idea that we could leave her behind and think politically in ways untouched by her is as improbable as Oedipus' hope that he could leave Corinth behind and live out his life elsewhere untouched by his fate.

If there is no dispensing with Antigone, then we must work through this figure, rereading her and working our way out from prior, now conventional receptions in order to find another Antigone who may have a different impact on democratic theory and may offer a different prod to our political imagination. That is the aim of this book. To promote a different turn to Antigone, however, we must first review the problems that arise when other political and feminist theorists invoke her.

In this chapter, I look at a few exemplary "turns to Antigone," assessing their aims and impact on political and cultural thinking. I focus here, in differing degrees of detail, on four thinkers who mobilize Antigone versus Oedipus – Jean Bethke Elshtain (the political theorist writing on Antigone and feminist theory in the 1980s), Diana Taylor (who assesses the gender politics of Latin American theater in the same period and since), Judith Butler (who begins in the 1990s trying to excavate a new Antigone for a feminist and queer theory of alternative kinship and then, later, after 9/11, mobilizes Antigone on behalf of an ethics of vulnerability and a politics of precarity), and Lee Edelman (who criticizes Butler's first Antigonean turn and deploys a Lacanian Antigone on behalf of a different queer theory).

Finally, after canvassing the limitations of the various turns to Antigone listed here, I turn to one important theorist of lamentation and political action who does *not* take his bearings from the classical heroine. I argue that an alternative turn to Antigone might do well to take its bearings from Douglas Crimp (art critic, AIDS activist, founding member of ACT UP). Crimp theorizes a politics of mourning beginning in the mid-1980s and yet when US feminists, since the 1980s, want to think about mourning and politics they do not turn to him. Why not? They turn to Antigone, or to the Madres of the Plaza in Argentina, as we will see. Or both. Why the relative neglect of the US experience with mourning around AIDS? And why, of all these political and cultural theorists of lamentation, is Crimp the only one who never mentions Antigone, notwithstanding his avowed interest in the politics of lamentation? This chapter will speculate as to why he avoids, while others embrace, Antigone for politics. Does he perhaps intuit the risks of classicization? If so, he may be right to worry. As we shall see here, those who turn to Antigone seeking to enlist her power soon find themselves subject to her power. And those who seek through her a politics of counter-sovereignty end up promoting an ethics and politics of lamentation that rejects sovereignty as violent: thus, their politics of lamentation collapses into a lamentation of politics.

ANTIGONE IN ARGENTINA: ELSHTAIN AND TAYLOR

Since the 1970s and in the last few years in ever-increasing numbers, feminist scholars have called for moving out of the shadow of Oedipus and the incest ban that founds the traffic in women (in structuralism) to Antigone who seems a more promising feminist figure.[2] Two feminists whose treatments of this classical figure have had possibly the greatest impact in political theory are Jean Bethke Elshtain and Judith Butler. Writing almost twenty years apart, these two deploy Sophocles' ancient tragedy in ways that mirror each other uncannily. Uncannily, since these authors' politics could not be more different, with Elshtain championing traditional family values in conservative journals like *First Things* and Butler endorsing alternative gay and lesbian kinship structures in outlets like *The Nation*. Still, both turn to Antigone, the woman who defies her uncle's edict to leave her traitorous brother unburied and later dies for her dissidence. In Antigone, Butler and Elshtain see, first, a figure to authorize a politicized feminism against the state (Oedipus, the king) and second, a lamenter who stands for a universal ethics or humanism that may have a political impact but is not itself primarily political.[3] Instead it seems to be primarily *a*political.[4] The question posed here then is: is it perhaps the move to Antigone – meant to figure or incite resistance – that drives feminists to universalism and lamentation as an ethics and a politics? Might a critical reading of the turn to Antigone, then, provide a lens through which to assess and perhaps even counter the phenomenon that some refer to as "left melancholy"?[5]

In "Antigone's Daughters" (1982), her first of two essays on Antigone, Elshtain expressed surprise that "Antigone has not yet emerged as a feminist heroine."[6] Elshtain argued that Antigone modeled a maternalist, care-centered social feminism that cherishes family ties as resources of democratic politics. Political without joining itself to official power structures, Elshtain's social feminism fit well with Sara Ruddick's "maternal thinking" (1980).[7] Elshtain did not assimilate Antigone to maternal thinking but she established an alliance between them: both opposed utilitarian statecraft on behalf of human dignity and care (1982: 310).

Elshtain's second essay, "Antigone's Daughters Reconsidered" (1989), published some years later, moves from a focus on US-based social feminism to a more universal, humanistic ethics and post-politics of lamentation and loss. Here the emphasis shifts from Antigone's divisive resistance against Creon to her powerful lamentations for her brother, cast in universal terms.[8] Elshtain's aim here remains anti-statist but, though she underscores yet again her commitment to a feminism poised for politics by its location in the "exigencies of the private" realm (1989: 229–230), she also insists now that Antigone is a "great representation of the *human* spirit" (1989: 231; emphasis added). Noting that "Antigone resists simple capture," Elshtain nonetheless captures her for a humanism of grief, connecting Sophocles' heroine to brave women who stood up to Nazis to bury their murdered male relatives during the Second World War and then to the Madres of the Plaza in Argentina who faced down an army to demand an accounting of those "disappeared" in the Dirty War.

The move from resistance to lamentation triggers a shift of emphasis as well – from Elshtain's focus on the unique singularity of persons (violated by state bureaucracy) to their equality (violated by murderous juntas) and from her specifically anti-statist social feminism to a transnationally iterated universal humanism with anti-authoritarian power. The latter's premise is the equal dignity of the dead, whose equality often seems easier to grant than that of the living.[9]

Elshtain's comparison of the Madres and Antigone in her second essay took hold, and well beyond the domain of political theory.[10] It was even embraced by some of the Madres themselves. The Madres marched as mothers, Elshtain claims, and they were brought into politics and its more universal promises (of human rights and dignity) reluctantly, moved by the immediate losses they suffered and protested at great risk to themselves. Elshtain celebrates the Madres and all those she calls the contemporary "daughters" of Antigone for resisting, while "reject[ing] both revenge and self-sanctimony" (1989: 233), never noting that the trouble with Antigone, as it were, is precisely her propensity, in Sophocles' rendering of the story, to call sanctimoniously for vengeance.[11] Reported by the sentry to have "called down curses on the heads of those" who desecrated her brother's body (427–428 [476–477]), Antigone is given to hot incitements, not soft laments. Her vengefulness disappears when Elshtain ennobles the Madres by comparing them to the classical Antigone. With this move, Elshtain puts the Madres above or beyond politics, linking them to an ideological maternalism that represents motherhood as timeless, universal, and natural, and tethering it to an ethics of care that is all these things as well. But Elshtain also does something else: comparing Antigone to the Madres, Elshtain softens and humanizes Antigone. The effect on Antigone of such maternalization is less often noted than are the ennobling effects of classicization on others by way of her. For example, R. Clifton Spargo notes that the Madres' dissidence seemed political *"until* they took on, for Elshtain as for others, 'the classical grandeur of Antigone'" (2008: 291; emphasis added).[12] But, we might add, conversely, Antigone would have seemed vengefully partisan had she not taken on the humanist halo of the Madres. Hegel prepared the way for this sanctification by making Antigone a saintly sister whose actions may have deleterious political effects but whose consciousness is in no way politically engaged or motivated.

Such apoliticality may add to rather than subtract from the political effectiveness of dissidents like the Madres, as Spargo points out. But the Madres' was not a naïve apoliticality; it was strategic, Spargo says. Insofar as the Madres not only acted as *mothers* (as Elshtain would have it) but more importantly *acted* as mothers (wearing "dowdy, old-fashioned maternal clothing for their protests," for example), "they were 'ironically' interpreting their own apolitical status" (2008: 130).[13] And this gained for their actions a certain political traction.

There is a difference, however, between noting the efficacy of such naïveté (as Spargo does) and falling for it as Elshtain arguably does, while also then turning it into a norm for political action as such. The Madres had few choices and were unspeakably courageous. The idea here is not to criticize them nor to argue there were other real and preferable vernaculars of resistance. It is, rather, to ask how and why an action in one context, performed by women acting in concert as mothers against a junta, should be wrenched out of context and turned into a norm and an ideology (of maternalism) that becomes a standard for politics as anti-statist politics everywhere. It is also to ask whether such anti-statist politics are well suited as a total politics to the democratic and neo-liberal institutions of contemporary Western democracies.[14]

Diana Taylor, in a study of the gender politics of Latin American resistance culture, goes yet further to analyze the *costs* of such performed political naïveté, especially when it genders feminine. In her book, *Disappearing Acts* (1997a), she argues that the Madres' self-effacing but powerful performance of powerlessness bought them some power, but it was also disempowering. Specifically, Taylor blames the "bad script" of "Antigone versus Oedipus" embraced by many of the Madres. The Madres represented motherhood as "universal, immutable and eternal," Taylor explains. They claimed their lamentations were in "the tradition of women's lamentations that dates back more than 2,500 years to Greek drama." They positioned themselves as mediators "between warring fathers and sons ... [T]hey even perpetuated the Oedipal framing of events by repeatedly asserting they had been made pregnant by their children [and they] identified restoration of their sons with restoration of the phallus" (1997a: 203; cf. 220).[15] The result? The women brought down a regime (though, Taylor suggests, the Falklands war played perhaps a more key role), but they did not win agency or equality for themselves. Their sons were left with little choice: they could not ally with their mothers, who had styled themselves as weak, and so the sons joined or replaced the fathers in power and left the women "on the sidelines, somehow marginal to the happy ending" (1997a: 203–204).[16] This, Taylor says sadly, was the predictable "political denouement of this national fantasy" (1997a: 204).[17]

Taylor sees more promise in classical *receptions*, in particular in Griselda Gambaro's Argentine rewrite of Sophocles' *Antigone* as *Antígona Furiosa*. Gambaro too wants to "'mine the canonic possibilities first expressed in classical art and feeling' in order to stage women's defiance" (1997a: 209), says Taylor. But, unlike Elshtain, Gambaro does not sanitize Antigone's passion and violence, nor does she classicize in a way that universalizes. Gambaro maintains a "tension between Sophocles' work and her own" (1997a: 210), going back and forth between the fifth-century Athenian and twentieth-century Argentine contexts, highlighting the frictions and not just the continuities between them.[18] Gambaro sets out to rewrite the canon, Taylor says tellingly, "with a vengeance" (1997a: 222).[19]

Still, Taylor cautions, even Gambaro simply "cannot change the role of Antigone, who is doomed to sacrifice herself time and again" (1997a: 222). That is, we might say, even the best vengeful classicizations will succumb either to humanist martyrdom or to what Carl Schmitt called "Hamletization," which is "the transformation of the figure of the avenger into a reflective, self-conscious melancholic," mournful, and incapable of action (2009: 19).[20] As we shall see, Taylor's concern, and Schmitt's diagnosis, seem to be borne out by Judith Butler's shift, partly by way of Antigone, from a citational politics of vengeful sovereignty to a "humanist" ethics and politics of lamentation.

BUTLER'S ANTIGONEAN TURNS

Although she is drawn to Gambaro, Taylor is nonetheless at best agnostic about whether "feminist writers [can] open up new roads for themselves through ventriloquism" (1997a: 222). Such rewrites or receptions seem more promising to Judith Butler, who emphasizes throughout her work

promise of practices of reiteration and resignification for progressive
.tics. It is ironic then that Butler is lured by Antigone into lamentation
: Taylor is not. This may be because Taylor charts the working and
reworking of Antigone scripts while Butler is herself a participant in the
reclamation of Antigone for ethics and politics.

Butler turns to Antigone several times in her work but I focus mostly on
two of her Antigone-related books, which I take to be exemplary.[21] The
first, *Antigone's Claim*, is an extended reading of Sophocles' play and of
previous deployments of it by Hegel, Lacan, and others; the other, *Precarious Life*, is more of a mourning-work of US violence after 9/11, and it
invokes Sophocles' heroine. As with Elshtain, so with Butler: the first
engagement with Antigone develops an anti-statist Antigonean politics
and the focus is on the conflict with Creon.[22] The second endorses a more
universal humanist ethics of lamentation in which the focus is on suffering.
Sensitivity to shared vulnerability and exposure, Butler argues, can move
us to cross the merely political lines of friend/enemy and inspire us to treat
all lives as grievable and human. Finally, as in Elshtain so in Butler,
Antigone's self-sanctimony and her calls for vengeance go unremarked.
I begin with the second of these two of Butler's books and work backwards
from a humanism of grievability to politics, from lamentation of sovereign
violence to an effort to claim sovereignty, from suffering to speech acts,
from the post-9/11 context of 2004 to the pre-9/11 world of 2000. The
differences between the two positions are sometimes subtle – the arguments sometimes even shade into each other, as when brief mentions of
Spinoza's life-centered *conatus* appear alongside the discussions of grief and
grievability that are central to ethics and politics in *Precarious Life*. Still,
there is a clear switch in rhetoric and tone from the playful, funny,
energetic, even impish engagement with Antigone in 2000 to a more
sober, earnest, and decidedly unwitty invocation of the tragic heroine in
2004's *Precarious Life* and since.

(i) Precarious Life

Precarious Life shows how the US media and state institutions establish
certain *hierarchies* of grievability, putting the lie to the old saw that we are
all equal in death. Some deaths seem to call for public and private grieving
and others simply do not. Some death circumstances are seen as political,
others are not. Some obituaries are published, others are not. Some bodies
are treated honorifically, others horrifically. Butler asks: "What are the
cultural barriers against which we struggle when we try to find out about

the losses that we are asked not to mourn, when we attempt to name, and so to bring under the rubric of the 'human,' those whom the United States and its allies have killed?" (2004a: 46).[23]

The issue here is not only the hierarchy of deaths but also what it evidences and re-secures. After 9/11, loss and mourning in the US were treated as occasions to restore the sense of sovereign impermeability pierced by the attacks. The sovereign response to grief was to seek out vengeance and violence to shore up sovereignty's damaged form. But why, Butler asks, must grief and loss license aggression? These can move us instead to cultivate *non*-sovereign modes of being that reject rather than cultivate violence. For Butler, Antigone is helpful here. Ignoring the aggression and violence to which she gives voice in grief, Butler highlights Antigone's importance as someone who "exemplified the political risks in defying the ban against public grief during times of increased sovereign power and hegemonic national unity" (2004a: 46).

For Butler, lamentation points away from sovereignty and toward vulnerability and mortality, common traits that limn the "more general conception of the human" toward which Butler works in *Precarious Life*, emphasizing our dependence on others and our vulnerability to them (2004a: 31). This primordial dependence on others means we are defined by vulnerability, which demarcates a range of possibilities from "the eradication of our being at one end [of the range, to] the physical support for our lives at the other" (2004a: 31). Notably the two end points of Butler's range of human commonality map onto Hannah Arendt's labor (in which we are governed by the time of mortality and risk eradication) and work (in which we insulate ourselves from the time of mortality by fabricating physical supports of life that outlast a human life). But what about Arendt's third element of the human condition: Arendtian action, a collective, non- or quasi-sovereign endeavor whose principle is natality?[24] Arendtian action also exposes us to vulnerability (if action goes awry, we may be hurt or misunderstood and, since it is collective, we are dependent on others and the good will of their "constant mutual release"); and action helps produce supports for life (what Arendt calls the "web" of human relationships) (1958: 216).[25] Missing from Butler's spectrum of the human in *Precarious Life*, Arendtian action is of interest here because it points beyond the sorts of sovereignty whose violence Butler worries about, but also beyond the grievability with which she replaces them, while nonetheless bearing the marks of both. Action, which expresses what Arendt calls the "ontological fact of natality" is a non-sovereign performance that works to reconstitute communities and inaugurate new realities.[26] Arendtian action exposes us to mortality, we may die in action, after all; but it is not about grievability. Arendtian action postulates not grievability but immortality, as its debt to Pericles' Funeral Oration might lead us to expect, actually.[27]

Although Butler mentions in passing in *The Psychic Life of Power* that passion and love are similar in their ek-static structure to mourning, and although she thematizes the idea of a "livable life" (as opposed to a grievable one) in *Undoing Gender*, her affective repertoire, especially since *Precarious Life*, is largely oriented to loss.[28] Focused on doing mourning otherwise, she says much less about the need to do otherwise than mourning as well. Again, here, we feel the absence of Arendt's third dimension of the human condition: action. In neglecting it, Butler does not follow the *Antigone*'s lure. Few do (Butler was one of those few, in her earlier *Antigone's Claim*). It is true, the play's protagonist is focused (almost) exclusively on the lamentations denied her by Creon, but it is important that the issue for her is not just the lamentations but what they stand for: the forms of individuality and membership they postulate (as I argue in Chapter 4), the arguments they enable (Chapter 5), and the life-giving solidarities to which they give rise and by which they are nurtured (Chapter 6). More to the point, the play was performed in the fifth century in the context of a larger festival of Dionysus that featured also comedies, satyr plays, and more. The play's focus on the *mere* life orientation of finitude was supplemented by the *more* life orientation of festival in the fifth century. Thus, mortality is counterbalanced by natality and this is evident in the play's context and also in the text itself. We see it in something the Chorus says at the play's beginning.

Relieved that Thebes has narrowly averted a destructive civil war, the Chorus asks, in effect, "now what?" and responds as follows:

Now let us win oblivion from the wars,
thronging the temples of the gods
in singing, dancing choirs through the night!
Lord Dionysus, god of the dance
that shakes the land of Thebes, now lead the way!   (151–154 [168–172])

These lines immediately precede Creon's first speech in which he responds to the recent emergency by declaring one brother a friend of the polis and the other its enemy. The former is buried with full honors, the latter left out to rot. With his edict, Creon seeks to steady the unsteady polis. The Chorus has just proposed that rather than remember who did what and make an example of them, it would be better to forget – in dance. Rather than steady the polis, the Chorus wants further to unsteady it, or to unsteady it otherwise, by way of communal release and abandon. Their call to Thebans to forget strife in dance would have been familiar to Athens, the "city of forgetting" which staged its theater in the context of precisely the sort of festival to which the play's Chorus calls Thebes.[29] That the call is unheard or rejected by Creon seems to forecast his downfall. He is too much in the grip of remembering wrongs. Butler's call to move past friend/enemy distinctions like Creon's by way of lamentation allies her with Antigone, the great lamenter, the very Antigone Butler had earlier struggled to overcome.[30] Together then, Creon in his commitment to unequal grievability and Butler in her commitment to equal grievability, together they occlude the festive forgetting that reconstitutes communities and to which the Chorus on behalf of Dionysus issues that call to natality and dance.

(ii) Antigone's Claim

In support of her depiction, in *Precarious Life*, of Antigone as a representative of grief for ungrievable life, Butler cites her own earlier book, *Antigone's Claim*, and this intimates she has not altered her position from the one Antigone to the other. But in fact there is a shift: in *Antigone's Claim*, the focus is not centrally on Antigone's willingness to risk herself to bury Polynices but also and more fundamentally on Antigone's own efforts to claim *sovereignty* against Creon.[31] Antigone may not in the end "achieve the effect of sovereignty she apparently seeks," Butler says (2000: 77), but sovereignty *is* what Antigone seeks. As Butler herself puts it, Antigone counters Creon's "sovereign speech act by asserting her own sovereignty" (2000: 11; cf. 23). An assertive politics that quests for power in *Antigone's Claim* gives way in *Precarious Life* to a lamentation of sovereignty's excesses on behalf of a (post)politics or ethics premised on human commonalities of vulnerability and mortality.

To put it another way, we might say, natality is little in evidence in *Precarious Life*. The price of the book's turn to equal grievability seems to be the displacement of a more political and natalist Antigone on behalf of a humanist and mortalist one. It may even be that Butler, like Elshtain, is drawn by Antigone (but also, of course, by events of the day: the Madres for Elshtain, 9/11 for Butler) from a politics that quests for sovereign power to a lamentation of power's excesses, and from sovereignty into "humanism," a term Butler often puts in scare-quotes to mark its non-identity with what usually goes under that name.[32]

Insofar as Butler and Elshtain are pulled out of politics and into a universalism and/or ethics of lamentation by Antigone, it is particularly ironic that it is Antigone who draws them in. Sophocles' protagonist does risk herself to cross the lines of friend–enemy in grief and she does declare the dead are all equal. But she also invokes the very hierarchies of grievability that Butler deplores in her name. As it turns out, there are some people even Antigone won't try to "bring under the rubric of the 'human'" (2004a: 46). When Creon tells her that Eteocles would not approve of her actions, that to honor Polynices is to honor Eteocles' enemy, Antigone does not respond with humanist universals. Instead, she quarrels about precisely where to draw the line between who is in and who is out of the circle of concern: "But it was his brother, not some slave that died" (617 [581]), she says, making clear to Creon the limits of her "humanism."[33] Thus, Antigone can be a pure figure of mourning only if we divest her of her divisive politicality – sometimes ugly, violent, difficult. Some even project it onto others. One obvious site of such projection is Creon, who is depicted by Elshtain and Butler as a tyrant who divides people rather than joining them together. We are alerted to another instance of such projection, when Butler overlooks the rough curses directed by Antigone at her foes, while taking particular note of the brutal curses Oedipus directs against his sons.[34] Even so, Butler's first Antigone is divisive, certainly more so than her second.

If for Elshtain Antigone returns us to the family over the state, for Butler in *Antigone's Claim* (four years before *Precarious Life*), Antigone's very forbiddenness as an incest shows how imbricated are the heteronormative family and state. In what we could take to be a direct rebuttal of Elshtain (whom Butler does not mention), Butler says: Antigone cannot *represent* "the normative principles of kinship, steeped as she is in incestuous legacies that confound her position within kinship" (2000: 2). This means we cannot simply treat her as a good sister (Hegel) or mother (Elshtain) as if that explains anything, "as if kinship furnishes a [prior] principle for action" (2000: 58). (This serves as a critique of maternalism as an ideology.)[35] But neither is Antigone outside of kinship as such. Instead "her action is the action of kinship, the performative repetition that reinstates kinship as a public scandal." The scandal is that she loves her brother/father too much and that for her, an incest, the distinction between father and brother is unclear. Only in Butler's later mentions of Antigone, after *Antigone's Claim* (and *Undoing Gender*), will Antigone's scandal become the scandalous mourning of friend/enemy alike, which inspires an ethics of grievable life poised to overcome statist distinctions between friend and foe.

Does a more divisive Antigone
begin to re-habilitate Creon?

In *Antigone's Claim,* however, Butler sees a different politics issuing from Antigone. Her scandalous act is generative: it "implicates her in an aberrant repetition of a norm." The norm is not a rigid law antecedent to practice but rather "a lawlike regulation of culture that operates with its own contingency" and so it is vulnerable to subversion (2000: 58). This is a postulate of norms as such (and of the "human" [2009: 94–95; 168]), a point on which Butler insists throughout her work, positioning herself beyond the powerful repetition or pure negation of the law that most Lacanians treat as the only two options. Butler's aim here is to break the grip of the Oedipal law and find the agency that remains in the universe of psychoanalysis after Antigone's famous "no" to Creon has been said. This is different from Butler's lamentation focus since 9/11. Butler says in response to Lacan: the "position outside life as we know it," which he identifies with Antigone (a position that is beyond life and death, beyond the limit, and beyond the human), "is not necessarily a position outside life *as it must be*" (emphasis added). The "position outside life," the Antigonean position, gives us not just "a perspective on the symbolic constraints under which livability is established," but also "a critical perspective by which the very terms of livability might be rewritten" (2000: 55).[36] This comes not from "a prepolitical opposition to politics, representing *kinship as the sphere that conditions the possibility of politics without ever entering into it*" (2000: 2; emphasis original), as Irigaray also intimates. Irigaray develops the reading in a distinctive way, finding in *Antigone* evidence of a prepolitical, prior matriarchal arrangement that might decenter patriarchy. But, Butler argues, by trying in this way to rebut Lacan on the totalizing quality of the Symbolic, Irigaray ultimately *recycles* his arguments rather than breaking out of them fully, for what institutes the distinction between matriarchal and patriarchal forms, at all, if not the Symbolic? Irigaray is thus stuck inside the very thing she seeks to get out of, Butler concludes. We are better off seeing Antigone's resistance in relation to her scandalous reiterations of Creon's discourse, her hybrid and shocking mixture – in her incest and her love of Haemon – of natal and conjugal family forms, and her mother-laden identification with and desire for her brother(s), Polynices (and Eteocles and Oedipus).[37]

"Is Lacan right," Butler asks, "that 'Antigone chooses to be purely and simply the guardian of the being of the criminal as such' 2000: (283), or does this criminality assert an unconscious right, marking a legality [which, presumably in a way different from Irigaray's matriarchy, is] prior to codification on which the symbolic in its hasty foreclosures must founder . . . ?" (2000: 55).

It is not entirely clear what Butler is thinking of when she refers, as she does here, to the Symbolic's *hasty foreclosures*. Foreclosure is an important term in her work before *Antigone's Claim* where it relates to same-sex desire foreclosed in the process of gendered subject formation and not, as here, to a legality prior to codification. But the term "hasty" is new (in *The Psychic Life of Power*, she describes foreclosure as a "preemptive [but still not *hasty*] loss" [1997: 23]). The term "hasty" seems to make the point that the Symbolic is more vulnerable to penetration and reiteration than most Lacanians think. Indeed this is Butler's modification of Foucault in her early work – that the Lacanian law of the father depends on performativity and a repetition that, "as imitation, works to contest and destabilize identity" and not, contra Foucault, to consolidate it (1990b: 13). This has been Butler's project throughout her work, to identify openings for resignification, iteration, subversion, to press for the aberrant repetition of norms, insisting on their weak dependence on the acts of subscription that others take as a sign of the norms' power and dominance. That is, her claim is that they need us and our compliance more than we need them to form us, to inform (on) us.

But why connect the Symbolic's vulnerability to *haste* in its foreclosures, when elsewhere Butler attributes its vulnerability to the incompleteness of its foreclosures and, in particular, to its disavowed but powerful dependence on subjects' rarely fully obedient re-performance of the Symbolic's laws in the social sphere? (There is always a gap, she says, between the norm and even our most obedient instancings of it.) The answer may be a sign of the power exerted by Antigone over her interpreter as Butler shifts focus away from Oedipus (in Freud and Lacan) and to Antigone.[38] In so doing, another subtle shift happens as well. In her turn to Antigone, Butler not only gains a heroine for feminism, but also a new antagonist: by way of Antigone, Butler is moved out of confrontation with the Oedipal paternal law, implacable, incontrovertible (even if also generative, in psychoanalysis), and is repositioned to face instead Creon and his edict forbidding the burial of Polynices. It is Creon's edict, after all, that is a *hasty* foreclosure, issued too fast and ultimately retracted. And Creon's is the sort of patriarchal power even a feminist can love – impotent, defeasible, ultimately regretful. In Creon, after all, we have a man who actually says he is sorry.[39]

This slip from Oedipus to Creon suggests one way in which (contra Taylor) pressing the cause of Antigone can alter and not just re-cement the Antigone versus Oedipus frame. If we note further that, as Mark Griffith (1998) observes, Creon at the end of the play is destroyed as a father and patriarch, but not as a ruler, then we may see further the attraction to

Butler of his displacement of Oedipus who, by contrast, loses his kingdom but retains his (flawed, incestuous) patriarchal power. Oedipus' power as patriarch is intact enough, as *Oedipus at Colonus* draws to a close, for him to end not by lamenting his loss of family but by cursing his sons and so securing the continuity of his line and/as the continuity of its curse. Creon's paternal law, more than the Oedipal one, is vulnerable to penetration and reiteration. In sum, the suggestion here is that if Butler returns to Antigone repeatedly, it is not only for the counter-sovereignty, resistance, and (later) lamentation that she expressly endorses. Butler benefits, more subtly, from the foe she thus gets to combat, a more defeasible foe than the father Antigone only laments and whose power is only enhanced and not dimmed by his death.[40]

Haste, then, is a productive term on which to focus here. But it does not tell us everything. For, in fact, the newly fragile Symbolic is not just the condition, it is also the product of Antigone's agency. On Butler's earlier account, the law is always "at risk of going off its course," and not just because the Symbolic's foreclosures are hasty but also because of the indefatigable power of words that Antigone finds the courage to utter on behalf of a "rival autonomy" that is much more than the mere "negation" to which Lacanians seek to confine her (2000: 65; 68).[41] The words she utters are Creon's, turned to new and subversive purposes when she, a daughter of incest, a woman, a dissident, speaks them. In sum, where Lacanians ask: "how does heterosexuality fatalize Antigone?" Butler wants us to ask: "what in Antigone's act is fatal for heterosexuality in its normative sense?" And what other pleasures and possibilities might arise in its place? It is not enough to pervert or reject or negate the norm; it must also be rearticulated. Later, in *Precarious Life*, all this will be upstaged by the need to mourn the norm's violence. But in *Antigone's Claim*, Butler argues that "Antigone is the occasion for a new field of the human, achieved through political catachresis, the one that happens when the less than human speaks as human" (2000: 82). Her actions prove fatal, it is true, concedes Butler but, she says, positioning Antigone as martyr for the cause, "this fatality exceeds her life and enters the discourse of intelligibility as its own promising fatality, the social form of its 'aberrant, unprecedented future'" (2000: 82).

Citing Lacan's own words, "aberrant, unprecedented future," Butler here positions herself vis-à-vis Lacan in precisely the way she says Antigone positions herself vis-à-vis Creon, borrowing and reiterating his language to make her "claim." Butler strives not to negate Lacan but to force a rearticulation.[42] She does this more than once but one more example suffices to illustrate the tactic: Lacan famously says that Antigone is a creature of monstrous desire. Butler takes that figure and turns it to advantage in a politics identified with the figure of monstrosity, catachresis, which makes sense of monstrosity by making monstrosity make sense.[43] Through catachresis, when the not human speaks as human it becomes human. This is no mere inclusion, however, for the human is itself altered.[44]

In sum, in *Antigone's Claim*, Butler insists that Antigone can transmit the Lacanian Symbolic and repeat the Oedipal curse in a way that "stops the future operation of that curse's chain" (though here the chain in question has become a bit more Creon's weakly linked one than Oedipus' iron clad one, as we just saw). But, by *Precarious Life*, the emphasis is less on stopping the chain than it is on Antigone's moving capacity to lament its operations and on her capacity, with her lamentation, which is now not citational or appropriative, to enact a counter-politics of humanist universals in opposition to the state's friend/enemy distinctions: a mortalist, humanist politics of grievable life.

ABSORBING THE LESSONS OF ANTIGONE:
EDELMAN, LATENCY, RESIGNIFICATION

If Butler seeks to open up a different future by way of Antigone (versus Oedipus/Creon), Lee Edelman sees instead in Antigone an invitation to reject the future altogether. Antigone is best read, Edelman (2004) argues contra Butler, not as a liminal incest who resists heteronormative marriage and points the way to the non-conventional attachments of new kinship forms. Instead, Antigone's marriage-to-death is what stands out: her rejection of all potential supporters and her monstrous embrace of death. She forces us to confront a radical anti-humanism from which tragedy's humanist receptions have for centuries shielded us with their focus on the redemptive powers of art, martyrdom, and love.

For Edelman, the fundamental divide is between anti-humanism – queer, anti-redemptive, anti-futurist, monstrous – and a humanism that is an ineluctably heteronormative, redemptive ideology of reproduction. From Edelman's perspective, the catachresis to which Butler turns recovers Antigone for intelligibility, rather than insisting on her opacity and monstrosity. Butler absorbs Lacan into her reading, but loses what he has to offer since in Butler, Edelman argues, resignification always bleeds into remediation and recuperation.[45] Developing this criticism of Butler, Edelman claims that when she allies Antigone with a future (i.e. kinship to come), Butler succumbs to the allure of the sacrificial Symbolic and falls into its ideology of "futurism." Futurism, Edelman's term, is the quest for human meaning and ontological status, tied not to kinship per se but more specifically to reproduction, and this with no small impact on those whose desire is enmeshed in non-reproductive sexual practices that are specifically resistant to futurism's domestications.[46]

Differences between Edelman and Butler can be parsed by way of the figure of the Child, central to Edelman's critique of the ideology of futurism which, he argues, incessantly invokes "the children" as an uninterrogatable reason to sacrifice ourselves for the future and in turn casts aspersions on the childless who are always under suspicion, suspected of standing outside the sacrificial Symbolic and of having no stake in the "future."[47] The Child comes up in an interview with Butler recorded in 2000 (when she was writing *Antigone's Claim*) in response to a question posed by Paul Rabinow. Rabinow asks Butler what he should do about his friends in Paris who insist gay couples must be raising psychotic children. He is mystified: "And these are thinkers, people who are socialists or communists or Trotskyites or leftists of all friendly bourgeois sorts who are defending all the right things in every other realm." Butler responds: "Your question brings us back to the sphere of liminality. What would it mean for the psychotic to speak and to make a claim, to go school and . . . I think that when you hold the view that such kids would be psychotic, and then the putatively psychotic kid comes over to your house – and wants a cookie, and wants to play with your kitten, tells you his feelings about balloons – there's a certain kind of *insistent mundaneness* that, I think, undermines that highly phobic relationship, maybe even lives in some kind of tension with it until it breaks open to something else, until it becomes unsustainable in some way." Paul Rabinow: "So you really are mildly optimistic?" (2001: 45–46; emphasis added).

She is. But sometimes a balloon is not just a balloon. Edelman refers to balloons as well, citing in his book an early scene in Hitchcock's *Strangers on a Train*, in which Bruno Anthony (played by Robert Walker) "punctures the balloon of cuteness that hangs like a halo above one annoying child" (2004: 121). Edelman says the scene casts as unspeakably cruel the villain (a homophobe's gay man), a "sinthomosexual" figure who visits wanton violence on the iconic innocent Child of the ideology of reproductive futurism. Uncharacteristically, Edelman, who does not normally bypass such details, does not pause to note the overtones of homoeroticism, pedophilia, and castration in this scene, in which the adult man punctures the boy's balloon with the heat of his lit cigarette. Still, the scene alerts us to the place of balloons in the repertoire of normal, idealized childhood and suggests that perhaps what comforts Butler's imagined phobic parents when the lesbian or gay-parented child shares his feelings about balloons is a reassurance subtly conveyed by the balloon: that this child has taken up his place in the "ideology of reproductive necessity" (Edelman 2004: 121). Edelman would focus on the betrayal, for queer politics, of this reassurance, while Butler sees enfolded in it a possibly radical agent of change. But there is something yet more powerful in the encounter, imagined by Butler, between the child and his friend's hostile parents. What makes the encounter potentially transformative is more than just the staged contradiction between the adults' phobic commitments and their experience of this child. What matters all the more, surely, is the fact that the child is seductive. He represents desire in the form of appetite (he wants a cookie), play (he wants to play with the cat), and sociality (he shares with the prejudiced adults "his feelings about balloons").

For Edelman, though, no such efforts to expand "the reach of the human" can deliver on the promise of real and equal inclusion. Instead, we must expand the field of the *in*human and insist on "enlarging what, in its excess, in its unintelligibility, exposes the human itself as always misrecognized catachresis, a positing blind to the willful violence that marks its imposition" (2004: 152; emphasis added). In an extended reading of Hitchcock's *The Birds*, Edelman invokes the birds as a marker of *in*humanity's expansiveness but, even though he does discuss Sophocles' *Antigone* as well, he neglects the complex role played by birds in Sophocles' play, in which birds are said to eat the carrion of Polynices' body and Antigone is herself likened to a bird bereft by her empty nest.[48] Carol Jacobs notes that when the sentry compares the mourning Antigone to a mother bird at an empty nest, the comparison gestures precisely in these two different directions: it both puts Antigone in the caring maternal role in relation to her brother (the mother bird) and in a more devouring relation, since birds are at that very moment feasting on Polynices' body (the vulture) (1996: 904).[49]

Such undecidability need not be a problem for Edelman, who wants to argue that the monstrous inhuman is always trying to break free of the grasp of the human. But it may be a problem nonetheless: where Butler takes catachresis, the figure of the monster, for her new "humanism," Edelman insists on the decidably anti-humanist Antigone. And he charges Butler with evading humanism's true monstrosity. Against Butler, and in effect reprising Diana Taylor's critique of the Madres' maternalism, Edelman insists on the limits of resignification, noting that even catachresis just catches us in the trap of rearticulation: resignifying a term like "human" does not, he says, efface or transcend the "prior uses to which it was put: no historical category of abjection is ever simply obsolete. It abides, instead, in its latency, affecting subsequent signification, always available, always waiting to be mobilized again" (2004: 115). Edelman departs from Taylor in one significant way, though: unlike Taylor, who worried that mobilizing Antigone versus Oedipus may be an inherently limiting move (part of the "bad script" of Antigone versus Oedipus), Edelman does not hesitate. His frustration apparent – *why*, he asks, must Antigone's readers always make a mother of this anti-maternal heroine?[50] Why must she be said to open a *future*? – he accuses Butler of an ameliorative reading that betrays queerness, but then stakes his own claim to Antigone: his is a fully monstrous Antigone that resists all domestication and turns no face to the future.[51] This is the meaning of her marriage-to-death.

Edelman's critique of Butler epitomizes a central debate within queer theory about the (im)possibility of remaking or rejecting the terms of intelligibility. Where Butler hopes for future kinship forms that repeat the law of kinship with a difference, Edelman calls for the renunciation of futurism, the embrace of the death drive with which he says gay people are in any case insistently identified, and the dethronement of the Child as the *arche* figure of hopeful politics. Edelman puts his position starkly: "The queerness we propose . . . knows nothing about 'sacrifice' now for the sake of future generations . . . " (2004: 31).[52]

Ironically, however, and in spite of his claim that old figures abide in their "latency, affecting subsequent significations, always available, always waiting to be mobilized again," Edelman seems to assume that his own monstrous Antigone, who rejects motherhood and reproduction, does break fully out of the old Oedipal frame when she entirely negates it with her "no!" (2004: 115). The resilience and latency of the old frame is made manifest, though, when at the end of a fabulous book-length screed against generational inheritance (*No Future!*), in which Edelman celebrates Antigone briefly and a host of others at length for turning "no face to the future," he affirms a lesson that he says is "bequeathed" to us by a queer character in a Hitchcock film (2004: 105; 109). It is a mere slip and we should not make too much of it. But it is nonetheless significant, for it shows how difficult it is to leave Oedipus behind, to think the future without the trappings of "futurism" – intergenerational kinship and its legal apparatus – which abide in their "latency, affecting subsequent significations, always available, always waiting, to be mobilized again" (2004: 115).[53]

For her part, Butler attends more to the act of inheritance than to the bequeathing. Antigone, who has no choice but to transmit the Lacanian Symbolic, repeats the Oedipal curse, but "by obeying the curse upon her, stops the future operation of that chain" (2000: 52).[54] How we inherit is more important than whether we do. By the time we get to *Precarious Life*, however, Butler's Antigone is more identified with lamentation than interruption. This might seem to vindicate Edelman's critique but, to be fair, Butler assumes that lamentation may itself constitute an interruption. My argument here is that if lamentation has interruptive powers, these are different from the ones on which Butler is focused, in any case, and they postulate a different reading of *Antigone* than the one provided by Butler: one in which we position Antigone's laments as part of an agonistic humanism, not an ethics and politics of grievable life.[55]

We have seen here that a certain pull from action and natality to lamentation and mortality exerts itself on those feminist and queer theorists who turn to Antigone. (If Diana Taylor escapes this fate, it is because of her own critique of and skepticism about this move.) In Butler we shift from an Antigone who stops the future operations of the paternal law in order to claim its power (as Butler says in *Antigone's Claim*) to one (as in *Precarious Life*) who laments its operations upon us. The claiming Antigone does not seek to stop sovereignty, she seeks to own it. From *Antigone's Claim* to *Precarious Life* and, most recently, *Frames of War*, Butler's earliest Antigone of rival citational sovereignty gives way to the humanist lamenter of the dead. This is the Antigone-effect.[56]

FRAMED

My aim here has been to highlight the magnetic powers of the "Antigone versus Oedipus" script, or frame. Like so many others who invoke Antigone versus Oedipus, first Elshtain, then Butler finds herself pressed from a politics of agonistic conflict in quest of (counter or anti)sovereignty into a humanistic ethics of lamentation of sovereignty's excesses. In her study of "frames" in *Frames of War*, Butler proposes that since frames have the power to inflect and subvert our purposes we may sometimes find that social change requires that we change the frame that sets the limits of what we can see and say. Our current frames of war seem to press us into violence, and so, Butler argues, we need to change the frame from one of sovereignty to one of precariousness. But the figure to whom she turns again and again on behalf of the new frame – Antigone – is herself, as we have seen, a figure of sovereignty *and* precariousness. Does the received

Antigone who props up the naïve Madres and is propped up by them, does that received Antigone, who laments her brother and brings down a tyrant, herself press Butler from sovereignty (the focus in *Antigone's Claim*) to precarity (the focus in *Precarious Life*)?[57]

When Butler broaches the problem of differential grief, noting that public grieving after 9/11 makes certain deaths but not others iconic, respectable, real, she says that the politics of differential grief is an issue "since at least the time of Antigone" (2009: 38–41), seeming to leverage the powers of classicization for her argument. But she also strives to avoid implication in the powerlessness that Taylor charges is the unavoidable effect of Antigone-framed resistance and that Edelman sees as necessarily the consequence of an ongoingly humanist appropriation of classics. Thus, Butler refers occasionally to the connections between lamentation and anger, loss and dissidence, mourning and resistance.[58]

Nonetheless, I have suggested, the frame exerts more power over Butler than Butler does over the frame. In this sense, the frame may appear to be rather like the curse that drives Greek tragedy. Those over whom it has power think they can rework, evade, or escape it, but almost invariably, no matter the lengths to which they go, they are drawn back into its orbit. But the power of the frame is also less determinative than that of the tragic curse. If feminists are lured by Antigone from action to mourning, that may be because of how they approach the play or because of assumptions they bring to it. In the case of Butler, even her first, powerful and more political, reading of Antigone sidesteps some of its more radical possibilities and leaves intact, if latent, certain elements of the "bad script" of Antigone versus Oedipus. Arguably, her focus on Antigone's speech acts (sovereign and citational) in *Antigone's Claim* leaves Antigone's lamentation in a kind of unprocessed apoliticality, empowered in/by its rawness to return later and exert its seemingly innocent force in *Precarious Life* (much as Butler would claim sex-gender norms operate when unsubjected to critical appropriation, redirection, and critique).[59]

Moreover, Butler, throughout her work, sees Antigone as an isolated, lone, suffering heroine, opposed to her sister and seeking glory for herself, a martyr to the proverbial lost cause. (For all his differences with Butler, Edelman sees Antigone the same way.) This captures and mirrors modern romantic and liberal imaginations but does little for our shared democratic futures. It may even feed a certain left melancholy in which activists are more pure but also less powerful.[60] This rather conventional Antigone slips all too easily into the self-indulgence for which Anouilh made her famous, a charge also often directed at Butler by critics who seriously mistake her politics of performativity for mere wardrobe choices and solipsistic fashion statements.

In *Frames of War*, Butler understands the importance of resisting the hero's allure: "Maybe the 'act' in its singularity and heroism is overrated: it loses sight of the iterable process in which a critical intervention is needed and it can become the very means by which the 'subject' is produced [as sovereign] at the expense of a relational social ontology" (2009: 184). This speculation, a critique again of Lacan and others, actually commits Butler, it seems to me, to a reconsideration of her earlier readings, especially her admiring treatment of Antigone's rejection of Ismene as a mark of the more famous sister's heroic singularity (2000: 27–28; 61–62). Evidence of what Butler calls a "social ontology" is apparent in the risk that attends Antigone's choice to cross the lines of friend/enemy in grief (as Butler wants us to do now), and in the lines of inequality that constitute her social world, apparent when Antigone *invokes* the very hierarchies of grievability that Butler deplores in her name. Antigone practices a politics of differential grief when she demands equal treatment for Eteocles and Polynices, but contrasts her brothers with slaves on whose behalf she would never protest the indignity of exposure. As I will argue in Part II of this book, this is just one sign that Antigone's laments are not universal. They are part of a vernacular that situates her in a particular form of life. Moreover, as we shall also see in Part II, there is heretofore unremarked evidence of a deep sororal connection between Antigone and Ismene that presses on us the responsibility to interrogate the palimpsests of reception that isolate Antigone and make of her a radical individual – something quite different from Sophocles' creation.

CRIMP, A ROAD NOT TAKEN?

Voltaire said that heaven has given us two things to compensate for the many miseries of life, *hope* and *sleep*. He might have added *laughter* to the list. (Kant, quoted in Critchley)

There is another model of political mourning not drawn upon by those whose turn to Antigone is tracked here. I close this chapter with the work of Douglas Crimp because in theorizing his ambivalence about mourning's promise for politics and insistently combining mortality and natality in his politics, he seems to avoid the Antigone-effect: his politics of mourning is never only that and it never collapses into a mourning of politics.[61] He recognizes that mourning may displace political energies but he acknowledges at the same time the absolute need to mourn.[62] Crimp learned that

lesson the hard way. After his father, with whom he had a vexed relationship, died, Crimp did not mourn. He soon acquired an eye infection that
blocked his tear duct making it impossible for him to cry and, as the
infection ran its course, the eye then gave forth liquids of infection that
could not be stopped. Crimp yielded finally to what he took to be his
body's demand to grieve a difficult loss.

That lamentation will not be denied is an Antigonean motif, but Crimp
does not classicize his experience. He is wary of romantic or tragic emplotments of the AIDS crisis and Antigone would seem to promise both. Emergency, crisis, catastrophe, which seem by their very nature to make survival
paramount and to narrow our focus from more life to mere life, also come
with scripts (or frames) or soon acquire them. As Marita Sturken points out,
AIDS soon came "to be associated with a heightened artistic awareness, a
tragic yet romantic early death, a sense of purpose," an invitation to transcendence (1997: 167). Crimp rejected such emplotments: "We don't need a
cultural renaissance . . . We don't need to transcend the epidemic, we need to
end it" (1987b: 7).[63] Wary of a tragic narrative in which artistic achievement
redeems – or in Nietzsche's terms "justifies" – individual suffering and loss,
Crimp demanded that art meet its social obligations and acquaint itself with
the political character of suffering. Between the humanist idealization of art as
"timeless and universal" and (the also humanist) capitalist commodifications
of art as a valuable resource for charitable fund-raising (Art for AIDS) lay a
third, obscured alternative: art as a collective political practice aimed at
transformation and social change. Seeking neither transcendence nor monet-
ization in response to the problem of AIDS, this artistic response grows out of
acquaintance with "individual lives, which are time-bound and contingent"
(2002: 29).[64]

In the 1980s, mourning was unavoidable in the face of devastating losses
but it was also dangerous: it threatened to absorb the much-needed
political energies of a nascent movement. In the wake of AIDS, says
Crimp, "people whose energies and resources had gone toward the invention of gay life either succumbed or turned their attention to dealing with
death" (2002: 13). It was important, Crimp argued, to mourn loss, while
not mistaking funeral gatherings for activist political action. "Public
mourning rituals may of course have their own political force, but they
nevertheless often seem, from an activist perspective, indulgent, sentimental, defeatist," says Crimp, noting the last words of Joe Hill: "'Don't
mourn, organize!'" (2002: 131–132).[65]

But mourning and activism are not necessarily opposed in the zero sum
way suggested by Joe Hill in his famous self-elegy. If many people think

they are, this may be due to Freud's influence, Crimp argues. For Freud, the normal mourning process requires a turning away from the world and this seems at odds with activism. Also, for Freud, Crimp says, the completion of mourning returns the mourner to normalcy and this also seems to be at odds with activism. Normalcy is usually what activists are trying to unsettle. Moreover, normalcy signifies differently in gay male grief practices, as Crimp points out. When Freud, who prizes the normal work of mourning, insists that mourning should not be interfered with lest it be aborted, he makes clear the quandary of gay men whose mourning is constantly interfered with (as was Antigone interfered with in hers, though Crimp does *not* make the comparison). Causes of death are hushed up and surviving partners silenced at funerals where families of origin demand that lost loved ones remain closeted in death as they were in life or work actively to return them to the closet from which they in life had emerged. Here Creon's treatment of the dead Haemon is evocative: when Creon takes his son home to his mother (having unclasped the dead Haemon from his corpse-bride), Creon re-establishes his own sovereign paternity post-mortem. He undoes the son's final living wish: to be married to Antigone in death. She is not a proper love object, in the grieving father's opinion.

There is another reading of Freud, however, that suggests that mourning and militancy are not only not opposed, they may even be co-implicated. As we saw in Chapter 1, we may read Freud as saying that mourning is a process that *begins* with withdrawal, with the ego wanting to die along with the "lost object," but it does not end there. As Henry Staten points out, Freud suggests that during the mourning process the ego "is 'persuaded' [as it were] by the sum of the narcissistic satisfactions it derives from being alive to sever its attachment to the object that has been abolished" (1995: 255). On this reading, mourning does not always come to its own conclusion; often it is interrupted. On Staten's reading, recall, the interruption is, however, enabling or productive, not abortive (or, better, perhaps it is both).[66] At some level, we may say, Crimp understands this (although this is not his reading of Freud). Hence his consistent demand for a militant combination of lamentation and festival: to grant mourning its place while also interrupting it with the pleasures of natality, luring activists out of mourning and back to life.[67]

Why hasn't Crimp's work been taken up by political theorists working on mourning politics? Why does the gay community's, and in particular ACT UP's, 1980s blend of lamentation and activism seem to lack the traction of Antigone and the Madres as a model for contemporary theorists of lamentation?[68] In Elshtain's case, the puzzle is easy to solve: her embrace of lamentation for politics postulates the heteronormative kinship structures opposed by Crimp. We might even hazard that lamentation is attractive to Elshtain as a politics precisely because one of its effects is to shore up the heteronormative family form that maternalist practices seem to postulate but also actually help (re)produce. Indeed, this was Taylor's critical insight regarding the Madres, that their commitment to lamentation drove them to *act* like mothers in some traditional sense that was not, however, authentically reflective of their roles in real life, nor authentically progressive, and the result was that maternity then acted on the women, who thought they could instrumentalize maternity but in the end were instrumentalized by it. (Perhaps this is another Antigone-effect.)

But what about Butler? In her case, the answer to the puzzle may have to do with a not always fully processed ethical anti-statism that has more in common with the Madres (whom she never mentions) than with Crimp (whom she does mention but whom she casts, as I will argue in a moment, in the role of Madre). The Madres mobilized a post-political ethical universalism (restoration of the dead to their families for proper burial) against the state, while Crimp and ACT UP fought to enlist the state to act on behalf of a sexual health politics that was different from the governmental emergency politics of a public health crisis.[69] Indeed, the crisis itself was political, they argued: the product of the government's wrongful evacuation of its role as caretaker of the public good. As Crimp put it, in no uncertain terms: "Scientific research, health care, and education are the responsibility and purpose of government and not of so-called 'private initiative,' an ideological term that excuses and perpetuates the state's irresponsibility. Therefore [every private initiative] should make clear that it is necessitated strictly because of criminal negligence on the part of government" (2002: 5).

Where Crimp wants to force the state to step up to its responsibilities, Butler wants to tell it to step back. She turns to Antigone, first, on behalf of a rival sovereignty and, later, on behalf of an ethics and politics of grievable life that seems inflected by the Madres though she never mentions them (but by now, twenty years after Elshtain, Antigone has virtually *become* the Madres and vice versa). Butler's aim in her first turn to Antigone is, as she herself says, to develop an anti-statist feminism and politics. If she mostly skips over the experience of ACT UP and the work of Crimp, that may be because the coalition is not anti-statist at all: its relationship to the state is more ambivalent than oppositional.[70] The aim of ACT UP in the 1980s was not just to oppose the state and expose the irresponsibility of government but to enlist the state's resources.[71] Like the Antigone of Butler's *Antigone's Claim*, but in far more statist fashion, AIDS activists like Crimp wanted sovereignty, and they tried to claim it. They did not want just to lament sovereignty's excesses.

In the context of the epidemic, what was needed was both for government to help and for it to get out of the way, for it to regulate less (opening trials and unapproved drugs for those who could not wait, which led to an unlikely but workable alliance with conservatives who favored market deregulation [Epstein 1996: 223]) and for government to do more (pressing pharmaceutical companies to make drugs available and affordable, running public safe sex campaigns, distributing condoms, supporting explicit safe sex manuals, deferring to gay community norms rather than moralizing against them, and so on). To accomplish all this, ACT UP had to, like Antigone, shout out or make visible emotions and actions cast as transgressive, and reject the temptation, historically identified with Ismene, to collude in keeping their actions a secret. Silence, ACT UP proclaimed, equaled death (as the group first proclaimed in a demonstration at the New York General Post Office in 1984, using a logo provided by the SILENCE=DEATH Project).[72]

ACT UP did not lament power, nor just rage against it, nor just seek inclusion. They did all of these. But they also *sought* power. Persons With AIDS (PWAs) democratized treatment and disseminated scientific knowledge. They turned themselves from patients into health citizens.[73] They became unapologetically impatient. Activists became fluent in the sciences of protease inhibitors, clinical trials, and statistical sampling and they won the respect, sometimes grudging, of members of the scientific community.[74] Moving from objects to subjects of knowledge, AIDS activists worked rifts in the scientific community, once they learned to speak its languages. When activists fought to open up clinical trials to patients cast as *imperfect* (those with other diseases, or who were unreliable in their medicine taking, and so on), clinical researchers resisted. But statisticians turned out to be more willing than clinicians to tolerate a little noise in their data (Epstein 1996: 248–250). That is, activists worked one model of good research against another. ACT UP anticipated Jacques Rancière's call to "indisciplinarity," a contestation of the division of the world into subjects and objects of knowledge. As Rancière puts it, "The apportionment of disciplines refers to the more fundamental apportionment that separates those regarded as qualified from those regarded as unqualified; those who do the science and those who are regarded as its objects" (2008: 3).

Crimp's call to combine mourning and militancy came out of this political practice. It was adamantly life-affirming: mobilizing, militant, passionate, and erotic – natal, angry, and funny – not unlike, even if not fully like, Antigone, as I read her below (and a bit like Antígona, as Gambaro renders her).[75] If Antigone is never taken up by Crimp as a model, this is probably not only because he was suspicious that humanist classicization was a mode of reconciliation with death rather than a commitment to combat it. It was likely also to some extent because she had been well and fully sanctified by Hegel as a non-erotic sister, and was at that very moment in the 1980s being maternalized by the Madres and their classicizing admirers, like Elshtain.[76] Besides, Hegel's and the Madres' quasi-Antigonean embrace of apoliticality for sororal ethics and maternal politics was too close to the position of passivity from which ACT UP was trying to break away on behalf of a fuller (more political, more erotic) portrait of gay male life (Crimp) and on behalf of the needs of the moment, which demanded autonomous aggressive activism and state action (Crimp, Epstein, Sturken). Crimp's politics were statist because, as Crimp argues, "[s]cientific research, health care, and education are the responsibility and purpose of government" (2002: 30).[77] But often also anti-statist because efforts like those of conservative Republican Senator Jesse Helms to defund AIDS preventative sex education make clear "how compromised any efforts at responding to AIDS will be when conducted by the state" (2002: 30). Warily, AIDS activists modeled a demanding agonistic enlistment of the state. Their civic demand that the state do its job – soliciting publics, generating and providing public goods – may be even more timely now in the neo-liberal twenty-first century than it was in the 1980s. That is, in the current context, anti-statism is easily turned to neo-liberal advantage, and facilitates the neo-liberal reinvention of the state from an institution charged with generating and securing public goods to a facilitator of private contracts.

(i) Butler, Crimp, and the quilt

Butler is not unacquainted with Crimp's work. She cites him in *The Psychic Life of Power* (1997: 212, n. 12) and *Frames of War* (2009: 39) in support of the AIDS Names Project quilt, which represents, for her, a politics of grieving ungrievable life. But Crimp is not as approving of the project as readers may infer from Butler's simple references to him. For Butler, "The Names Project Quilt is exemplary, ritualizing and repeating the name itself as a way of publically avowing limitless loss" (1997: 148).[78]

The quilt exemplifies the politics of grief for ungrievable life: it names, makes real, and binds together the unnamable and mostly liminal people who died of AIDS. Crimp acknowledges the necessity of mourning and the power of shared lamentation to establish the equal grievability of queer lives, but he ranks this second to the insistence on tending in a more natalist fashion to queer world-building: communal, alternative, proudly inaugural, life-affirming, state-enlisting, sovereignty-seeking.[79] Indeed, Crimp criticizes the quilt at length in the very same essay Butler repeatedly cites in simple support of the quilt.

Crimp worries about what the quilt covers. True, the names (and sometimes ashes) sewn into the quilt's panels publicize a death and constitute a community around that death's acceptance. But the quilt also attenuates "the difference between those of us who must learn to accept these deaths and those who still find these deaths acceptable. And who can say," Crimp asks (in his essay, "The Spectacle of Mourning," provocatively first delivered at a 1991 panel discussion called "The Names Project: The Transforming Power of the Forbidden Stitch"), "whether or not the Names Project quilt might cut both ways?" (2002: 201).[80] Seeming to empathize with the plight of Persons With AIDS, the quilt may nonetheless at the same time work to satisfy a certain homophobic desire: "That many in our society secretly want us dead is to me beyond question. And one expression of this may be our society's loving attention to the quilt, which is not only a ritual and representation of mourning [as Butler will later argue it is] but also stunning evidence of the mass death of gay men. It would, of course, be unseemly for society to celebrate our deaths openly, but I wonder if the quilt helps make this desire decorous" (2002: 199–200).[81] Making gay male *deaths grievable*, Crimp worries contra Butler *avant la lettre* we might say, is less an achievement than making gay male *lives acceptable*. The two are connected of course, this is Butler's insight, but in making the former a proxy for the latter, Butler may bypass some of the more vexing elements of the politics of lamentation.[82]

Crimp worries that the quilt undoes the passion and anger of activism. Insofar as the quilt enables acceptance of loss (that is, insofar as it functions as a conventional kind of transitional object), Crimp worries that it might reconcile gay community members to the inevitability of loss at precisely a moment when insisting on the non-necessity of such loss was of foremost importance, politically.[83] The risk is that we let go of the rage and righteous anger that feed political protest, activism, and self-organization. "We Have Turned Our Anger into a Piece of Quilt and Red Ribbons" read one ACT UP poster (Sturken 1997: 173). The concern is that the quilt works to "sanitize and sentimentalize gay life," refolding queer lives into its warm, heteronormative embrace. Indeed, the quilt's power certainly seems to derive in no small part from its association with the maternalism criticized above: historically, in the US, quilts are made by women, they are objects of comfort not antagonism, and they represent and constitute women's care practice within a certain patriarchal kinship structure. Reprising Edelman's critique of Butler, we may well ask: can this homey icon of motherhood be resignified from a mainstream maternalist object to a transitional object with the power to bring all kinds of people in to grieve ungrievable life? For Crimp, the answer – both yes, and no – depends on how we position the quilt in our politics and culture.

We might work to decenter the quilt, by making it just one part of a broader political practice of symbolization and resignification so that other elements might offset the quilt's more deleterious aspects. And we might work to challenge the quilt's propensity to essentialization by generating plural and contending representations of it (as I will do in Part II with Antigone). This precisely is Crimp's strategy: he decenters the quilt and pluralizes it. He pluralizes its meaning when he treats it not just as a memorial to individual lives lost, but to a world threatened. Looking at it, he says, he sees not just individual panels sewn together but an erotic world full of people "from the bars and the bath houses, from the streets and the parks" (2002: 199). Marita Sturken follows in these footsteps when she interprets the quilt agonistically, claiming it rejects "somber meditation on death" and is "colorful, playful and funny" (1997: 194). If the quilt is a maternal object, Sturken sees in it a new kind of mother, more raucous than most mothers we know, more undecidable than sentimental.[84] And Crimp also decenters the quilt: he admires other forms of AIDS memoria which focus not just on death and disease but on life, vitality, eroticism. For example, he endorses the AIDS memoire film *Danny*, as a worthy effort to represent a gay person with AIDS as not just a victim but also as a life force, not just diseased but also beautiful and sexual, not moved just by *penthos* but also by *thumos* – not just human but also gay, in other words: not just mortal but also natal.[85] *Danny* pairs the mortalism of lamentation with the hunger of desire and contributes to an archive of representation that contests the co-optation of AIDS memoria by those who might experience satisfaction rather than remorse over gay male deaths (2002: 99–101).[86]

Butler does not take this agonistic tack. Her several examples of a lamentation that goes beyond friend/enemy distinction are layered one on top of the other (newspaper obituaries, pronouncing unpronounceable names, the quilt) and there is no friction between them (as there is in Gambaro by contrast). That is, this is not a pluralization: the quilt is not decentered; it is re-centered. Where friction is discernible (as between Butler's two Antigones, as I have shown, or between her and Crimp, as I am arguing here) she does not thematize it, and even obscures it.[87] Without friction, though, we get a sentimental quilt and perhaps even a sentimental politics of shared feeling.[88] In her earlier *The Psychic Life of Power*, Butler was closer to Crimp: "The emergence of collective institutions for grieving is thus crucial to survival, to reassembling community, to rearticulating kinship, to reweaving sustaining relations." Referring in particular to Queer Nation's famous "die-ins," Butler says these call to be "read as life-affirming rejoinders to the dire psychic consequences of a grieving process culturally thwarted and proscribed" (1997: 148). Already here, however, we see the longing for a grieving process unthwarted and not proscribed. This will become, later, grief for ungrievable life. Already here in *The Psychic Life of Power*, the emphasis on survival and re-emergence contrasts with Crimp's emphasis on an adamant natalism in spite of disaster. It is a difference of emphasis. By the time she writes *Precarious Life*, Butler's emphasis has shifted even further, away from political collectivities and toward the binding power of grief.[89] A certain Antigone, the conventional one, seems to have won.[90]

(ii) The politics of beautiful death

Like Derrida, Crimp is willing to bring politics even to the quilt, the name, the eulogy; that is, insistently to desentimentalize and hunt out every rapprochement with death on behalf of what it remainders: in this instance, a queer natality that demands recognition and repudiates remediation.[91] ACT UP's challenge to the (re)productive workings of even death and burial and their supposed universal post-politicality comes across in a powerful photograph: that of a young man, perhaps it was David Wojnarowicz (1954–1992) who, protesting with ACT UP, wore a leather jacket featuring the words: "If I die of AIDS – forget burial – just drop my body on the steps of the FDA." He was not alone. Another AIDS activist, Terry Sutton, was famous for saying, "when I die, don't put me in the damn quilt." They did, though, and wrote on his panel: "He hated this quilt and so do we" (Sturken 1997: 187). The most terrible thing in death, from a humanist perspective, is to instrumentalize a corpse, to defile its dignity by putting it to use, to treat it as an object or dispose of it as a mere thing. But the message of these two activist PWAs is that, humanism be damned, the most terrible thing is to be dehumanized in life, cast outside of the social contract's circle of concern only to then be rehumanized in death, returned to full human dignity with a decorous burial.[92] Here, burial, which claims the register of dignity, seems more like use – a cover up of an (ontological) crime. For these activists, the proper burial that promises dignity in death constitutively supports an unjust social order, folding them into its ground. Such sentimental absorption, its post-mortem enlistment of the dead on behalf of a heternormative humanism seems best opposed by non-burial, but non-burial seems to instrumentalize the corpse and offend against its dignity too.[93] How can we ease the grip of the binary between good dignity and bad instrumentalization? We may begin by taking note of the binary's productive power, how it supports the idea that politics ends at death, and stages death as post-political, thus obscuring the ubiquitous politics of death and burial.

An enhanced sensitivity to the politics of lamentation and burial can come out of engagement with Sophocles' tragedy if we rework the received Antigone and the "Antigone versus Oedipus" frame. As Crimp would be the first to point out, this is a battle of representation. As Butler would agree, it is a battle over frames. Representation and reframing require pluralization and democratization. When Crimp says that "every image of a PWA is a *representation*" and calls on activists to "formulate [their] demands not in relation to the 'truth' of the image, but in relation to the conditions of its construction and its social effects" (2002: 99; emphasis original), he invites us to take the place *not* of the lamenting sister of Sophocles' play and Hegel's reception, but of the gods whose place *she* took.[94] The gods in archaic Greece were gods of representation. As we saw in Chapter 1, they took it upon themselves to provide heroes with a beautiful death.[95] Their divine unguents and elixirs, traces of Egyptian practices of embalming, remain with us still. They are the pictures, film, interpretations, and media that play a part in (what was always, in its own way) an agonistic politics of representation.[96] Crimp takes up their task when he criticizes Nicholas Nixon's photographs of the ravaged suffering bodies of people with AIDS. Instead of the wasting bodies frequently depicted in abjection, Crimp wants a "body too much" (to employ Thomas Elsaesser's term, central to my reading of Fassbinder in the next chapter). And so he endorses the manifesto, "No More Pictures Without Context," which includes the following: "We demand the visibility of PWAs who are vibrant, angry, loving, sexy, beautiful, acting up and fighting back" (2002: 86).[97] Something like the rage and calls to vengeance that ring through Antigone but are muted in Butler and go missing in Elshtain's somewhat sanitized second renderings of her are what Crimp tries to hold on to here. He does not want to let go of the rage and righteous anger that drive or feed political protest, activism, self-organization, and communal self-care. He does not want to let go of the beautiful death.

Crimp's demand to circulate natal and not just mortal images of PWAs is one we may level at *Antigone*'s readers, interpreters, stagers, and viewers as well. If the jury is out with regard to such innovative receptions, as Taylor says of Gambaro's efforts in this direction, that is surely, as Taylor would agree, no reason to stop pluralizing Antigone. It is rather a reason to redouble our efforts to do so in an effort to break or at least pluralize the frames by way of which we have received her until now. As with the quilt and death practices, so too with Antigone: we do well to decenter and pluralize Sophocles' protagonist, releasing her from the grip of the Madres and vice versa. Absent such intervention, the conventional Antigone of lamentation retains the power to derail radical efforts like Crimp's to build new worlds, and leaves them at risk of being refolded into the mortalist humanism that projects like the Names Project quilt may well exceed but cannot help but vehiculate nonetheless.

There are those who share my concern that Antigone's centrality to political theory may not be an entirely good thing, though not all would identify her legacy of anti-statism and maternalism as the problems. Some propose we should move from Sophocles to Aeschylus (tragedy) or to Aristophanes (comedy). I shall argue in Part II, however, that Sophocles' *Antigone* may prove to be a transitional object and as such is not as dispensable as recent calls to turn elsewhere might suggest. That is, we may yet do well to turn to *Antigone*. Deepening not dismissing this text, we may avoid its sentimental lure and sidestep its solicitation to mortalist humanism.

FROM TRAGEDY TO MELODRAMA: GENRES OF GENERATIONS

AIDS killed almost an entire generation, but it was not disease alone that cut the ties between past and future that nourish politics and community. In the 1990s, argue Chris Castiglia and Chris Reed, "a powerful concentration of cultural forces" turned AIDS into "an agent of amnesia, wiping out memories not only of everything that came before but of the remarkably vibrant and imaginative ways that gay communities responded to the catastrophe of illness and death and sought to memorialize loss" (2011: 3). Leaving the non-normative past behind, forsaking its legacies and wisdom, was figured as maturation, and responsible citizenship through marriage and military service became markers of what was cast as a now well-earned inclusion in the system of social equality.

The disruption of generational time and the ensuing problem of inter-generational legacy are also the points of departure in Greek tragedy, where incest confuses lineage and curses or plagues destroy whole kinship lines. But tragedy is not the only genre that addresses such issues.[98] As I turn now to look at Rainer Werner Fassbinder's contribution to the film *Germany in Autumn*, I note that in 1978 he shared with the ACT UP activists who came soon after a suspicion of tragedy as a politically regressive mode of emplotment. Fassbinder staged his critique of heteronormative citizenship before AIDS, and in response to a different crisis, but his use of melodrama invites us to reflect on both the limits of tragedy for politics and the promise of melodrama for reinterpreting Antigone.[99]

CHAPTER 3

"Antigone versus Oedipus," II: the directors' agon *in* Germany in Autumn

The *Trauerspiel* is conceivable as pantomime; the tragedy is not.

Walter Benjamin

Traditional tragedy [is] an inappropriate mirror for contemporary experience. Our modern world may well be, whether we like it or not, the world of melodrama.

Redmond O'Hanlon

In many ... respects the melodrama is the inheritor of many tragic concerns.

Geoffrey Nowell-Smith

The mourning play both repeats and transforms, restores and irremediably dislocates, the agonistic trial in which tragedy has its model ... one would be tempted to say that it overturns the tragic court of appeals and reinstates the initial verdict, were there any decision. Precisely that, however, does not take place: there is no final verdict ...

Samuel Weber

Having looked in Chapter 2 at the effects of mobilizing Antigone versus Oedipus in feminist and queer theory, I move here in Chapter 3 to study the tactic again, but this time in a different context. In the film, *Germany in Autumn*, Antigone is once again invoked against a too highly controlled and violent political order that carries within it unacknowledged generational injustices. *Germany in Autumn* (1978) is focused on Sophoclean themes: political violence, dissident protest, and state-legitimation in the context of a problematic inheritance – not the incest of Oedipus but the horrors of Nazism. Given this book's aim of assessing the promise and limitations of invoking Antigone (as feeling, *phonê*, lamentation, dissidence, maternal power) versus Oedipus (as sovereignty, governance, rationalism, patriarchy), this film is especially useful because it also unsettles the binary of Antigone versus Oedipus, staging instead an *agon* between two quite different Antigones in two sequences made by two different directors. The opposition of Antigone versus Oedipus becomes an *agon* between two Antigones: the active dissident (and sovereign political actor) versus the vulnerable lamenter. Where in Chapter 2 we saw how those who enlist the former are led to the latter (tracked by way of the shift from *Antigone's Claim* to *Precarious Life*, for example), here we see them set against each other by two directors with very different views about the prospects for Left politics in West Germany in the late 1970s. What is at stake between them is precisely the concern thematized in Chapter 2: how to enlist the power of lamentation for politics without allowing that politics of lamentation to collapse into a lamentation of politics?

But the film also presses us beyond the questions of Chapter 2. As we shall see, one of the things in play between the two directors is a politics of genre that I have thus far only tentatively broached by way of references to sentimentalism and dramaturgy. In this chapter, genre comes to the fore: the film's master director Alexander Kluge emplots the events of the day as tragedy, while Rainer Werner Fassbinder in his own sequence melodramatizes them. Comparing their approaches invites, necessarily, some reflection on the genre politics of tragedy and melodrama, which positions us well to turn, finally, in Part II, to close readings of the dramatic text whose impact and legacy have been the focus of Part I.

Melodrama may seem to be just the film version of sentimentalism, criticized above for its self-absorption and for flattening distinctions between suffering and death that we do better, politically, to preserve and explore. But where sentimentalism emphasizes sympathy and fellow-feeling, melodrama explores isolation and incommunicability which, in Fassbinder's sequence, are dramatized as the predictable political effects of the state's expansion of its power as it responds in controversial ways to one emergency (terrorism) but not to another (the open secret of West Germany's incomplete denazification since the end of the war). My aim, in any case, is not to press the cause of melodrama as the best genre for politics but rather to argue that there are things to be learned from it and that its invitation to decenter tragedy as the political genre par excellence is worth accepting.[1] More to the point, I will argue that what Fassbinder offers us when he mobilizes a melodramatic Antigone against Kluge's tragic one, is not a brief for melodrama but rather an example of "genre-switching," a practice that helps us reconsider the uncontested privileging by political theorists since Hegel of one genre in particular: tragedy.

NOTHING TO DO WITH SOPHOCLES? "ANTIGONE FEVER" IN *GERMANY IN AUTUMN*[2]

[O]ne generation cannot free the next. (Chorus, *Antigone* [596 (670)])

Asked "whether he had asked his father – the former president who refused to launch a full-scale invasion of Iraq after driving Saddam Hussein from Kuwait in 1991 – for advice on what to do" when contemplating invading Iraq ten years later, President George W. Bush "replied that his earthly father was 'the wrong father to appeal to for advice ... there is a higher father that I appeal to.'" (Rupert Cornwell)[3]

[T]hese sons ... did not identify with the official optimism of the West German economic miracle, they also did not have a genuine stake in any (socialist) alternative. Instead, they identified with the latent emotions, the ones that the forced optimism and strident efficiency tried to hide. Seeing the fathers' cover-up, seeing through it, but being sons by flesh and blood, they also had to deal with their own internalisation of the father, whose hidden guilt and shame ... returns in the son as self-destructive melancholy. (Thomas Elsaesser)[4]

Germany in Autumn is a patchwork quilt of a film that consists of several different sequences, made by various directors, all sutured together by director Alexander Kluge. The film, which documents the events of Germany's "hot autumn" of 1977, emplots events of the day in classically tragic, Sophoclean, terms, as we shall see, invoking Antigone as a model mourner and admirable civil disobedient several times. My aim here is to track and assess the effect of Kluge's "turn to Antigone," and I do this in part by attending to one sequence in detail: Fassbinder's. Just as certain panels in the AIDS quilt contest the quilt's larger mission of unity in mourning, so too Fassbinder's sequence stands out, as Thomas Elsaesser (2004) also argues, for its agonistic contestation of Kluge's narration of the events. Elsaesser focuses on the directors' *agon* with regard to the politics of (de)Oedipalization, about which more below. But, I argue here, theirs is also a contest over genre. Fassbinder's use of melodrama in his sequence counters Kluge's classicizing focus on tragic, Antigonean treatments of themes of lamentation and resistance. Thus, Fassbinder's sequence invites us to consider the limits of tragedy for politics and points to the possible promise of the much-maligned genre of melodrama. It is important that Fassbinder does not abandon Antigone, he intensifies and queers her: he counters Kluge's final sequence depicting Left mourning politics at a Red Army Faction funeral with an ambiguous collapse that leaves spectators wondering: is Fassbinder subverting the Antigone-effect? Or merely acting it out?

The film's vignettes were made by members of Germany's New Left cinema in the immediate aftermath of the hot autumn of 1977, a season of political uncertainty in Germany amidst Red Army Faction (RAF) kidnappings and murders, a violent airplane hijacking, and the development of enhanced state counter-terror measures (widespread wiretapping, search and seizure, new hotlines for people anonymously to inform on "suspicious" neighbors, and the turn from diplomacy and negotiation to the use of special forces to rescue hijacked hostages) that were part of a war on terror.[5] Kluge classicized Germany's hot autumn, recording the political events of that season through the prism of father–son rivalries and a politics of generational succession punctuated by the lamentation and resistance of Antigone figures who are, for the most part, just as caught in the trap of violence and vengeance as their male counterparts. The film revisits several times the themes of Sophocles' play, in particular the politics of burial – focusing on the debate at the time regarding whether and how terrorists deserve to be buried and asking after the moral and political obligations of bystanders who (like Sophocles' Ismene or Haemon) witness casual or state-licensed violence and must decide whether or how to act in response.

Giorgio Agamben's well-known claim that "the routine yet surreal soccer match in Auschwitz between the SS and Jewish members of the *Sonderkommando*" recurs daily (quoted in LaCapra 2004: 178), seems overheated, even melodramatic, when he says it now. But forty years ago in West Germany, it was almost true. In mid-1970s Germany, former SS members operated more or less openly as members of the country's industrial and political elite, much as members of the Argentine junta would go on to do as well.[6] Mapping this hasty foreclosure of the Nazi past by post-war democratic West Germany as a problem of fathers and sons (not difficult with 60s and 70s youth quizzing their parents about what they had done during the war), Kluge's *Germany in Autumn* mobilizes as an alternative to it a humanism born of the natural sentimentalities of kinship (featuring non-rivalrous sisters and moving father–daughter fidelities), rural neighborliness (a pub owner offers to provide food for the funerals of the RAF terrorists), and universalism or good Samaritanism (good Samaritans come to the aid of strangers in at least two sequences, while Fassbinder, in his, throws a would-be houseguest out of his apartment in the middle of the night).[7]

The movie opens with the official, honorific funeral of Hans-Martin Schleyer, a German industrialist (Chairman of the German Federation of Industry and a Director of Daimler Benz) and former Nazi, who was

kidnapped and murdered by the RAF in 1977. The movie closes with the
hotly contested funeral a short while later of three RAF members –
Andreas Baader, Jan-Carl Raspe, and Gudrun Ensslin who committed
suicide or were murdered in Stammheim prison when plans to negotiate
their release via hostage trades failed (the German government refused to
negotiate over Schleyer, and the hijacked airplane passengers held hostage
at Mogadishu were rescued by German special forces). "Hotly contested"
means there were public objections to allowing the bodies of Baader,
Raspe, and Ensslin to be buried in any cemetery, and calls were made to
dispose of their bodies in the sewers. With their terrorism, they had
crossed the line from human to animal and could be treated like refuse.
But they are finally buried in a protest ceremony depicted at the end of
the film. The two funerals (of Schleyer, the industrialist and former Nazi,
and of Baader, Ensslin, and Raspe) are coded by *Germany in Autumn* as
official versus transgressive, state-approved versus state-policed, and they
are made central to the story of the hot autumn as Kluge bookends the
film with them.

   It is impossible for anyone familiar with Sophocles' *Antigone* to miss
the film's many references to Sophocles' play, in which Antigone's two
dead brothers are given disparate treatment by Creon, their uncle and
the new ruler of Thebes: Eteocles buried as a hero, Polynices left out to
rot, then later buried hastily and without fuss. History itself seems to be
always already scripted by Sophocles. Slavoj Žižek (referring to the
historical events, not the film, but his views are shaped by the film
which shaped the reception of the events then and now) identifies
Gudrun Ensslin with Antigone since Ensslin shares with Lacan's Antigone a determination not to give way on her desire, he says.[8] Others
follow the prompt in a different direction and assign that role to
Ensslin's sister who is shown in the film trying to find a place to bury
her sister and her comrades when it seems no one will have them. The
reverberations to Sophocles in *Germany in Autumn* are unmistakable as
we watch Ensslin's father, a pastor, join with her sister to seek, at first
without success, a burial place for Ensslin, Baader, and Raspe. This
seemingly doomed quest inverts the story, told in Sophocles' *Oedipus at
Colonus*, of Oedipus' journey in the company of his daughters to seek
his final resting place. In the film, a friend of the Ensslin family
recounts the difficulties faced by the father: "Father Ensslin tried hard,
despairingly hard, to find graves. In Stuttgart itself he had unbelievable
problems convincing the citizens or anyone at all to bury these three
terrorists – in any case, people who stand outside society – within the

city walls, or within the community. Outside on the land, all right, but not where so-called normal people are buried."[9] Marking the line between human and inhuman, the dividing power of city walls returns us also to Sophocles' *Antigone* in which the city walls should fail fully to insulate the people from the body of Polynices, left out to rot, and that of Antigone, buried alive.

Germany in Autumn makes the reference to *Antigone* most explicit in a comic-tragic sequence written by Heinrich Böll and directed by Schlöndorff, which the film carries at its moral center.[10] The sequence depicts a Broadcast Commission meeting debating whether to show a film version of Sophocles' *Antigone* as part of a series called *Youth Meets the Ancient Classics*. With the German public in the middle of a debate about whether and how to bury the bodies of three RAF members, all three said to have committed suicide and one of them a woman, this ancient play, which turns on burial, resistance, and suicide, and features women acting politically in transgressive ways, seems to anticipate the 1970s political scene, so much so that one of the board members suspects the director has altered the ancient script to inflame the events of the day: "Is that really Sophocles' ending?" he asks, only to be reassured that yes, it is.

The deliberations of the television executives are punctuated by clips of the proposed broadcast. In one, Creon delivers a speech whose significance to the film's framing is unmistakable: "As to Eteocles . . . there shall be such funeral / as we give to the noblest dead . . . But as to his brother Polynices . . . it has been proclaimed / that none shall honour him, none shall lament over him" (cited in Blumenthal-Barby 2007: 143).[11] Do such turns to Antigone offset or (as I argued in Chapter 2) reinforce the Oedipal frame? The latter appears to be the case as the play's own often overlooked father–son rivalry is highlighted in the last moments of the scene. Having decided that "it is not a good time for *Antigone*," the executives leave the room, when onto the television screens pops the messenger who describes in tight close-up how Haemon tried and failed to kill his father, Creon, and then killed himself (like Baader and Raspe). This unviewed scene, shown to an empty room in a seeming error of broadcasting, calls film viewers' attention to the parricide (Schleyer) and filial suicide (Baader and Raspe) at the center of the film and events of the day, and underlines continuities between the fifth and the twentieth centuries.

The prism of father–son politics is everywhere in *Germany in Autumn*. Kluge opens the film with a scene of paternal bequest, reading aloud a letter written by Hans-Martin Schleyer to his son the night before his murder by the RAF. The letter signs off *"dein Vati,"* interpellating the viewer into the position of the son as we listen to the now-dead father warn – from beyond the grave – of doom if the constitutional state cannot learn how to deal with terrorism.[12]

Later, the film features yet another important *père–fils* pairing: the son is the Mayor of Stuttgart, who uses his executive power of decision to clear the way, against public opinion, for Ensslin's family to arrange her burial, along with Baader and Raspe. The mayor, who makes "a quick decision and clean choice" (as he himself puts it in the film) to allow for the burial, is named ... Rommel.[13] The father is Field Marshal Erwin Rommel, a point underlined by film footage showing the mayor, thirty years earlier, as a young boy standing near the coffin of his famous father, the general who was forced to choose between exposure as a traitor and the more honor-preserving suicide for which Hitler would host a state funeral and celebrate his general as a national hero.[14]

The father–son motif offers Kluge a way to depict the varied directions taken by the second generation in the aftermath of Nazism. Rommel's son works within the system while the RAF members seek to topple it. He is a mayor of a small city, they are part of an organization with transnational ambitions. He represents humanism, they pursue politics terroristically.

But the father–son framing also depoliticizes, Thomas Elsaesser argues: Kluge's psychological Oedipalization cast "the German protest movement [as merely] anti-authoritarian rather than egalitarian, [as merely] caught in the ruses of patriarchy ... " (2004).[15] In Elsaesser's view, none of the usual turns to Antigone (as daughter, resister, lamenter) can undo this Oedipalization. To break the spell of the father–son dyad, we need, Elsaesser says, to turn to yet another turn to Antigone, one that is subtly embedded in the film, and points us in a different direction. He finds it in Fassbinder's sequence: "Paradoxically, the part that most challenges any kind of Oedipalization is not the Schlöndorff/Böll segment [about whether or not to show *Antigone* on television], but the one directed by Rainer Werner Fassbinder, featuring Fassbinder himself, along with his lover Armin Mayer and his mother Lilo Pempeit" (2004). In his sequence, Elsaesser argues, Fassbinder "cast[s] doubts on ... a founding myth of West German democracy": the idea "that (masculine) ideals of self-discipline, responsibility and citizenship had done away with the authoritarian personality" (2004). Against them, Fassbinder shows himself "alternately naked and wrapped in an untidy bathrobe, restless and sweating, in his sombre Munich apartment, frantic about the news blackout, cynically incredulous about the Stammheim [RAF] suicides, in fear of possible police raids and house searches, on the verge of a nervous breakdown, finally collapsing on the floor in a fit of uncontrollable hysterical weeping" (2004).[16]

That collapse is brought about not only by news events but also by what those events have brought about: a self-destructive paranoia and regimen of drinking and drug taking (a relapse) that contribute to Fassbinder's undoing. However, Elsaesser does not see those final moments of despair as Jacques Rancière might: as a miasmic collapse brought on by the turn to ethics, over-exposure to Antigone, and inadequate engagement in actual political struggle.[17] Quite the opposite: Elsaesser sees important Antigonean resistance here. He refers to this as "'a body too much': violent, obese, naked, grossly material" and says that when Fassbinder exhibits his body in this way, he "assaults the viewer" and demands "an Antigone to mark the site where mourning has not taken place" (2004).[18] Elsaesser's claim, then, is that the Fassbinder sequence returns us to a politics obscured or undone by Kluge. Depicting German manhood as impotent, queer, vulnerable, and paranoid, Fassbinder intervenes in the gender and sexual politics of West-German liberal democracy after fascism. When he interrogates his mother about terrorism and the (in)capacity of the rule of law to deal with it, Fassbinder interrupts the frame put in place by Kluge, who opened *Germany in Autumn* with a reading of Schleyer's letter of paternal bequest to his son, outlining the challenge posed to the constitutional state by terrorism. The contest here is not only about constitutionalism and its possible limits. For Elsaesser, it is crucial that Fassbinder poses these questions about law to a mother not a father, thus making "the primary incestuous mother–son bond so over-explicit that it effectively de-Oedipalizes the lineage from (guilty) father to (guilty) son."[19]

However, there is also something else going on in the *agon* between these two directors. If Elsaesser is right to argue that "Fassbinder's self-display is an act of resistance, and a double Antigone gesture, partly directed at the film that Alexander Kluge has bound him into" (2004),[20] de-Oedipalization may not be the only thing in play. Fassbinder's sequence is also the one that issues the starkest genre challenge to Kluge. If we think of Kluge's father–son framing not just as an effort to psychologize, but also to classicize — to emplot events of the day as tragedy — then Fassbinder's resistance to that framing may also be seen as part of a contest about genre and its political implications.

TRAGEDY AND MELODRAMA – ASYMMETRIES OF (DE)CLASSICIZATION

There is no generic system without a hierarchy of genres. (Jacques Rancière)

Elsaesser does not distance Fassbinder from tragedy. In fact he compares Fassbinder to Antigone, and calls the sequence "antigonising." But Fassbinder, who rages at everyone he encounters, polices the borders of his apartment, and ends collapsed in a heap on the floor, is at least as much Creon as Antigone, perhaps even more so. Seemingly incapable of resistance, he storms around the apartment, bullies his lover, interrogates his mother, and retreats into alcohol and drugs.[21] There are no heroic radical fists raised in the air, no sung anthems of the Left. Still, when we see Fassbinder insisting, in an interview, that if his films contribute to the destruction of conventional marriage, that is fine with him, we recognize Antigonean themes: his position, uttered boldly, is anti-conjugal, anti-heteronormative. But, when we attend to the fact that these utterances appear in a flashback as he is on the telephone frantically trying to retract his words and prevent them from being made public, Fassbinder appears rather unheroic – small.

And maybe that is the point. With this failed retraction, Fassbinder calls attention immediately to the curious genre of his sequence. It will not feature figures who are larger than life, but rather those who are trapped and boxed in by powers beyond their control. It will not make tragic heroes of the Red Army Faction and villains of Germany's public figures, nor vice versa. It will not replay that Oedipal script. Instead, Fassbinder announces he wants to reject that inherited script: out with conventional marriage, out with futurism (*à la* Edelman), out with fathers and sons. But there is more going on here yet. With the tight shots of his face as he sweats and tries to take back his words but finds he cannot, Fassbinder announces with his images that he also wants to reject the Oedipal *genre*: out with tragedy; this is melodrama.

Where Kluge, in the film as a whole, and Böll and Schlöndorff in their sequence, do all they can to accent the rather remarkable continuities between the contemporary and classical conflicts, celebrating resistance and radicalism, Fassbinder – rather like Gambaro – accentuates the frictions and discontinuities between past and present.[22] But he goes further than Gambaro and switches genres, moving from tragedy to melodrama.

Fassbinder's sequence features virtually all the traits of melodrama which, as Peter Brooks says, "generally ends in resignation," with characters "emerg[ing] as lesser human beings for having become wise and acquiescent to the ways of the world" (1976: 77). These traits include hyperbole (Fassbinder shouts and storms and collapses), externalization of inner/psychic violence (he sweats and vomits and collapses), acting out (he hectors his mother and berates and roughs up his lover, Armin), a sense of being overwhelmed by outside forces (he expresses his felt impotence in the face of news blackouts and state power several times on the telephone to his ex-wife in Paris), paranoia (he expects his apartment to be searched at any moment by the police or invaded by spies and he acts accordingly), a *mise en scène* of confinement (he seems never to leave the apartment), and a move from the big city to a small town (the sequence opens with him arriving from Paris and he says more than once that he wishes he could go back to Paris but he needs to finish his work first), with the attendant biases and prejudices a big city dweller might expect to find among rural counterparts (Armin in the apartment repeatedly expresses small-minded political views which enrage Fassbinder, who batters him and belittles his views when speaking on the telephone to his ex-wife).[23]

Melodrama provides Fassbinder with genre cues that dramatize the effects on citizens of the state's expansion of its power. It gives expression to their affective responses to heightened political pressures and new forms of violence. It gives him a way to enact the call to the rule of law, repeatedly in his discussion with his mother, not as a sober, principled, or reasoned (shall we say academic) conclusion to a dispassionate argument about the *Rechtsstaat*, but as the only recourse for those caught in an overheated political crisis in which all parties and institutions, including the state, are acting out in ways that are affectively charged. Fassbinder explored the genre of melodrama throughout his work, but the challenge it poses to tragedy's supposed superiority as a high culture genre is made clearest in *Germany in Autumn* in the context of his *agon* with Kluge.[24]

The alternative, which may *seem* to embolden dissidents, the classically Antigonean option of resistance and lamentation promoted by Kluge, Schlöndorff, and Böll, seduces with its symmetry; but symmetry is not mere, innocent form: as Elsaesser says (referring to Maier's *The Unmasterable Past* [1988]), "symmetry, balance and repetition" set up "their narrative to achieve almost 'classical' closure," detracting from the singularity of Antigone's act and mastering "the German past by letting it metaphorically slide into [a] master-narrative of fathers and sons" (2004). The Oedipal narrative masters the unmasterable. It seems to offer resources for resistance, but in fact only domesticates new events by returning us to old familiar narratives of psychoanalysis or to old familiar structures – of tragedy.

But there is a further, historical rather than structural problem with *Germany in Autumn*'s turn to Antigone. When Kluge turns to tragic forms, references, and themes, seeking to dramatize various universalisms, he does so in quest of resources with which to counter both the German Nazi past and the emerging present of the German security state. But when he turns to tragedy, he inadvertently mobilizes not a transnational or universal set of values but a very German drama. Indeed, his tragic emplotment under-writes the very sense of Germanness that Kluge seeks to attenuate here. German national identity is bound up with classicism and in particular with that country's role in the formation of the discipline of classics, with its history of philological recovery and restoration of ancient texts in the nineteenth century. In 1970s Germany, a television series called *Youth Meets the Ancient Classics* is itself a device of nationalization. It offers a way to reach back behind Nazi fathers to earlier generations of Germans for whom *Bildung* and enlightenment, not militarism and genocide, were the essential loci of German identification. Kluge plays right into this univer-salism as nationalism (his Germany gives unique expression to humanism's universal high culture). Fassbinder, however, knows (at some level) that reaching for Antigone, the tragic play or the tragic heroine, can only reinstall the master narrative and its dialectic of enlightenment versus barbarism. And that master narrative obscures disturbing overlaps, docu-mented by Katie Fleming, Suzanne Marchand, and others, between the nineteenth-century philologists' identification of Germany with ancient Greece, sometimes cast as pure racial forebear, and the Nazis' tendency to idealize the ancient Greek and Roman worlds.[25]

When Fassbinder turns to emplot the hot autumn not as tragedy but as melodrama, we can see some awareness of the limitations of tragedy. Rather than try to reach behind Germany's Nazi past to a cultural resource that is not unimplicated in ideologies of racial superiority, Fassbinder takes the low road. While Kluge romanticizes the German countryside, Fassbin-der stays in his apartment. While Kluge celebrates neighborliness, Fass-binder worries that his neighbors may inform on him, after he hears radio broadcasts of government calls for people to report anything suspicious.

Kluge, it is worth noting, not only expresses a preference for tragedy (mixed, as always, with comic elements) when he emplots *Germany in Autumn* as a drama of fathers and sons; he, further, embeds in the film a subtle critique of melodrama as politically useless or stifling. In a move unnoted by Elsaesser, Kluge may even, just possibly, chide Fassbinder for his melodramatic emplotment of events Kluge prefers to classicize as tragic.[26] Whom, if not Fassbinder, might Kluge have in mind when he records one of the RAF eulogies (delivered by a woman): "If you are truly outraged, you won't shout but will consider what to do." Fassbinder in his sequence shouts for thirty minutes straight and ends in a pile on the floor, infant-like, wrapped in the arms of his battered lover, collapsed into drug use, rage, paranoia, and abuse under pressure of events in the hot autumn of 1977. This opens Fassbinder to the critique leveled at Benjamin by Adorno: that Benjamin was seduced, as James Martel puts it, by the "cult of futility, wine and magic" (2011: 33). Doesn't Fassbinder's sequence make clear the destructiveness of such seduction? Does it not make clear that melodrama is anti-political: debilitating and nothing but a self-consuming artifact?[27] If melodrama is a democratic genre, does it not worryingly stage a democracy of resignation rather than engagement? This is the risk of melodrama: that depicting paralysis, it paralyzes – like Baudelaire's wine poetry, like the *Trauerspiel* that also captured Benjamin's attention.[28]

For his part, Kluge may fall for tragedy's promise of resistance only to be drawn into its eternal return of the same. But, we might say in his defense, contra my own critique here until now, and contra Elsaesser, that Kluge also tries to point beyond it. His final shot, unanticipated by Sophocles (except in Irigaray's rendering of his play), is of a young mother and daughter (or perhaps two sisters) hand in hand, leaving the RAF funeral, with a lively dirge playing in the background; it is Joan Baez's tribute to Sacco and Vanzetti (which does point us again to the eternal return of the same, however, with its implication, when played here, that the state just keeps killing its enemies). Elsaesser misses it but this concluding shot may itself be the sort of de-Oedipalizing gesture he thinks only Fassbinder provides: the woman and the girl, hand in hand, seem to break with tragedy's usual formulas and promise the possibility of a different future than that of the politics of fathers and sons that dominate the film. (Though, again, we may be directed here, as earlier, to *Oedipus at Colonus*, which leaves Antigone and her sister, Ismene, to walk off, on their own, fatherless, after Oedipus dies.)[29]

So we end with these images: the unlovely Fassbinder on the floor in Armin's arms and, later, the lovely woman and the girl walking away – two non-reproductive couples. Of course Kluge's film does not quite end there.[30] The very last bit of film posts the following thought: "suicide is the last resort of those who see no other options." And suddenly we are back to tragedy after all. And we are reminded of the politicality and not just the resignation of melodrama because, unlike Kluge, Fassbinder never accepts the official *fact* of suicide. Melodrama is the genre of suspicion and Fassbinder, the melodramatist, is staunchly incredulous of the state's claims. He sees the state as itself melodramatic, a party to the struggle, not its neutral overseer. In this, he is after all like Antigone, though unlike her he is reduced, not ennobled, by the state's violent grandiosity.

Melodrama, with its emphasis on isolation, paranoia, affect, and suspicion, provided Fassbinder with the perfect generic frame with which, first, to contest the goings-on and then, second, to depict the collapse of democratic citizenship under conditions of real or contrived emergency. In his hands, melodrama is a critique of irresponsible state power and it is also a rather empathic depiction of what can happen to people deprived of the bracing cold air of civic freedom. Fassbinder may not depict heroic agency but he offers a politically salient exhibition of the conditions under which such agency is undone. Moreover, by melodramatizing events Kluge preferred to classicize, Fassbinder performs a kind of agonistic genre-switching that could work as a device of spectatorial awakening, and call attention to the subtle working of genre on those interpellated by it.

RE-EMPLOTMENT OR GENRE-SWITCHING AND/AS POLITICS

Democratic theorists may not want to privilege the genre of melodrama as essential to democratic theory, but democratic theorists do well, in my view, to follow Fassbinder's lead and enlist melodrama to offset tragedy. Taking this genre seriously helps to pluralize Antigone, beyond the tragic genre and the Oedipal script. And it presses us to reconsider texts and arguments we may have thought we settled. For example: with melodrama's genre traits in mind, we might return to reappraise Butler's *Precarious Life*. Where in Chapter 2 that book appeared to collapse into ethics, we might now see Butler in that book as occupying something like Fassbinder's role in *Germany in Autumn*: externalizing vulnerability, rejecting the normalizing violence of marriage, focusing on lives and deaths cast as marginal by sovereign powers, *Precarious Life* is an emotional, revelatory, sometimes overheated, and personal text. Both worldly and inward in its orientation, its frame both expansive and tight, it longs to establish new connections but it is also closed in, forced to operate in a world newly narrowed by Bush's vengeful sovereign response to 9/11.

Both Butler's book and Fassbinder's sequence were produced in close proximity to traumatic events, and it shows.[31] The chapters of *Precarious Life* were written not long after 9/11 and US responses to it. Fassbinder's sequence was produced right after the events of the hot autumn. Both are raw and, both wager, something can come of that. Both, albeit to different extents, carry traits of melodrama. (We might say the same of Agamben and his overheated prose, too.)[32] Neither seeks to claim sovereign power; both are more interested in the psychic costs of power than in how to gain it. But where Butler is drawn, perhaps even in spite of herself, to a universal humanism of lamentation, for Fassbinder, such an aspiration is perpetually thwarted by the paranoia engendered by new state forms and assemblages.

We could go even further and give an Elsaesserian reading of Butler – in which the most "Antigonising" of her texts is not the one explicitly linked to the Sophoclean referent (that is to say, not *Antigone's Claim*) but rather the one in which Sophocles is less evident, the one that seemed more ethical than political, more lamentational than resistant, more, we can now say even if Elsaesser might not, melodramatic than tragic. Reading *Precarious Life* as melodrama, we could contrast it with the more conventionally tragic *Antigone's Claim* and move beyond the question of the power of "Antigone versus Oedipus?" posed in Chapter 2, and beyond even Elsaesser's displacement of Antigone with an Antigonizing alternative, to ask after the potential power for democratic theory of genre-switching: that switch in expectation, reception, and readerly cues that occurs, as here, when we re-emplot a text in a new genre, when we approach it with different genre cues in mind than before.[33]

The consideration of melodramatic emplotment for democratic theory offered here is meant not to replace tragedy, but to call for a certain genre infidelity in support of the agonistic humanism on whose behalf I seek here to interrupt "Antigone."[34] Genre-switching or, perhaps better, genre-bending may open us up to a more alien Antigone than the paradoxically childless figure of maternal mourning so removed from natality that she can only say "no," or parody others or lament ceaselessly so as to haunt sovereign power but never fully to claim it.[35] Switching genres, that is, can be an emancipatory tactic of interruption.[36]

THE BATTLE OF THE BROTHERS

Ironically, we are drawn by Elsaesser's reading of this film into seeing in it a battle of sorts between Fassbinder and Kluge, between Antigonizing versus Oedipalized politics or, on my own reading, melodrama versus tragedy. The irony is, of course, that Elsaesser has thereby returned us once again precisely to the "battle of the brothers" that he, with his quest for a de-Oedipalized politics, wanted to exit. Blaming Kluge for emplotting events as tragedy's eternal return of the same, Elsaesser is in the end seduced by that very frame, even as he tries to diagnose its power and sketch an alternative. Such is the power(lessness) of the "Antigone" frame, even when it is converted, as it is by Elsaesser, to "antigonising." It emplots political struggles as tragic drama and offers for our identification murderous men and lamenting women (and, sometimes, vice versa). But the idea of genre-switching, pressed on us by melodrama's seemingly odd re-emplotments of political struggles, may help us reach beyond the battle of the brothers.

Each new performance, each new citation of Sophocles' *Antigone* gives this tragedy new life, but each also threatens merely to fall into old patterns of reception, without interrupting them. The reception context has been too well prepared by generations of philosophers, political theorists, and feminists working in psychoanalysis, criticism, or performance. However, the old receptions are not only habitual; they are often valued and fiercely defended, for Antigone the solitary, principled heroine is thought to be absolutely essential to resistance politics, from Texas to Athens to the West Bank. She may be. But she is not without her limitations. Resisters need more than resistance politics and, as they grapple with questions of equality, singularity, modernity, and more, they may find some release from Antigone's gripping "no!" and even some political orientation toward something more affirmative in *Antigone*, if they can only interrupt the received, canonical "text" and perhaps even apprehend and overcome our failure to be receptive to its other possibilities until now.

PART II

Conspiracy

Introduction to Part II

We saw in Chapter 2 that Diana Taylor was agnostic but not optimistic about whether a new or differently performed *Antigone* might avoid the Antigone-effect tracked in Part I. We might take Taylor's conclusion – "we won't have new answers until we have more choices" – as an invitation to pluralize *Antigone*, develop new readings, incite new performances. This will be the work of Part II. If we are going to endlessly reperform the gesture of turning to Antigone versus Oedipus (or even if we hope to break this perpetual cycle of reperformance), we need a different Antigone, one who does not just immerse us in a politics of *lamentation* premised on shared finitude but also inaugurates an insurgent *politics* of lamentation that solicits out of us a potentially shared natality.

Conspiracy is the theme that will help us to make this move. It comes from Walter Benjamin whose *Origins of the German Tragic Drama* (or *Trauerspiel*) (2003) picks up, as I have already intimated counter-chronologically, where Fassbinder leaves off: with the mourning or martyr play that is melodrama's low-culture cousin. Extending Benjamin's own arguments, we saw in Chapter 3 how melodrama, modernity's democratized *Trauerspiel*, might have potentially transformative or, at least, interruptive powers. But Benjamin offers us still more.

In Benjamin's account of the *Trauerspiel*, we find suggestive resources by way of which to receive anew Sophocles' great tragedy. There is surely a great deal of irony in this, for Benjamin, after all, is the one who insisted on the differences between the two genres, and charged that the *Trauerspiel* was brought down partly by the efforts of its purveyors to be "measured by the models of classical tragedy."[1] Invoking Aristotle, they sought evaluation by standards they could never meet. It is their "gesture of submission" to the classical ideal that Benjamin rejects. But the account he gives of the traits unique to the *Trauerspiel* does not just evidence the distance between that genre and classical tragedy nor only attest to the failure of the Baroque to rise to the standards of the classical. As it turns out, the traits of the *Trauerspiel* serve surprisingly well as genre cues for classical tragedy itself.

TRAUERSPIEL AND/AS TRAGEDY

For Benjamin, the sovereigns of the sixteenth-century German *Trauerspiel* travel a certain route: operating in a world "of fallen nature without any visible sign of grace" and "without stable authority," they are weighed down by a "ubiquitous guilt" that, in Samuel Weber's parsing, "drives those who rule to become first, tyrants, and then, often martyrs" (2008: 141). In this process we see that "power changes character," but it does not do so unaided: "it detaches itself from rulers and evolves upon those who know how to exploit the weaknesses of others." Perhaps, Weber concludes, this is why "the most characteristic figure of the Baroque, who completes the triad of its 'political typology,' alongside the tyrant and the martyr, is the intriguer, the schemer, or perhaps better: plotter." The sovereign's unraveling is aided by plotters who surround him, serve him, know how to manipulate him, and help to secure his ruin. It is the plotter who makes things happen.

It is striking how well this typology illuminates Sophocles' play, which features all three of Benjamin's types: tyrant, martyr, and plotters, as we shall see. Moreover, once we are alerted by Benjamin to the constitutive role of sovereign guilt and intrigue in the *Trauerspiel*, we see them at work also in this fifth-century tragedy, and not only in the obvious places. For example, at the end of the play, Creon claims the guilt for the tragic events is all his. But he does not elaborate on the nature of that guilt and not many critics think about its sources and significance. Benjamin invites us to think more deeply about this when he notes that guilt in the *Trauerspiel* (but maybe not just in the *Trauerspiel*; that is its exemplarity, we might say) comes from the ruler's experience of a gap or "antithesis between the power of the ruler and his capacity to rule" (cited in Weber 2008: 287). This is the situation of Creon, though the disenchantment that plagues Benjamin's modern rulers is not, in his case, the cause or occasion: the sometimes tragic demands of sovereignty are.

For Creon, ruling in the aftermath of civil conflict entails decisively positioning the polis with one of the two rivals for power, honoring one brother, dishonoring the other. The guilt that will soon destroy his rule attaches to such sovereignty-defining decisions: to honor Eteocles and leave Polynices out to rot; to punish Antigone for her disobedience and dismiss Haemon's pleas on her behalf. Creon's decisions accent the gap between his power and capacity as ruler, and the guilt that ensues (to which Benjamin sensitizes us) works through the action and drives it. Creon cannot enforce his decrees and in time comes to see them as in error. These acts, which Creon will seek too late to undo, will be his undoing. If Creon soon becomes a tyrant, might that not be a sign of the guilt to which he will only later lay claim? Might it not be his guilt that accounts for his refusal to brook dissent or disagreement until finally he cracks, only to become a martyr of his own aspirations? First too decisive, then seemingly utterly incapable of decisions, and finally unable even to commit his own tragic suicide, Creon is led away by others, as he wonders why no one has yet killed him. He is past giving orders, it seems. And his soldiers are past following them. As we shall see in the chapters that follow, they were never quick to do so, in any case.

Creon shows some awareness of his men's uncertain loyalties, when he says: there are those who are "grumbling against me in the dark" (291–292 [330]). These men who serve but do not quite obey Creon might be the very sort of plotters who, Benjamin argued in the context of the *Trauerspiel,* enable the king, even carry out his orders, but are all the while plotting against him and ultimately, through their machinations, bring about his downfall.[2] But there is in Sophocles' play an even better candidate for the role of "plotter" or, perhaps more accurately, there is an even better plotter: the messenger who is always, it seems, one step ahead of his king. Perhaps his most important machination, heretofore not appreciated as such, is his exchange with Eurydice, within whose hearing he first mentions Creon's devastating news – the loss of Haemon. Eurydice responds, to what we may now with Benjamin's help see as the messenger's plotting lure, when she asks for more detail. The messenger obliges though (or perhaps because) he could not fail to know what would follow. After hearing from him about the sequence of events outside the city that ended with her only remaining son dead, Eurydice kills herself. Creon, even now carrying his son's body home, intending to break the news to his wife and lament with her, arrives to find her dead. That the messenger's speech quickens the unfolding of events is not a new idea. But the idea that the messenger might not be just a vehicle of such unfolding (a tool of the gods, always already the first plotters), but a plotter in his own right who secures such unfolding, is one pressed on us by Benjamin. It is Benjamin who provides the new light by which to see that when the messenger's speech hastens events along, he may be himself hastening them, eagerly pressing events to their logical, tragic conclusions.[3]

Benjamin presses on us throughout his work the idea that, like the messenger, we have both more and less agency than we think. We may be hopelessly embedded in structures and fantasies, discourses and iconographies, beyond our control but there is hope nonetheless.[4] Small alterations, not always intended, may open up chasms of change – this is what Benjamin calls weak messianism.[5] With this in mind, we may not only read anew, seeking new resources in texts we had not approached the same way before, as I will be doing in the chapters that follow. We may also enter into conspiracy with those received texts, in keeping with James Martel's argument in *Textual Conspiracies*, or yield to their conspiracy with us. To the *Trauerspiel* type, plotter, Martel adds the idea of "conspiracy." For Martel, the "plotter" of the *Trauerspiel* prefigures in a way the idea of conspiracy that comes later in Benjamin's work by way of Baudelaire who, Benjamin says, "'conspires with language itself'" (quoted in Martel 2011: 7). Noting that Benjamin saw in Baudelaire a "latter day version of the *Trauerspiel* dramatists" (2011: 7), Martel suggests that through his work on Baudelaire, Benjamin came to see some promise in conspiracy as a mechanism of change. Connecting the Benjaminian idea of conspiracy with language to Machiavelli's discussion of conspiracy in *The Prince* and his enactment of conspiracy in his plays, Martel points out that conspiracy has its own rhetorical figure: *adianoeta*.[6]

Adianoeta is a sort of pun or double entendre that carries "two separate meanings, one 'obvious' and one more subtle." Most democratic theorists are suspicious of conspiracy because it undermines the publicity on which they assume democracy depends, but *adianoeta* underlines the value and significance of publicness for both politics and theater, since it plays to (at least) two crowds and seeks to constitute still more: "As a rhetorical figure, *adianoeta* is particularly understood to mean that various members of an audience will understand the same words differently, some let in on the ironic nature of the figure and some not" (Martel 2011: 98).[7] This need not undermine publicity as such (it may, but it needn't necessarily); it sets in motion a rivalry among possible publics.

— Conspiring with the canon, as it were, we let ourselves in on its secrets. We may find in it resources and energies that feed new politics and constitute new publics rather than just mirror, reconfirm, or resecure old states of affairs. Plotters in the *Trauerspiel* press events to their logical tragic conclusion but conspiracy can press events to their illogical conclusions, thriving on their subtle rather than obvious implications, breaking their imperatives, and exploding their logics to open the way to what Arendt called "new relations and new realities." Thus, although more could be said about which of Sophocles' characters might fit the typology provided by Benjamin, I leave such questions aside: my aim is not to subsume the text to Benjamin's categories. It is rather to find in Benjamin but also in others some levers to incite new readings and dislodge old ones. Benjamin and other modern and contemporary figures such as Arendt, Cavarero, Rancière, Loraux, Fassbinder, Lacan, Williams, and Schmitt, incite, as we shall see, a new "reception" of Sophocles' *Antigone*. Reception here means that the text is re-birthed by later receptions and alien contexts.[8] In the chapters that follow, I develop a reading of Sophocles in a fifth-century context that is always already immersed in nineteenth-, twentieth-, and twenty-first-century contexts that include Benjamin's plotters and conspirators, Fassbinder's agonistic genre-switching, and more.

In Part I, we assessed the promise and limits of various turns to Antigone and their implication in a politics of *lamentation*. The central aims were to note the workings of lamentation, mourning, or grieving as political practices, to account for political, feminist, and queer theorists' recent endorsements of lamentation as a politics, and to assess the fitness of grievability or finitude as an ontology for politics. The idea of lamentation as politics often slides, I argued, into a lamentation of politics, as such. Lamentation's connection to humanism, ethics, and sentimentalism suggested that theorists who turn to mourning often do so seeking refuge from sovereignty rather than new ways to enlist it on behalf of their cause.

Here in Part II, the focus is on the *politics* of lamentation. Lamentation is seen not primarily as an affective or expressive practice nor as the centerpiece of a mortalist humanism but, more fundamentally, as a political vernacular which, like other vernaculars, is plural, various, contested, partisan. The focus in the next three chapters is on Sophocles' play, along with some interpretations of it. The idea is to treat lamentation as a kind of performative utterance, to look at what is said and done by way of lamentation: the curses uttered, the positions taken, the fidelities owned, the vengeances called for, the appropriations performed, the conspiracies enacted with others, and with language. In part, the aim here is to highlight how much of the canonical text had to be sidelined or overlooked in order to secure the humanist/sentimental Antigone: universal lamenter of the dead or strident and unsubtle agonistic actor.

One way to map what I find in Sophocles is by comparison with Benjamin's own journey, traced by Martel, from plotters to conspiracy. As we shall see, the sequence of the three chapters in Part II moves from (i) plotting and conspiracy in Creon's world (Chapter 4) to (ii) Antigone's conspiracy with language (Chapter 5) to (iii) plotting and conspiracy in

Antigone's world (Chapter 6); (though these are not in keeping with the chronology of the play, as I note). In the first of these three chapters, Chapter 4, the focus is on Antigone's effort to undermine Creon's rule by burying the brother whose traitorous body (deemed so by Creon) has been condemned to the indignity of exposure. There are plotters who take her side: soldiers who look the other way or fail fully and quickly to follow Creon's orders. Antigone also combats Creon on a second front: while she fights to defend her aristocratic privileges and meet her kinship obligations, Antigone's ire is directed at Creon not just for his exposure of Polynices but also, more broadly, for conspiring with the new democracy of the day. Creon makes the accommodations she refuses to the new democratic polis. Together, they represent the two strategies that, Mark Griffith argues, were adopted by elites in fifth-century Athens: Creon (as we shall see) accommodates himself to the new order and adopts its values. Antigone adamantly resists democratic encroachments. Right at the beginning of the play, Antigone makes clear she will not conspire with democracy like Creon. She rejects such conspiracy, preferring to plot in the dark with her sister and then, later, to violate Creon's law in the bright light of the noon-time sun.

In Chapter 5, however, we find there are other options between plotting and open resistance. We are now at a much later point in the play and something has changed. Antigone's resistance to the democratic polis is unmodified but she has made some adjustments, or extended herself in new ways. She has moved into conspiracy with language and it with her. Here she openly solicits the support of the Chorus, then more subtly she issues appeals to Creon's soldiers, the larger polis, and the audience that witnesses her in the theater and since. Something like *adianoeta* is clearly at work when she gives a dirge for herself that is not just a lamentation but also an open secret of political critique aimed at Creon. Antigone's dirge is nothing less than an argument against the democracy with which Creon seems to have more or less made his peace. Words that he hears as mere self-indulgent lamentation are, I argue below, freighted with other meanings that go over the unsubtle ruler's head, seeking, soliciting, constituting publics elsewhere. In Chapter 6, as we shall see, focusing on two earlier scenes (Antigone's two scenes with her sister), Antigone begins by way of intrigue and ends with full-on conspiracy. She plots in the dark (her first scene with Ismene) and later moves to conspire with her before finally conspiring with language, in the *adianoeta* of her last scene with her dirge.

In her second and final scene with her sister, in which Antigone quarrels with Ismene about who can claim credit for the burial of Polynices, Antigone speaks in sotto voce conspiracy with her sister, in Creon's presence, wresting one more victory out from under him. But Antigone is not engaged here as she will be later in her dirge in an effort to solicit a public that could become her co-conspirator. The words spoken do not, like those of her later delivered dirge, voice a critique; here Antigone enacts sorority, not citizenship. (Or better: she enacts sorority as a different sort of citizenship, or tries to.) If we return these scenes to their ordering in the play's chronology, we may then – by way of these three scenes, two of them staged in front of Creon but none of them addressing him directly – see a movement: from secret plotting to risky sororal conspiracy to out-spoken solicitation of publics by way of conspiracy with words in Antigone's dirge.[9] That is to say: the sororal Antigone, with whom I end Part II, is not the one with whom Sophocles ends. Noting this, we are reminded not to invest too much in sorority.[10] Still, some focus on Antigone's sororal plotting and conspiracy enables us to see that the play offers us a critical and conspiratorial Antigone we have so far failed to receive. And thus we learn – both in the play and in our own ongoing reception of it – that conspiracy requires not just whispers and subtle wordplay but also hearers and publics willing to step up or allow ourselves to be swept up in response to the calls that occasionally come our way.

What we get from Benjamin (with Martel), then, is his sorely needed rescue from the tendency to affiliate such strategies of plot and conspiracy with the so-called "weapons of the weak," a move that would simply return us to the Antigone (or Ismene) of Part I, the humanist lamenter who finds strength in weakness and acts in fidelity to finitude.[11] That is, without Benjamin, we could read Antigone's sotto voce appeals to Ismene as a sign that Antigone is getting more conventional – more feminine, less in your face, less radically public. But, I argue, she is better seen here as enacting conspiracy. It may sometimes be hard to tell the difference between these two but the fact that Antigone will move from this sotto voce conspiracy with Ismene to her out-loud conspiracy with language in her next scene's dirge, suggests a trajectory that speaks in this interpretation's favor. This reading shows Antigone learns persuasion (in their second scene together she succeeds with Ismene, as we shall see in Chapter 6), and she also comes to aspire to yet more (as we shall see in Chapter 5): she conspires to constitute or solicit publics by conspiring with language itself. Because her mode of action is conspiratorial, while so many critics turn to her for open heroics and adamant announcements, her conspiracy and its lessons have for the most part until now been missed. The genre cues of classical tragedy, shaped by romantic conceptions of individuality, have also played a role in obscuring from view Antigone's conspiracies with language.

CONSPIRACY'S GENRE? *ANTIGONE* AS MELODRAMA

A theoretical discourse is always simultaneously an aesthetic form, a sensible reconfiguration of the facts it is arguing about. (Jacques Rancière)

Yet it is still necessary to distinguish between *Trauerspiel* and tragedy, to separate them so that the specific quality of the tragic is not lost and the seriousness of a generic tragedy does not disappear. (Carl Schmitt)

As I have already been suggesting by way of Benjamin, one way to account for the new readings developed here is by way of genre-switching which (as we saw in Chapter 3) impels the reader to attend to new genre cues and awakens us to the text anew. Prioritizing the guilt of fragile sovereigns, the place of plotters and their intrigues at court, looking for coded speech and whispered communications, staying alert to *adianoeta*, we are directed by the genre cues of *Trauerspiel* and melodrama to a new *Antigone*. In the chapters that follow, I will not argue that Sophocles' play is a melodrama but I will suggest that if we approach it with some sensitivity to that low-culture genre's cues (as I have already begun to do here, briefly, with Benjamin's *Trauerspiel* traits and with Fassbinder's Antigone still in mind as well), we will find new texture and detail in Sophocles' play and, most important, we will be empowered to reclaim it from rather than – as some will worry – cede it to the other side of melodrama: the sentimental weepie.

The idea of rereading or re-emplotting *Antigone* (or any ancient tragedy) as melodrama may be greeted with some skepticism or resistance so it is worth noting that is not without precedent among classicists. Donald Mastronarde makes the case for melodramatic reception in relation to Euripides, a playwright some see as the most hospitable of the classical tragedians to such genre-bending: "the application of the term [melodrama] to Euripidean drama is usually another way to describe his work as non-classical or non-Sophoclean or not fully tragic," says Mastronarde, before concluding that the move to look at genre has some benefits for critics (it is useful as a "heuristic device, for the help it gives us in differentiating various tones and emotional effects, the mixture and juxtaposition of which is a key to much of [Euripides'] dramaturgy") (2010: 62).[12]

Elizabeth Craik makes a case for approaching even Sophocles this way in "*Philoktetes*: Sophoclean Melodrama."[13] Like Mastronarde, Craik too seems to expect that the turn to melodrama will encounter resistance from classicists; hence the care with which she broaches the idea: "It may be argued that some of the effects in the *Philoktetes* are strikingly reminiscent of Euripidean practice in some late plays: and that, while in Euripides they would be immediately recognized as melodramatic, in Sophocles they invite less comment" (1979: 16).[14] Craik extends melodrama to Sophocles but not without reinscribing a high–low culture distinction that positions Sophocles, the patrician, above Euripides, playwright to the masses.

Such classed distinctions are subject to change, however. Tragedy is a high-culture genre now in the West, but in fourth-century Athens, it was a more undecidable thing: low culture in its association with the democracy that birthed it and therefore a cause of concern to conservative critics like Plato, but nonetheless available to be seen as partial to elites in its airing of critiques of democracy. Aristotle, who was less dismissive of the genre than Plato, nonetheless reports that "[p]eople say" that tragedy is addressed "to crude spectators," it is "vulgar" and "inferior," while epic "is addressed to decent spectators who have no need of gestures" (*Poetics*, 1986: 1461b26–1462a5).[15] Tragedy as it is received in the fourth century plays the role of what Benjamin calls pantomime and identifies with tragedy's low-culture cousin: *Trauerspiel.* Seeming to channel today's complaints about melo-drama's excesses (what Elsaesser called, without complaint, its "body-too-much"), Aristotle goes on: "It was for an excessive style that Mynniscus dubbed Callipides an 'ape' and the same opinion was also held about Pindarus. As the latter actors stand to the earlier so does tragic art as a whole to epic" (1986: 1462a).

And, although Plato earlier seems to merge tragedy and epic when he says in Book X of the *Republic* that Homer is the first of the tragic poets, his treatment of the two actually privileges Homer as a uniquely inaugural figure over the tragic poets whom Plato casts as mere imitators of epic. Indeed, in Book III, Plato characterizes tragedy and comedy as forms of poetry that proceed wholly by imitation (2000: 394c), by contrast with epic poetry, which is superior because it mixes narration and imitation.[16] In Benjamin's terms, again, we might say that tragedy in the fourth century plays *Trauerspiel* to epic's *Tragödie.* If melodrama's low-culture status is a historical contingency subject to change, that status should not be reason for its dismissal. (It is not a good reason, in any case. Why shouldn't we employ low-culture genre traits to reopen sedimented high-culture texts?) Surely it makes sense that a so-called low-culture genre merits consideration by democratic theory, especially when that genre is one that calls attention to affect, body, subjectification, thwarted agency, and the quest for eman-cipation, often amid covert double-speak or in circumstances of isolation.

Melodrama may, indeed, be the democratic genre par excellence. "[F]amously said to be written for people who could not read" (Williams 2004: 116), melodrama, Peter Brooks explains, is also anti-grandiose; the

Good question

genre levels (1976). Melodrama's anti-grandiosity is evident in its granting of a central place to members of the lower orders, servants, criminals, workers, queers, women. Indeed, in Sophocles' play as I approach it, the women (not just one woman, but rather the women) are central as are the plotting messenger and sentry.[17] Beyond that, though, *all* the traits of melodrama listed by Brooks are discernible in *Antigone*, especially as I will read the play here: hyperbole, sound, tone, secrecy, machination, double entendres, forces closing in, overwrought speech and feeling (perhaps even the trait we noted in Chapter 3, the protagonists' being recently returned from more worldly to provincial settings, is here: the play begins after the sisters have returned from their travels with Oedipus). In Chapter 4, as we shall see, it is hyperbole that alerts us to the broad reach of the politics of lamentation. In Chapter 5, the focus is on Antigone's dirge and its conspiracy with words, but also – as we shall see – on the keening sound and embodied practice of lamentation: loud, wordless, and self-lacerating. And in Chapter 6, the key to a new reading of the play is taking seriously the possibility of secrecy and double-speak in the private or isolated world of women. These along with a certain overwroughtness – an example of which is surely Ismene's "I'm forced, I have no choice," (66 [79]) but there are many more, including Antigone's "Creon, what more do you want than my arrest and execution?" (497 [555–556]) and "oh god, the voice of death. It's come, it's here" (933–934 [1025]) – are all hallmarks of melodrama.[18]

Some will object that a melodrama-inflected approach cheapens tragedy. This book contests the distinction between high and low culture that undergirds such objections. I have already indicated that I am not alone in suggesting we take melodrama seriously for classics or democratic theory. I turn now to read *Antigone* with democratic theory's concerns and melodrama's genre cues in mind. This is a genre-switching of sorts; a reassessment of the play by way of its partial re-emplotment from tragedy to melodrama. There is no reason, however, to limit the various interpretative strategies employed here – contextual, historical, dramaturgical, deconstructive – to this single one. Still, attending for a moment to genre and genre-switching, we may keep in mind Benjamin's observation that Shakespeare and Calderón managed to transcend the limits of their genre – *Trauerspiel* – to produce true tragedies.[19] Being open to reading *Antigone* as melodrama (but not just as that), I am in effect suggesting that others who have produced true tragedies may have descended, as it were, from their genre, to inadvertently produce true melodrama, or at least to have left us a melodramatic subtext.

CHAPTER 4

Mourning, membership, and the politics of exception: plotting Creon's conspiracy with democracy

[I]n a curious way, to focus upon the disobedient and the process of disobedience is to accept the perspective of the established order. It is a concession that it is the [wo]man who appeals beyond law that is in need of explanation.

Robert Cover

The task that remains to me then is to outline an authentically conflictual reading of tragedy, one that upholds both poles at the same time, the politics that prescribes forgetting and the mourning that regenerates memory.

Nicole Loraux

Politics is not made up of power relationships; it is made up of relationships between worlds.

Jacques Rancière

Turning now from Part I's focus on the politics of *lamentation* to look in detail in Part II at the *politics* of lamentation, I begin by setting Sophocles' *Antigone* in the context of fifth-century burial politics in Athens.[1] Approaching the play in this context we find not a mortalist humanist Antigone but rather a partisan political actor. I read Antigone's burial of her brother, Polynices, (but also other actions of hers) as a performance of elite objections to the classical city's emergent democracy. Creon, on this reading, represents not sovereignty or the rule of law run amok, or not just that, but also and more pointedly a different elite tactic: he conspires with the new democracy and adopts many of its causes as his own. He is one of "the newer breed of elites who," Mark Griffith argues, "are willing to work within the democratic system and to shape their own claims and choices to conform with what is 'good for the city'" (2010: 123). Seeking to enlist sovereignty for his causes, Creon accommodates the polis' needs. Antigone, by contrast, will not work with the opposition. Thus, the two protagonists represent the two strategies that, Griffith notes, were adopted

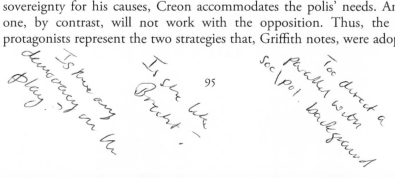

by fifth-century Athenian elites faced with the new democracy's establishment: some resigned themselves to the new democratic polis and its values, while others stayed reactive to them and refused all compromise as complicity or collaboration.[2]

Playing out this conflict, Antigone and Creon illustrate – by way, in particular, of funerary and family law and practice – the political and psychic costs of the fifth-century democracy's profound political changes. Some of these can be seen as developments of innovations first introduced by Solon 150 years earlier, altered by Cleisthenes, and later, further, by Pericles.[3] Under Pericles' leadership, burial styles were fundamentally contested in the 440s and 430s, as David Roselli (2006) shows. The play, written in the late 440s BCE, reflects this fundamental contestation but, contra Roselli, I find it unnecessarily limiting to treat the play as if it is simply about burial styles. It is also about all the things that might drive or underlie a shift in burial practice. Moreover, the play goes beyond offering "a striking example of social disturbance resulting from a woman's mourning," as Josine Blok puts it (2001: 106). Perhaps, better, it offers an insight into why a woman's mourning should be so socially disturbing. Through the issue of funerary practice and female lamentation, Sophocles' *Antigone* explores conflicts between honor-based versus law-based conceptions of justice, individuality and replaceability, aristocracy and democracy; Homeric honor versus democratic unity and membership.[4]

These claims about the play's larger political concerns are not undercut by the fact that the question of burial and mourning in Sophocles' play seems to address a prior, more fundamental question of friendship and enmity, for the politics of mourning in the play are not confined to Polynices – nor to Antigone for that matter. Although Creon prohibits Polynices' burial in order to punish his treason – Polynices attacked the city with a foreign army to claim the throne from his brother, Eteocles – the assumption that the play is centrally about Polynices and his burial unduly narrows our sense of the play's scope. Contra those who see Antigone as an example for those today who seek to lament politically or grieve ungrievable life (enemy dead, those who die of AIDS, those who are disappeared by military rulers), the play repeatedly explores the question of how permissibly to grieve not just ungrievable life but grievable life as well. The problem of when and how to mourn arises *several* times – in relation not only to Polynices but also to Antigone, Haemon, Eteocles, and Eurydice. This suggests that the play does not get embroiled in the problem of burial because of the politics of enmity.

Rather, it takes up the problem of enmity in order to broach (in a distancing way, starting with the burial of an enemy) broad political problems of which burial politics are a synecdoche.[5] The key to the reading here, then, is to decenter burial – it is just one issue among others – and to decenter Polynices as himself just one among others in need of burial or mourning.

Antigone does demand the right to bury her brother, but what is she doing when she does that? She does want to mourn and bury her brother but beyond that his death, his body, also provide an occasion for Antigone to object to the democratic order of the day. In her laments for her brother but also, as we shall see, in her dirge for herself and elsewhere, Antigone memorializes the family's dead in heroic terms (in terms of the dead's individuality, the loss to the surviving family, and the need to avenge a wrong), exhibiting fidelity to natal over marital family, clan over polis. She gives expression to an elite concern in the fifth century that the democracy sends soldiers to die in war while offering only a pretense of the memorialization and honor they deserve, a pathetic substitute for the real (Homeric/heroic) thing that only their families or clans, but not the democratic polis, can provide.[6]

These political stakes of Antigone's actions are obscured by those who see her in Hegelian terms, as a defender of private right against public law and also by those who see in Antigone a model of dissident politics as singular heroic action. Slavoj Žižek focuses on Antigone's "no!" and on her stammering repetition of the tautology of her brother's kinship location in her (in)famous final speech, which I discuss at length in the next chapter. Žižek follows Lacan, who points out that Antigone's love for Polynices has nothing to do with his traits, but is simply premised on his being her brother. He is who he is who he is for Antigone, Lacan says, and Žižek agrees. Butler brilliantly argues against Lacan that Polynices' singularity is less tautological than might first appear because Antigone's references to her beloved brother are dangerously and productively doubled: her brother, whom she calls son of her mother, is not only Polynices, as so many assume, but also, of course, her father, Oedipus, who is also a son of Jocasta and whom (although Butler does not say this, Derrida does) Antigone also does not get to bury (2000: 60–61).[7] But to what might Antigone say "yes"?[8]

Against Žižek, Judith Butler rightly notes that Antigone does not "simply say 'no,'" although "negations riddle her speech" (2000: 68). Butler and I differ regarding what it is that Antigone says yes to, however. To incest, to a different kinship, to anomalous desire, as Butler suggests?

Certainly there is much in the play that is illuminated by Butler's turn to this figure of incest to argue against structuralist and psychoanalytic assumptions about kinship. But Antigone's identification with incest can figure something else too: the charge of incest is an old one leveled against aristocrats, those clannish families that are said to protect their power and privilege by marrying inward, blending the marital and natal family and bearing the less than optimal children that result from such endogamy. That is, incestuous is how the natal family form looks from the perspective of the conjugal. Of course, the charge is also made that aristocrats marry exogamously, manifesting disloyalty to the polis when they seek to acquire through marriage to a foreigner the wealth and soldiers they need to advance their power at home. Antigone shows her familiarity with such marital politics when, late in the day, she positions herself between the two ill-fated marriages of her family, her father's endogamous incest, which destroyed him, and her brother's exogamous marriage to a daughter of the Argives, which enabled him to raise there an army to try to reclaim the Theban throne (863–871 [951–958]).[9]

If Antigone acts on behalf of an aristocratic form of life under pressure in the mid-fifth-century democratic polis, does Creon identify with the democratic or does he at least model an elite complicity with the new democratic form? Creon's contemporary detractors will undoubtedly object to the idea of connecting him to the democracy, noting that he exhibits few of the standard democratic virtues, and they would be right. But contemporary readers tend to think democracy is more a matter of procedure than substance. Reading procedurally, interpreters such as Martha Nussbaum see no evidence of democratic leaning in Creon, who after all does not deliberate nor consult with the people or the elders, and is hard pressed to take counsel from anyone (Nussbaum 1986; cf. Euben 1997). But, I will argue here, Creon _metonymizes_ _democracy_ substantively. His ban on lamentation and his repeated emphasis on the harms of individuality represent the fifth-century democratic view. That these are unaccompanied by other more positive traits also judged democratic in classical Athens may highlight the fact that Creon, for all his complicity with democracy, retains aristocratic traits; or, more powerfully, it may suggest that the play casts democracy in a critical light.[10]

Another reason for the mis-judgment of Creon is commentators' assumption that his *kerygma* against burying Polynices is obviously tyrannical or unjust. As Helene Foley points out, it was the specific measure of leaving the body out to rot that was the problem: "Contemporary Attic punishments of traitors involved casting the body outside the city's borders, throwing them below into pits and gorges, or casting them into the sea. Creon, on the other hand, left the body exposed and created pollution" (1995: 134).[11] Even Christiane Sourvinou-Inwood, who actually reads Creon as otherwise democratic, accepts the view that his *kerygma* is at odds with her reading. She resolves the problem it seems to pose by suggesting that Creon's *kerygma* is an "error." He errs in leaving Polynices exposed rather than dishonoring the body in accordance with Attic norms for the treatment of traitors. On my reading, however, no such resolution is needed. Creon's excess is precisely what marks him as conspiring with the democracy. If Creon's treatment of Polynices exceeds the bounds of the permissible, that is perfectly compatible with the claim that Creon represents Attic norms which are in Sophocles' play, as we shall see, represented hyperbolically, through the lens of the rival world view with which they contend. From an elite/heroic perspective like Antigone's, Creon does not depart from, he rather instances, democratic practice when he mistreats the dead and prohibits burial, as we shall see.

Moreover, insofar as democracy would appear tyrannical to mid-fifth-century Athenian elites, Creon's apparently tyrannical traits are fully compatible with his character as representative of, or complicit with, the democratic order.[12] Creon begins in statesmanlike voice (his first "ship of state" speech is Periclean).[13] If he becomes tyrannical over time, that may signal a defect of character; or it may suggest perspicacity: he sees that his struggle with Antigone is about more than a burial and a body. Within the framework of the play, their struggle is about the terms of collective coexistence and the recalcitrance of a rival form of life. Creon aims to clarify the terms of Theban membership when he promotes one brother as an honored son and denigrates the other as an enemy. One brother besieged the city; he "thirsted to drink his kinsmen's blood and sell the rest to slavery," says Creon of Polynices (201–202 [225–226]), while the other sought to defend it (208 [233]; cf. 313–314 [326–327]) and so, as Antigone points out, Creon "graced one with all the rites, [and] disgraced the other" (21–22 [27–28]).[14] Eteocles is given an official honorific burial in which Antigone participates but Polynices is left out to rot. Creon may mean by these measures to consolidate the lines of Theban membership. But the issue of which brother's side Thebans should take is distinguishable from the larger question of whether and how a brother should be mourned; how we mourn is a deeply political issue to whose history in Athens I now briefly turn.

So Sophocles merely exaggerates?

Is not Thebes used as the counter-image of Athens

REGULATING LAMENT

In the sixth century BCE, legislation is passed first by Solon at Athens, but then throughout Greece, restricting mourning and burial practices. Over 150 years before Sophocles wrote *Antigone*, one of Solon's polis-forming legislations called for restraining what Plutarch calls the "wild and disorderly behavior" of women in grief (1960: 21.5), as well as the "breast beating and lamentation at burials."[15] Commentators today stress that "*women's*" mourning – loud, keening – was cast as "excessive." At the time, families burying their dead might have turned to *threnon exarchoi*, who sang the *threnos*, "a formal lament." These "professionals" "probably existed throughout antiquity despite possible efforts by Solon to abolish them by banning the singing of prepared dirges" (Garland 1985: 30). Kinswomen performed *goos* (a personal and more improvised sort of dirge) which, when lamenting men killed in battle, focused on "the plight of the bereaved" and not on the "heroic feats" of the dead or their contribution to the public good (Holst-Warhaft 1992: 114). Both forms of lamentation featured calls for vengeance and both were subject to Solon's regulations, which were quite specific. The *prothesis* "was to be held indoors and the *ekphora* could only take place in silence and before dawn" (Taxidou 2004: 176).[16] The *prothesis* gave "the bereaved an opportunity to indulge in shameless self-pity by bemoaning the effects upon their own lives occasioned by the loss of the beloved" (Garland 1985: 30). This practice is not so much an expression of authentic feeling as an orchestrated ritual.[17]

There may be many reasons for Solon's innovations, including the need "in the newly formed democratic polis" to "diminish the power of the aristocracy" for whom funerals were a way to flaunt wealth (Taxidou 2004: 176).[18] As Gail Holst-Warhaft points out, however, reining in the wealthy was not the only aim: (i) Solon set out to take charge of practices of remembrance in order to end cycles of vengeful violence that were seen as a threat to the new polis form (funerals were a locus of clan strife, especially in the case of a murdered relative).[19] (ii) The emerging city aimed to reorient mourning away from its focus on the lost, irreplaceable life and toward that life's honorable dedication to the good of the polis. These two aims are connected insofar as (i) the thirst for vengeance is whetted, not slaked, by the belief that dead relatives are (ii) irreplaceable.

The aim seems to be to shift away from Homeric dirges' focus on the unique individuality of the dead, the loss to the surviving family caused by the death, and the call to vengeance.[20] Homeric mourning features "[e]xtravagant, out of control behaviour, including loud wailing, tearing the hair, and lacerating one's face. This is a common initial response to death, especially by men but also by women" (Holst-Warhaft 1992: 113–114). Note that excess mourning, later attributed to women and cast as feminine from Solon to Pericles and beyond – Socrates tells his male friends not to weep over his impending death like women or he will be forced to send them away, as he did Xanthippe (*Phaedo* 117d–117e) – is in fact a trait of both men's and women's mourning in Homer. There are gendered differences noted in surviving vases, but they suggest different customs of physical expression not an opposition between loud, showy lamentation and more decorous mourning.[21] At issue in the later ban, then, are formal practices of mourning (*threnos*) led by women (*threnon exarchoi*) and the practices of loud wailing and self-laceration (*goos*) previously conventional, now gendered feminine and cast as excessive.[22] Both focus on the family's loss rather than on the city's gain from the death being mourned.[23]

Given the privatization of the *prothesis* as well as its diminution (from nine days in Homer for Achilles to one day under Solon), we might expect to see forbidden practices of lamentation go underground, as it were, or take new forms. Indeed, it does seem possible that this is what happened when the late fifth century witnessed new developments in funerary practice. People (it may not have been women, specifically) began to place "in cemeteries, graves, pits or rivers the small folded lead plaques known as *katadesmoi* (curse-tablets)," most commonly in the graves of "those who died young or violently" (Garland 1985: 6).[24]

Subtly or overtly the forbidden lamentations remained and retained traits the new polis form tried to erase.[25] The laments aroused the passions of those left behind, highlighted the unique individuality of the lost life, and called for survivors to avenge the deceased. Solon in the early sixth century saw the practice as threatening to the new polis form. By the 440s, when Sophocles wrote *Antigone*, the threat had shifted but it was not diminished: Athens was now democratic and "the dead bodies mourned were more often than not the bodies of young men who died at war," no longer defending the polis but rather expanding the Athenian empire (Taxidou 2004: 30).[26]

Prohibition was not the only strategy in fifth-century Athens. Eventually institutions of exception were established as well. One, referred to as a "concession" by Larry J. Bennett and William Blake Tyrrell, allowed for the bones of the dead to be displayed for two days ("twice that allowed private funerals") in the agora and families could here mourn as they wished but on the third day the polis took over and the mourned became simply "the dead," nameless members of the city to be buried publicly (1990: 443).[27] Also on offer were alternative funerary practices and two new genres of loss – tragedy and the Funeral Oration.[28] "Female lamentation gradually becomes suppressed," Laura McClure argues, "just as the epitaphios or public funeral oration becomes increasingly important in consolidating political identity at Athens" (1999: 45, cf. chapter 1). Funeral Orations, delivered by men not women, glorified the dead for their contribution to the city's greatness but also insisted on their replaceability. "The *epitaphios logos* is the polis' substitution of public praise for private mourning," Gail Holst-Warhaft says (1992: 124), though it might be more apt to say the epitaph substitutes one kind of public mourning, that of the classical city, for another kind of mourning, elite or Homeric, which is also public, if not polis-centered. Homeric mourning's focus on the hero's beautiful body, embodied pain, and survivors' bereavement is replaced by the classical city's focus on gorgeous speech, oratory that moves and pleases its audience without calling for vengeance.[29] With this substitution is launched a new economy of substitution, in which no one is said to be so uniquely singular that his loss should be seen as devastating to family or city or to require recompense. In this moment, we might say, Athens treats every soldier as an "unknown soldier." The *patrios nomos*, paternal ancestral law, set out rules for the public commemoration of Athenian war dead who were collected from the battlefields and divided up into their tribes, a social ordering established by Cleisthenes in 508 and treated today by Jacques Rancière as foundational to democracy because Cleisthenes' new political groupings were no longer birth-based; they were more arbitrary and contingent (2007). The bodies were then cremated. Their ashes were put into common tribal coffins and displayed in the city. The names of the dead were listed on marble tablets. A big public oration was given in the public graveyard and the dominant note was praise, not lamentation (Blok 2001: 106).

Tragedy, the genre of devastating loss, also became important, perhaps to compensate for the loss of loss (mourning practices), as it were, or to balance with its larger-than-life characterizations the smaller-than-life lot to which Athenian combatants were now consigned.[30] But tragedy could also go too far. The first tragedy, now lost, *The Capture of Miletus*, authored by a little-known tragedian named Phrynicus, triggered "an epidemic of uncontrollable grief" for Athens' sacrifice of Miletus to the Persians (Taxidou 2004: 97). For this, Phrynicus was fined a thousand drachmas and the performance of the play was prohibited by law. This puts some pressure on the common notion that Athenians shed tears at the theater that they were not allowed to shed elsewhere.[31] Instead, the episode suggests, tragic theater, this new institution of exception, was also a regulated, disciplined domain within which some subversion was tolerated. Permitted, approved, if still also transgressive, tragic theater was a relatively safe venue that allowed and even occasioned emotions like, but not the same as, the emotions once solicited by female mourners, some of whom were "professionals," not unlike the actors who performed in the dramas.

In tragic theater, emotions once exercised in now forbidden mourning rites were transformed into something else and exercised in moderation in a polis-centered and policed form. Thus, while the audience was watching Sophocles' *Antigone* and perhaps even feeling the justice of Antigone's cause, they were participating as spectators in one of the institutional forms that sought to mark her defeat and to enable the victory that I shall now argue her antagonist, Creon, hyperbolically sought.[32]

ANTIGONE'S LAMENTS: HOMERIC MOURNING IN DEMOCRATIC ATHENS

With these contextual details in mind, readers today may find Sophocles' *Antigone* opens up to them in new ways. Again and again, the play stages encounters between archaic/Homeric versus classical mourning practices cast as excessive versus well-judged, respectively. The distinction between these two kinds of mourning and their (im)propriety is just one way the play marks a larger divide between two paradigms of political culture: aristocratic Homeric/heroic individuality (and the elite community it postulates) and classical democratic community (and the forms of individuality it permits). Other markers in the play point to shifts in citizenship legislation (in 451/0, from aristocratic patrilineal to democratic bi-parental); changes in the mechanism for distributing civic responsibilities from an aristocratic principle of worth to a democratic practice of randomization by lottery; and, more generally, a shift from an heroic ethics and politics of individuality and distinction to a democratic ethics and politics of interchangeability and substitution.[33]

When Antigone is accused of burying Polynices not once but twice in the play, she is said to act excessively. This is the classical city's judgment of Homeric mourning, that it is "excessive."[34] When Antigone complains to Ismene that their brother Polynices is "to be left unwept, unburied, a lovely treasure for birds that scan the field and feast to their hearts' content" (28–30 [35–36]), Antigone re-cites the plight of Patroclus in the

Iliad: "unwept, unburied" (22.386).[35] Does she imagine herself – are we to imagine her – an Achilles, fated to die early and bereft of a brother/lover?[36]

Also, Antigone's two recorded mourning speeches – one for Polynices (at the second burial) and one for herself – are both clearly marked as Homeric, the first conventionally so, the other hyperbolically.[37] We hear about the first of these two laments from the sentry who witnessed it. He describes Antigone in terms that call up all the forbidden elements of women's lamentation:

And she cried out a sharp, piercing cry, like a bird come back to an empty nest [*in Homer, an iconic representation of the mother in mourning*] peering into its bed, and all the babies gone [*bereavement*] . . . Just so, when she sees the corpse bare she bursts into a long, shattering wail [*loud, keening*] and calls down withering curses on the heads of all who did the work [*vengeance*]. (423–428 [471–477])[38]

Later, as Antigone approaches the cave to which Creon has consigned her, she mourns again, this time for herself. When she describes her "future life immured in the cave as 'bereft'" (Rehm 1994: 182, n. 12) and goes on to wail that she will never marry or have children, she is, in Nicole Loraux's words (written in the context of an argument about Euripides' play), "like a Homeric mourner [who] weeps in advance over her future life" (1998: 63). Antigone is not a professional mourner, she is not engaged in the more formal laments [*threnos*] first outlawed by Solon. *Goos* is the term used by Sophocles to describe Antigone's plaint. She does call for vengeance as she is led to the cave in which she will die, though the call is muted by comparison with her earlier lament for Polynices (she may doubt the justice of her cause now the gods seem to side with Creon): "Very well: if this is the pleasure of the gods, once I suffer I will know that I was wrong. But if these men are wrong, let them suffer nothing worse than they mete out to me – these masters of injustice!" (925–928 [1017–1021]).[39]

Here, also like a Homeric mourner, Antigone focuses on the unique, irreplaceable lost life of her brother. This seems to mark a shift from her earlier account of herself. Antigone is normally thought of as speaking on behalf of the gods of the underworld when she argues that the dead are all radically equal and, regardless of their deeds in the human world, must be buried. She does cite the gods. But her sentiments about the equality of her brothers' claims to honor in death also recall Homer. As James Boyd White points out, citing Simone Weil: in the *Iliad* "Homer describes Achaean and Trojan deaths . . . in identical terms, expressive of identical feelings" (1984: 39). He so well recognizes "the equal humanity of the people who must suffer on both sides" that, as Weil puts it, "'One is barely aware that the poet is a Greek and not a Trojan.'" White adds: "A death is a death. Trojan or Achaean" (1984: 39–40). This is Antigone's view. On it is premised her refusal to differentiate as the democratically identified Creon wants her to between Eteocles and Polynices.[40]

Antigone's earlier refusal to take seriously the friend–enemy distinction in the name of equality among the dead shifts to a focus in her final dirge on her brother's unique individuality. She ends by claiming a particular devotion to her brother, to whom she refers as "my own mother's son" (466–467 [521]). This phrase, "my own mother's son," is much remarked upon by Luce Irigaray, Judith Butler, and others. For Butler, as I noted above, the formal kinship location – son of my mother – is productive because it highlights, contra structuralism, the polysemousness of kinship, its ambiguous character, its vulnerability to slippage. (The term, as noted, refers not only to Polynices, but also to Eteocles and to Oedipus, Antigone's father/brother, as well.) Irigaray interprets the phrase as indicating that for Antigone the issue is less about Polynices than about access to the forbidden maternal in this increasingly patriarchal order of kinship premised upon taboos of incest and homosexuality. The phrase is worthy of remark for another reason as well. In Homer, paternity is definitive for kinship and there is no such thing as bastardy. Against that background, to call someone a brother would not connote a shared mother. Only in that context, in which the hearer would not infer a shared mother from the stated fact of fraternity, does the specification of a shared mother add information. That information is rendered redundant and unnecessary in Athens by the citizenship law of 451/0 (passed almost ten years before Sophocles wrote *Antigone*) which, "on Pericles' proposal, require[ed] that candidates for citizenship be born from two freeborn native parents" (Lape 2003: 54).[41] Thus the phrase "my own mother's son" may be another marker of the elite/Homeric Antigone's alienness to democratic Athens, the audience or addressee of the play.[42]

What follows from the specific irreplaceability of Polynices? No child or husband, Antigone says, could have moved her to the same self-sacrifice. "A husband dead, there might have been another. A child by another too, if I had lost the first. But mother and father both lost in the halls of Death, no brother could ever spring to light again" (909–912 [1001–1004]). One can always remarry or have more children, but a brother (whose parents are dead) cannot be replaced, she says, seemingly justifying her act. She will accept no substitutes.

I discuss this speech in detail in Chapter 5, where I argue that the polis' regulation of laments is part of an education into a new economy of citizenship whose centrality to the play is signaled subtly by this speech's much noted but seldom analyzed citation of a story told by Herodotus in his *Histories*. Here it is important to note simply that when Antigone insists on the irreplaceability of Polynices, she establishes herself as one who prizes singularity over substitution. Pericles, by contrast, as we shall see further in Chapter 5, saw the city's dead in far less singular terms.

Creon approves a democratic economy of substitution that Antigone goes out of her way to reject, as when he defends his treatment of Antigone, saying that if Haemon cannot marry Antigone, there are "other fields for him to plow" (569 [642]).[43] But Ismene stands up for the uniqueness of her sister: "Perhaps, but never as true, as close a bond as theirs" (570 [643]). Creon is unmoved by Ismene. Like her sister, she too stands for an order of rank and an economy of individuality he rejects. Haemon's suicide shows Ismene was right: he will not accept a replacement for Antigone. Thus, the argument for an economy of substitution, which one critic identifies with democracy as such, is made or its power is instanced more than once but each time it fails.[44]

It is important to note that Creon's attitude is not just misogynist. He expects men, too, to accept their own substitutability, to be self-disciplining and law-abiding, to give up their heroic ambitions. The play opens in the aftermath of the heroic single combat of Eteocles and Polynices. This style of contest is subtly contrasted by Creon with the unity of the hoplite line in which each shields his neighbor from harm and follows the orders given. The hoplites fought in phalanx formation and lived and died by an economy of substitution: when one fell, one from the next line would move in immediately to take his place. This is Creon's model of good citizenship.[45] The good man, Creon says to Haemon, one fit to rule and be ruled, is "staunch in the storm of spears, he'll stand his ground, a loyal, unflinching comrade at your side" (665–666 [743–745]). But "whoever steps out of line" (667 [746]) invites "Anarchy" (672 [752]) which "breaks the ranks of spearmen into headlong rout" (674–675 [754]).[46] Those who "last it out . . . owe their lives to discipline." Such men "live by law" (675–677 [755–757]).[47]

Here Creon collapses hoplite order and law, opposing them to anarchy, dissidence, disorder. Rather than grant that Antigone represents a rival order, possessed of its own values (vengeance, aristocracy, Homeric honor), Creon treats her as a merely anarchic force. This is the very anarchic or dissident Antigone, now revalued as a positive force, who is called upon by many contemporary feminist and democratic theorists to re-energize a justice exhausted by legalism and betrayed by state power. But this is Creon's view of Antigone (as Robert Cover points out in the service of a different argument in *Justice Accused* [1975]), which casts her action only in negative and disruptive terms.[48]

The politics of democratic Athens and the cultural context of Antigone's resistance are also in play when the *Antigone* subtly calls attention to what M. I. Finley (1973) identifies as the central institutions of ancient democracy: "the lot and remuneration – the lot to assign public offices and remuneration for participation in the assembly" (cited in Saxonhouse 1996: 101).[49] When the soldiers find that Polynices has been buried against Creon's edict and on their watch, they know someone must tell Creon what has happened. No one volunteers because they all fear his wrath. Who wants to be the bearer of bad news? They fell asleep on the job, after all. And yet the king must be told. So the soldiers draw lots and, the sentry reports sarcastically, "I got the prize" (275 [312]). Casting lots could be read as a sign of the soldiers' cowardice and avoidance of duty and they do indeed "stare at the ground" and hang their "heads in fear," according to the sentry (269–270 [305–306]). But it can also be seen as the opposite. In fifth-century Athens, almost all officials were chosen by lot, a practice first introduced more limitedly by Solon in the sixth century BCE (Solon introduced appeals and some use of lottery; citizen courts came later). Indeed, the men judging the plays performed at the Dionysian Festival had themselves been chosen by lot. Submitting to lot therefore need not be seen as an avoidance of responsibility, but as a conventional mechanism for its distribution.[50] More subtly, there may here be a careful critique of fifth-century democratic Athens, a quiet suggestion that this conventional mechanism of responsibility distribution is for cowards or makes cowards of those who rely on it.

A critique of the second quintessentially democratic institution, payment to the poor for public service, is also aired. When Creon rashly accuses one after another of taking bribes and betraying the public good (as he sees it), he voices a familiar critique of the democratic practice: once the polis pays *for* public service, the door is opened to prize payment *over* public service and suspicion of corruption is rife.[51] Sophocles' genius may have been to find a way to broach such criticisms in front of an audience vulnerable to them and yet garner from them prizes for it, too. Most important for us, however, these references to two of the democracy's institutions may be the play's alert to us that other democratic innovations are at issue in this drama – the regulation of mourning which is part of the reshaping of citizenship in conformity with the needs of the democratic polis.

That Creon might represent the democracy's views is one plausible interpretation of the Chorus' welcome of him as "the new man for the new day" (155–157 [174]). It might also help further to explain Creon's initial bewilderment at Antigone's resistance, since the fifth-century democracy counseled and expected civic obedience, a view voiced by Creon when he says "that man the city places in authority, his orders must be obeyed, large and small, right and wrong" (670–671 [748–751]).[52] But there is one oddity here. Democratic Athens did not forbid kinswomen from mourning; it limited laments *to* kinswomen.[53] Why then would Sophocles use Antigone, a kinswoman, to explore a ban that would not have applied to her? Why ban *goos* to make us think about the forbidden *threnos*? There may be exaggeration for effect here. Where in Athens mourning is narrowed from the community at large to kinswomen exclusively, from public female-led performances to public male-led performances and private female mourning indoors, so in Sophocles' Thebes where *that ban is assumed to be already in effect* (it informs the expectations of the characters throughout the play, as we shall see further in a moment), the *new* restriction, Creon's edict, narrows things even further and thereby restages the old debate and reanimates it. This may be the play's way of suggesting that those who think only Creon's ban is extreme miss the extremity of the current restrictions: the Athenian restriction of mourning to kinswomen was tantamount to the prohibition of the practice, *tout court*, since the practice underwent huge transformations once it excluded the women for whom mourning was a central activity, the professional mourners who knew best how to move people in their grief. Or Sophocles' point may be more conservative. He may approve the Athenian regulation rather than criticize it, showing its reasonableness by comparison with Creon's more extreme prohibition.[54] Either way or both, the play invites readers or viewers to revisit and reassess the fifth-century regulation of mourning and the democracy's post-heroic citizenship practices.

Many tensions between Homeric/heroic and democratic paradigms are referred to repeatedly in the play. But it is mostly through mourning practices that the tensions between the two are explored as in this, her final scene, when Antigone bemoans her fate at length and Creon archly comments on her plaint: Antigone says, "No one to weep for me, my friends, no wedding-song – they take me away in all my pain . . . the road lies open, waiting. Never again, the law forbids me to see the sacred eye of day. I am agony! No tears for the destiny that's mine, no loved one mourns my death" (876–882 [963–969]). To which Creon says, "Can't you see? If a man could wail his own dirge [*goos*] *before* he dies, he'd never finish"

(883–884 [970–971]). This is not just "scornful," as Charles Segal says, though it is that too (1995a: 249, n. 22). More significantly, Creon here sums up the classical view of Homeric/elite mourning: it is excessive and self-centered. Those who go on and on when mourning others may as well be mourning themselves; it is all about them. They put the good of the city second to their own bereavement. The play represents this point of view hyperbolically: Creon airs the charge that Homeric mourning is *self-indulgent* – endless, excessive, and without regard for the good of the city – in response to one whose mourning is literally self-indulgent; Antigone here actually does *sing her own dirge*.[55]

As we shall soon see, this is where Creon tries to interrupt her: "Take her away, quickly!" (885 [972]).[56] But the soldiers delay, perhaps exhibiting in their plotting way the sympathy Haemon has claimed the people have for Antigone and surely illustrating for the audience the impotence of Creon whose orders never seem to be followed as given. The soldiers extend to Antigone the hospitality Creon denies her and, in her "tragic overliving," Antigone manages to do what Creon here expressly forbids, to exercise her "stranger's rights." She sings her own dirge and is finally silenced, when Creon admonishes the soldiers a second time: "Take her away. You're wasting time – you'll pay for it too" (931–932 [1023–1024]).[57]

Antigone's dirge is our central concern in Chapter 5. For now, it is enough to note that Antigone's laments regarding the life she has forgone, her losses, her singular attachment to her irreplaceable brother, the downfall of her family, and her calls for vengeance contrast sharply with Creon's regulation of funerary practice and his focus on the (dis)service of those now dead to the city. Creon, like Pericles, collectivizes lament, and presses grief into the service of the city.[58] Together, Creon and Antigone, in contrast, suggest that if the democratic Oration moves us too quickly out of mourning and does too little for the dead because it instrumentalizes them for its own ends, Homeric laments fail to move mourners along quickly enough, allowing them to wallow in endless dirges impervious to the polis' larger needs.

These are the two poles in contention. But there are other options as well. Antigone is not alone in her lamentations. Concerns about the destabilizing powers of lamentation are expressly raised, for example, when Eurydice, Creon's wife, hears of her son's suicide. Thus, the play's focus is not "how to solve the problem of Antigone?" as most other readings assume (though they might not all share in the quest for "solution"), for the problem is not confined to Antigone.

Eurydice reacts strangely to the Messenger's report that her son, Haemon, is dead of a suicide committed in his father's presence. The Chorus asks: "What do you make of that? The lady's gone, without a word, good or bad" (1244–1245 [1373–1374]). The Messenger joins in the Chorus' concern: "I'm alarmed, too," he says.[59] He worries, however, not about Eurydice's well-being but about the well-being of the city: "But here's my hope – faced with her son's death she finds it unbecoming to mourn in public. Inside, under her roof, she'll set her women to the task and wail the sorrow of the house. She's too discreet. She won't do something rash" (1246–1250 [1375–1380]). The stakes are clear: will Eurydice indulge in forbidden public, loud Homeric wailing or confine herself to the private, less "unbecoming" household-centered grief that good polis judgment since Solon recommends? (In the Gibbons and Segal translation, the line reads: "She's not without good judgment and won't do wrong" [2003: 1335–1336].) The messenger is confident; the Chorus is not: "I'm not so sure. To me, at least, a long heavy silence promises danger, just as much as a lot of empty outcries" (1251–1252 [1381–1383]). The Chorus calls the "empty outcries" potentially dangerous while also calling them empty, which simultaneously suggests the opposite. They are empty insofar as they cannot bring the dead back. But they are not at all empty insofar as they can restart a cycle of vengeance and destabilize the city. Loud lament can make citizens not only admire those who gave sons to the city but also, even at the same time, wonder at the wisdom of sacrificing the city's sons to war.

In her private household, off the streets forbidden to her, Eurydice did not mourn quietly with her servants, as the Messenger hoped (the Chorus member's worry that "a long heavy silence promises danger" was perspicuous), nor did she call loudly and publicly for someone to avenge her son's death, as the Messenger feared. The Messenger reports to Creon that, inside, she raised "a cry for the noble fate of Megareus, the hero killed in the first assault, then for Haemon, then with her dying breath she called down torments on your head – you killed her sons" (1302–1305 [1427–1431]). Eurydice ends her life cursing the husband she blames for her pain. Even in her death, "the dead, the woman lying there, piles the guilt of all their deaths on you" says the Messenger to Creon (1312–1313 [1436–1437]), surely seeking still further to manage the trajectory of events. When Eurydice kills herself on the sacrificial altar, in the household, away from the public streets and yet cursing her husband out loud, she dies a death that stands somewhere between the two orders in contention here. Like Antigone, Eurydice curses and calls for vengeance; unlike Antigone, Eurydice wails indoors. But Eurydice's cries and words are mobile. Through the

Messenger, they leave the confines of the palace.[60] This woman accepts her confinement, but her words do not.

Eurydice's corpse appears as well. "See for yourself!" the Messenger says as servants open the palace door to bring her corpse to Creon on its bier. "[N]ow they bring her body from the palace" (1293 [1419]). The shift from aristocratic to democratic practices is not costless. Sophocles' *Antigone* opens the palace door to reveal the cost of polis life and membership. Its name? *Eurydice*, which means *"wide justice."*[61] Wide justice highlights the narrowness of two rival paradigms, Homeric and democratic, whose contest makes a plaything of Thebes. Eurydice haunts all forms of narrow justice.

If she does so, it is surely because she crosses boundaries. When she kills herself by dagger, for example, she violates tragedy's gendered division of death in which, as Nicole Loraux argues in *Tragic Ways of Killing a Woman* (1987), women die by noose and men by dagger. But Charles Segal sees something other than a cross-dressed suicide here: he reads Eurydice's death by dagger as a sign that she takes female self-lacerative mourning to an extreme. It is an interesting possibility but it also, notably, works to recuperate Eurydice for femininity. Rather than stand somewhere between the Homeric and democratic orders, Segal's Eurydice represents the extremity of female mourning. And Antigone is her double. She, too, on Segal's account, represents extreme self-laceration: when Haemon's blood spurts onto her, she looks as if she had self-lacerated, Segal suggests. I will pursue a less recuperative interpretation of Antigone's suicide in Chapter 5. For now, it is worth noting that when Segal puts Antigone and Eurydice together as two self-lacerating women, even though Antigone does not "self-harm" in lament, he not only goes against Loraux's mapping of the gendered pattern of suicide in tragedy and effaces the differences between these two suicides (one by dagger, one by noose); he also recuperates Antigone and Eurydice for a binary, gendered framework even though the play itself offers not a binary but, rather, a spectrum of plural possibilities in lament.[62]

Tragedy has traditionally "been read as charting the linear development of a progression, from darkness to light, from barbarism to civilization, from blood vengeance to democratic jurisdiction," says Olga Taxidou, but tragedy does not in fact represent a straight, linear path. The "emphasis on mourning tends to throw up the contradictions" (2004: 178). That contradictions are thrown up by tragedy is clearly right. But Sophocles' *Antigone* (one of Taxidou's examples) is not undone in its aspiration to plot a linear development by its focus on mourning. Rather, it

focuses on mourning in order to throw up the contradictions and con-
testations that roil fifth-century Athens.

ANTIGONE'S UNDECIDABILITIES IN CONTEXT

The idea that the play explores tensions between two paradigms –
Homeric/heroic and classical democratic – by way of each one's practices
of mourning and membership seems to support Michelle Gellrich's claim
that we should see "the crisis of the play in terms of the undecidability of
criteria for absolute judgment" (1988: 72). But that undecidability is not
just structural, as Gellrich seems to suggest, it is also historical. The reading
offered here, I want to suggest, contestable but historically located, occupies a middle position in recent classics debates about the merits of
referential versus polysemous approaches.

For Helene Foley, the polysemous nature of ancient Greek tragic texts,
their dramatic character, and their dependence upon reception from a
diverse, unpredictable audience all militate against referential interpretations that decode the plays as position-taking arguments in an ideological context.[63] For Richard Seaford, by contrast, the focus on
ambiguity is "in danger of becoming a disabling cliché" (1995: 203).[64]
The "civic Dionysus of the *Antigone*'s fifth *stasimon* was for the Greeks
not . . . a quasimetaphysical principle [of ambiguity] but inherent in the
imperative to perform his collective cult" (1995: 207).[65] Thus, Seaford
argues, the *Antigone* does not fan the flames of a never-ending tragic
ambiguity but rather performatively (re)establishes a cult that channels a
"controlled ambiguity" that serves the needs of the polis (and does not
also undo it). Why, however, should we assume that ambiguities aired by
the play are controllable by cult worship and do not also exceed it? And
what warrants privileging the play's fifth *stasimon* (which points to the
cult) over what comes after: the suicide of Eurydice and the scene of
Creon's grief?

Positioned somewhere between Foley and Seaford, the reading
developed here is focused on particular elements of historical context and
necessarily draws selectively on elements of this complex play. No single
character is taken to represent, against Foley's caution, "a clearly defined,
logically consistent, and easily assimilable viewpoint" (1995: 144), but
neither is ambiguity celebrated as such, against Seaford's caution. Instead,
each of the contending positions, democratic versus Homeric, is seen
through the other's critical lens, the position of each amplified and
criticized by surrounding characters (as when Ismene argues for Antigone's

singularity and irreplaceability, for example), and the partiality and insufficiency of both contending forms of mourning and membership are on display.[66]

Thus, Antigone's dirge is endless and self-indulgent, Creon says, and so it seems to be. It ends only when Creon tells the soldiers for the second time to take her away. If we grant Creon's claim some weight, we may see that Antigone is depicted through a critical democratic lens as admirable but also self-indulgent and disinclined to consider things from the other's point of view.[67] And Creon's treatment of the body goes beyond the pale, Antigone says, and it does. This is not just Antigone's perspective: the sentry mentions its decay and its stench and Tiresias is horrified to find Polynices' flesh on the city's altars. Creon's action represents in hyperbolic form what, to a heroic or aristocratic point of view, looks like the democracy's generally excessive violation of the bounds of the permissible when it comes to the treatment of the dead. By depicting a recognizably democratic (or democratically-affiliated) figure failing to bury properly in a way that exceeds even the permissible impropriety called for by a dead man's treason, the play airs the charge that the democracy disrespects the dead, *tout court*. From a heroic or aristocratic perspective, what Creon did in this exceptional case was not atypical of what was routinely done in Periclean Athens: the bodies of the dead were treated improperly, their ashes thrown into communal coffins.[68] Depriving the dead of their proper rites, the democracy may as well be leaving them unburied.

Another aristocratic complaint, that the classical city lacks the power to truly enforce its agenda, lurks in the fact noted by Tiresias that the body exiled outside the city by Creon keeps returning to the city in spite of his decree. If Polynices deserves as a traitor to be cast out of the city, Creon's *kerygma* has not secured that just desert but has on the contrary undone it precisely by leaving the body exposed. As a result, the exiled body keeps returning to the city in bits and pieces as carrion. If the work of burial in part helps survivors move on, then the fact that this unburied corpse keeps turning up like a bad penny may be a way of showing how in the absence of proper burial, survivors cannot move on. The dead body's return in bits and pieces to the city suggests also that Creon's problem is not (just) his overzealousness but, again recalling a classic critique of democracy, his ineffectiveness. Notwithstanding his power as ruler, he simply cannot keep Polynices out of the city. Similarly, Antigone resists confinement within the household. In other words, the descendants of Oedipus can neither be kept out nor in.[69]

Does this reading then leave us with the empty undecidability Seaford worries about? On the contrary, we are left with a deep criticality, one that finds both sides worthy and wanting.[70] That both lead characters come to a bad end need not mean the views they aired are delegitimated or overcome. The views surely outlive their bearers. But neither does the play, on this reading, offer us characters that are mere historical referents. Instead, the play airs through its two main characters and others, too, concerns about the costs of a particular democratic form of life while insisting as well on the limitations of its chief rival. These concerns are rendered visible by the binary of "Homeric/heroic versus democratic" used here, but there is also contiguity, mutuality, and slippage in what I have suggested thus far is a fairly binary set of terms. This is most obvious perhaps in Haemon, upon whom I have not focused, who argues for moderation and pleads Antigone's cause. But it is also true of Creon who, on this reading, is a somewhat liminal figure, combining aristocratic birth with democratic fidelities.

Creon articulates elite not democratic values when he voices vengeance as the law of his ideal household: "That's what a man prays for: to produce good sons – a household full of them, dutiful and attentive, *so they can pay his enemy back with interest*" (641–644 [715–717]; emphasis added) and when he, possibly vengefully, grounds his rule on the vengeful treatment of Polynices' body. Also, his mistrust of those who take pay for public service may (contra my argument earlier) be read as a marker not of his democratic accommodation but of his *in*complete affiliation with the democracy of the day. And, in choosing to bury Polynices first before tending to the then still living Antigone, Creon may be seen as taking his cue from the heroic Antigone, not the democracy: he is instructed by the Chorus to "free the girl from the rocky vault and raise a mound for the body you exposed" (1100–1101 [1224–1225]), but he follows Antigone's order (first the dead, then the living), not that of the Chorus leader. Because Creon rushes first to bury the dead Polynices and then to release Antigone – as the messenger reports to Eurydice (1196–1205 [1318–1328]) – Creon reaches Antigone too late. He had left enough rations to sustain her for a while and so might have assumed there was time to tend first to Polynices. In delaying, Creon privileges his sense of time (there is yet plenty) over Antigone's (which has always already run out). He may underestimate her agency (or, like a good plotter, he may secretly count on it).[71]

If Creon departs from type more than Antigone, this may fit his character; he grows and changes for worse and better over the course of the play in ways his antagonist seems not to. Or perhaps his conspiracy

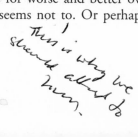

with democracy is just that: a conspiracy out of which at times his
elite values emerge and take over. Alternatively, even his shifting from
one table of values to another may fit rather than interfere with the claim
that he conspires with democracy. With his lack of consistency or back-
bone, he personifies the aristocratic critique of the democracy, just as
Antigone in her seemingly stubborn unchangeability may personify the
democratic critique of aristocracy. (Though she does change, as we shall
see in Chapters 5 and 6, to the consternation of some her devotees.)

Another slippage: H. A. Shapiro points out that Creon buries Polynices
in Homeric style, "with the burning of the body and the raising of the
mound" (2006: 131). Notably, however, this is not on Creon's own
initiative: the Chorus leader *tells* Creon to bury in this way: "Go ... raise
a mound for the body you exposed" (1100–1101 [1224–1225]). Still, Creon
listens. Working with material evidence, Shapiro argues that the play's
Homeric references would not have been lost on the fifth-century audience. He draws conclusions different from mine, arguing that Creon
represents Achilles (the bulk of the play does not support this, in my
view), comparing Achilles' desecration of Hector to Creon's treatment of
Polynices. On the reading developed here, however, Creon is no Achilles.
Creon may be moved by rage against Polynices, but if so then Creon
evidences the dependence of the democratic view he mostly represents on
elements of a Homeric ethos that the democracy both admires and
abjures.[72] Thus the play troubles the binary of Homeric versus democratic
in which it also traffics and whose contention it stages. But beyond these
contiguities and slippages, the binary is finally and most importantly
troubled in the interruption of both the codes in contention here by a
keening grief that stands out for its violation of all the expectations the play
and its contexts have set in place: Creon's grief.

CREON'S GRIEF

If Creon is finally harshly undone, that may be not just to show the
depth of his offenses (on this account, they may not be as deep as some
readers think and they are surely not deep in the way many readers have
thought), but also to give him occasion to mourn.[73] This is needed not
just to give him his just deserts, as most readers might think, but
because his mourning will either add another instance to the spectrum of
possible mournings explored by the play, or it may topple the spectrum
entirely. The laments of Antigone, Haemon, and Eurydice all partake of
the Homeric practice in which the bereaved keen loudly, prize the

individuality of the lost person, call for or try to exact vengeance, or commit violence on themselves or others in response to loss. They contrast with Creon's polis-centered and initially measured judgment of Antigone's dead brothers, with his proper disposition together with Antigone of Eteocles' body, and with his elegiac lament for Haemon. But when the losses cut closer still, Creon is tested: will he cleave to the strictures of democratic mourning or will he give in to the sort of lamentation the polis seeks to constrain?

Hearing of Eurydice's suicide as he stands with Haemon's dead body in his arms, Creon shrieks loudly and engages in what can only be called excessive public bereavement: "I shake with dread! Why has no one stabbed straight into my chest with a two-edged sword? Desolate me, *aiee*! Desolate the anguish that is now mixed into me!" (Gibbons and Segal 2003: 1306–1311 [1394–1397]).[74] Creon seems to partake of the very practice he had forbidden. He mourns like a woman; his lament is loud, wailing and pained. (Here, surely, he is haunted by Haemon's earlier line that if he, Creon, is a woman, then yes, Haemon's concern is all for him.) But Creon's lament differs from the outlawed laments in one important respect: he looks to no further violence or vengeance to restore a social or political equilibrium: "And the guilt is all mine – can never be fixed on another man" (1317–1318 [1441–1442]).[75] He is, he insists, solely responsible for what has happened. Unlike his son and his wife, he does not curse others and does not commit suicide; he only wishes for death. (One could note acidly that here, as elsewhere, he seeks to delegate to others rather than act himself: the plaintive "Why has no one stabbed straight into my chest with a two-edged sword?" takes the place of the self-inflicted, heroic suicide.)[76] How should we understand Creon's departure both from the code of the permitted, official funerary practice (his loud grieving cry of "*aiee*!" is ill-judged by that code's standards) and from the prohibited Homeric modes of mourning (he absolves all others rather than curse them)?

These departures may bespeak Creon's continued commitment to his sovereign mission to wean Thebes from vengeance and end cycles of violence. On this reading, Creon, who seems to be utterly destroyed, does not quite lose himself. He does not yield to the passions he sees as most destabilizing to the city and so he ends the play as he began, pressing himself into service on behalf of the public good, modeling as much as he can what he now sees as the appropriate comportment in mourning for Theban citizens: Creon's grief models something like the "concession to familial loss and grief, loosened from normal curbs on public display" which the fifth-century polis came to allow (Bennett and Tyrrell 1990: 443). Perhaps this "concession" is what Creon extended to Antigone when he allowed her a share in lamenting Eteocles, though he did not offer the same to her for Polynices. Creon here avails himself of something like that practical concession and does not go beyond it. The play ends with his grief, incomplete or interrupted by the Chorus, leaving to others (including the audience) the final work of mourning and burying the dead. From this vantage point, the play enacts the drama of Athens' "concession," telling a story of how it came to be.[77] The "concession" is formally similar to the other Athenian institutions of exception: like tragedy itself and the rituals of the cult of Dionysus, the concession permits the impermissible while seeking to safeguard against its excesses by binding or limiting it in space and time.[78] The concession permits some limited mourning inside the city, while tragedy and Dionysian ritual permit its expression and seek to offset it with festival outside the city. Recalling here Creon's failed efforts to keep Antigone in and Polynices out, we may see the play as asking: can the city succeed when it turns to institutions of exception to keep mourning in or out?

There is also another possibility. Creon begins the play representing the triumph of the Periclean polis. He is repeatedly exposed to but unmoved by the Homeric/heroic laments of those who resist his rule. When he finally experiences grief, it is visited upon him with such abundance and intensity that it exposes the inadequacies of both of the practices in contention here. The play explores the conflict between two economies of mourning and membership (with various permutations represented by the contiguities that complicate Creon and also by such figures as Ismene, Haemon, and Eurydice), but ends siding with neither. When it ends with Creon's code-defying grief, does it softly suggest that no economy of mourning and membership, and no institution of exception, is up to the task of voicing or managing the grief we seek in our politics to express, contain, or channel, that the *différance* of Creon's grief undoes them all?

If Charles Segal and other (post)structuralist readers of the play miss both the concessive and ruptural properties of Creon's grief, that is because they work within and against a binary framework in which it is Antigone who is positioned as ruptural – she is wild nature – by contrast with Creon, who represents the order of civilization without concession. These readers take their bearings from the structuralist opposition of the raw and the cooked, but also from the Chorus' characterization of Antigone as wild and passionate and from Creon's view of Antigone as needing taming. In this as in so much else, however, Creon and the Chorus may mislead.

They – as fifth-century democrats might – cast Antigone as outside order altogether, rather than as a metonymic marker of a rival order. This is hegemony's tactic – to act as if it has no rivals in the human world. Some of Antigone's contemporary admirers fall for it when they cast her as a metaphor for dissidence as such.[79]

Meanwhile, historicists too miss the significance of Creon's grief. Bennett and Tyrrell miss it because they assume Antigone not Creon represents the democratic view, and so they overlook the possibly concessive trait – iconically democratic – of Creon's grief. Also, for them as for other historicists, there is no apparent historical referent in the historical context for a seemingly aneconomic grief, the disorderly "*aiee!*" that seems to rupture the historical practices evidenced by the material culture they study.

The concessive and ruptural readings of Creon's grief, it is worth noting, do not force upon us a choice. The concession to private lament takes a risk: it opens to view a rupture that threatens to exceed temporal and spatial boundaries to which the polis seeks to confine it. That is, the Athenian "concession" to familial grief restages that recurring issue: the capacity of institutions of exception – tragedy (Goldhill), ritual (Seaford), and concession (Bennett and Tyrrell) – to manage fires of disruption or loss without also fanning their flames. Focusing on the play's performance of grief highlights the concern that exception-institutions like these cannot turn to totally constructive purposes the very forces and emotions those institutions seek to contain, manage, elicit. What if these forces and emotions, like the children of Oedipus, will neither be kept out nor in?

We might be alerted to the ambiguity of the line delineating the interpretative choice between concession and rupture by the fact that the play ends with Creon grieving, but with the two bodies of his family members yet unburied. Who will bury them? Leaving the question open, the play exceeds the boundaries of its performance and interpellates the audience into this task. The central problem depicted in the play is in the end uncontained by it, and this violates or at least puts at risk the *mission* of tragedy as an exception-institution that stages or occasions but also contains prohibited forces and emotions. We do not know whether Haemon and Eurydice will be buried, nor by whom, nor how (in what manner). The responsibility is, in a way, left to us. Will we take it up as polis members, rendering the dead anonymous? Or will we memorialize them by name and assert their singularity? The fifth-century audience faced these questions with some awareness of Phrynicus, whose unhappy fate constitutes the limit of too much grief, and the promise of the festival's dance and ritual whose happy events constitute the limit of too little.

Earlier in the play, Creon accused Haemon of taking the woman's side (meaning: Antigone's) in the conflict. Haemon responded to his father: "If you are a woman, yes – my concern is all for you" (741 [829–830]). That reassurance, with its poisoned implication that Creon was something other than manly, is now realized as Creon is unmanned, deprived of his family and power. (We may recall here Griffith's point, noted above, that Creon, who loses his paternity but keeps his kingdom, inverts the fate of Oedipus, who loses his kingdom but maintains his – vexed – paternity.) Creon is led away: "Take me away," he says to his attendants, "quickly, out of sight. I don't even exist – I'm no one. Nothing" (1320–1325 [1445–1446]). Is his loss inexpressible? Certainly it defies or exceeds the strictures to which he sought to confine others in their losses. Antigone, who in her lamentations chafed against the democracy's strictures, helped to make apparent the grievousness of loss. But, ironically, the grief Antigone is usually taken to personify – raw, wild – is on this account voiced by Creon. It is not really raw or wild, though: its condition is the conjugal family form's promise of male – head of household – power, now withdrawn.

The Chorus may then reassure somewhat with its sense of worldly order and hard-earned wisdom (which, however, always comes too late, it says) (1348–1353 [1466–1470]). Or we may recur to its earlier extended invitation, noted by Seaford, to leave behind grief by joining the Feast of Dionysus to dance all night, to find forgetting in festival.[80] But the trace of Creon's grief, which animates, sustains, and undoes the codes of lamentation and resists containment to any institution of exception, is hard to forget. Creon's grief is both concessive and ruptural and suggests that no amount of history, polis commemoration, sovereign reasoning, ritual feasting, juridical concession, tragic theater, worship, or codes of lamentation can fully remediate mortality whether via substitution (the democratic Oration), memorialization (the Homeric laments), or exception (tragedy, cult, and the concession or familial exception). Some political orders find better ways than others to acknowledge or make meaning out of human mortality. Our debt to Sophocles is his invitation, still fresh and unfortunately still much needed, to look hard at the myriad ways in which we silence the grief that in our politics we yet do so much to generate.

To be clear, such acknowledgment does not imply an embrace of the fact of finitude as ontology or raw matter out of which to generate an ethics or a politics, as mortalist humanists would do. Instead, it supports an agonistic humanism committed to living up to Hannah Arendt's insight: the fact that men are mortal does not mean that we are born to die. The fact that we grieve does not mean grief or grievability should be the center of our politics.[81] Lament, as *différance*, is not a basis for politics but is a sign of the partiality of our codes of grief and of the limited ability of our codes of grief to control or redeem our losses by embedding them in economies of meaning that are supposedly themselves impervious to rupture and interruption.

To grieve bears a double meaning to which theorists of grievability are not so alert: it means both to express grief and to litigate or seek redress for a wrong. Thus, to grieve is both extra-political, as many theorists of lamentational politics would have it, and also fundamentally political: it means to take sides and fight against wrongdoing, as is sometimes done in litigation (but not only or primarily in litigation). The term connotes mourning, resistance to injustice, rectification of wrong and vengeance for it. Efforts to disentangle these were evident in the feminist turn to Antigone, as we saw in Part I, Chapter 2, as Antigone was depicted more as a lamenter than as an agent of vengeance, more as someone torn by loss than one driven by rage. Attending here to the *politics* of lamentation, we have seen how Creon conspires with the democracy of the day, only to be outdone, outmaneuvered. Antigone also plots and conspires, first with the sister she is usually thought to disdain and then, as we shall see, also with language – and language with her – in ways that may yet still speak to us. Turning now to look at these conspiracies in reverse order, beginning with her final speech, we will see in Chapter 5 that her lamentation is always and inexorably political – even partisan. The speech that is often taken to exemplify humanist universals of mourning and lamentation is laden with double entendres, parody, and more. Grieving in the double sense of that term, lamenting her losses but also litigating a wrong, Antigone's dirge moves beyond the courtroom of grievance and the sentimentalism of grief to seek out publics that Creon aims to repress and marginalize on behalf of his own view of public order. She may yet inaugurate new publics still.

CHAPTER 5

From lamentation to logos: *Antigone's conspiracy with language*

> A tribe has two concepts, akin to our "pain." One is applied where there is visible damage and is linked with tending, pity, etc. The other is used for stomach-ache for example, and is tied up with mockery of anyone who complains.
>
> Wittgenstein

> In order to qualify as illegal torture, physical pain "must be equivalent in intensity to the pain accompanying serious physical injury such as organ failure, impairment of bodily function, or even death," – a legal memo authorizing abuse [and torture] of prisoners approved by George W. Bush, primarily authored by John Yoo.
>
> Andrew Sullivan

> And she cried out a sharp, piercing cry . . .
>
> Sophocles, *Antigone*

> So the simple opposition between logical animals and phonic animals is in no way the given on which politics is then based . . . The logos is . . . the account by which a sonorous emission is understood as speech, capable of enunciating what is just, whereas some other emission is merely perceived as a noise signaling pleasure or pain, consent or revolt.
>
> Jacques Rancière

The regulation of laments in fifth-century Athens is one context in relation to which we can usefully read Sophocles' *Antigone*, but there are others. If Chapter 4 proposed a new reading of *Antigone* in historical context, here in Chapter 5 history intrudes (as Carl Schmitt might say) on Sophocles' text, and the result is a strange torsion that opens other new and surprising dimensions of the play, amplifying its overlife and not just, as contextualists might assume, its original life in context.

I detail further here the argument that the regulation of laments, and the counter-assertion of what we may call the right to have rites, is part of a politics broader than burial policy: the regulations are part of a classed and gendered socialization into a new economy of citizenship that domesticates desire, longing, pain, and loss. Sophocles' play calls attention to the costs of that education project. (Whether or not he argues against such socialization is a separate question.) The key to this reading is Antigone's much-noted but little-analyzed final part of her final speech about why she violated Creon's edict. In this chapter, I look in detail at her speech, which Creon tries twice to interrupt and which modern critics consider possibly inauthentic and certainly problematic. The speech – a dirge in which Antigone, a mythic figure and tragic character, airs her suffering and casts about for the right frame in which her story should be told – cites a historical event reported by Herodotus and so introduces historicity to mythopoesis. One challenge, then, is to take interpretative cues from the historical context while maintaining some fidelity to the play as simultaneously mythic, tragic, and historical as well as a philosophical palimpsest, enlisted in the nineteenth, twentieth, and twenty-first centuries by seemingly everyone: philosophers, psychoanalytic theorists, feminists, dramatists, and political activists.

Antigone's dirge also leads us back to mortalist humanism, specifically now by way of the politics of pain and voice. Instead of the fact of finitude or vulnerability, some theorists and critics turn to voice or vocality as the basis of a humanism. Humans or creatures are said to be united by susceptibility to certain sounds. The sound of suffering, a-linguistic and sonorous, is said by some to provide the universalism that diverse, fractious forms of speech fail to deliver. Others see in language and speech precisely the opposite: not division but rather the objectivity or at least intersubjectivity and publicity that are better able than pain, which is in their view ineluctably private and subjective, to deliver on real universality. For those who see universalism in vocality, pain, or sound, what is remarkable about sharp, piercing cries like those that punctuate Antigone's lamentation for her brother, is that they have the power to move *any*one, not just members of a shared linguistic community. They not only cross the lines of friend/enemy (as Antigone is said to do when she seeks to bury Polynices), they also cross the lines of otherwise incommensurable linguistic communities. This "vocalist humanism" reiterates elements of the mortalist humanism discussed above and I return to it later in this chapter with that in mind. First, arguing that Antigone's lament is well approached as a speech act, not as raw sound or wild nature, I explore in detail what I take to be her conspiracy with language.[2]

ANTIGONE'S DIRGE: PRIOR RECEPTIONS

In her final speech, Sophocles' Antigone introduces a new reason for her violation of Creon's edict against burying her brother, Polynices. Having claimed that the dead are all equal and are owed proper rites, she shifts in her final speech to say she acted as she did out of fidelity to a *law* that directed her to hold Polynices "first" in honor, and insists she would not have done the same for any husband or children she might have had because her brother alone is irreplaceable. This *law* conflicts with one earlier invoked by Antigone, which calls for the dead to be treated equally regardless of their deeds in life. Antigone's law of the irreplaceable brother also seems uncharacteristically cold and calculating and so lovers of the play such as Goethe, Kitto, Jebb, and others reject this final speech as inauthentic.

When read in historical context, however, Antigone's dirge is less conflicted, less chilling, and more politically telling. It parodies Pericles, mimics Creon, and cites a story told by Herodotus about Darius. These references help make sense of Antigone's otherwise odd "law" of the irreplaceable brother, but it is important that the desire to explain what is explicable not lead us to explain *away* what may be an instructive tension in the play.[3] In Antigone's two seemingly incompatible laws – of equality and singularity – we find a commitment that is exemplary for contemporary democratic theory and practice, though she herself was, of course, no democrat: *to the absolute equality of all members as such – such that no one person's good or life can be exchanged for another's – combined with an insistence on the absolute singularity, irreplaceability, dignity of each and every individual life in a democracy . . . such that no one person's good or life can be exchanged for another's.* That is, the inconsistency that seems to be a dramatic flaw may nonetheless be a political plus, for Antigone's two laws are the twinned, agonistic commitments of democracy.[4] (It is, in any case, not a dramatic flaw, as I shall now argue, but rather a textual detail that rewards interpretative attention.)

On the verge of death, Antigone recounts her suffering, speculates about its causes, and mourns the life she will not get to lead, the marriage and children she will never have. She begins in dialogue with the Chorus, singing a *kommos* in which she contests the terms in which her story will be told. Here again she calls to mind Achilles, who sought reassurance in advance that he would gain his promised *kleos* in exchange for his death.[5] Seeking clues to her own *kleos*, Antigone tries to have a hand in shaping the story that will be told of her acts after she dies.[6]

But the Chorus resists her efforts and thus seems to provide some support
to Creon who disparages her when he observes that she is singing her own
dirge. "Can't you see?" he says, interrupting her performance: "If a man
could wail his own dirge *before* he dies, he'd never finish" (883–884 [969–
971]). The line is funny. With his pun, Creon mocks what he casts as
Antigone's self-absorption – if her dirge is endless it is, he intimates,
because, like most people, and certainly like most elites, she cannot say
enough about herself – and he mocks her heroism: noting that singing an
unending dirge allows a man to put off death indefinitely, Creon demotes
Antigone from a heroic actor who does not fear death to a more ordinary
human who seeks to defer it. But Antigone will soon (perhaps even driven
by Creon's insult) give the lie to Creon's implication that she does not have
the true hero's taste for death. She does not wait for the slow demise to
which Creon sentences her. Nor does she linger, waiting for rescue. She
takes matters into her own hands and kills herself. Self-indulgent she may
be, but she is no coward.[7] Moreover, yet again in a seemingly impossible
situation, she finds a way to act. When she dies "by her own will," Nicole
Loraux notes, "Antigone change[s] execution into suicide" (1987: 312).[8]

Antigone's dirge for herself, like the one she wanted to perform for her
brother, is prohibited.[9] When Creon interrupts her sung *kommos* with the
Chorus, he tells his soldiers, "Take her away, quickly! Wall her up in the
tomb, you have your orders" (885–886 [971–972]). But the soldiers do not
listen and Antigone goes on, now speaking rather than singing her lines
and no longer in the company of the Chorus. It is only after her lines 891–
928 (978–1021) that the Chorus leader comments on her wild passion and
then Creon again steps in to interrupt her, repeating to the guards his
earlier instruction: "Take her away. You're wasting time." He adds, "You'll
pay for it too" (929–930 [1023–1024]), and this time they listen. However,
like the plotters they may be, they move slowly and thwart his will even
while carrying it out. Antigone has time to insult Creon one last time –
"see what I suffer now at the hands of what breed of men" (940–942 [1032–
1033]). The soldiers' delay, Creon notes bitterly, will cost them.

What occurs during this "wasted" time? In the second part of her now
twice-forbidden dirge, Antigone introduces a new reason for her dissidence. She has said all along she buried Polynices because the gods and
divine law demand it: her brother deserves proper burial regardless of his
deeds in lifetime because the dead are all equal. But here, in her final scene,
she cites another reason for her actions, she calls it a law and, although she
has not mentioned it before, she says here that she defied Creon because
this law *exclusively* commands her fidelity: her brother is uniquely singular.

What she did for Polynices, she says sliding into apostrophe to address him directly, she would have done for no other family member: "A husband dead, there might have been another. A child by another too, if I had lost the first. But mother and father both lost in the halls of Death, no brother could ever spring to light again. *For this law alone I held you first in honor . . .* " (909–913 [1001–1005]; emphasis added).[10]

Antigone's speech offends many of the play's readers, but Hegel, one of her most famous admirers, is not among those.[11] In the *Phenomenology of Spirit*, Hegel singles out Antigone's speech for special attention. He admires it and builds his account of ethics around it, prizing the brother–sister relation named by its "law" as one of unique, unerotic equality, ignoring – as Derrida and others also point out – the incest that marks Oedipus' family and is the obvious obstacle to Hegel's idealized Antigonean family romance.[12]

The very same speech that Hegel admired for its exemplarity is famously rejected by others as artificial or offensive, a betrayal of Antigone's otherwise admirable character. Hegel's contemporary, Goethe, called the speech "*ganz schlecht*," and longed for the day when a philologist would prove its inauthenticity (2005: 227). Kitto rejects it as a "frigid sophism" (1966: 30). And Jebb wrote, soulfully and rather transparently: "I confess that, after long thought, I cannot bring myself to believe that Sophocles wrote 905–912 . . . The composition [of 905–912] is unworthy of Sophocles" (cited in Fleming 2006: 185).[13] Michelle Gellrich calls these critics the "cut and paste scholars" (1988: 56–57). Overall, what troubles them is the speech's seeming introduction of inconsistency into a character – Antigone – whose aesthetic unity they admire. This heroine of love and family seems here to be a ruthless calculator. An action that began on behalf of the equality of the dead is brought to a close by invoking the singularity of *this . . . dead . . . one.*

In the diametrically opposed judgments of Hegel and Goethe, we find crystallized their different assessments of romanticism. When Hegel finds exemplary the very same speech Goethe will around twenty years later reject as inauthentic, Hegel sets Antigone up as the bearer of a law of the family that is, in his view, more reliable than the Romantics' barometer of inner feeling. Goethe celebrated in Antigone the very same romantic anti-authoritarianism that Hegel regarded with suspicion.[14] For Goethe, Antigone represented precisely inner feeling: love. But, if Goethe's Antigone really is, as she says of herself, "born to love" (523 [590]), then what to do with her final controversial speech in which she ranks those she loves? Goethe rejected as inauthentic the very same speech whose law seemed to Hegel exemplary.

The speech is now considered original to the text but Antigone remains deeply marked by Goethe's interpretation. Working in Goethe's still powerful wake, most see Antigone in similarly romantic terms and most do not dwell on the speech. Most also follow Goethe in a different way. Almost all seem to assume we must choose between Antigone's two stated laws. Either she is a loving devotee of the equal claims of the dead on the living, or she is singularly devoted to her singular brother. Goethe is drawn to the former. Lacan, who calls Goethe the "Sage from Weimar" and dismisses his reading in a quick aside, is drawn, as is Hegel, to the latter. The convergence of Lacan and Hegel may be surprising since they are otherwise so different: Hegel rejects the possibility that desire figures at all in Antigone's acts, while Lacan identifies Antigone with nothing but desire. But as Miriam Leonard rightly sees, there are other affinities between Lacan's reading and Hegel's: for example, both see Antigone as lacking access to normal moral life and position her at the limits of moral experience (2005: 118–119).[15]

Still, Hegel is invested in Antigone's purity, while Lacan is drawn to Antigone because she is scandalous. Her offensive speech carries in it a "suggestion of a scandal" (Lacan 1992: 256). He finds evidence in Antigone's final speech for his claim that S1, which anchors the signifying chain of S2, S3, S4, and so on that it also releases, has finally been reached by Sophocles' heroine. The equality of the dead belongs to the realm of the Symbolic, where equivalences are traded and words give order to things. That is Antigone's stock in trade for most of the play. But in her final scene, Antigone has arrived finally at S1 itself, the point of no return, the site of an absolute incommensuration. As Catherine Belsey puts it: Antigone "is driven to die … by an 'unwritten and unfailing' law (lines 450–457), which in Lacan's account is 'not developed in any signifying chain'" (2003: 10).[16] By the end of her life, Antigone is focused significantly on the one irreplaceable indivisible thing: Polynices. This is the thing that makes everything else for her meaningful, even possible (though I shall argue in Chapter 6 that Ismene plays this role for her as well, that Antigone does well by her in the end, and then resets her sights on Polynices). Thus for Lacan, even in this apparently calculating speech which so offends so many, Antigone does not calculate. It is Creon who impresses himself into the order of calculation and commensuration that Lacan calls the "service of the goods." Antigone's dirge, by contrast, is the speech of uncompromising desire and perhaps this is the real source of offense, for desire is a terrible thing to contemplate.

Yannis Stavrakakis (2007) points out, contra so many of Lacan's inter-preters, that Antigone is not Lacan's last word on desire. It is however fair to say, I think, that desire *is* Lacan's last word on Antigone.[17] For him, she represents the fidelity to desire that is uncompromising. Thus Lacan finds great significance in the speech that Goethe and others find offensive. What they judge inauthentic, Lacan sees as a synecdoche for authenticity itself, or at least for irreducibility. With this, however, Goethe's romantic, singular Antigone, or something like her, actually triumphs, now using as evidence for it the very speech that once seemed to betray it.

Analogously, Samuel Weber notes that the same speech taken by Lacan to represent what "he calls 'absolute individuality' is in fact eminently *divisible* and divided, never at home" (1991: 58; emphasis original). Antig-one's tautology, in which she becomes fixed on her brother who is what he is (ad infinitum), is itself unstable: the name that for Lacan "fixes the thing remains a signifier and the individual it names remains suspended in respect to the separations and demarcations which it depends on but which will never be realized in their entirety," says Weber (1991: 58). The discord of the signifier inheres even in Polynices' name, Weber points out, which as we saw earlier means *many quarrels*. But inherent discord is a trait of all names, as such. And so, Weber concludes: "There is always a remainder, an excess or a lack; the signifier is never reducible to a deter-minate relation, it is essentially detachable from each of its possible and even inevitable attributes" (1991: 58). When Judith Butler, as we also saw earlier, notes that Antigone's reference in her dirge to "my own mother's son" refers to two people, not one, for it fits not only Polynices but also Oedipus (and, we could add, Eteocles as well), she makes a similar point, rejecting the indivisibility of Polynices proclaimed by Lacan and Žižek, and finding a remainder precisely here, in this name for *remains*.

Another contemporary reader of the play, Christiane Sourvinou-Inwood, finds Antigone's final speech offensive on different grounds. The speech marks Antigone as a "bad girl" who flouted the gender and democratic ideologies of the day when she wrongly prioritized her natal or birth family over her conjugal family (1989).[18] Against Sourvinou-Inwood, Helene Foley, in "Tragedy and Democratic Ideology" (1995), points out that the husband and children Antigone supposedly forsakes do not actually exist, they are merely hypothetical, while the brother she ranks higher actually does exist (or did). This matters, Foley says, and she is not wrong: grandstanding about how your real-life brother takes priority over a hypothetical marital family you might have one day had *is* different from choosing him over actual others. Still, Haemon, Antigone's betrothed, was real and, for most critics, ranking the dead Polynices above the live Haemon is a problem, as is the act of ranking as such, whether actual or hypothetical.[19] So the hypothetical nature of Antigone's reflection does not quite rescue it from being problematic.

But Foley's interpretation does open a possibility she does not herself consider. The hypothetical nature of Antigone's reflection is surely what marks it as a *law*, as Antigone herself knows for she names it such. All law is hypothetical, after all, generated (by contrast with an edict like Creon's *kerygma* against burying Polynices) for cases that do not yet exist.[20] Thus, the hypothetical character of Antigone's speech cuts both ways. It may not apply to a particular case – indeed, one can almost hear in Foley's defense of Antigone the disclaimer: "*no actual husband or children were harmed in the making of this speech.*" At the same time, however, of course, *all* husbands and children are put at risk by a law that privileges the mother's natal over the conjugal family as such, and this is one of the things at stake in this speech.

Sourvinou-Inwood is not wrong, then, to see that the issue here involves tensions between conjugal and natal family politics, as we shall see in more detail below. But her reading is moralistic and urges judgment – "bad girl" – rather than reflection on the issues here involved. The speech has three historical referents, only one of which has to do with kinship politics, per se. I turn to these now but, as we shall see, the historicity of Antigone's dirge does not settle its meaning but rather propels it, in the play and beyond, to reach past its context and even beyond reference entirely to address issues of import to democratic and feminist theorists now.

ANTIGONE'S DIRGE, RECONSIDERED

The forms of social interlocution that have any impact are at once arguments in a situation and metaphors of this situation. (Jacques Rancière)

As we have seen, Antigone's dirge offends those who expect consistency of character: when Antigone ranks family members she seems to betray her commitment to the equality of the dead. And she offends almost everyone with a moral sensibility when she treats some family members as mere goods that can be replaced. But the offensiveness of Antigone's speech surely also has partly to do with its character *as* a reason-giving speech. A parody of reason-giving (what kinds of reasons are these? Child or husband I might have had another ... ?) it calls attention to the politics, promise, and violence of reason-giving. I turn now to look at the speech in detail in relation to three contexts, one historical (Pericles), one textual (Creon), and one historical and intertextual (Darius as portrayed in Herodotus' *Histories*). All are part of Antigone's *agon*, part of her effort to frame her story and control the field of interpretation by which she will be judged. That is, her dirge is not mere lamentation and it is neither inauthentic (Goethe) nor hyper-authentic (Hegel or, in a different way, Lacan) but is rather, on the reading developed here, a canny and fraught speech act delivered by a political actor positioned precariously at the juncture of myth, tragedy, and history. It is Antigone's conspiracy with language and it is language conspiring with her.[21]

(i) Parodying Pericles

As we saw in Chapter 4, there are interesting intertextual resonances between Antigone's dirge and Pericles' Funeral Oration as reported by Thucydides. The Oration memorializes the dead by collectivizing lament and by focusing on the dead's contribution to the polis, and not – as in Homer or in laments identified with women in the fifth-century polis – on the unique individuality of the dead and the grievous loss to surviving family and comrades. In Homer, vengeance, suicide, or appetite (as in the funerary feast and games) alleviate the ache of grief and return survivors to life.[22] In fifth-century democratic Athens, other seemingly more stable responses are encouraged: the Funeral Oration offers the dead the immortality of the polis and directs grieving Athenian parents to the solace of other children.

Thucydides' version of the Oration came roughly a decade after Sophocles wrote *Antigone* but, as some classicists have argued, the Oration surely captured themes current in the earlier discursive context when Pericles was *strategos* in Athens.[23] Pericles' Oration urges parents – if they are still of childbearing age – not to mourn too long over their lost sons but to have more children to replace them: "Some of you are of an age at which they may hope to have other children, and they ought to bear their sorrow better; not only will the children who may hereafter be born make them forget their own lost ones, but the city will be doubly a gainer. She will not be left desolate and she will be safer. For a man's counsel cannot have equal weight or worth, when he alone has no children to risk in the general danger" (1881: 2.44).[24]

When Antigone says that a husband or a child can be replaced, Goethe is horrified. But is she cold? Or does she call attention to the coldness of an emergent civic ideology that offers the bereaved the cold comfort of

So she doesn't really mean it?

replaceability? Parody certainly seems to be in play when Antigone points
out that Polynices is irreplaceable because his parents are dead: being dead
means Polynices' parents are, as it were, too old to have more children,
much too old. They are beyond the slim consolations of the Oration.
When Antigone insists on the specific irreplaceability of the lost brother,
she opposes a more general fifth-century Athenian claim that individual
lives are replaceable; that past lives may be forgotten if future ones take
their place.[25] The parody is lost on modern readers because most read
Antigone as dead serious; earnest, shrill, determined, perhaps mad, but not
wry, funny, or arch. This, however, is a mark not of fidelity to the text but
of bewitchment by its canonicity.[26] Critics may miss it, but Antigone's
parody of Pericles is funny ("But our parents are *dead*. They *can't* have
more children"). She lampoons Pericles' civic ideology which treats men as
replaceable and sends them to war while depriving them in death of the
individuating rites and loud lamentation that they, from a heroic
perspective, are properly owed.

But in he lin content / ot he an / Chapter ?

(ii) Mimicking Creon

Antigone's second allusion is to Creon. Earlier in the play, Creon had
dismissed Ismene's concerns that Haemon, his son and Antigone's
betrothed, will suffer if Antigone is put to death. No other match will
provide "as true, as close a bond as theirs," Ismene warns (570 [643]). This
is nonsense to Creon who thinks that if Haemon cannot marry Antigone,
there are "other furrows for his plow" (569 [642]).[27] In her offensive
speech, Antigone takes up that male position for herself. If she ranks a
brother above a husband that is, she all but says, because there are other
furrows for *her* plow, as well, or . . . other plows for her furrow. She can
always have another husband. If there is scandal in her speech, then, the
scandal may not just be that she betrays her loving character by stopping to
calculate (as Goethe and others worry), or that she risks heroic epitaph in a
Thebes that forbids it, or that she suddenly claims to be acting exclusively
out of loyalty to a heretofore unmentioned "law" of singularity in tension
with her defining commitment to the equality of the dead. Here the
scandal of her speech is that she claims for herself a prerogative Creon
would reserve for his son and perhaps for all sons.[28]

Antigone does not succeed fully in this, however. She is reappropriated
for the conjugal family she rejected in life when Haemon, finding her
dead, kills himself to marry her in an iconic marriage-to-death that
vindicates Ismene's warning that Antigone is singularly suited to him.

but she could be married

With this marriage-to-death, Haemon re-positions his betrothed in the conjugal family's subordinate role.[29] The contention over her suicide and its meaning begins almost immediately, as the Chorus weighs in on Haemon's side: "He has won his bride at last, poor boy," intones the Messenger, seemingly sealing the deal for Haemon (1241 [1370]).[30]

Giving their own meanings to Antigone's suicide, Haemon and the Chorus highlight the dependence of Antigone's act on its reception. Her act's singularity, on which Slavoj Žižek and Jacques Lacan insist, is like all performatives dependent for its meaning on its perlocutionary force, that meaning-producing dimension of action that exceeds the actor's agency, intention, and context and exposes even the most autonomous actor's heteronomy (a point made clear by Gayatri Spivak in her seminal work on political suicide).[31] Butler, too, when she celebrates Antigone's suicide as an admirable and winning rejection of conventional conjugal ties, overlooks the subsequent marriage-to-death whereby Haemon reclaims Antigone for the conjugal family form.[32]

Using her final moments of life to frame her act, Antigone calls attention in her dirge to this very issue: natal versus conjugal kinship politics. Right before Creon interrupts her dirge, Antigone positions herself between her mother's and her brother's doomed marriages, her mother's incestuously confined to the natal (she married her own son), and her brother's exogamously tethered to a foreigner.[33] Antigone says: "O mother, your marriage-bed, the coiling horrors, the coupling there – you with your own son, my father ... O dear brother, doomed in your marriage – your marriage murders mine ... " (863–871 [951–957]).[34] It is right after this that Creon breaks in with his first, ultimately ineffective, interruption of his niece. Why? Was it something she said?

After Creon's interruption, Antigone resumes her dirge, but she does not return to continue the *kommos* with the Chorus; she moves into the final spoken monologue portion of her dirge. Since her voice and meter change at this point, and since it is at this point that she moves to underline her brother's irreplaceability, some, like Goethe and Jebb, find reason to argue that this speech is in fact a later addition. Others, like Peter Burian, explain the seemingly odd shift here by noting that at this point Antigone no longer looks for frames with which to press for her story to be told, and moves instead to give some reason for her actions. If those reasons are less than fully persuasive, that is because she reaches for them under pressure as death approaches. The text does support Burian's reading, but it also directs us to consider yet another possibility: what if, by way of her reason-giving, Antigone is nominating yet another frame

by way of which her story should be told? What if, having been rebuffed
by the Chorus, she now bypasses them and speaks directly to her
audience, to us, and offers with her reason-giving something more than
reasons? Indeed, it is notable that when Antigone moves out of her
kommos with the Chorus to *rhêsis*, from song to speech, she returns to
her theme of natal versus conjugal family tensions. She cites, albeit
without naming it, a story told by Herodotus in his *Histories* (1996:
3.119 [221]) about a woman famous for privileging natal over conjugal
family: the story of Intaphrenes' wife.

(iii) Citing Herodotus

In Herodotus' story, a woman referred to only as Intaphrenes' wife reasons
similarly to Antigone and earns the admiration of a powerful king. The
story is usually told in the briefest terms by those few of Antigone's
interpreters who take note of the citation.[35] Intaphrenes' wife is asked by
the ruler, Darius, to choose which one of several male relatives she would
like to save lest they all be put to death on account of the husband's
suspected treason. The wife chooses to save her brother because, she
explains, with their parents dead he alone is *irreplaceable*.[36] The king,
impressed with her reasoning, rewards her by saving not just the brother
she asked for but also her eldest son.

   To anthropologists, the story is a familiar illustration of the universal
gift of generation.[37] Intaphrenes' wife is given by Darius precisely the two
elements needed for social reproduction in a matrilineal structure: where
fathers vary but the mother does not, the mother's brother operates as a
male head of household, he is the only male that the offspring share, and
the son represents a future, the next generation. But there is more to the
story than this. If we look at it closely, we find that it serves as a legend
for the play.

   Herodotus reports that Darius suspected Intaphrenes of plotting treason
against him and had Intaphrenes and all his male family arrested and
sentenced to death. Intaphrenes' wife "came to the palace and began to
weep and lament outside the door, and continued so long to do so that
Darius, moved to pity by her incessant tears, sent someone out to speak to
her" (1996: 3.119 [221]). "'Lady,' the message ran, 'the king is willing to
spare the life of one member of your family – choose which of the
prisoners you wish to save.'" The woman thinks over the offer and
then informs the messenger that if she could only have one family
member, she would choose her brother. "The answer," Herodotus reports,

"amazed Darius, and he sent again and asked why it was that she rejected her husband and children and preferred to save her brother, who was neither so near to her as her children nor so dear to her as her husband." The woman now responds with the *argument* that earned her the admiration of the king and the puzzlement of readers through the ages: "'My lord,' she replied, 'God willing, I may get another husband and other children when these are gone. But as my father and mother are both dead, I can never possibly have another brother. That was the reason for what I said.'" In classic parable fashion, the supplicant's words find favor with the king and "to mark his pleasure, [he] granted her not only the life she asked, but also that of her eldest son. The rest of the family were all put to death" (1996: 3.119 [222]). The end.

Dewald and Kitzinger, two of the few classicists to compare Herodotus' story in any sustained way with Sophocles' play (though even their essay is only eight pages long), ask why the king would take pleasure in the woman's anti-patriarchal reasoning. They suggest that it is because the husband, who is seen by his wife as replaceable, is in this case charged with treason. Here being anti-patriarchal with regard to her husband means being differently patriarchal: loyal to Darius. In this vein, we may speculate further that when Darius, known for toying with his subjects, asked the woman to *reason* her choice, his aim was to interrogate her loyalties. When he asks "Isn't the husband more dear?" he means: "You asked for your brother but are you sure you are not, nonetheless, still loyal to the traitor Intaphrenes?" With her carefully crafted responses to his questions, the woman announces her fidelity to her natal not her conjugal family, reassures Darius, and wins her brother back. Dewald and Kitzinger conclude that the woman outfoxes Darius: "Darius has invited her to negotiate the most basic familial bonds . . . and she has risen to the challenge" (2006: 124–125). But there is a flaw in this reading.

If loyalty to natal over conjugal family is what reassures the king, then why does Darius seem needlessly to complicate matters by throwing in the eldest son, a remnant of the conjugal family, a son of the traitorous Intaphrenes who will extend the father's longevity into a future? If Dewald and Kitzinger do not ask after this that may be because they share a structuralist assumption that if Intaphrenes' wife has a brother and a son, she has all she needs: a stable male head of family and a future – the saved son. This forces us to conclude that although her family will be slaughtered by Darius, Intaphrenes' wife leaves the palace a satisfied customer. A post-structuralist might wonder, however, about that saved son: is he a remnant, a *restance*? It is a question to which I will return.

For now, it is important to note (although *Antigone*'s readers do not stop to note this) that the story of Intaphrenes' wife is about a woman who laments too much and a sovereign's determination to put an end to it. With her family condemned to death, Intaphrenes' wife sets up camp outside the palace and wails.[38] Her tears are "incessant." The sovereign, Darius, seeks just like Creon does in *Antigone* to end a woman's laments. But Darius does not respond as Creon does, with prohibition, threats, and edicts, even though the person on behalf of whom the woman laments is no less a traitor, in Darius' eyes, than is Polynices in Creon's. Darius seeks to end the woman's lamentation, which like Antigone's dirge had gone on so, so long, with inducements. He is said, after all, to "pity" her.[39] Pick one, he says, and I will release him.

Whea! This is little different from what parents today say to whining children: "Stop crying. If you tell me in words what it is you want, then maybe I can help you." The parents assume that the child is whining *for* something and so the child's want can be verbally articulated without loss. But the crying of the child may not be referential at all and may call for a different sort of response. This is Wittgenstein's point when he asks us in *Zettel* to imagine a tribe that mocks rather than cares for those whose pain has no visible referent (2007: §380). He means to show by way of contrast that for us it is not a referent (*pain*) but rather pain *behaviors* such as crying or writhing that normally elicit responses like tending and pity.[40] We care for people with headaches even though we cannot see their pain. But Wittgenstein's example also undermines his point. For once we do stop to imagine a tribe that mocks pain with no visible referent, we soon realize this is no crazy counterfactual. We are that tribe. This is how we, in our own culture, often respond to pain that is psychic. Thus, we do not need to "imagine" what would happen in such a circumstance; we already know. With their pain behavior ignored, misinterpreted, or dismissed by those around them because it lacks the sort of visible or physical referent normally taken as a sign of pain's veracity, sufferers of psychic pain find ways to corporealize their pain and make it count. Practices like cutting or self-laceration make psychic pain visible and give it a referent: pain becomes a something rather than an anything or nothing (to borrow again from Wittgenstein) and commands attention.

When parents demand that children stop whining and state what they want, do the parents demand a referent? Maybe. But we also demand something else or, better put, the demand for a referent is itself a demand for something else: it aims to restructure desire. The demand is for the child to replace the infinite needs postulated by whining with the finite and satisfiable needs that we call wants and are postulated by speech. We insist nothing is lost in translation from need or pain to want, we even reward the act of translation, often by giving the child what is then asked for. And so we are mystified when the whining persists, as it sometimes does, even after the named want has been satisfied.[41] We then assume a certain recalcitrance on the part of the child, as indeed did Pericles when he said of the Samians to whom he was ruthless: they are "like children who have been given food, but cry nonetheless" (Aristotle, *Rhet* 1407a; cited in Vickers 2008: 17).

What to do in the face of such recalcitrance? This is Darius' project. When Darius says to Intaphrenes' wife, "Pick one and I will spare that one," and she responds, she stops keening. Her reply – *what* she says – may be less important than the fact that, as Herodotus says, "She thought about it and replied." Her wish is not yet granted – it has not yet even been articulated – but already there is no more wailing. She is moved from lamentation, which is inconsolable, into an economy of commensuration in which consolation or at least compensation is possible.[42] Thus, what Samuel Weber says of Antigone seems to apply equally well to Intaphrenes' wife: she calculates the incalculable. What she experiences as the infinite pain of lamentation and loss is recorded with/translated into a specific, satisfiable request – the brother.[43] We may even see this as a shift (recalling the two modern meanings of grief, noted in Chapter 4) from lamentation to litigation. *Please spare my brother*, she says.

But that is not enough for Darius. The move away from lamentation must be a move into *logos* if it is to be secure. Or at least that is one way to read the king's next request: can Intaphrenes' wife explain *why* she chose in this way? *Why* the brother and not the husband who is more dear and the children who are more near? Again the woman answers. Here we get the argument about the brother's irreplaceability so recognizable to the discipline of anthropology, and so familiar to *Antigone*'s readers. Here, it may be that what pleases Darius are not her reasons, but *that* she reasons. When Intaphrenes' wife calculates and ranks, she shows she has left the keening abyss of need and entered into a finite, logocentric economy of reasoning and exchange.[44]

On this reading, then, Darius wants her to be reasonable. And she obliges. Intaphrenes' wife is by way of this set of exchanges with Darius moved from a sovereignty-disrupting aneconomic realm of need and desire into a sovereignty-governed and sovereignty-supporting economy of reason or *logos*, what Lacan calls the service of the goods.[45]

This approach to the story of Intaphrenes' wife may be further supported by another story about Darius told by Herodotus right before this one. According to Herodotus, when the Persians took control of a plateau through which water flowed from one large river into five smaller ones, Darius dammed the gorges below and stopped the water from continuing on its way to the land of five tribes who relied on it. The result?

[A] great deal of suffering among the tribes, because they used to rely on this water and now they cannot use it. It is all right in the winter, when the god sends rain on to their land as he does everywhere else, but in the summer when they are planting their millet and sesame, they need water. Since they receive no supply of water, they make the journey to Persia, taking their wives with them, and there they stand at the entrance to the king's palace and bellow loudly and bitterly. The king then gives orders that the sluice-gates blocking the river which flows into the territory of the tribe which pleads most forcefully are to be opened and when their land has soaked up enough water to become saturated, these gates are closed and the king gives the order for the next loudest pleaders [and so on] ... My information is that he opens the gates only after he has exacted from them a great deal of money, over and above their regular tribute ... (3.117 [217])

The tribesmen and their wives appeal to the ruler whose actions are responsible for their plight. The water the tribesmen once prayed for now has to be paid for.

Taken together, this story and that of Intaphrenes' wife show us a king who controls both the waters of nature and the tears of women. Both fall, or not, in response to sovereign power. (Notably, Darius is the ruler of whom Herodotus says, "Everything was filled with Darius' power" [1996: 3.88 (208)]). The men bellow, they do not lament, they plead but do not keen, and from them Darius demands money not reasons. But in both vignettes, the supplicants are sent on their way once they learn to acknowledge the king's power and play by his rules (of paying or reasoning). True, Herodotus reports that those who bellow loudest are the first to get what they came for and this seems at odds with the idea, suggested here regarding Intaphrenes' wife, that Darius wants to teach his subjects orderliness, reasoning, and deference to sovereign economies.[46] But the narrator adds as an aside that he has it on good authority that in fact it is not the bellowing but rather the under-the-table payments that are doing the real work.[47]

The *a*symmetries between the story of Intaphrenes' wife and Sophocles' *Antigone* are illuminating as well. Antigone too will give reasons – her brother is irreplaceable, her parents are dead – but she, unlike Intaphrenes' wife, gives those reasons in a context where it is already too late and they cannot therefore do the work of reasons: persuade, make clear, yield understanding. By citing (*after* Creon has ordered her to stop speaking) Intaphrenes' wife, a woman who laments a husband but saves a brother, Antigone, a woman who laments a brother and foregoes a husband, shifts the frame of the viewer from herself to Creon: with her citation, she puts Creon on trial to his face, in his presence.[48] Darius offers inducements, rewards, and gifts. But Creon seeks to tame Antigone by blows as he tames animals. He is a less gifted ruler than Darius. And Antigone is a more willful antagonist than Intaphrenes' wife. Citing the story of Intaphrenes' wife, Antigone aims not to give reasons but to fault Creon.[49] And she finds that he is no Darius.[50]

If this reading has force, then Antigone's law of the irreplaceable brother may let us know that the issue is not, contra Hegel and Lacan, the very thing she seems to say it is – the uniqueness of her irreplaceable brother and her (dis)passionate attachment to him. Instead, her reference to the irreplaceable brother covertly directs attention to Intaphrenes' wife, another woman whose keening, like Antigone's, ill suits the needs of sovereign power. Such covert communication – *adianoeta* – is not out of character for Sophocles' protagonist and is not unknown in classical and even archaic sources.[51] We shall see yet more examples of it in Chapter 6. With this covert reference, Antigone indicates – in Creon's presence and after he has ordered her taken away – that the issue at hand is political; and it is not merely about whether or how to bury Polynices but rather about sovereign efforts to move subjects from the infinitude of loss and violent abyssal vengeance into a finite and more governable economy of wants, appetites, and their satisfactions.[52] Ironically, in Herodotus, the orders of reason and vengeance are commingled in the very moment of Darius' effort to privilege the former over the latter. He socializes the lamenting wife into reason's economy but he also arrogates to himself the right to vengeance: Darius will kill Intaphrenes and most of his family to repay treason.

Why, then, does Darius spare the life of Intaphrenes' son? Does he not thereby open himself to precisely the sort of future vengeance he seeks to curtail in others and reserve for himself? The question presses us to yet another reading of Herodotus' story.

We may be helped in answering this question by Adriana Cavarero, who opens her book on the corporeality of voice with a discussion of Italo Calvino's striking story, "A King Listens." In the story, a king, surrounded by the deadening and instrumental talk of his spies and servants, is attracted by the voice of a woman singing. In Benjamin's terms (we might say, drawing again on Weber and Martel), the spies and the servants are the indifferent "plotters" of the *Trauerspiel* while the woman's voice, which lures the king away from them, is conspiratorial. The woman is never seen, only heard, and this leads us to note a detail we have not yet considered in the story reported by Herodotus: when Darius makes his offer to Intaph-renes' wife, Darius has not seen, he has only heard her. He has been listening to her keening outside his palace, just like the king in the Calvino story. Both rulers respond to the voice of a woman and even though the one sings and the other keens, it could be said that, for both the kings in question, these women's voices emerge "from the world of the living that is outside [or at least less inside] the deadly logic of power" represented by courts, plotters, and their intrigue (Cavarero 2005: 2).

Darius has not seen the woman's face but he has heard her voice and her vocality, as Cavarero would say, carries her uniqueness.[53] (Similarly, to anticipate the arguments of Chapter 6, we may surmise that what renders Antigone newly open to Ismene after their first quarrel is hearing her sister keen for her, as she stands accused before Creon; only after those keening sounds are heard, is Ismene brought before Creon, held together with the sister whose fate she already laments.) The keening voice of Intaphrenes' wife has called out – to Darius, or maybe to the universe – and this may generate in Darius a desire to respond. He is open to her, sort of.[54] True, Darius stays fortressed in his palace and unlike Calvino's king, who bursts into song, Darius merely sends out a messenger. But for Darius, on this reading, this is a reaching out. And, true, where Calvino's king "occupies himself only with sounds and totally overlooks the semantic" (Cavarero 2005: 6), Darius allows his fascination with sound to bleed into a demand for semantics. Still, he does feel pity. And so, from this interpretative angle, we may consider the possibility that when Darius asks "Which family member do you want?" he is asking (as Calvino's ruler longs to as well): "Who are you?" The woman responds with her longing for her brother. This only adds to the mystery for Darius, or else he is not fully up to her call – not able to rise to her "vocal perspective" (in Cavarero's catachretic phrasing [2005: 6]), and so he asks for more: why the brother? When Darius asks Intaphrenes' wife to reason her response (without realizing the violence of his request, let us say) he *incites* her into rationality itself.

As Judith Butler explains in a reading of Foucault: "Rational self-reflection is not a spontaneous effect of rationality. It is incited by an other, delivered through discourse, in the form of an address and [it] arrive[s] as an incitement, a form of seduction, an imposition or demand from outside to which one yields" (2005: 125). When Intaphrenes' wife risks rational self-reflection to answer the question: "Why choose the brother?"

she yields to Darius. She gives an account of herself (in Butler's titular phrase) and Darius responds with a gift.[55] Not just the brother she asks for but also the eldest son.

It is a gift of mis-recognition. Perhaps Darius thinks his gift can assuage her suffering. But things are not so simple, for the gift he gives is what *he* would want: a son, to continue the paternal line, to alleviate the ache of the father's mortality by carrying the paternal name into the future. The importance of sons to the fathers is well known to the women of Greek tragedy and myth. That is why, from Procne to Medea, women angry with their children's father kill the children, because the women know they are the *father's* children (as Cavarero, elsewhere [2009], also points out).[56] Like them, like Antigone, Intaphrenes' wife prioritizes natal over conjugal family. Noticing this, we return to that remainder we earlier set aside. Darius is said to have "rewarded" the wife's reasoning by sparing *also* the life of her eldest son. But this reward leaves alive a remnant of the nearly destroyed conjugal or procreative family, an overliving son who may, like Orestes, one day seek vengeance, perhaps against Darius, who killed his family, perhaps against his mother, who privileged her blood family over his. If the saved son is a gift, he is surely a gift that will keep on giving.[57] The son is futurity itself, with its promise of vengeance and joy (though under the circumstances the promise is a bit more heavily weighted on the side of vengeance than joy).[58]

Notably, Intaphrenes' wife has asked for no future, however. Like Antigone whose name means "no progeny," this woman has expressly asked for *no* children. Thus, like Haemon, who tries to give Antigone and himself a future by forcibly marrying Antigone in death, Darius' "gift" presses Intaphrenes' wife into futurity by maternalizing her against her expressed wishes. Dewald and Kitzinger read this as a story in which the woman outfoxes the king but surely things are not so simple. The king's gift – his addition of the son to the requested brother – complicates matters.[59]

Perhaps then Antigone's citation of the story of Intaphrenes' wife publicizes not only that her plight is about the ban on laments (parodying Pericles, our first reading of the citation), that her fidelity is to natal over conjugal family structures (mimicking Creon, our second reading), and that Creon falls short of the standard of governance set by Darius (citing Herodotus, our third reading). Perhaps with this citation Antigone continues the mission of the *kommos* that Creon interrupted: referencing the story of Intaphrenes' wife, Antigone continues the *agon* over the meaning of her story even as she is pressed (by Haemon's and the Chorus' post-mortem appropriations, by Creon, by the Chorus in the *kommos*, by the polis that hosts tragedy, by later readers of the play) into the service of futurity and its romance, in which husbands' love and children fulfill us and we must, as everyone does, live out the curses of our fathers and sacrifice ourselves for future generations. With her dirge's parody, mimicry, and citation, Antigone contests these appropriations, and tries to frame, in her own terms, the meaning of her life and death.[60]

THE MEANING OF LIFE AND DEATH

Creon interrupts Antigone because he is aware that her dirge is an effort to frame the meaning and significance of her act, to secure her legacy in opposition to his effort to do so. The decisive making of meaning is something Creon considers to be his right (though of course the Chorus claims it as well). This after all is what drives him throughout: the quest to own the power of definition (who is friend, who is enemy?) and to control the dissemination of meaning – "Follow my orders closely," he tells the Chorus (215 [240]). For Creon, Antigone's dirge is not just, as I have argued until now it is for him, long, excessive, and yet further evidence of the narcissistic self-indulgence of elites in a democratic polis that presses laments into service on behalf of the larger collectivity. It is that. But it is also, like all dirges, a bid for immortality.

Immortality is precisely what Creon wants to deprive Antigone of. Creon wants Antigone to die quietly, away from the city and without fanfare.[61] She wants the Chorus to tell her story as she wants it told. She tries making the case that she is like Niobe, the ceaselessly lamenting goddess petrified into rockface. The Chorus rejects the frame. Antigone might be flattered by the comparison, they say, but it is inapt – Antigone is a mortal, not "a god, born of gods" (834 [925]) – and it is in any case not for her to make the case: "of course, it's a great thing for a dying girl to hear" (836–838 [927–928]), but her story will be told by others, after her death. Antigone responds as if she has been mocked, abused, and perhaps she has been or perhaps she merely takes offense. In either case, the Chorus stands its ground. Simon Goldhill notes the *kommos'* departure from the usual function of consolation: this Chorus does not only console, it also condemns (2012: 110). But he neglects to note that the parties are soon reconciled. They meet on common terrain when the Chorus asks: "I wonder . . . do you pay for your father's ordeal?" ("Will you accept that frame?" they ask) and she responds, "There – at last you've touched it, the worst pain" (856–858 [945–947]). They agree: hers is the story not of divine *hubris* struck down by the gods but of a curse stubbornly wending its way through a family line.

But Antigone is not only chastened, or at least she is not fully chastened by the Chorus, I want to suggest. She does back away from the comparison to Niobe and she does accept the Chorus' proffered Oedipal frame for her story. But their truce is shortlived. She soon tries something else. After Creon ends her *kommos* by ordering that she be taken away, she moves into *rhêsis* and broaches the law of the irreplaceable brother, an adianoetic reference that quietly signals her ongoing determination to tell her story as she wants it told. Denied the comparison to Niobe and not fully content with the Oedipal frame, though she sees its undeniable truth, she reaches for another frame: what about (the unnamed but clearly referenced) Intaphrenes' wife? She laments ceaselessly as well and she is firmly in the human world. This proposed frame is uncontested: unremarked by the Chorus and unnoticed by Creon.[62]

Creon wants the meaning of Antigone's story to be about his own ruling edict, the friend/enemy Polynices, and Antigone's dissidence (the play's readers ever since have for the most part obliged Creon on this).[63] The Chorus wants the story to be the final chapter in the legend of Oedipus, and they want it told later, after her death, and not by her. Antigone wants it to be about all the other issues explored here. She finds a way: when she names the law of the irreplaceable brother as her motive, Creon misses the law's covert message (and maybe the Chorus does too) which directs our attention past the brother and toward the politics of the situation: the sovereign cessation of laments, the struggle between kinship forms, his own style of governance, his plotting with democracy, and Antigone's appropriation of the right to signify. Her speech seeks to control the field of signification, but Creon, just like his son Haemon, seeks to have the last word. This was foreshadowed in Creon's first exchange with Antigone, when he asked her to respond to the sentry's charges: "You, tell me briefly, no long speeches – were you aware a decree had forbidden this?" (446–447 [495–496]).

Antigone goes on to give several long speeches. But she fails, in the end, to secure the meaning of her death. For Lacanians, she is the revolutionary suicide, a heroic subject of conscious death, a subject with remarkable fidelity to the Real; for Žižek, Antigone is a proto-totalitarian, anti-Habermasian figure who does not want to argue with Creon and sticks stubbornly to her decision; for some political or feminist theorists, she is an anti-statist representative of the private realm's virtues (Elshtain) or, for still others, a heroine of the public (Dietz, Douzinas). For Butler, Antigone models alternative kinship structures yet to come, but for Lee Edelman,

Antigone exhibits a valuable antipathy to child-centered kinship as such. This is the field of contestation into which the reading of Antigone tendered here enters, not unwarily, for Antigone's passion is something about which her devotees are quite passionate.

WORKING THE INTERVAL: THE CORPOREAL VOICE

[T]he acoustic sphere is the kinship between song and the language of birds. (Benjamin)[64]

Against those who would treat Antigone as a representative of extra-political mortalist or monstrous (anti)humanism, I have argued that her dirge and her death are political acts that rework vernaculars of meaning and solicit publics over the head of Creon in whose presence all of this happens. Against those who seek in lamentation a universal humanism of sound and cry, I have argued that Antigone's dirge is a partisan political intervention. However even if Antigone's words are political, that may leave intact the mortalist humanist claim that voice or lamentation eludes politics. Like a dog whistle, the sound of the lamenting cry may operate as *adianoeta* does, calling to hearers on a different register than words and soliciting us into an extra-political universalism. But *phonê* and *logos* are not as easy to untangle as this objection implies. Parody, mimicry, and citation postulate not just worded repetition but also intonation and inflection. That is, analytically distinguishing *phonê* and *logos*, though useful, misleads us into thinking of *phonê* and *logos* as parallel and distinct logics. What if instead they inspirit and interrupt each other?

When Nicole Loraux identifies the sound of grief with marginalized women's laments, she seems to collapse sound and lamentation, or at least to focus on the wordless aspects of lamentation. It is the voice or sound or music, not the script or words of lamentation, that she studies in *The Mourning Voice* (2002b). But in that book, she actually calls attention not just to *phonê* in place of *logos* but also to *phonê*'s eruptions into *logos*. For example, she points out that the name, Ajax, is a homonym; in addition to the hero's name it is also a word, *alas*, and onomatopoeiacally a sound of lament, *aiai*, a point subtly noted by the Chorus of sailors in Sophocles' play by that name when they say "Ajax of the mournful name" (cited in Loraux 2002b: 39). Elsewhere, Loraux notes a similar slippage from semantics to sound when she casts the shift from the city's word, *aei* or "always," which connotes the eternal city of Pericles that is worth dying for, to the lamenter's cry, *aiai*, as a shift from meaning to sound and from politics, which she sees as the realm of sense, to an anti-political encounter with meaning's aporias. But if *phonê* erupts into *logos*, might not *logos* erupt into *phonê* as well? If the *aiai* of lament breaks through the *aei* of the city, then might not listeners also hear the *aei* of the city in the sound of the *aiai* of lament? If the civic "always" is riven by universal cry, might not universal cry be riven by the civic always? Hearing lament in Ajax's name, we may also hear his name in cries of lament. Each is the trace of the other. Politics may be riven by mortalist humanism but mortalist humanism is riven by politics as well.

A similar possibility is explored by Adriana Cavarero when, in *For More Than One Voice* (2005), she deconstructs the binary of *phonê/logos* and argues that *phonê* does not only disrupt *logos* from outside, as it were, but also inspirits it from the inside.[65] In Plato and elsewhere, Cavarero tracks *logos*' denial of its dependence on voice, its claim to be superior because immaterial, abstract, anti-corporeal. We could add to her arguments, since *logos* has other strategies as well. It neutralizes or appropriates *phonê* not only by casting it as mere voice (non-sense, noise), but also by bringing *phonê* into the fold of sense, as when *phonê* is figured as onomatopoeia, which combines sound and word into an undecidable unity and blurs the distinction between Symbolic (studied by semantics) and Semiotic (studied by phonology). An evocative example is Loraux's tragic *aiai,* with its multiple connotations of "forever" or "always" as well as the sound of pain. But Loraux and Cavarero differ on an important point: replaying the difference between Goethe and Lacan, Loraux hears universal equality on the register of cry (Antigone's first law); Caverero hears singularity (Antigone's second law). Furthermore, Loraux's orientation in her discussion of sound and song is more toward pain and Cavarero's is more toward pleasure.

For Rousseau, in the *Essay on the Origin of Languages* (1997), the word that sounds like what it is is doubly protected against the alienation that Rousseau feared of presence through language and writing. But what for Rousseau is a sign of presence is for Cavarero rather a ruptural power because of voice's *corporeality.* Voice's corporeal emanations, like the cries emitted by Antigone "like a bird at an empty nest," introduce alienness into the situation rather than insulating us from it. Even where *logos* seems to establish its hegemony, abstracting reason from the body and accounting for *phonê* by way of onomatopoeia, nonsense, and more, *logos* remains, Cavarero says, dependent upon unruly voice, which is its alien register, its embodied materiality, its undecidable supplement: its *différance.* In short, what Loraux sees as shifts between *phonê* and *logos* (even as she describes the former interrupting the latter) are for Cavarero signs of a mutual inhabitation that both inspirits and ruptures *phonê* and *logos.* Where

Loraux is drawn by voice into a possible humanism, Cavarero finds in the bodily organ evidence of an undeniable sexual difference.

Jacques Rancière pushes the *agon* of *phonê/logos* in a slightly different but overlapping direction when he posits *phonê* as part of the political situation, not prior to or apart from it. Rancière does not identify *logos* with politics and *phonê* with anti-politics, as Loraux does. He does not insist on their mutual inhabitation, as Cavarero does, nor does he see them in relation to a politics of sexual difference. Instead, he insists these are simply two kinds of sound distinguished by a political partition of the sensible:

> The simplest opposition between logical animals and phonic animals is in no way the given on which politics is then based. It is ... one of the stakes of the very dispute that institutes politics ... Politics exists because the logos is never simply speech, because it is always indissolubly the account that is made of this speech: the account by which a sonorous emission is understood as speech, capable of enunciating what is just, whereas some other emission is merely perceived as noise signaling pleasure or pain, consent or revolt. (1999: 22–23)

Phonê is the name for the sonorous emissions of the excluded, and *logos* is the name claimed by the included for their own sounds. When Rancière's political actors seek equality, they appropriate the *logos* that excludes them. They do not claim commonality with their oppressors as mortals, as Loraux says. Instead, Rancière's political actors aim to be able to say that "from being 'mortals' they have become 'men'" (1999: 25). And they stage their dissensus using the very same tactics Antigone uses in her dirge: *parody, mimesis, citation.*

Parody, mimicry, and citation are possible because of the excessiveness of language, what Rancière calls its "literarity," which is normally domesticated by way of figurations, like onomatopoeia, which name that excessiveness and give it a function.[66] But *adianoeta* is one of those rhetorical counter-strategies that enable dissidents to mobilize the excessiveness of language in a different way, aiming to disrupt the dominant order, what Rancière calls the police order. It is uncanny that such excess or literarity, along with the parody, mimicry, and citation enabled thereby, should be most evident in a triply allusive speech that is also a speech of suffering and a crux (a speech suspected of inauthenticity) which, like all cruxes, is much suffered over by critics.[67]

Like Lacan, Rancière is drawn to scandalous speech. But where Lacan saw in Antigone's offensive speech the "suggestion of scandal" because the speech's purity suggests she has reached the limit point of desire, for Rancière the scandal is in the speaker's contaminated mimetic thieving entry into *logos*. The scandal is political because, Rancière says, criticizing Habermas: "Politics' penchant for dialogue has much more to do with literary heterology, with its utterances stolen and tossed back at their authors . . . than with the allegedly ideal situation of dialogue" (1999: 59).

Stealing from the dominant language might mean we engage in mere mimicry, though. Is that a dead end, as Žižek seems to suggest when he distinguishes, in Donald Pease's parsing, "the radical aspect of Antigone's ethical act and a merely performative reconfiguration of one's symbolic condition" (2009: 199)? Such "marginal configuration of the predominant discourse would nevertheless remain within the social order that it would simply reorganize," says Pease in support of Lacan and Žižek (2009: 199).[68] (This, it will be recalled from Chapter 2, is Lee Edelman's critique of Butler: that she mistakes the merely performative reconfiguration for the more truly radical act.) But there is another option: a truly political Antigone (rather than an ethical and/or monstrous one) might evade the trap of radicality versus complicity by practicing a mimicry that is self-overcoming. "Through transgression," Rancière's political actors "find that they too, just like speaking beings, are endowed with speech" (1999: 24).[69] Sometimes political actors succeed in shifting the terms of the current partition and gain some adjustment in its partition of the sensible. Since Rancière's focus is on efforts to change the dominant order, he may orient us to the question of success or failure on that front. But sometimes we have another aim – to live otherwise.[70] The action of dissensus may fail in instrumental terms while nonetheless succeeding for, in such action, equality is enacted and experienced. Butler points this out: "in the asking, in the petition, we have already become something new" (2004a: 44).

The *agon* of dissensus and consensus is what Rancière calls *politics*, and it provides the perspective from which he criticizes Edmund Burke and Hannah Arendt for binarily opposing universal human rights to the rights of citizens. Human rights are said to be empty and citizen rights are never full enough to fulfill the equality demands of the stateless. Rancière criticizes Burke and Arendt for what he says is their forced choice between the universal's identity of human/mortal and the civic's identity of citizen. Instead, Rancière argues, there is a third (I would call it an agonistic) option in which we work "the interval [itself, I note, a musical term] between the two identities," using parody, mimicry, citation. These are interstitial rhetorical devices that move between the serious and the comic, the internal and the external qualities of language. These devices allow democratic actors to reconfigure distributions of public and private, universal and particular, mortal and citizen. Such reconfiguration is always

I like her politics, I like her exploration of Antigone - but the two are uncomfortable suite.

Argument occurs - each layer supercedes the last

needed because even the universal, Rancière says, "is incessantly privatized by police logic" (2007: 61–62).

Critics have for centuries interpreted Antigone as embracing one or another identity – for example, private (family) goods versus public (polis) goods and as a strictly oppositional figure. But once we unpack the many levels of Antigone's speech, we see she works with a sophisticated repertoire and seeks to engage, if not Creon, then certainly others (the soldiers, the Chorus, Ismene, us, and more).

Moreover, Rancière's idea of "working the interval" invites us to see that Antigone is not simply, as may have seemed in Chapter 4, a defender of aristocratic privilege against democratic encroachments. Instead, we may now see, she inhabits the two identities whose contention is staged here – Pericles' polis-centered lamentation and the women's laments outlawed in the fifth-century polis – and she then works the intervals between them. Approached from this perspective, the play opens up: we see how, first, Antigone performs the accepted rites for Eteocles, in complete accordance with the logocentric polis' funerary requirements. Then later, when she keens and calls for vengeance over the body of her other brother, Polynices, Antigone performs lamentations, to a "T," as they have been outlawed by the fifth-century polis: keening in broad daylight and loudly calling for vengeance. Finally, in her third and final performance of lamentation, her dirge for herself, she does exactly what Rancière's political actors do when they work the interval between the identities whose oppositional logic might otherwise have frozen them. Her dirge neither conforms to the expected form nor simply violates it. Instead, she parodies, mimics, lampoons, and cites the stories, figures, and speech of the powerful, insinuating her views into their discourse, not absolutizing them, as Žižek says, nor losing hold of her capacity to make sense, as Dewald and Kitzinger argue.

Staging dissensus by working with materials provided by the city of consensus, Antigone conspires with language to work the interval between lamentation and *logos*, singularity and equality, between the infinite *aiai* of tragedy and the finite *aei* of the city. She does not cease to make sense; she seeks to make a new kind of sense. She suffers for this but she is not defined by her suffering. She dies but she is not defined by her mortality. As we saw in Chapter 1, Nietzsche cast her as natal, not mortal, and so he accented other aspects of her character, inviting us to see in her, perhaps, a different (post)humanism than the new mortalist humanism that is now being developed, often in her name.

Following Nietzsche's lead, we may see that this tragedy does something other than provide resources for our deeply conflictual time by soliciting us to an extra-political ethics of mortalist humanism: in *Antigone* we find elements of an agonistic humanism that works the interval between word and cry, natality and mortality, equality and singularity, and can be extended further, even perhaps to (re)working the interval between human and animal. Friction, not seamlessness (recalling Taylor's appreciation of Gambaro) is a trait of this work.

"Working the interval" is also a good response to the philosophical reception of *Antigone* which has historically claimed Sophocles' protagonist for humanism as well as anti-humanism. Agonistic humanism might, better than the mortalist humanism to which Loraux ultimately turns, respond to Loraux's occasionally expressed longing for a politics that is beyond the binary by which her account is often gripped: neither a polis politics nor a mortalist humanist, tragic, anti-politics. "What if the word 'political' had more than one meaning?" Loraux asks, expressing dismay that such a politics is only imagined (1998: 93). But no politics can be real with*out* being imagined.

THE "HAMLETIZATION" OF ANTIGONE?

[Hamletization is] the transformation of the figure of the avenger into a reflective, self-conscious melancholic. (Carl Schmitt)

Carl Schmitt coins the term Hamletization in the context of his reading of Shakespeare's play, but it could apply to Antigone, as she has been until now received, as well. Her play, no less than his, depicts an avenger thwarted. In Shakespeare's play, the protagonist is beset by melancholy and is incapable of decisive action. In Sophocles' play, the protagonist is, if anything, too decisive, not indecisive. (It is Creon who indecisively leaves Antigone buried alive to die or not as the gods will it; Antigone by contrast takes matters into her own hands when she tends to Polynices, when she kills herself.) If her vengeance is thwarted, it is partly because no one responds to her calls and she is overpowered; it is not, that is, for lack of trying. And yet, it is for her mourning that she is most remembered now. Today, she and Hamlet are the two great protagonists of mourning or melancholy. Antigone's conspiracy with language, tracked in detail here, goes for the most part unremarked by modern and contemporary critics who seem to want, rather, to be moved by her keening. They overlook the fact that, in her keening lamentations, she does not just move others to share in a feeling of finitude that renders friend/enemy distinctions nugatory. She calls for vengeance and distinguishes repeatedly between friend and enemy to her cause. In sum, the Hamletization of the avenger that occurs, on Schmitt's account, within the pages of Shakespeare's script has crept up on Sophocles' *Antigone* over time.

For Schmitt, the Hamletization of Hamlet is a result of an intrusion of history into the text that prevents the play from following the pattern provided by the usual tragic or mythic sources (Greek or Norse). The usual outcome would allow for retribution against, or exoneration of, the mother. But, Schmitt argues, Shakespeare is unable to decide the guilt or innocence of Hamlet's mother because either choice would have put the playwright too directly in the way of the tender politics of James I's succession. (James's mother, Mary Stuart, was suspected of collaborating in the murder of her first husband whose murderer she then married "in unseemly and suspicious haste" [Schmitt 2009: 16].) The result of the blockage is Hamlet's famous indecision. History distorts the play and leaves its mark. For Schmitt, this distortion elevates the play from mere *Trauerspiel* to true tragedy.

In *Antigone*'s case, the intrusion of history (in the form of Herodotus' story of Intaphrenes' wife) also causes a distortion, forcing on the protagonist late in the play a motive for her acts that conflicts with her character and her cause as they are earlier defined.[71] Is the seeming inauthenticity of Antigone's dirge for herself a mark of history's intrusion? Importantly, Schmitt says that where such intrusion and distortion occur, the effect is scandal, and, as we have seen, this is precisely the term used by Lacan to describe Antigone's offensive speech. Indeed critics through the centuries have been scandalized by Antigone's law of the irreplaceable brother (seeing it as more *Trauerspiel* than tragedy, we might say — that is, they see it as a low motive unbefitting the otherwise high tragic heroine). Ironically, on the reading developed here, allowing this intrusion to have its impact actually works to de-Hamletize Antigone. We can see how a speech that looks like fraught, unbalanced lamentation (although the Chorus recognizes she is *auto-nomos*, like her father) is a nuanced performance of thoughtful conspiratorial action with political ramifications.

We need not insist, as Schmitt seems to, on the "reality" of history versus aesthetics, in order to profit from the comparison with his reading of *Hamlet* and from the terms his analysis usefully generates. In particular, we may find helpful here the distinction he develops in *Hamlet or Hecuba* among allusion, mirroring, and intrusion, these being three ways in which history exerts a certain pressure on tragic theater.[72] It is in the crucible of the last that true tragedy is formed, Schmitt says, for only the last has the necessary distorting effect. The other two, allusion and mirroring, are traces of historical events in the play of different levels of importance.

Strikingly, allusion, mirroring, and intrusion map well onto the three registers of meaning explored in this chapter: parody, which alludes, mimicry, which mirrors, and citation, which instances intrusion. If we go on to focus on the three terms' relation to history, as Schmitt does, we may see an example of allusion in the references to lot and remuneration, mentioned in Chapter 4. An example of mirroring may be Creon's prohibition of Antigone's lamentations, if this indeed recalls the fifth-century ban, as I argued in Chapter 4 and here, further, in Chapter 5. An example of intrusion, an intersection of history and theater that undoes, or in this case, redoes, the play's meaning, is arguably the law of the irreplaceable brother. That is, the story of Intaphrenes' wife (who laments in confrontation with sovereign power and lives) intrudes into the play and forces its tragic hand, undoing the inherited bewilderment or dismissal of Antigone's law of the irreplaceable brother to disclose her not at all indecisive intervention into the *politics* of lamentation. Breaking the old frame of lamentation versus politics that has for so long contained Sophocles' protagonist, we find, finally, a not at all Hamletized Antigone but rather a conspiratorial one.

One might expect that more precise historical contextualization of a work of art would deprive it of its ability to address future generations, divesting it of its "universality" rather than enhancing its capacity to speak to us now. I return to this question in the Conclusion. For now, it is important to note that, in this instance anyway, the contrary is the case. Historical contextualization along with attention to the play's prior receptions creates an overlife for the play beyond its context, and it does so not by invoking so-called universals like "finitude," as humanists enamored with the tragic and its universality have done for centuries (as we saw in Part I). Instead, we now see, the play's urgency for contemporary readers is intensified by demonstrating the work's way of "working the interval," something that comes to the fore when we trace the intrusion of history into the play.[73]

But there is also another effect: history's intrusion may, as Schmitt says it does in *Hamlet*, create a kind of excess in the play, an "extimate" dimension that finds expression in what Eric Santner, parsing Schmitt, calls a "manic proliferation of theatricality that culminates in the triplification of levels of play-acting in the third act of *Hamlet* . . . " (Santner 2011: 152). Evidence of this in Sophocles' play may be a play within a play, staged for Creon by the sisters, this one an effort not (as in *Hamlet*) to find out whodunit, but rather to obscure the answer to precisely that question. I turn now to that scene, noting now that the reading I develop requires taking seriously the role of voice in performance, the power of intonation, the impact of double entendre, and the pressure of a certain untimeliness, in which Ismene, read in historical context, turns out to be more modern than the sister more often embraced by modern and contemporary theorists of politics or feminism.[74]

CHAPTER 6

Sacrifice, sorority, integrity: Antigone's conspiracy with Ismene

Ismene: Such wretched straits.
Oedipus: Hers [Antigone's] and mine?
Ismene: And mine too, my pain the third.

Sophocles, Oedipus at Colonus

The scenes looked at in this chapter come earlier in the play than Antigone's dirge, the scene we just examined in detail in Chapter 5. If the ordering of these chapters violates the play's chronology, that is for two reasons. First, having established the context of burial politics in Chapter 4, it made sense to move immediately in Chapter 5 to discuss Antigone's dirge. Second, the earlier scenes I look at now here, in Chapter 6, include one in which Antigone conspires with Ismene, or so I will claim. That claim is easier to establish if we have in place some appreciation of Antigone's capacity to conspire with language and it with her, and this appreciation postulates the close reading of her dirge that was the focus of Chapter 5. Thus, the non-chronological ordering is necessary to undo several settled elements of interpretation and reception and to make room for a more agonistic engagement with the play.

Perhaps no element of *Antigone*'s reception history is more settled than the belief that Antigone's sister, Ismene, is an anti-political character who lacks the courage or imagination to act when called upon to do so. Critics split the two sisters into active and passive characters, treating them respectively as heroic and withdrawn, courageous and cowardly. The contrast highlights the exceptionality of Antigone, dramatizing her (in)human boldness in the face of impossibility. It also calls attention to the dimensions of tragedy most favored by humanists and anti-humanists alike: the tragic thwarting of human aspiration and the isolation of the tragic hero by forces beyond the control of any individual, be these the gods, powerful men, or the cursed fate of one's family line. For humanists, tragedy performs the paradoxically impossible when the art form makes meaning out of man's insignificance. For anti-humanists, tragedy is the

151

non-redemptive genre that explores human ambition, desire, or compulsion but then confronts the protagonists (and the audience) with the inevitable demise that destroys human illusions of grandiosity.

Humanist and anti-humanist receptions converge in their tendency to orient readers and spectators away from tragedy's political implications and toward an ethics, or what Nicole Loraux calls an anti-politics of shared suffering (2002b: 26–27) or (what Lacanians call) desire. Still others, including Loraux in her earlier work, seek the politics of tragedy in the fifth-century context or in its later receptions.[1] Often neglected is tragedy's own exploration of the problem of political agency as action under conditions of (near) impossibility. Those who do seek in tragedy some instructive exploration of political agency, political theorists, tend to fasten on the humanists' solitary heroine of conscience in Sophocles' play, or on Creon, the isolated (anti)hero, as exemplars of political action; and this distracts attention from those elements of most concern to democratic theory: solidarity or action in concert among equals. Indeed, political theorists vary in celebrating or faulting Antigone, but virtually all agree she lacks any interest in mobilizing others or constituting a public. Both classicists and democratic theorists, even those who admire her, criticize her for being too self-centered or principled to a fault.[2] She is often contrasted with Haemon, who knows how to argue reasonably, it is said (e.g. Nussbaum 1986 and Tully 1995), though making the case for this character as a model of deliberation requires delicately sidestepping his attempted parricide and his violent self-destruction.

The interpretation of *Antigone* offered in this chapter, developed as a close reading of the text, adds to the possibilities of political reception by highlighting dimensions of political agency heretofore unnoted in the play. This is done by homing in on the moments when, as I argue, Antigone plots and conspires with her sister. Developing further the contrast of word and sound and exploring their intimacy, work begun in Chapter 5, I attend not just to the text but also to possible subtleties of tone and performance to generate new interpretative options. Also, in this chapter, I intensify the focus on action rather than suffering, solidarity over heroic isolation. The emergent interpretation is promoted assertively in order to establish its viability against the likely incredulity of readers, but of course this reading is, like all readings, partial and contestable. It highlights certain dimensions of the text and not others. I will argue in its favor, however, on interpretative grounds and also on political and dramaturgical ones. The aim is to intervene not only in the play's philosophical and philological reception history but also in its dramaturgical reception. That is, this reading has implications for the play's staging and performance, suggesting that in this instance the repertoire, to use Diana Taylor's terms, may find new bearings in the archive (and not only vice versa).[3]

"WE ARE NOT BORN TO CONTEND WITH MEN" – ISMENE'S RECEPTION HISTORY

In the play's first scene, Antigone knows what she has to do but she does not just go out and do it. She turns to Ismene seeking help and, notwithstanding centuries of interpretation that treat Ismene as a passive, compliant character, Ismene puts up quite a fight when she hears her sister's plans.[4] In this chapter, I read the play through the prism of this first scene, in which Antigone tries to plot with Ismene and then responds to Ismene's entreaties by rejecting her sister and swearing to an abiding inhospitality to her forever more. "I'd never welcome you in the labor, not with me" (70 [83]).

Antigone's apparent brutality toward her sister seems to conflict with Antigone's later claim that she was "born to join in love, not hate" (523 [590]). And Ismene's late effort to share her sister's fate seems out of place given her character-defining refusal in the play's first scene to defy Creon's edict. These puzzles are solved by the reading developed here, in which the sisters act in coordination beneath the radar of Creon's sovereignty.

Turning later to read the play with and against Alenka Zupančič (1998) who interprets the play elaborating Jacques Lacan's account of ethics, I argue there is a case to be made for treating Ismene and Antigone as plotters and conspirators who act ethically and politically. One benefit of this approach is that it shows how driven are conventional interpretations by certain contestable humanist assumptions about heroic individual agency, politics, and sovereignty.

Lacan does not grant ethical agency to Ismene. In this, he is not alone. For centuries, Ismene has been cast as the inert drab backdrop against which her more colorful heroic sister stands out. Antigone is active, Ismene passive; Antigone is heroic, Ismene cowardly, are the refrains of the conventional readings.[5] Slavoj Žižek preserves them:

We must oppose all attempts to domesticate her, to tame [Antigone] by concealing the frightening strangeness, "inhumanity," *a-pathetic* character of her figure, making her a gentle protectress of her family and household who evokes our compassion and offers herself as a point of identification. In Sophocles' *Antigone*, the figure with which we can identify is her sister Ismene – kind, considerate, sensitive, prepared to give way, and compromise, pathetic, "human" in contrast to Antigone, who goes to the limits, who "doesn't give way on her desire" (Lacan) and becomes, in this persistence in the "death drive," in the being-toward-death, frighteningly ruthless, exempted from the circle of everyday feelings and considerations, passions and fears. (1989: 117)[6]

The splitting of Ismene and Antigone recurs even when the conventional takes on the two sisters are revalued, and Ismene is rendered more, not less, attractive than her beautiful sister.[7] Jill Frank (2006) argues insightfully that Ismene is not withdrawn, weak, or incapacitated; she is patient and bides her time. Antigone, by contrast, is too quick to act, too fiery, too thunderously loud to be truly effective. Mary Rawlinson criticizes feminists for deriding Ismene's focus on survival in favor of Antigone's heroic martyrdom. Ismene's this-worldly orientation is actually more valuable to feminism than her sister's sacrificial desire, Rawlinson concludes.[8]

But Ismene does more than survive. She acts creatively in response to a series of "forced choices," and this is in keeping with, not in opposition to, what Alenka Zupančič casts as a Lacanian ethics of creativity and "forced choice."[9] Indeed, I argue here that Zupančič's treatment of Lacan invites an assessment of Antigone's supposedly ordinary sister different from the one he and his followers, like Žižek and Zupančič, themselves give. When Ismene, who wants to die with Antigone, agrees to go on living without her, Ismene does not (contra Lacan, Žižek, and various feminist readers of the play) simply choose survival and avoid death. Instead she performs what Lacan calls an ethical act: she confronts her own limit and does not back down. Her limit is not death but rather a living death: to go on living in the house of her sister's killer, Creon. This is Ismene's second forced choice and she does not avoid it. As we shall see, she does not avoid the first forced choice pressed upon her either, and in relation to that one she is creative.

The first forced choice, set in motion by Creon's edict, is cast by Antigone as a choice between flagrant disobedience or cowardly withdrawal: will Ismene help bury Polynices, or not? As we shall see, Ismene finds a way to act otherwise.

A close reading of the text suggests that the two sisters act in concert in ways that complement rather than compete, or complement *and* compete. Sophocles' readers and viewers, from Hegel to Lacan and from Segal to Goldhill and Butler, have thus far failed to detect the sororal solidarity at work in this play.[10] Why?[11] Antigone's solidarity with Ismene, and Ismene's transformation, call into some question the remnants of the heroic, ruptural model of action by which even progressive theorists of politics remain bewitched.[12] An alternative Antigone, solidaristic and sororal, is important to democratic and feminist theory, however, because her commitment to Ismene expresses a commitment to life, not just death. This Antigone was indeed, as she herself says, "born to love," and she presses on us a question: what assumptions about sacrifice, heroism, and agency may perhaps blind us to sororal and other solidaristic forms of agency and their powers, both in the play and possibly in the world around us?

The play's subtleties are worth attending to, as democratic and feminist theorists continue to work through our centuries-long relationship with Antigone, her readers, and her receptions. Antigone is not just the familial heroine of burial and the guardian of the dead celebrated by Hegel for her service to the brother, nor is she a witness protesting the injustice of her brother's reduction to bare life, as readers of Giorgio Agamben might put it. Nor again are her actions best seen as vindications of would-be extra-political universals, such as the ontological fact of mortality which positions us all as mortal, vulnerable, or grievable. Antigone may be all these things, but she is also – and more importantly for democratic and feminist theory – a partisan sororal actor in concert who sacrifices herself not just for the disgraced, "ungrievable" dead brother, but also for a living equal: her sister. Antigone avows the sacrifice when she tells Ismene to go on living and says, "My death will be enough" (547 [617]). And Ismene subtly acknowledges her sister's gift by ceasing at that point to remonstrate with her and accepting her own fate. The idea that political action is heroic has blinded us to the sisters' actions in concert and perhaps also to conspiratorial and even sororal powers in the world around us. Such limited views of political agency are well tested by rereading the very play that has to some extent undergirded them and whose conventional interpretation is undergirded *by* them.

The idea that Antigone's death is a sacrifice is not new. In nineteenth-century Germany, philosophers from Hegel to Schelling, Goethe, and even the composer Felix Mendelssohn, approached Antigone through a sacrificial structure typical of their Christian moment. In the Christianized Germany of the 1840s, Sophocles' heroine was identified with Mary Magdalene who put herself at risk to care for the dead when she took Jesus' broken body down from the cross (Geary 2006). Antigone's sacrifice for her dead brother was available to be appropriated not on behalf of the anti-statism in the name of which this heroine has so often since been redeployed but rather on behalf of the sort of uncompromising and selfless loyalty and devotion that stood as a particularly central virtue of modern Christianity and was useful to the still-new state form. This is the Antigone Friedrich Wilhelm wanted to see in his court theater in 1842, not the dissident transgressor of Creon's law. Something like this Christian Antigone is taken up by Lacan and his heirs to this day as a forceful model for transgressive desire and for dissident politics. Feminists have been drawn to this heroic Antigone as well, perhaps also (even if unwittingly) to the power of her self-sacrifice.

Antigone's sacrifice is usually assumed to have been on behalf of the much-talked-about heroic and dead brother, Polynices, not for the sake of the still-living, quiet, and anti-heroic sister, Ismene. I document the text's suggestions that we do well to look past Polynices and reconsider this portrait of Ismene. The dead brother is one object around whom the sisters connect and contend, rather than a crucible that only divides them. And we unearth the sororal collusion at the play's center by attending less to formal law and more to practice; less to the edict against burying Polynices (the focus of so much of the *Antigone* scholarship) and more to the two transgressive burials of Polynices (the focus of very little of the scholarship). This helps cast Ismene's subtle agency into sharper relief, while also treating the two burials as distinct. Rather than, as is usually done, casting the first as a failure that is corrected or completed by the second burial, we see each as accomplishing something unique, each enacting a particular, exemplary kind of relationship not only to the dead but also to the living.[13]

I turn now to a close reading of Sophocles' text in relation to the classics commentary, then to extend that reading further and consider its political implications in light of Lacan's and Bernard Williams's very different but overlapping treatments of ethics as the impossible negotiation of tragic dilemmas or forced choices. I close with a discussion of distinctively sororal power in the play and in its reception, establishing some critical distance between this work and Simon Goldhill's (2006, 2012) recent calls to explore the power of sorority for thinking politically. One way to look at this intervention is to understand it as positioning Antigone somewhere between the heroism with which Bernard Knox identified her forty years ago, and the citizenship with which (sublimation into which) Julia Lupton has more recently argued Antigone should be affiliated.

"I DON'T DENY A THING" — THE PROBLEM OF THE TWO BURIALS

Creon's edict prohibiting the burial of the traitor, Polynices, is violated twice. The first time, at night, unwitnessed, someone performs a symbolic burial ritual – the body is not buried, but dusted. The story of what happened that first time is told to Creon by a sentry, a sighted man who did not see it, in a scene that mirrors a later scene with Tiresias, a sightless man who sees all. Creon accuses both men of selling out for money. In both instances, the charge is false and Creon's impatience with both characters is a clue that he will misread the signs they bring to him. In the case of the sentry's first scene, the signs have also been misread by critics ever since.

The sentry explains to Creon that he and his companions, posted by Creon to guard the body and prevent anyone from burying it, somehow failed to see something that must have happened right before their eyes. Someone came in the night and sprinkled dust over the body of Polynices, in clear violation of Creon's edict. Creon suspects the guards of corruption and sends the sentry back to his post at the corpse site with strict instructions to find the offender (they also re-expose the corpse, though it is unclear whether they were instructed to do so).

The sentry soon returns to Creon with a prisoner: Antigone. Although the sentry congratulates himself on apprehending the culprit, his success is not a product of good detective work, but rather of good fortune. There was a second violation of Creon's edict – a second burial. And this time Antigone was caught in the act; the guards witnessed her performing the rites for Polynices. In the ensuing scene with Creon and in centuries of interpretation since, the assumption is that this second act of burial was committed by the same person who performed the first. In fact, the mystery of the first burial is never solved.

The text does not explicitly contradict the assumption that Antigone committed both violations, but it does offer some suggestions that it might have been worth looking elsewhere for suspects, perhaps beyond the obvious or maybe right at the obvious (a counsel also apt in Oedipus' case, in that later Sophoclean tragedy). The subtle suggestions in the play become more forceful once we ask: *why* was Polynices buried a *second* time? Readers have over the years provided answers that support Creon's assumption that Antigone performed both burials, preventing the mystery of the first burial from becoming too pressing. For example, noting that in the first burial the body was only dusted, but that in the second Antigone pours libations, Jebb infers that Antigone must have returned because she had earlier forgotten the libations and needed them to complete the rite (1966: 114).[14]

Another possibility is that since the corpse had been unburied by the guards after the first burial, Antigone wanted to reperform the ceremony, to undo their undoing. This is Gilbert Norwood's suggestion – that Antigone's performance of the second burial is a mark of her stubborn obsession with keeping her brother's body covered (1928: 140, cited in Rose 1952: 251, n. 7). Seeing the body re-exposed, she buried it again and so opened the line of events that ultimately lead from one death to the next. The sentry's claim that Antigone, upon seeing the body called down curses on the heads of those who had done "the work," may be seen to support Norwood. If Antigone cursed those who had unburied Polynices, this intimates she knew about the first burial presumably because she herself had performed it. However, the work she curses might be not the un-burial, but simply the work of outlawing the burial, leaving the body unburied, guarding it, and so on, all of which led to the decay and decomposition that are cause enough for Antigone's cursing when she arrives, possibly for the first time, at the site.

Yet another reason for a second burial could be that Antigone's aim was not yet achieved. If her goal was not only to bury Polynices but also to stand up to Creon, she had reason to return. Indeed, this is Creon's perspective, which continues to frame critical receptions of the play: "This girl was an old hand at insolence when she overrode the edicts we made public. But once she had done it – the insolence, twice over – to glory in it, laughing, mocking us to our face with what she'd done. I am not the man, not now: she is the man if this victory goes to her and she goes free" (480–485 [536–542]). On a reading that accents Creon's claim, Antigone does not *want* to get away with her crime and is dismayed to think she has done. When she realizes the soldiers might never catch her after the first burial, she comes back to do it again precisely so as to get caught in the act. This reading is not contradicted by the text, but neither is it given much support. Antigone never boasts about the two burials, nor is she represented in such unheroic terms that it is really credible that she would try once to defy Creon, fail (or forget the libations!), and have to try again. Still, this reading has one merit: it shows the issue may not just be about Polynices. On this reading, Polynices is also an occasion for a political clash Antigone seeks to stage.

More suggestively, we might treat Antigone's second burial of Polynices in psychoanalytic terms. I have explored this possibility elsewhere (2013), suggesting that Creon's edict disables Antigone's mourning, and Ismene's refusal to help Antigone do the work of burial makes matters worse. Without Ismene's help, Antigone cannot lift the body. This deprives Antigone of the fuller satisfactions burial provides survivors, and leaves Antigone trapped in melancholy. Failing to bury Polynices again and again, she can achieve only a mere simulacrum of the proper rites, and so she acts out a repetition compulsion that might have gone on forever had it not been interrupted finally by her arrest. This interpretation finds support in – or lends support to – Stanley Cavell's claim that there is, in Elisabeth Bronfen's words, "a repetition compulsion at the heart of the tragic theme" (2008: 287; citing Cavell 1976: 310). (This, arguably, is what melodrama homes in on and intensifies.)

This last is similar to the reading offered by J. L. Rose, who maintains that the solution to the problem of the second burial is solved by close examination of Antigone as a tragic character obsessed by one idea: "Antigone's complete absorption in one idea or interest is manifested in her passionate support of what she considers right and in her courageous love of her dear ones," says Rose, drawing on A. C. Bradley's discussion of Shakespeare's tragic characters (Rose 1952: 221; citing Bradley 1929: 20) and further splitting the two sisters: "Strength and conviction and intensity of feeling attain in [Antigone] a great force. When she is brought into conflict with a selfish person, like Ismene, the utter unselfishness and self-sacrifice of her nature stand out clearly ... " (Rose 1952: 221).

Thus, it is possible to resolve the mystery of *why two burials?* without departing too far from conventional interpretations. But the focus on solving the problem of the second burial has distracted attention from the rather more productive problem of the first. And there is some evidence to suggest the first burial was not performed by Antigone.

First, when Antigone is caught and then brought before Creon, she does not only confess, she also is said not to deny violating Creon's edict. Confession and non-denial are not exactly the same thing, as Judith Butler has also pointed out in the context of a different argument (2000: 8; 33; 2004b: 161–173). "We interrogated her," the sentry says, describing the scene at the corpse site, "charging her with offenses past and present – she stood up to it all, denied nothing" (434–435 [482–484]). Again, when Creon asks if she buried the corpse, she says: "I did it. I don't deny a thing" (443 [492]). What shall we make of these non-denials? They could be the civil disobedient's classic confession, which takes entire responsibility, and is anticipated by Antigone's earlier admonition to her sister in the play's first scene to "shout" the crime out "from the rooftops" and "tell the world," rather than hide it and keep it a secret (86–87 [100–101]). Or we could see some care, some crafting in the language. Does "I did it" go to the second burial (434–435 [483–484])? And does her "I don't deny a thing," which is not the same as "I did it," go to the first burial?

If Antigone did not perform the first burial, the sentry's charges might be the first she has heard of it and she might well be confused, as she stands there accused, first by the guards, then by Creon. "*What* past offenses?" she might be silently wondering, denying nothing, but not affirming anything either since she did not in fact commit all the crimes with which she is charged.

Confusion may be evident in her posture as she stands accused before Creon. After hearing the sentry's report, Creon says to her: "You, with your eyes fixed on the ground – speak up" (441–442 [489–491]). *Eyes fixed on the ground* is how the sentry describes himself and his comrades when they realize after the first burial someone must go tell Creon his edict has been violated: "one man spoke out and made us *stare at the ground,* hanging our heads in fear" (269–270 [305–306]; emphasis added). In the context of the play, this is a posture of cowardice, out of character for Antigone. Perhaps, then, it is a sign of something else. Might Antigone avert her face from Creon to hide confusion?[15] While the sentry speaks of an earlier burial she knows nothing about, she may listen and think about how to handle the questions that will inevitably follow.

When Antigone says "I cannot deny it," is she wondering: *"Did someone else bury Polynices before I got there? But who?"* She does not know; the first she heard of that first burial, she was standing in front of the sentries, called to account for "offenses past and present" (434 [483]). Antigone has no way to find out more. She can't ask her accusers. She thought she acted alone, but now it seems perhaps there is another. She won't betray that secret supporter by calling attention to the mystery of the first burial. Nor will she lie and say she did it.[16]

More to the point, the style of the first burial is not at all in keeping with Antigone's character. Her *shout-it-from-the-rooftops* attitude is hardly in evidence in the secret nocturnal performance so quietly performed that the guards miss it.

Did someone else bury Polynices? But who? Who has motive, opportunity, and with whose character is this particular performance of the crime well-fitted? The Chorus hazards a guess to Creon: "could this possibly be the work of the gods?" (278–279 [316]). But the possibility is so thoroughly dismissed by Creon that no character in the play and few critics since dare revive it for serious consideration.[17] "Stop – before you make me choke with anger – the gods! You, you're senile, must you be insane ... Exactly when did you last see the gods celebrating traitors? Inconceivable!" (280–281, 288–289 [317–319, 326–327]). Creon is cutting: "Tell me, was it for meritorious service [that] they proceeded to bury him, prized him so?" (284–285 [321–322]). Insisting Antigone is responsible for both burials, Creon makes it unthinkable that anyone *else* – divine or human – might be responsible for the first one. If we assume, as the sentry clearly wants us to and as Creon does, that Antigone performed both

Criticism as detective fiction.
causal level

burials, then the case is neatly solved.[18] Antigone is a lone burial zealot and we need not worry, as the Chorus does, about the gods.

But there is also another possibility, less thinkable to the Chorus, and less imaginable to audiences through the ages: *what if Ismene did it?*

"keep it a secret" — if ismene did it

If Ismene did it, we no longer need to puzzle out why Antigone might have buried Polynices twice, nor why the gods would intervene. Instead, we have *two sisters, two burials*. And each is done in the characteristic style of each sister.

The first, Ismene-like, subtle, *sub rosa*, quiet, under cover of darkness, performed exactly, to a "T," as Ismene counseled Antigone to do it in the play's first scene: "Then don't, at least, blurt this out to anyone. Keep it a secret" (84–85 [98–99]). Indeed, the furtiveness of the first burial is noted in the sentry's report: "someone's just buried it, then run off" (245–246 [278]).

The second, true to Antigone ("Dear god, shout it from the rooftops . . . tell the world!" (86–87 [100–101]), is performed with loud, keening, and vengeful cries out in the open, in the noon-time sun: "the sun stood dead above our heads, a huge white ball in the noon sky, beating, blazing down," the sentry tells Creon (415–417 [460–462]).

But how can this be? Didn't Ismene express horror and shock at the thought of defying Creon? Didn't she try to dissuade Antigone from committing this very act? Didn't she opt for human over divine law? Didn't she express confidence that the dead would forgive her this very choice?

Ismene did indeed say all these things. But she said still more. At the end of their harsh and typically sororal exchange in the first scene, Ismene declares her love for Antigone.[19] Perhaps alone on stage, perhaps in her sister's silent presence, Ismene says: "Then go if you must, but rest assured, wild, irrational as you are, my sister, you are truly dear to the ones who love you" (98–99 [114–116]). How should we read these lines? How should they be performed? Historically, the lines have been taken to convey a passive declaration of unconditional but resigned love for her impossible impetuous sister. But imagine this: Ismene says the lines thoughtfully, as if a new idea is coming to her, a plan is forming: "you are truly dear to the ones who love you" is not a regretful apology, not a request for forgiveness or understanding, not an indulgent or resigned "whatever you do, we love you anyway," but a statement of still emerging resolve and a reflection on what love *calls* for. Ismene may with these words show a plan in formation,

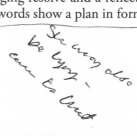

she was also can try to find

an intention to do something – to stop her sister from the rash act that will surely bring about her death. What if this suggests something has shifted in her?[20] Reflecting on her love for Antigone, confronted with her sister's intransigence, Ismene may resolve to *do* something about it.

If she buried Polynices first, before Antigone could do it, Ismene may have hoped to save her sister from her fate, to make it unnecessary for her to take on Creon and risk her life. To do this, Ismene had to go beyond her keenly felt limits. Some limits were stubborn. Just like her sister, Ismene too is unable to lift the body alone. She can only give it, at best, the ritual dusting the sentry describes to Creon. Unlike her sister, Ismene is not inclined to transgress Creon's law. She sees no honor here, only danger and reckless disobedience. So she takes the smaller risk of a stealthy nocturnal act. Still, she gives up the idea that women are "not born to contend with men," that submission is the sisters' lot (61–62 [75]). If she did bury Polynices, she did it not for political principle but for her sister, possibly for her brother, and possibly for herself as well. Although Ismene did not show it at the time, we may infer from the sentry's description of the first dusting of Polynices (as "just a light cover of road-dust . . . as if someone meant to lay the dead to rest and keep from getting cursed") (255–256 [290–292]) that Ismene may well have been unsettled to hear Antigone say that the sister, who refuses to act, will incur "the hatred of the dead, [who] by all rights, will haunt you night and day" (93–94 [108–110]). When the sentry says the dust provided was just enough to avert this fate, the hint is clear. Perhaps Ismene thought a secret nocturnal burial would be enough – just enough – to rest Polynices' soul (and, not coincidentally, a nocturnal act conforms more closely to the polis' new restrictions on funerals). Perhaps it would be enough to stop Antigone taking the risks of public transgressive action. (Was there perhaps also a tad of sibling rivalry in Ismene's doing it first? Perhaps no more than in Antigone's need to do it better – louder, more heroically.)

This reading accounts better than others for the cries emitted by Ismene when Antigone is taken prisoner (491–492 [548–549]). Ismene would mourn her sister's fate, in any case. But she would surely mourn it all the more passionately had she put herself at risk to avert it. Her cries are so loud and unsettling, Creon comments on them: "I just saw her inside, hysterical, gone to pieces. It never fails: the mind convicts itself in advance, when scoundrels are up to no good, plotting in the dark" (493–494 [549–552]). These lines are commonly taken to be more of Creon's late onset, Captain Queeg-like paranoia by readers who through the ages assume Ismene's incontrovertible innocence and passivity. But if she is not innocent, then Creon's lines may signal a quintessentially tragic stumbling on a truth just barely out of reach: his tragedy is, as he rightly senses, in the hands of plotters.

Creon shows some perhaps dim awareness of the twinned and complementary character of the two burials and the two buriers when he says, first of Ismene, that she has been "plotting in the dark" (494 [552]) and then adds, regarding Antigone: "Oh but I hate it more when a traitor, caught red-handed, tries to glorify his crimes" (495–496 [552–554]). One sister was quiet and surreptitious; the other flaunted her crime flagrantly. Accusing Ismene "of an equal part in scheming this, this burial" (489–490 [547–548]), Creon sees not just resistance but a plot, for which at this moment he intends to punish both women while distinguishing their levels of culpability in it. He is focused here on the planning or plotting (in which he believes Ismene is implicated) and the action (of Antigone), but his words work as a perfectly tragic double entendre. He could just as well be speaking of two crimes, two burials, the first performed in stealth, "in the dark," and the other, "caught red-handed," out in the open. If the sisters' guilt is "equal," as he insists, in spite of the fact that, as he says, one only planned the deed while the other carried it out, it is because Creon senses something else may be the case: their crimes though not identical are actually not that different: *two sisters, two burials.*

This is the moment at which Creon commands that Ismene, until now in this scene heard but not seen, be brought from the palace: "Bring her here!" (491 [548]). Antigone responds by frantically trying to distract him. Like someone seeking to save another from a raging bull, she waves a red flag in his face and calls his wrath upon herself: "Creon, what more do you want than my arrest and execution?" (497 [555–556]) and sure enough, he falls for it: "Nothing. Then I have it all" (498 [557]). To which Antigone, still protecting her sister by focusing the bull's enraged gaze on herself, says: "Then why delay?" That is, why wait for Ismene to be brought from the palace? And then to keep his focus, Antigone provokes him further: "Your moralizing repels me … Enough. Give me glory …" (499–502 [558–561]), she says before goading him one last time. Turning to the Chorus, she calls him a tyrant who rules by fear (505–507 [565–567]). But her effort to monopolize his wrath falls short.

"I DID IT, YES" – ISMENE SPEAKS

The question of Ismene's fate is not settled by the time she arrives on the scene. As she enters, Creon turns his attention fully to her, once again stumbling, unknowingly, on some truths: "You – in my own house, you

So why doesn't Sophocles tell us that Ismene perf. the first burial?

viper, slinking undetected, sucking my life-blood! I never knew I was breeding twin disasters, the two of you rising up against my throne. Come, tell me, will you confess your part in the crime or not? Answer me. Swear to me" (531–535 [597–603]). Having indeed slunk, undetected, to perform the first burial of Polynices, Ismene now speaks out loud: "I did it, yes – " (536 [603]).

Why has no one for hundreds of years or more taken her at her word?[21] She confessed. Not only does she not deny it, she actually owns it.

Perhaps her confession is overlooked because on other readings, which treat Ismene as a quiet passive woman who cannot think of challenging Creon's authority, this late effort to share her sister's fate seems wildly out of character. As Creon (whose perspective will subtly frame the critical reception of these scenes for centuries) said earlier, she must surely be "hysterical."

Ismene also abets those who claim she lacks agency, for no sooner has she confessed than she seems to take it back: "I did it, yes – if only she consents – I share the guilt, the consequences too" (536–537 [603–605]). Why the proviso "if only she consents"? If Ismene did do it, then why does she need Antigone's consent? If Ismene did not do it, then why does she say she did?

Most critics focus on the last question and try to account for how it is that Ismene here shows a courage that, on their readings, she earlier lacked. But focusing on the first question – why the proviso, "if only she consents"? – we may find a clue to the puzzle's solution in the play's first scene. Ismene has refused to help Antigone bury Polynices and has tried to persuade Antigone away from her course using every possible rhetorical tactic, reminding her of the ignominious fates of their father, mother, and brothers, underscoring their limitations as women and underlings dependent upon the hospitality of their uncle, and urging her sister to see her course of action is extreme. Antigone listens but is undeterred. And then, impatiently, harshly, she says, "I won't insist, no, even if you should have a change of heart, I'd never welcome you in the labor, not with me" (69–70 [82–83]). This withering rejection may still ring in Ismene's ears several scenes later. Ismene may have it in mind when she confesses her act and then seeks her sister's permission to confess. Ismene says, in effect: *I did have a change of heart. I did the labor. But because of what you said earlier, I won't confess without your consent.*[22] *Won't you welcome me in after all?*

In Creon's "will you confess your part in the crime or not?" Ismene may hear an echo of Antigone's earlier: "Are you worth your breeding, Ismene, or are you a coward for all your royal blood?" At first, Ismene seemed unable to rise to the challenge. Seemingly frozen within the binary terms of Antigone's forced choice – hero or coward? – Ismene chose inaction. But then Ismene saw her way through. She is neither-nor, a quiet actor willing to take some risks but not powerful enough to stem the tide of events. And now here, confronted with Creon's either-or, she again seeks a third way. Will she confess or not? Not for her the heroics of isolated autonomy. She will confess but in order to do so, her sister must consent.[23] And Antigone says yes, and no.

Antigone acknowledges her sister in intimate terms, extends protection to her sister, *and* refuses to allow her to confess. When Ismene earlier asked Antigone to keep her own transgressions a secret, Antigone mocked her sister, but here her gift to Ismene is the very secrecy Ismene earlier wanted (though of course she now claims not to want it; tragic belatedness is in operation here too). For Antigone has now decided. She will sacrifice herself for her sister. The sisters then argue in front of Creon about whether Ismene should share Antigone's fate. The argument is won by Antigone, who never utters her sister's name again. Antigone is often criticized for this. It is a sign of her coldness, critics say.[24] But what if the erasure of Ismene is Antigone's gift to her, the gift of survival to the sister who initially sought to survive?

"WORDS ALONE" – THE SISTERS' SECOND FIGHT

If Ismene did it, then the final scene between the two sisters takes on an incredible dramatic pathos (536–560 [604–631]). From the perspective of a sororal agonism, Antigone's accusations against Ismene operate as a double entendre that is nothing short of brilliant. Instead of a set of flat accusations leveled unlovingly to her unjustly despised sister (the dominant reading[25]), Antigone's words in this scene convey a series of complex realizations and strategies. Perhaps for the first time, it is dawning on Antigone that Ismene, now ready to share her punishment, may be the performer of the first burial, still unexplained. When Ismene says "I did it, yes," Antigone may hear her. Antigone, after all (on this reading) is the only other one present who *knows for certain that she did not herself* perform the first burial. Antigone's response to Ismene, who went beyond her limits in the first burial, is to go beyond her own limits now: Antigone affirms the path she earlier demeaned as cowardly: that of survival.[26]

When Ismene says she wants a share in the deed, and Antigone will not consent, does Antigone belittle her sister? Or does she affirm her? Butler says Antigone wants the deed for herself. But intonation is everything.

And, indeed, the same words, differently delivered, could support either possibility: the line can be said with loving regret or with sneering disdain: "No, Justice will never suffer that – not you, you were unwilling. I never brought you in" (538–539 [605–607]).

But then, surely the next lines suggest only disdain! "Who did the work? Let the dead and the god of death bear witness! *I have no love for a friend who loves in words alone*" (542–543 [610–612]; emphasis added). These words may signal heartless rejection. But there is another possibility. With these words, Antigone neutralizes Ismene's confession, calling on the gods and the dead to negate Ismene's words, "yes, I did it." Only Ismene's second phrase "if she consents" is left standing. And Antigone will not consent. The words of Ismene's confession thus cease to function as (possible) truth statements and become, by dint of Antigone's dissent, the mere empty vessels Antigone accuses them of being: words alone. Notably, Antigone's own words here are wounding, hence critics' distaste for the heroine in this scene. There is an interesting paradox here: the blunt force of Antigone's words belies her dismissal of mere words as powerless.[27]

Antigone's dramatic, indeed melodramatic speech may speak to the largeness of her character in Creon's newly small post-heroic Thebes. But it may also signal something else: a staged theatrical performance internal to the play whose addressee is not actually Ismene but rather Creon, who is himself right there. In this scene, Antigone plays out the sisters' divisions rather than their unity for Creon to witness. It is surely to him that the exculpatory "I never brought you in" (539 [607]) is addressed. It is not, after all, news to Ismene. Ismene is the one person who would know it is false. Antigone did try to bring her sister in and Ismene refused her.

When Ismene begs "Oh no, my sister, don't reject me, please, let me die beside you, consecrating the dead together" (544–545 [613–615]), Antigone responds with: "Never share my dying, don't lay claim to what you never touched" (546–547 [615–616]). We can imagine her saying these words as a cold, demeaning rejection, but we can also hear them said with great tenderness, resignation, and sacrifice. It is a delicate but not impossible line to walk, accenting the former for Creon, the latter for Ismene.

This approach is supported by the fact that when Ismene insists further on dying with Antigone, Antigone responds in a way that seems calculated to remind her sister that Creon is present. "What do I care for life, cut off from you?" (548 [618]) Ismene says, recklessly making dangerously known once again her love for her sister. And Antigone, sensing the danger, moves to bring her to her senses: "Ask Creon: Your concern is all for him" (549 [619]). Is this not a coded way of saying *pssst; he is right here*? Ismene does not completely understand yet but, sensing the change in temper, she latches onto the falseness of the charge: "Why abuse me so? It doesn't help you now" (550 [620]). She is trying to sort it out. She asks the question to herself as well, not just to Antigone. *Why does my sister talk like this if it will not help her?* It won't. But it is a good question. It helps us see that Antigone may have a different aim: to help Ismene. And this Antigone makes clear immediately: "You're right," she says, "if I mock you I get no pleasure from it, only pain" (551 [620–622]). This line is least attended to by critics and indeed cannot be made sense of by most conventional readings. Here Antigone hints broadly that her martyr's goal is now also to save Ismene, who should go on living. And it works. Ismene gives in; her next line accepts Antigone's subtle instruction: "Tell me, dear one, what can I do to help you, even now?" (552 [622–623]). Antigone's answer is straightforward: "Save yourself. I don't grudge you your survival" (553 [624]).[28] It is a gift, a shift from her earlier position when she did indeed begrudge Ismene's focus on survival. Here that focus is affirmed not mocked, though. When late in the day Antigone says, "My death will be enough" (546 [617]), it is clear the option of survival is not what it once was: Ismene is asked to go on living in the household of the man responsible for her sister's death. "Save yourself" is a rough gift indeed.[29]

These lines may convey Antigone's insistence on protecting her sister. *Don't be a fool*, she virtually whispers. (Simpson and Millar [1948] call it an "aside.")[30] *Be quiet. Let me handle this.* Then out loud she accuses her sister of being all words and no action. But methinks she doth protest too much. Why the harsh charge? She is desperate to neutralize Ismene's response to Creon. Perhaps Antigone suspects there *was* an act and not just words, in fact a wordless act, the first burial of Polynices, yet to be explained. Ismene did it. Antigone sees that but cannot say it. Creon is right there. In this sisterly exchange, the sisters reperform their quarrel from the first scene, but this time it is a theatrical performance for Creon's benefit.[31]

What does Creon know of sisters? Or of conspiracy? He falls for it, or at least the Chorus does – but are they complicit? He is softened up by the sisters' performance for the Chorus' query: "Ismene too?" they ask when Creon rages that Haemon cannot "save those two young girls from death" (769 [865]). "No, not her" he concedes (waffling like a democrat, elites like Antigone might have said) (771 [867]). Ismene will live.[32]

melodrama when she wails
& subtle when she wants

On this reading, Ismene is not, as Antigone charges, all empty words and no action. On the contrary, as the double entendres might have suggested to a knowing audience, especially one composed partly of women, Ismene's words are well earned by her quiet courageous actions: first, perhaps, the first burial of Polynices, which Antigone may now suspect and credit as a worthy act and, perhaps second, the attempt to die with her sister, also a worthy act. Antigone's too loud words are necessary to stop Ismene from confessing, to neutralize what Ismene has said, to render her actions invisible, to make it thoroughly unthinkable that quiet little spineless Ismene could ever be the one who did it, the one who first buried Polynices.[33]

The same motivation, the desire to protect Ismene, may motivate Antigone's later melodramatic cries that there is no one left to mourn her, that she is "the last of a great line of kings" (941 [1031]).[34] If she goes out of her way to diminish her sister, that is because Antigone does not know that Creon will soon crumble. She thinks he will go on ruling Thebes and Ismene must survive in his household. If he thinks Ismene is nothing, Creon may let her survive.

If Ismene did it, then, Antigone becomes much more of a tragic heroine than on other accounts, but also much less so. She is surrounded by words whose meanings exceed her grasp, enmeshed in relations she does not fully appreciate or understand. In this, she is much like Creon in this play, and like Oedipus in his, as Simon Goldhill's account of Sophoclean irony should lead us to expect. Ismene's actions also stage for Antigone the heroic scene in which Antigone, by absolving her sister, outwits Creon, as she will soon do again, with her suicide.[35] That is what Antigone does; she outwits.[36] She helps Ismene by mastering the opacity for a moment, redeploying it using *adianoeta* to save her sister in a way that makes sense of Antigone's otherwise strange claim that she was born to join in love, and ridding us of the problem, much wrestled with in the literature, that she is inconsistent: sister dutiful to Polynices but not to Ismene.[37]

If Ismene did it, then her insistence, at the end of the play's first scene, on the love she bears Antigone is significant. These are not empty words. That Antigone might have mistakenly thought so had she heard them at the time is part of Antigone's tragedy. Arrogating to herself alone the right of action, and thinking her acts alone – brazen, bold, provocative – *qualify* as action, she sees in the words of others only the emptiness of non-performance ... until nearly the end of her life. In the end, the charge sticks to Creon, who shouts and warns about consequences he ends up trying to undo, but not to Ismene. Late in the action, Antigone awakens to the truth of Ismene, suspects her action, respects her power in stealth (so different from her own), and offers her the protection that love demands, the sort that suits the recipient. Playing out a sororal enmity that is as false as it is convincing to Creon, Antigone saves her sister's life and leaves alive a remnant of the natal family.[38]

If Antigone saves Ismene, then she reminds us again of none other than Intaphrenes' wife, the woman whose words Antigone will in her next scene obliquely re-cite. As we saw in Chapter 5, Darius, having sentenced Intaphrenes and his family to death, responds to the wailing of Intaphrenes' wife by offering her the opportunity to save one relative. She chooses her brother and explains her choice with such clever reasoning that Darius is moved to "reward" her by freeing not only her brother, as asked, but also her eldest son. Re-citing the story here, Antigone toys with Creon. She cites only the part about the irreplaceable brother, but she surely calls to her audience's mind the whole of the tale. In so doing, she puts the lie to her claim in that very same dirge that she is the last remnant of the Oedipal line. For the re-cited tale calls to mind not only the saved brother but also the remnant son, reminding the audience if not the unsubtle Creon of none other than the remnant sister: Ismene.

As noted in Chapter 5, others (Weber, Dewald and Kitzinger) have pointed out that Antigone is not really like Intaphrenes' wife. The latter acted prospectively and was able to save her brother from Darius' death sentence, but Antigone's brother is already dead and all she can wrest from sovereign power (and she fails) is the right to bury him. These readers forget about the woman's son, unasked for but released by Darius to mark his pleasure at the woman's reasoning. These same readers also overlook Ismene and do not notice that, without Antigone's interventions on her sister's behalf, and without the Chorus' protestations, Ismene (regardless of her implication, or not, in the first burial) too would have been killed by Creon. Thus Antigone does act prospectively. She succeeds, no less than Intaphrenes' wife, when she saves her doomed sister. Ismene is the remnant of the remnant, the unasked for unaccounted for gift, to whom we are directed by Antigone's subtle reference to the story of Intaphrenes' wife. Darius throws in the eldest son, a dividend that exhibits the abundance of his power (and possibly his cunning). Creon, by contrast, characteristically simply gives in. Questioned by the Chorus, deceived by Antigone, and distracted by the sisters' coded conversation, Creon relents and Ismene lives.

170   *Conspiracy*

If Ismene did it, and if Antigone sacrificed herself for her sister, then we have here the story of two women partnered in their difference – one brazenly bold, the other possessed of a quieter courage – both plotting and conspiring in resistance to overreaching sovereign power but acting also in love or loyalty for each other. The sisters do not form a democratic collectivity (they may well represent the fifth-century aristocracy's views, as I argued in Chapter 4) or a feminist solidarity, per se. But – on this reading – the sisters care for each other in turn: each guesses at the other's sacrifice in quiet isolation, and each utters the lines and performs the acts that both suit and extend her character. Read in their sororal solidarity, the sisters exhibit a fuller range of virtues, character, desperation, and hope than is discernible to readers who assume Antigone acted alone, which is to say almost all of the play's readers.

disguise   If this sororal conspiracy has been almost invisible until now, that may be because readers and spectators do not admire conspiracy as a mode of action and they have trouble imagining a female agency that is agonistic-ally and solidaristically sororal and not merely subject to male exchange. And most critics internalize Creon's perspective. Even those critical of him as a tyrant share his view of Antigone as an anarchic, wild, trans-gressive flouter of law.[39] Romantic lovers of transgression may find heroism in this, liberal and left readers may see here a prefiguration of the dictates of conscience and integrity they admire, and others may disapprove of what they see as disrespect for authority and public order. But all share Creon's perspective.

Simon Goldhill is captured by it too when he notes how beholden are Antigone's feminist readers to "the myth of the heroine [Antigone, which] is constructed with all the inspirational force and selective blindness of hero worship" (2006: 160). For Goldhill, this hero worship ought to give way to an unblinking assessment of Antigone's unpalatable rejection of her sister. Feminists ignore this at their peril, he says. Goldhill is right; relinquishing our habitual reading of Antigone as heroic (solitary, autono-mous) opens the play up. What we see, however, when we do so, is not, contra Goldhill, a really unkind and unheroic Antigone that should discomfit feminists, but something else that has remained undetected for even longer: a sororal solidarity less discernible perhaps in the *logos* of the sisters' talk than in the *phonê* of their intonation; an agonistic sorority that is solidaristic, not merely subject to male exchange, infused with love, anger, rivalry, complicity, mutuality, devotion, and care. To see this, we must set aside the Creonic framing that has become hegemonic, in which heroic action alone, solitary and disruptive, counts as action.

In getting round Goldhill's call for an unblinking assessment! she has uncovered a different play,

"LET HER CHOOSE" – LACAN'S ETHICS AND/AS
FORCED CHOICE

how loose or tie the knot? (Ismene)[40]

I wonder, Sister, are you still crouching like some used, forgotten toy in a corner of his Palace? (Jina Politi)

Antigone, who says she was born to die, seems tailor-made for Jacques Lacan.[41] From Lacan's perspective, Antigone is not opposed to Creon (as Hegel says) but is rather dependent upon him. Creon provides the occasion for her to meet her antecedently formed death wish.[42] In her being-toward-death, she is able to resist the lure of choices we normally mis-take for ethical ones.[43] For Lacan, a properly ethical choice abjures the conventional "service of the goods" which orients us to mere want satisfaction, and defies the governance of ethical codes. Both are alien: the service of the goods tames our desire into feeling (wrongly) satisfied by the faux-satisfactions of endless chains of goods, while ethical codes hold us to account by principles that have nothing to do with the particular shape of our unique personality, which is betrayed by the demand for universality. Lacanian ethical action resists both of these, says Paul Allen Miller: it "is Kantian in its devotion to a pure concept of duty, but psychoanalytic in its predication on a highly individualized desire that cannot be generalized, with regard to its content, into a universalized maxim" (2007: 83).

  This approach, equally critical of both Kantianism and utilitarianism, calls to mind Bernard Williams's critique of both Kantianism and utilitarianism on behalf of an alternative ethics that is immaterial, code-defiant, and personal (in Smart and Williams [1973]). Williams too sees the tragic or forced choice as a formative and sometimes destructive choice that calls for ethics, not for goods or codes, nor for politics.[44] And Williams too sees that the tragic situation breaks the grip of the everyday. But Lacan affirms this rupture, for it forces into the forefront our own unique desire, while Williams regrets it, for it threatens to destroy us. For Williams, such moments are best avoided, for they threaten our integrity, while for Lacan, our openness to the tragic choice situation forces us beyond our mere traits to a more existence-affirming awareness.[45] Still, these two very different thinkers, one psychoanalytic, the other an acute practitioner of philosophical psychology, converge in their judgments of Antigone.[46]

  The echo to Lacan is unmistakable when Williams casts Antigone in *Shame and Necessity* as death-bound in a way that precedes and exceeds Creon's edict: "Creon's obstinacy does not simply elicit a noble response

from Antigone. It triggers a ready and massive self-assertion and the fact
that her end can mean what it does mean (and still more, what it has come
to mean) is in a sense Antigone's good luck" (1993: 86–87). Antigone was
fated to die unnaturally, in any case. Creon just gave her a reason. For
Williams, however, such self-assertion is not, as in Lacan, the rupturing
manifestation of a desire that knows no law; it is the assertion of self by a
person who is a law unto herself, as we all are or might be.

    Both thinkers focus on Antigone's uniqueness rather than her partisan-
ship, and so both stress her solitariness rather than her sorority, her massive
self-assertion rather than her sotto voce conspiracy. But Lacan's ethics
provides a way to read past that. The way is prepared by Alenka Zupančič's
elaboration of Lacan's ethics of creativity and forced choice. With this
definition of ethics, Lacan turns to Antigone, Zupančič points out. Drawing on her own and Lacan's readings of the play, Zupančič argues that
Lacan's idea of an ethics of "absolute choice" should be understood in
connection with his concept of the "forced choice," of which there are two
kinds: the first, she calls "classical," the second, "modern" (1998: 110).
Antigone is seen in relation to the classical. The modern is exemplified by
the heroine of Paul Claudel's 1911 melodrama, *The Hostage*, Sygne de
Coufontaine, also discussed by Lacan. But, as we shall see, the forced
choice labeled "modern" fits Ismene well.

    The classical "forced choice" model captures Antigone's predicament
and has a familiar structure. The example given by Lacan is "Your money
or your life," in which the two terms are asymmetrical. In Zupančič's
words: "If I choose the money, I lose both. If I choose life, I have life
without money, namely a life deprived of something." In this forced
choice, one of the two options, life, "is not simply one of two alternative
possibilities but is [also] the indispensable condition of the choice itself."
Does this mean we should choose the money, then? Not quite, says
Zupančič: "This minimal structure already allows us to deduce the ethical
figure to which it is related. It could be defined as the ability *to choose where
there is no choice*" (1998: 109–110; emphasis original).

    In other words, the impossible choice *is* possible. There is a third
term that makes it so, "something which exceeds life."[47] It can be many
things, anything that serves as an "ultimate point of identification for the
subject," as his or her "ultimate support" (Zupančič 1998: 110). Costas
Douzinas (1994) captures it when he refers to Antigone's "I-must."
Alternatively, it may be the Lacanian S1 that anchors the signifying
chain and is not itself subject to that chain's metonymic trade-offs and
translations. Or it is a principle, idea, commitment, or affiliation without

which life would no longer be what it is, without which life would no longer be worth living. It may be what Bernard Williams calls "integrity." It may "appear, for instance, as a 'point of honor' but [whatever it is] it is always something in which the subject recognizes his/her own being – something which determines the subject beyond life and death" (Zupančič 1998: 110). This is what makes sacrifice or martyrdom possible. This, for Lacan, is what Polynices is to Antigone, the one irreplaceable thing that is the ground of all else (citing Lacan 1986: 279). (On our reading thus far, Ismene could also be seen to occupy that place for her sister.)

It is essential to an ethics of forced choice that the tested subject does more than simply yield to the force of the choice.[48] Caught in the snare of the forced choice, Antigone, Zupančič argues, is not merely re-active, she is creative. No mere passive resister or civil disobedient, Antigone not only says "*no* to Creon and is willing to pay for it with her life" (that presumably would be merely to submit to the force of the choice); she creates "a new possibility there where the options seem to be exhausted" (1998: 111).[49] We might think this "new possibility" refers to her sororal solidarity, but Zupančič is not alert to that. Her Antigone is only ethical, not political, and it is because she is ethical that, when she is confronted with the forced choice that defines ethics, she not only makes the impossible choice, she does so in a way that "*forces others to choose*, confronts *them* with a forced choice" (1998: 111; emphasis original). It is not entirely clear what precisely is ethical about passing along a forced choice to others and not much detail is provided by Lacan nor by Zupančič regarding the specific elements of Antigone's ethical creativity. But Žižek is helpful here. Parsing the same point as Zupančič, Žižek says that (for him, for Lacan), "[a]n ethical act is not only beyond the reality principle ... it rather designates an intervention that changes the very coordinates of the reality principle." It "is not simply beyond the good, it redefines what counts as good." The example to which Žižek here turns is Antigone, "the standard case of civil disobedience" whose act does not simply violate positive law out of fidelity to "a more fundamental law." Her civil disobedience is "more radically performative" insofar as it "defies the predominant notion of the good" (Žižek 2000: 671–672).

There is a further case to be made for Antigone's politicality, though. Žižek and Zupančič do not make the case but Sophocles' text rewards those who return to it with their Lacanian questions in mind.[50]

When Antigone is subjected by Creon to a forced choice, she may seem simply to pick one of the options presented. For example, in response to the edict that forbids the burial of Polynices, which presents her with the forced choice – leave your brother unburied or bury him and die – does not Antigone choose the latter? So it seems, but there is evidence of creativity in the *way* Antigone conducts herself under pressure. After all there is more than one way to bury Polynices: we know that from the three very different burials given him.

Thus, the issue may not be whether or not Antigone buries Polynices: that anemic framing is Creon's *are you with me or against me* way of presenting it. The issue is *how* she does so. Antigone buries Polynices, owns her deed, and sings her final dirge seeking to frame her own and not Creon's understanding of her act for posterity. When she avows her crime, frames her actions in heroic rather than democratic terms, when she cites Herodotus' story of Intaphrenes' wife, all of these are *part of her* act and show she has not limited herself to the small question of obedience but has embraced the larger ethical or political situation and reformulated it.[51] She performs the burial of Polynices in a way that she hopes will recast the situation. She will, she tells Ismene, perform the burial heroically, publicly, and the people of Thebes, confronted with their own forced choice, will celebrate her for it (Zupančič 1998: 113).[52] Creon will come around, or not. Either way, she will have glory and the implication is that, as a result, the awful choice that staged all of this for her will lose its force henceforth. This, more than any of the traits Zupančič looks at, is Antigone's creativity, surely. Note though that her creativity here is not merely ethical; it is also political. Aiming to create "a new possibility there where the options seem to be exhausted" (Zupančič 1998: 111), Antigone makes public an act criminalized by Creon and through first plotting and then conspiracy, she solicits the support of a public possibly cowed by him, yet sympathetic to her.

These maneuvers are made in the context of other forced choices imposed on her along the way and already analyzed here, but if we return to them with Lacan's rubric in mind we can now see them in yet another new way. For example, when Antigone says "I did it; I don't deny a thing" in response to Creon's interrogation, she does so, we may now note, in response to a forced choice with which Creon confronts her. When Creon asks Antigone if she violated his edict, he has a specific way of asking. He frames this question as a forced choice that rules out any heroism: "Do you deny you did this, yes or no?" Her only choice is to deny, or not (441–442 [491]). The only affirmation on offer is that of double negation, that of non-denial. Thus, as we now see with the help of Zupančič's rubric and in addition to our earlier reading, something creative is going on when Antigone responds with "I did it, I don't deny a thing." With these words, she rejects the forced choice that seeks to limit her to (non)denial. Ignoring it, she says "I did it," and then, in case Creon fails to get the message of her reframing, she makes clear her rejection of the vernacular of denial – "I don't *deny* a thing," as in: *I don't do denial*. Thus, she not only claims responsibility for the forbidden act, she rejects his framing of her act; she rejects the double negation – non-denial – to which he tries to confine her.[53] She fastens on a more heroic affirmation of her act, something she will pick up on later when, in dialogue with the Chorus, she tries to connect her situation first to Niobe, then, in the face of the Chorus' incredulity, to Intaphrenes' wife.

And then there is the last forced choice, imposed on Antigone at the scene of her entombment: after Creon has told his soldiers to take her away and wall her up in her tomb, he adds: "Abandon her there, alone, and *let her choose* – death or a buried life with a good roof for shelter" (885–888 [973–974]; emphasis added). Once again, we might think that Antigone fails to contravene the terms of the forced choice. After all, she chooses one of the two options, death rather than buried life. But to see things this way is, again, to stay inside the forced choice framework Creon favors, and to miss the very thing he wants to obscure. Antigone finds a third way. Although she will in the end die a quick death by her own hand, she uses the moments that follow Creon's pronouncement of her "free" choice – "let her choose" – to sing the dirge for herself in which she compares herself to Intaphrenes' wife and frames her action as one of fidelity to a law of singularity mentioned here by her for the very first time.[54]

Thus, "the fact that her death can mean what it does mean" is not simply, as Williams puts it, a matter of "good luck" (1993: 86–87). It is a consequence of Antigone's creativity: she responds to the forced choice thrust upon her by constructing for herself something like the elongated beautiful death of Homer's heroes. Before her immurement in the cave, Antigone participates in the *agon* over the meaning of her actions, a privilege Creon seeks to reserve for himself when he restricts her to menus of predetermined options. He tries to economize. She is excess. When he says "take her away, you're wasting time," he diminishes her dirge as mere impotent delay – she is trying to buy time, he charges, but it won't work. Rather than grant to her, as later executioners will to their victims, the right to respond to the question: "have you any last words?" Creon mocks Antigone for her use of words. As we saw in Chapter 5, he suggests that she means to defer dying, that she does not have the true hero's taste for death. But she will put the lie to that with her suicide.

In response to her effort to frame the meaning of her act and bequeath her conspiracy to others, Creon not only mocks Antigone for her use of words. He also anticipates. After saying it is her choice how to die, he makes clear the falseness of the choice: either way, "dead or alive she will be stripped of her rights, her stranger's rights, here in the world above" (890 [976–977]). It is for these, surely, that Antigone fights in her moments of overliving – for the right to make meaning of her life, to tell her story in her own way, promoting her cause and preserving her memory.

Most receptions of the play have not risen to the lure of Antigone's creativity, staying rather within the domain of the forced choices that she seeks to transform: public versus private, male versus female, order versus anarchy. In sum, if Antigone forces a forced choice on us, we have so far managed to evade it.

Recall, however, that for Zupančič, Antigone's creativity lies specifically in her making the impossible choice in a way that "*forces others to choose*, confronts *them* with a forced choice" (1998: 111). Zupančič argues that within the frame of the play, three people are solicited by Antigone into the structure of the forced choice – Ismene, Creon, and Haemon – and all three fail. (She leaves out the public, mentioned above, though they fit her account and they fail too.) As coldly as Creon, Antigone makes the stakes clear to Ismene: we'll soon see what you're made of, she says to Ismene: "Worth your breeding, or a coward." And, Zupančič says, Ismene "makes the wrong choice (or rather she refuses to recognize that there is a choice)" (1998: 111). Or better, we might say on Zupančič's behalf (for this is not our reading), Ismene refuses to recognize that the choice is inescapable, that it has force, that it is for her, that it forces itself on her.

Faulting readers of the play from Hegel onward, Zupančič goes on forcefully to claim: this is no "solitary 'isolated' sacrifice that [Antigone] owes her brother and her gods." Instead Antigone sees her choice "as something which very much concerns others and not solely as a private act" (1998: 111). Thus, when Ismene says she is unable to help bury Polynices and expresses her fear for Antigone, Antigone responds in ethical terms: "Don't fear for me. *Set your own life in order*" (83 [97]; emphasis added).[55] She even invites Creon "to resubjectivise himself as a master, but instead Creon tried to *reaffirm* himself as the master" which, Zupančič points out, "is not at all the same thing" (1998: 111). Ismene "understands the stakes of the choice" but fails to rise to its challenge. She "panics." Creon, too, is said to "panic" (1998: 111–112). The charge rings truer in his case than in hers. Ismene is distressed in the first scene, but there is no evidence in the text of panic. And she, unlike Creon, does rise above the choice Antigone forces upon her. Ismene reformats the situation she faces though Zupančič does not see this and indeed Zupančič and Žižek both obscure Ismene's creativity by repeating the familiar lines about Ismene – gentle, normal, uninspired, cowardly – so as better to highlight, by contrast, Antigone's exemplary heroism.

Ironically, Zupančič's focus on the failure of Ismene and Creon to take up the invitations issued by Antigone reinstates the very thing Zupančič says she is trying to overcome: the idea that Antigone's is a "solitary 'isolated' sacrifice." On Zupančič's reading, Antigone may try but she never succeeds in enlisting others to her side. On the reading developed here, however, Antigone succeeds in making (contested) meaning out of her acts. And Ismene finds her own way. Burying Polynices surreptitiously, Ismene does not duck the choice, nor does she pass the forced choice on to another. She breaks its spell, choosing neither flagrant disobedience nor meek inaction. She does not consent to leave her brother unburied nor will she allow herself to be drafted into a disobedience she considers inconceivable. She does what Zupančič admires as quintessentially ethical and which I have been suggesting here is surely better understood as political insofar as it effects a re-partition of the sensible: Ismene creates "a new possibility there where the options seem to be exhausted" (1998: 111).

However, the limiting, contested binary of obedience versus dissidence reasserts itself when Ismene's act is covered over by Antigone's act – the second burial. That may be why Ismene so often disappears in the play's pages, invisibly unimportant except as a point of contrast to the heroine. The strident act renders the subtle invisible.[56] The grand gesture obscures the quiet work of conspiracy. If her aim was to save Antigone the trouble of transgression, Ismene fails. But this is not her only forced choice. In her final scene with Antigone, she faces another forced choice and here failure is not an apt term for what occurs.

"WHAT DO I CARE FOR LIFE, CUT OFF FROM YOU?" – ISMENE'S MODERNITY

And ultimately, I think that this is just what queer critique must do: use our history and presently quite creative work with pleasure, sex, and bodies to jam *whatever* looks like the inevitable. (Elizabeth Freeman; emphasis original)

Ismene's last forced choice is different in structure from the one described by Zupančič as "classical." Indeed, it bears an uncanny resemblance to the one she calls "modern." By contrast with the classical forced choice captured by *your money or your life*, the modern forced choice is captured by *freedom or death*. Here it appears that we have a choice but really we do not, since choosing freedom under threat of death is hardly a free choice. Zupančič explains, quoting Lacan: "'in the conditions in which someone says to you *freedom or death!*, the only proof of freedom that you can have in the conditions laid out before you is precisely to choose death, for there, you show that you have the freedom of choice.'" The strange thing about the structure of this choice, Zupančič says, is that "the only way you can choose A is by choosing its negation, the non-A: the only way the subject can stay true to his Cause is by betraying it, *by sacrificing to it the very thing which drives him/her to make this sacrifice*" (1998: 115; emphasis original).[57]

The example given by Lacan and analyzed by Zupančič is that of Sygne de Coufontaine, the heroine of Paul Claudel's 1911 play, *The Hostage*. Confronted with a forced choice of the modern sort, Sygne comes to realize that she cannot choose death in order to preserve her "reason for living" because death would be the easy way out and the situation (which is as contrived as most melodrama, and may be seen as a fable of the forced choices of the French aristocracy in post-revolutionary France) demands something else of her. She is asked to marry a man she detests in order to save the life of the pope she is harboring from Napoleon's forces. The man who seeks to marry her is a Jacobin named Turelure who had her aristocratic parents executed before her eyes during the Revolution and now says that if she will not marry him he will apprehend the pope. If she marries Turelure as he demands, she will save the pope but she will marry someone she detests, thus violating the sacrament of marriage, and cede to him her family's aristocratic title and land.

Sygne's first instinct is to kill herself; her second is to fight Turelure even if it means everyone in the house including the pope will be destroyed.[58] But there is something about the situation that presses Sygne further. Her family's priest, Badilon, asks her to take the hardest course of all: "[S]he is asked not to sacrifice herself for the Cause (something which she would do without hesitation), but to *betray*, to sacrifice this Cause itself, to give it up . . . " (Zupančič 1998: 115–116; emphasis original). Badilon says to Sygne as she wrestles with her decision and considers her honor, for which she is willing to sacrifice her life: it is good "to have something of one's own; for then have we something which we can give" (cited in Zupančič 1998: 116). True sacrifice calls for her to give up not her life but her reason for living. She must sacrifice and live.[59] She will marry Turelure and live as his wife to save the pope. She will be his hostage. Her deep resistance to the course she chooses manifests itself corporeally. Toward the end of the play, she is beset by a facial tic, an involuntary twitch that mimes the head-shaking gesture that normally means *no*.[60]

Zupančič argues, following Lacan, that it is only with modernity's loss of a possible faith in an afterlife and its redemption, that we get the idea that ethics may demand not the sacrifice of one's life but of one's reason for living.[61] We certainly get something like it from utilitarianism, the modern social theory that casts as moral (not ethical, per se) any action that brings about greater pleasure over pain. Early utilitarianism would surely say that Sygne must insert herself into the situation to bring about the socially preferable outcome, regardless of the individual suffering she may undergo as a result.[62] Indeed, some might argue that utilitarianism is, arguably for this reason, and notwithstanding its avowed secularism, deeply sacrificial in structure.

Against the utilitarian view, Bernard Williams (Smart and Williams 1973) argued that such sacrifices cannot be morally required, for the one thing that morality cannot ask of us is to give up who we are. Our integrity is the postulate of ethical life; it cannot be positioned as one of its calculated trade-offs. Williams recognized we are sometimes put into such situations – he had a deep appreciation of Greek tragedy – and wrote about the need to face such tragic situations with integrity. He understood that in the modern world of plural values, such tragic situations were an ineliminable feature of moral life. But he found repugnant to morality the utilitarian demand to consider our obligations in calculative and ultimately sacrificial terms. On this point, Žižek (2000) is in agreement.

For Williams, Sygne's tic would be a significant symptom, marking the regret or remorse that Williams sees as properly attending the sacrificial choice when it is made, as it may be, under duress. To be clear, then, the problem with utilitarianism, for Williams, is not its recommendation of self-sacrifice, per se, but its claim that when such sacrifice is called for (by the felicific calculus), it is the right thing to do, without remainder. Utilitarianism, Williams argues, is committed to the idea that any regret manifested by the moral agent who acts in the utilitarianly best way is irrational. In short, the problem with utilitarianism, for Williams, is its refusal to grant regret the moral salience it deserves. Utilitarians would fail to see or grant the significance of Sygne's tic.

The subject of integrity that grounds ethics and politics for Williams is for psychoanalysis a result of the subject's fortressing within layers of painful psychic defense (that enable some elements of subjectivity). In the context of Lacanian psychoanalysis, in which a great deal of what makes us who we are numbs us to the Real, the idea of giving oneself up, sacrificing our integrity, may seem promising. The goal of psychoanalysis is, after all, precisely to dis-integrate the subject. But to call this ethics is another matter and to intimate from it a politics (as contemporary Lacanians seem to want to do) is yet another matter, still.[63] We need not, however, adjudicate the questions of ethics and integrity in order to gain new interpretative insight from the structure of Zupančič's "modern" forced choice. For in Sophocles' *Antigone* there is one character who comes close – awfully and anachronistically close – to this "modern" position, the position in which "the subject is asked to accept with enjoyment the very injustice at which he is horrified," and that character is – Ismene.[64]

It is Ismene who says in the first scene, "I'm forced, I have no choice" (66 [79]) and who sees the "madness, madness" (68 [81]) of the situation. It is Ismene who is asked to remain living when she would rather die, to dwell in the household of her sister's murderer, and to depend upon the hospitality of a man who has usurped her parents' place. When she begs to be allowed to die with her sister, "What do I care for life, cut off from you?" (548 [618]; cf. 566 [639]), Ismene makes clear the difficulty of going on. But Antigone, playing Badilon to her sister's Sygne, says *no*. There is something about the situation that calls for Ismene to live. The exchange with her sister is, for Antigone, painful: "You're right," she says "if I mock you I get no pleasure from it, only pain" (551 [620–621]). That pain is not just a marker of the difficulty of acting out a feigned derision for the sister she loves. It is also recognition of the fact that Ismene, fated to live, will suffer a martyr's life no less than Antigone will suffer a martyr's death.

Thus, we see that what Zupančič maps in temporal terms, classical and modern, marks the difference between the two sisters in this classical play. Both sacrifice, both extend themselves, but one is more otherworldly and oriented to death and the other is more this-worldly and oriented to life. Both act not just ethically but also politically. They plot together, diverge, come back together, conspire, plan, and stage the scene of Antigone's final conspiracy with language. Why then are critics of all stripes unified in seeing these two women primarily as (un)ethical actors or solitary political (anti)heroes and never as partners in action in concert, never as conspirators?

Zupančič's distinction between classical and modern forced choice helps us to extricate ourselves from that sedimented reading and further to develop neglected dimensions of sorority and conspiracy in Sophocles' *Antigone* and its reception history. But, scripting the two kinds of choice in temporal terms, Zupančič oddly limits the reach of her rubric, ironically claiming periodicity at the very moment at which she proposes the promise of classics for late modernity.[65] Since her temporalization is belied by the co-incidence in the play of both kinds of forced choice, classical and modern, we could criticize her terms and simply correct them by de-temporalizing them. Or we could find in that very temporalization an invitation to anachronize the play, to see it as simultaneously classical and modern, lift it out of its timeline of so-called origin (classical) and subsequent linear (modern) reception history and conclude that *Antigone* is both more modern and (because) more classical than we thought, and vice versa.[66] The conclusion makes sense since this play, perpetually restaged and reread, has a constitutive role to play in the formation of modern continental philosophy and democratic theory since Hegel. That constitutive role has been authorized by the claim that the play is a canonical, classical text – an original – even while its recirculation in copy after copy, interpretation, and performance, secures and evidences its inexorable modernity.[67]

"ὦ κοινὸν αὐτάδελφον ἰσμήνης κάρα" – "ISMENE-HEAD"

Gemeinsamschwesterliches! (Hölderlin, *Trauerspiele des Sophokles*)[68]

In a recent paper on Ismene, Mary Rawlinson focuses on Ismene as a better model for feminist politics than her more renowned sister. Ismene privileges the world of the living, Rawlinson argues, and she looks toward the future. "Why should we feminists valorize Antigone's embrace of the dead brother over the living sister?" she asks. Rawlinson guides us to the other sister, but when she picks one to be the heroine (even if it is the other one), does she not remain captive to the hero model that Simon Goldhill says has wrongly gripped feminists until now?

Goldhill also makes the case for Ismene. Criticizing Irigaray and Butler, he argues that they allow Ismene to be shut up with the women while embracing Antigone as a model for a feminist politics based on the purity of blood (Irigaray 1985a) or on its contamination (Butler 2000). Either way, Ismene is erased by feminist readers of the play and by its heroine. When Antigone calls herself 'the last remnant of the house of your kings' (40–1), Goldhill says, "Ismene is written – spoken – out of the family line. This silencing is all too often repeated, rather than analysed, by the critics" (2006: 157).

For Goldhill, the relevant context for taking Ismene seriously is the shifting politics of the fifth century in which "[t]he general frame of the city-state, on the one hand, and the specific frame of Athenian democracy, on the other, change the structuring politics of the personal." As "key institutions of the family, like burial, and key terms of family affiliation are taken over by the State ... brothers can become a civic, political symbol," not just a familial-political one (2006: 148). From the brothers whose conflicts were central in heroic epic to the new political claim of equal citizenship as fraternity, something like Derrida's "phalloc-racy" is evident, Goldhill says, but "against the claim of fraternity, sisterhood also changes as a normative term. Sisterhood learns to speak" (2006: 148).

As we have just seen, however, by tracking the coded communications that pass between Ismene and Antigone in front of Creon, *how* sisters speak may be the more fundamental issue, not *whether* they do. (Goldhill himself takes on this phrasing in his recently published book, which includes a revised version of his essay, to which I respond in more detail below.) Goldhill provides support for this thought when he notes the odd way in which Antigone addresses her sister, in particular, the alienness of Antigone's speech in her address to her sister whom she calls, in the play's opening words, *autadelphon* ("ὦ κοινὸν αὐτάδελφον Ἰσμήνης κάρα," "Oh dear sister of the same womb, [something like] *Ismene-head*"). This may well point to the doublings of incest in this perverted family context, as Miriam Leonard points out (2005), or to the contortions to which sisters are driven by institutional tensions in a time of transition, as Goldhill persuasively argues and as I myself suggested in Chapter 4, focusing on different elements of the play than those on which he focuses. But it may also suggest another possibility worth considering: like many intimates, plotters, and conspirators, might these sisters have a private language, a coded way of speaking between themselves that eludes the understanding of outsiders? Sorority may be as untranslatable and elusive as the play's famously difficult first line.[69]

Sororal power can be belittled, of course, as Creon mocked and belittled the daughters of Oedipus. But, as the Chorus knew, sometimes powerful forces are underestimated by their belittlers.[70] These sisters may bury the brother, as Hegel required of (one of) them, but they do not only do that. Or better, in burying the brother, they also do something else. It matters that there are two of them, not just one, for as they act in agonistic concert they hint at an alternative politics, and an alternative to Hegel's dialectic. In *Skirting the Ethical* (2008), Carol Jacobs sees how Antigone must escape and exceed the negativity of the Hegelian dialectic. She does not pause to note how this excess may be rooted not in Antigone's heroic autonomy, but in her sororal conspiracy. In her individuality Antigone is, as Hegel would rightly note, fated to mere negativity and little more. In their sorority, however, the sisters' twinned negotiations of their forced choices model a tragically doomed *politics* that is, notwithstanding its tragic character or perhaps even because of that, a more serious force and a more powerful example to feminists now than the individual and sacrificial politics of conscience for which Antigone is traditionally celebrated even by radical feminists. I have argued elsewhere that statist law and politics ascribe dissidence to individual actors where there are in fact networks and concerted actions doing the work of politics (2006). It is ironic that feminists who often seek to stake out anti-statist politics fall into the habit of seeing like a state in their receptions of Antigone, often missing the concerted, solidaristic action and celebrating the lone hero (who may, however, as Irigaray insists, long for connection). Such misreadings are shaped by conflations of heroic agency with agency as such and are enabled by Creon's perspective, which so many readers of the play unconsciously adopt, rather than interrupt. They further are misled by a failure fully to apprehend the politics of agonism, in which not only struggle and rivalry but also mutual respect and equality – even care – are characteristic elements.[71]

The move to mark the sororal agency in this play should not be mistaken for a normative effort to promote sorority as a privileged site of agency.[72] It is rather an effort to exhibit the benefits of a more agonistic, conspiratorial, and political (that is, less moralistic, less heroic, less senti-mental) approach to the texts and contexts of classics and politics on behalf of the plural and surprising sites of agency we may find. That we find here an agonistic sorority is not reason to privilege sorority as a site of agency everywhere, as some feminists might argue. Indeed, it is necessary to enter a still further caution by way of conclusion: the move to sorority, contra Goldhill, may turn out only to restage rather than interrupt the fraternity or phallocracy we seek to contest. The sisters are sisters, after all, by virtue of the Oedipal contract, which claims kinship is prior to politics even while it mobilizes one form of juridically secured kinship against others not so favored. This suggests we may not be able to break the spell of Oedipus or phallocracy simply by moving to sisters rather than brothers. This is what Peggy Phelan means when she notes that Antigone and Ismene are "cast firmly in an Oedipal tragedy" in which the "desire two women feel for each other" can only appear as "sororal love" (1997: 16). Embedded in the "Law of the Social," Phelan argues, sisterhood is not enough. But surely it is a start. Or at least it is what we encounter here, when the form it takes is one of agonistic mutuality, pleasure, care, rage, cooperation, and rivalry, and not simply, as Phelan herself assumes, along with almost everyone else, a "speedy abandonment" of one sister by the other (1997: 15). Phelan attributes that abandonment to "a Sophoclean Oedipal blindness" that renders "the allegiance that might pass between women" unimaginable.

She hopes the play nonetheless "suggests, while not realizing, another way to play this drama," one that may "point to a different form of theater sisters might one day invent . . . a new theater of desire" (1997: 15–16).[73] My aim here has been to highlight the ways in which this theater has always already been invented, by conspiring sisters who perform it, or by the tragedian who (re)invented them, or by the language that took charge of them, and to suggest that the failure thus far to see this promise with*in* Sophocles' great tragedy is a fault not just of the play but of our own reading and spectating practices.[74]

ADIANOETA AND THE IRONIES OF RECEPTION

Words often understand themselves better than do those who are using them. (Schlegel, quoted in Goldhill)

Simon Goldhill has recently responded to my criticisms of his 2006 essay with his own critique of mine on Ismene and so I end this chapter with a response to his just-released *Sophocles and the Language of Tragedy* (2012), which attends to linguistic structures, rhetorical figures, and reception contexts in its readings of tragic drama. In his book, Goldhill shifts his attention from his own earlier essay's emphasis on sorority, as such, to call for more of a focus on sorority's varied and vexed workings, in the play, in feminist politics, and in the world at large. Responding to my reading of sorority in the play, charging that it is anachronistic and willful, Goldhill positions himself in this most recent book somewhere between those feminists who ignore Ismene entirely (Irigaray and Butler, blinded by "hero worship" for Antigone [246]), and myself, whom he charges with overemphasizing sorority in a "drastic redrafting of Sophocles' play," which features "a new image of sisters who despite their bitter arguments really love each other" (247).

While in his earlier version of this argument, to which I responded above, Goldhill emphasized contra Butler and others that it is important to bring Ismene in so that at last "sisterhood learns to speak," here, in his book's revised version of that argument, he emphasizes, as I did earlier as well, that "it is worth our while to look carefully at *how* sisterhood learns to speak" (248; emphasis added). The "tragic myth of Antigone" (but no longer the play?), Goldhill goes on, "offers a profound way of thinking about myth and feminism productively through a critical gaze at the politics of sisterhood." A critical gaze is called for because invocations of sorority tend to exclude others along established lines of (racial, class, geographic) privilege.[75] I agree. This is one of the reasons I cautioned against mistaking a reading of sorority in Sophocles for a normative promotion of this sort of relation for feminism.[76] There was also another reason for caution against such idealization: sorority's dependence on the patriarchal, Oedipal contract.

But let us return to the play from the tragic myth, for it is the play that has been harnessed to, and in turn licences so many of, the basic questions and assumptions of continental philosophy and contemporary feminist theory. At stake for Goldhill, it seems to me, in his own reading of the play, is his central claim that Antigone is isolated and unable or unwilling to enter into collective relationships. Perhaps most striking in his account are the parallels, unthematized by him, between his reading of Antigone's relationship with the Chorus and her relationship with Ismene. The Chorus responds to the hero, who confronts us with the problem of "excessive commitment," by trying "to assimilate, comprehend, negotiate with excessive, demanding, transgressive individuals," says Goldhill, and thus the Chorus was "good for Athenians to think with, politically" (132–133). Writing about Antigone's *kommos* with the Chorus, he sees the Chorus' "flowing relationship" with her, by turns consoling and condemning. But he focuses solely on their many moments of divergence and not at all (as I have done here, in Chapter 5) on their one moment of convergence. He underlines the Chorus' failure finally to reintegrate Antigone into the social order (132). She resists them and stands alone, he says.

Similarly, he notes how Antigone's relationship with her sister is one of pairing and separation, emblematized by *lusis*. He notes that in the play Antigone twice uses the word *non* in her initial exchanges with Ismene "to bring the sisters together" (32) – (Ismene also uses the term at line 50 to talk about "our" father) – but that the sisters' closeness soon falls apart. He sees in Sophocles' staging of the sisters a "difficult and unresolved claim of sisterhood." Difficult and unresolved because Ismene speaks but Antigone, typically, does not listen. In their final scene together, we hear the "language of communality claimed [Ismene] and denied [Antigone]" (241). In the play's first scene, Antigone and Ismene disagree and their eventual separation is prefigured, "anticipated in a fascinating habit of Antigone's language. She never uses a first-person plural verb to refer to herself and another person," Goldhill says (31). Antigone uses linguistic forms that stress her isolation from others – not "ours," but "yours and mine," and this, he argues, "constantly anticipates the separation of the sisters away from a 'we' into a contrasting 'you' and 'I'" (32).[77] In her exchanges with Ismene, Antigone confines herself to what we might (taking a cue from Michael Oakeshott [1991]) call collecteds (which are summative, you and I) rather than collectives (which are more organic, we).

This insight regarding Antigone's language is valuable but how should we read it? If we think beyond Antigone's own conspiracies with language and attend rather to how language conspires with her (and with us), we may speculate that, although she never says "we," she may nonetheless act out of a desire to do so. That is, the desire for a "we" may inspirit her "you" and "I"; or it may not. This is one question with which to return to the text. There are others, as well. The challenge is to attend to her language while resisting the nominalism that often results from such attention. And so when Goldhill charts Antigone's linguistic habits, he invites us to ask: does her use of "you" and "I" testify to her inability to join up with others, and signal her final, isolated fate? Or is it a marker of the social situation that intervenes repeatedly into her efforts to join up, and interrupts her desire to do so? In what sort of mood, with what sort of affect does she say "you" and "I"? Tenderly? Resignedly? Brashly? Confrontationally? Sarcastically? Might the terms "you" and "I" mean more than one thing at once? Might they point not only to division, but also to other forms of commonality or sorority that are different from Ismene's model? Might "you" and "I" undergo some sort of transformation over the course of the play, beginning as markers of sororal differentiation, then operating as markers of an enacted union, perhaps even with their plural, signifying power bringing the sisters *in*to a union they (and the audience) never sought nor thought possible? When in the end one sister dies and the other survives, might each nonetheless be transformed precisely by the "you" and "I" whose plural powers go missing when Goldhill reads it as a univocal linguistic marker?

In Antigone's sorority with Ismene, Goldhill sees a progressive deterioration from would-be union to isolation and estrangement. Ismene recognizes "that she and her sister are a pair ["now we are two"] – the dual again," but, says Goldhill, this "is part of an ominous narrative of paired destruction." It may be. But it may also – at the same time – be part of a narrative of agonistic sorority in which the sisters work through their collected versus collective self-understandings, two or more different kinds of joining, by quarreling with and providing cover for each other. When Ismene disappears and Antigone dies, this may signal division, again. Or not: on my reading, it is possible that Antigone dies not just for Polynices' sake but also for Ismene's. And this reading may have force whether or not Antigone understands herself in this way, as a martyr. That is, there is evidence for it in the sisters' situation, and in the language and the speech acts that work their way through them.

This seems to fit rather well with Goldhill's own innovative characterization of Sophoclean irony. Earlier in his book, he says such irony is different from the traditional, reassuring sort of irony where the audience securely knows something about the significance of an actor's words, about which the actor himself is ignorant. Instead, Goldhill finds in Sophocles a "flickering irony," a kind of irony that implicates the audience in the doubts and uncertainties and fissures of tragic language and leaves "the reader in a far more uncomfortable position than the strong model of dramatic irony presupposes" (27; cf. 250–254). Goldhill chooses *lusis* to illustrate this point, while I focus on other key moments in Sophocles' text, but Antigone's "you" and "I," ironically, seems to provide us with a common stage on which to think together about these issues. Perhaps another way to make clear the differences between our approaches is to pose the question like this: through what figure should we read this "you" and "I"? Goldhill reads these lines through the figure of irony (which he recasts innovatively); I have proposed not just irony but also *adianoeta*, which, as I noted earlier with James Martel, means "that various members of an audience [and later readers and critics] will understand the same words differently" (2011: 98). (This fits as well with Froma Zeitlin's point about tragedy and discrepant awareness, also noted above, though it is more subversive, less tethered than on her account to the city's pedagogic purposes.)

I think the readings I develop in this book, because they are attuned to *adianoeta*, are also more attuned to the sort of irony Goldhill theorizes in his book and could therefore be seen for the most part to support Goldhill's own position. Why does Goldhill not see this? In my view, it is because he insists too strongly on the singular meanings of the terms he traces. But it may also be my fault: it may well be because I present the reading of the sisters' sorority in what may seem to be a rather intentionalist frame, as if Antigone is fully in charge of her words (if not of their impact) and is finally victorious in a traditionally tragic sort of way. It may seem that I am claiming here that Antigone is quite deliberate when she puns, mimics, and parodies her way through her dirge, for example, or speaks sotto voce to Ismene (and to the audience, and the guards, and the Chorus) in Creon's presence. But this is not and need not be the case. This may be Sophocles or even language itself conspiring through her. (As I suggested at the end of Chapter 4, many possible and even conflicting conspiracies are arguably discernible in the play.) There is no reason to assume that Antigone's various speech acts are hers in some authorial or intentional sense at all. If I have in my readings attributed to her a variety of possible motivations, hidden thoughts, and strategies, that is because reimagining the play this way seemed to help make room for new readings that might rival older, more established ones.

More to the point, as I suggested throughout, Antigone may be engaged in the various efforts I attribute to her while nonetheless saying more (or less!) than she is aware of at each moment. For example, she may reach for Intaphrenes' wife blindly, without full awareness of what it will mean to recirculate that story in her own context. Or, as I suggested in Chapter 5, Sophocles may put that story there, in her mouth, as it were. Or, as we also saw earlier, when Antigone moans and laments, she may call to mind Ajax, but this need not be seen as a choice of hers, nor as a reference. This is language (and even the non-linguistic world of sound and cry) conspiring with her, working through her, even with and against her – agonistically. For this reason, I have insisted that Antigone (and Sophocles as well!) conspires with language *and* that it conspires with her (and with him). Hence too my alert to readers at the beginning of the chapter and article on Ismene: "The emergent interpretation is promoted assertively in order to establish its viability against the likely incredulity of readers, but of course this reading is, like all readings, partial and contestable" (cf. 152 above; Honig 2011a: 31).

Goldhill wants to argue that even though Antigone "famously claims" that she was born "'to join together in mutual bonds of duty and obliga-tion' rather than to 'join together in hatred,'" this is ironically undermined by her linguistic utterances in the rest of the play because "joining together with others, ironically enough, is exactly what she finds hardest to do" (2012: 32). The audience is not "in" on the joke but is, rather, vulnerable to it, just as she is made vulnerable to it, as well, by her apparent lack of self-awareness. My own reading suggests a different irony – in which the audience (as Goldhill wants) is once again not "in" on the right or real meanings of what is said, but in which, contra Goldhill, Antigone's commitment to joining together with others is *not* so thoroughly under-mined. It is subtly at work throughout the play, inconsistently, and it is always an object of struggle for her. But if we attend to it, we may see that it is possible that she is, in her second scene with Ismene, returned to joining rather than division. In this scene, the irony is in the situation which compels Antigone to distance herself from her sister at a moment of great closeness (in ways that find precedent, as already mentioned, in Penelope's and Odysseus' *ad.anoeta*).

There is no shortage of ironies here: Antigone, who began demanding flagrant disobedience, ends with sotto voce conspiracy, first in her scene with Ismene and then in her dirge for herself. The voce is so sotto that, though its speaker succeeds in one respect, she fails in the other: Ismene does live, but Antigone does not secure her own *kleos*. The story as she wants it told is not told. Or, put less intentionally, her story as it might have been told is not told. Her martyrdom has for centuries been assumed to be obviously for her dead brother and not for her living sister. Her effort to frame her act with reference to the story of Intaphrenes' wife has been dismissed as offensive and inauthentic. Her devotion to life disappears beneath her devotion to death, and her quest for sovereignty disappears as well. There is irony too in the fact that Antigone's agency, powerful if also thwarted, is virtually unsuspected and that the argument for it even seems "cheap," as Goldhill says.

The charge of cheapness is linked to that of anachronism and the value of the classical is raised by way of the contrast with mass-mediated modernity. When Goldhill says that the idea suggested here, that the sisters have an intimacy that subtends or exceeds or grows out of their conflicts, is the product of a familiar "Hollywood family cliché," he not only reinstalls a distinction between high and low culture that this project seeks, with Benjamin's help, to attenuate. He also inexplicably attributes to Hollywood a cliché that was certainly at home in the fifth century. The Muses and Erinyes were sisters, and since the Erinyes were sisters in vengeance, they already modeled sororal vengeance in concert.[78]

A final irony is this: when Goldhill calls mine "an extra-ordinary act of willful reading against the grain," he uses a term – willful – that Sara Ahmed has claimed recently as a cardinal feminist virtue (2010). I do not want, with this observation, to risk sliding from irony into political correctness. Goldhill sets the standard in Sophocles scholarship. As my various citations to him above make clear, I am indebted to his work, and where we disagree, he is always "good to think with." Let me end, then, with one final expression of that debt. Goldhill is right: the reading presented here *is* willful – pressing its case forward against other rivals, trying to make room for itself, amassing the evidence, seeking to reach beyond the established structures and figures of language, pluralizing them and the genres of reception. I cannot resist noting, however, with what I take to be Goldhill-inflected Sophoclean irony, that it is a bit unclear whether it is me or the reading that he calls willful. Either way, it is certainly fair to say that it may well be that Antigone has had her effect on me, too.

Conclusion

Every reading of a classic is in fact a rereading.

Italo Calvino

Does my reading of Sophocles' *Antigone* alter our understanding of the canonical source in order to make it user-friendly to late-modern readers and spectators, as Slavoj Žižek might worry? Žižek articulates this concern in discussing law rather than canonical texts, but the point can be extended: "[W]hen we change legal norms [or canonical texts] to accommodate them to the new demands of reality . . . we a priori deprive the law [or canonicity] of its dignity because we treat legal norms [canonical texts] in a utilitarian way" (2000: 673). That may be. But sometimes, rather than instrumentalize the law or the text, we may find alternatives or nuances that testify not to our contemporary partialities and insistences but to those of prior receptions. From what perspective could we know that our newest readings are mere easy-going accommodations and earlier ones more rigorous and authentic? The received *Antigone*, in which sisters are split and the paternal law may stumble but carries on, may itself be an example of an earlier, reassuring reading in need of a certain less reassuring overcoming. Our new readings may not be "self-confirmation[s]" (Goldhill 2012: 247) but rather the hard-earned products of new perspectives, alien genres, and innovative interpretative resources. We may even think of Sophocles' text as poised for self-overcoming. Why should we assume that the strict paternal reading (of the law, or the text) is the one with fidelity to the original text or the Real, while the seemingly more capacious one, the conspiratorial or the sororal one, say, is the product of "retroactive rewriting"? As I have tried to suggest throughout, the reverse might just as well be true. Or, better, new readings may seem to exemplify new demands of reality but need not be left there; they may just as well expose old demands of reality, as exemplified by prior readings.

Still, Žižek provides classical reception studies with a valuable warning. When he says of the law, not of classics, that the "total availability of the past for a subsequent retroactive rewriting" erases "not primarily the hard facts, but the Real of a traumatic encounter whose structuring role in the subject's psychic economy forever resists its symbolic rewriting" (2000: 676), he invites some reflection on the scene of classical reception. The contemporary focus on the reception, interpretation, rewriting, or restaging of classical texts tends to treat those texts as endlessly malleable, not as also resistant to their receptions. And yet sometimes the texts exceed and resist the demands of their interpreters.[1] When the texts (or other survivals) are recalcitrant, when we encounter their remainders, when they accost us with their alienness, the interpretative encounter may be less hermeneutic and more traumatic. The result may be a rift in thought or an opening in conceptualization, or a heretofore unconscious investment may be brought to the fore. It is because they have such powers that classical materials and their reception are of more than antiquarian interest to us. It is in part because Antigone has such powers that we cannot just dispense with her or Sophocles' play but must instead rework the play and the palimpsests of reception that frame, secure, and limit our Antigonean inheritances.[2] In the context of centuries of reception that cannot be undone it is, in my view, a necessary and potentially radical thing (and not just a conservative one) to return to the text, even while acknowledging the impossibility of doing so (i.e. we can access the text only as heirs of Hegel, Nietzsche, Lacan, and others, even – or perhaps I should say especially – if we have not read them).

Conspiring with the text (and its context and its reception history), I have argued for an Antigone who not only resists but also quests for sovereignty, who is oriented to life not primarily to death, who acts on behalf of both singularity and equality, sometimes in concert with others, plotting, conspiring, and navigating her way through *logos* and *phonê*, mimicry, parody, and double entendre, which also work their way through her. This Antigone gives expression to a certain aristocratic recalcitrance in the fifth century, but she may nonetheless be important to democratic politics and culture now. In Chapters 1 and 2, I tracked the Antigone-effect, the slide – evident in various modern and contemporary Antigonean turns – from a conflict-centered reading of the play to a mourning-centered one and asked whether the received Antigone, since Hegel, might not exert a certain gravitational pull in the direction of lamentation-centered ethics or politics.[3] True, Hegel's own reading of the play resists that pull and is focused on the play's (supposedly single) central conflict, personified by Creon versus Antigone. But the slide to mourning as the new humanist universal is nonetheless an extension – perhaps even a correction – of Hegel's reading.

Hegel identifies Antigone exclusively with a private lamentation rooted in a gendered household powerful enough to undermine both the polis and the post-polis state form that will, for Hegel, later embody universality. Since Hegel, however, others influenced by him accept his account but revalue it. They welcome the pull to the lamentation he worried about, finding in it (something like) the universality he sought elsewhere. Underlining the partiality of the state's perspective, they cast lamentation as the new universal. In universal mourning, we – all slaves, no masters – confront our finitude in ways that constitute us as ethico-political subjects of equality. In these post-Hegelian receptions, Antigonean lamentations become the universal against which both private and public chafe. Indeed, many today find in lamentation a truer, more humanist universal than any identified by Hegel: we relate variously to Hegelian rationality but, it is said, as mortals we all mourn for others and ourselves.

Against such mortalist humanisms, identified with Loraux, Butler, and White in Chapter 1, I argued there and in Part II's Chapters 4, 5, and 6 that those who find in lamentation an extra-political resource obscure what is actually, for political theory, more productively viewed as a fractured and contested set of practices, one instructive instance of which are the politics of mourning and funerary practice in the fifth century. In Chapter 4, I tracked the fifth-century *agon* between two kinds of death practice, and assessed shifting aristocratic and democratic political implications of each one, then and now. I noted that Antigone's laments are in no way private, as such. They stand for and belong to aristocratic practices marginalized in the fifth century and recast as private in opposition to new forms of publicness generated by the fifth-century democracy. I situated this reading in the context, then and now, of invocations of emergency politics, in which renewed efforts are made to delineate the inside and outside of political community. Death ritual serves as an occasion of such delineation and its contestation opens up the ways in which the politics of burial are the politics of community life itself. In Sophocles' tragedy, a community in transition incapable of policing its boundaries is bedeviled by an incestuous family line that will not be kept in or out.

But the play exceeds its emergency setting. How to bury Polynices is the central question for Sophocles' title character, but it need not be seen as the central question for the play's audience and readers. Instead the central questions for us, surely, are: how should we bury Polynices, Antigone,

Eurydice, Eteocles, and Haemon? And what are we doing when we do that? That is, rather than staging the question of how should the polis treat a traitor, Sophocles' *Antigone* can be seen to ask: how should the polis treat others (from traitor to polis hero, from dissident resister to mourning mother) in life and in death?

In Chapter 5, I suggested the divide between Creon and Antigone might also involve tensions between *phonê* and *logos*, thematized in the period in Herodotus' *Histories*, cited (possibly *avant la lettre*, as it were) by Antigone in her final dirge, which conspires with language to mount a critique of Creon in his very presence. Those who associate women's laments with the sound and cry of pain miss this critical dimension of lamentation. I went on to ask after the gender politics of identifying Antigone's power with either the *phonê* (Irigaray, Cavarero) or the *logos* (Jebb, Goethe) of lamentation, noting that each is enlisted by these thinkers to undergird a humanism (phonocentric and logocentric, respectively) of pain or reason whose universalism is classicism's postulated premise and product. And I argued that each is always already inspirited, interrupted by the other. I suggested that Antigone's two laws, of equality and singularity, and her seemingly impossible simultaneous commitment to both might – even in their seeming impossibility – inform a democratic theory project that seeks not to interrupt one with the other (for example, by prioritizing *logos* over *phonê* or vice versa), but rather (borrowing Jacques Rancière's terms) to "work the interval" between them. And throughout, I have noted the importance to the play – and to agonistic humanism, more generally – of themes of *thumos*, pleasure, and eroticism, not just hunger, loss, and death.

In Chapter 6, I pursued traces of other seemingly impossible simultaneous commitments and found evidence in the play of conspiratorial concerted action that has long been overlooked. This may even be the "intrigue" that Hegel identified as women's way of suborning the state's proper universality. But intrigue has different, less pejorative connotations in the context of Benjaminian conspiracy with language. I suggested that our failure to consider these conspiratorial dimensions of the play until now may be due, at least in part, to the philosophic and genre expectations we bring to the play, what Noël Carroll, writing in the context of film theory, calls our "criterial prefocus" (1999: 35). Tragedy orients readers and viewers to individuated heroes, motivated by principle or conscience, who act out a singular dissidence or suffer stalwartly and in isolation what is doled out by the gods. Our eyes are trained further in these directions by post-classical Christian ideas of martyrdom and self-sacrifice, and by modern philosophic and liberal assumptions about subjectivity and politics that privilege heroes of conscience over (what Jason Frank calls) the democratic sublime's action in concert (2010).

In arguing for a new Antigone who might interrupt the received ones, a certain irony has become apparent to me: over fifty years' worth of readings of a text we take to be radical, a text often taken as a founding text of radicalism, are culturally or aesthetically rather conservative. And a new possibility has emerged: an alternative Antigone who may interrupt our contemporary assumptions that radical politics is limited to dissidence or lamentation. This new Antigone does not only protest and mourn sovereignty's excesses. She also plots and conspires; she quests for power and seeks to infiltrate and claim sovereignty.

Antigone's inescapable impact on democratic theory and practice in the late twentieth century and since (and here I refer to both the exemplary character and to the play) means we cannot rework fundamental assumptions about agency, law, and politics without interrupting dominant receptions of the play. This has been one of this book's driving motivations. But it may not be enough to recraft or reinterpret Antigone, as I have done here, using historical, literary, and interpretative approaches. It may be that such recraftings necessarily involve re-emplotment and genre-bending, as well. Indeed, it is arguably through genre-bending that I have got this far. Surely one way to describe the new readings offered here is to say that I have enlisted the criterial prefocus of genres other than tragedy to illuminate Sophocles' *Antigone*. These include detectival mystery, comedy, and *Trauerspiel*, and most of all, melodrama, the genre of plot, conspiracy, paranoia, and embodiment.

"The trauma that is summarized in *Antigone*," Jacques Rancière says (with not a little melodrama), "is without beginning or end" and so, on behalf of a more emancipatory conception of politics, he recommends a return to Oedipus and away from Antigone (2006a: 5).[4] Rancière is in effect recommending a return to tragedy as conflict and away from tragedy as suffering (and as we saw in the Introduction to Part II, that distinction, Elizabeth Craik suggests, slips easily into a genred distinction between tragedy and melodrama). Some might argue that the readings of *Antigone* developed here have done precisely what Rancière calls for, maintaining a focus on conflicts and coalitions rather than on suffering and solitude. But that is imprecise. In fact, the readings developed here challenge this binary by refusing to cede lamentation to the humanists who see in shared suffering a new universalism that might (in place of the previous, now discredited, contender, reason) help them to bypass or overcome some of our most intractable conflicts. Instead, I have argued that lamentation (no less than reason!) is itself an essentially contested and politicized practice. This is the case in fifth-century Athens, where lamentation is split along class lines. And it is more generally the case that lamentation provides a vernacular hospitable to all kinds of arguments, communications, expressions, and affects. Its position now as a humanist universal is an (always contestable) achievement underpinned, ironically, by a play that belies it.

I have in Part II of this book tried to deconstruct the action versus mourning binary without allowing the former simply to collapse into the latter (such that action becomes mourning). Approaching the *Antigone* through the genres, figures, and tropes of conspiracy, especially melodrama, we have been oriented not just to Antigone's (singular heroic) "act" as Lacanians and most others are, but to her various acts, which are several and distinct. In Chapter 4, I looked at her burial of Polynices, an open act of civil disobedience that includes her effort to bring her sister in on the act, and her confession and *agon* with Creon when she is brought before him. Here Antigone fits quite well the conventional heroic model of action. These scenes provide the prism through which she is mostly read today, as an actor who wants "her speech act to be radically and comprehensively public" (Butler 2000: 28) just like Creon's. But, it is important to note, even here things are more complex than that: these acts begin not with public speech but rather with the whispered plotting of two sisters in the dark.

Why privilege the public act over the private communication, the broad daylit performance over the stealth of moves made in the dark? Democratic theory has long had a preference for the former over the latter, as James Martel also points out, but we need not recommit to that. Doing so, we miss out on the stealth dimensions of even public acts. Seeing their stridency but missing their subtlety, we may miss their conspiratorial nature, their double entendres, and more. Worried about conspiracy, we miss its openness: *adianoeta* is the figure of the open secret, after all, the sort that everyone knows, even if no one acknowledges it openly. The open secret has the power to generate new modes of being and alter existing realities. It is from the standpoint of the enlightened public sphere of deliberative democracy that plotting and conspiracy are demoted. But we may press against that hierarchy and pluralize the registers of political engagement that "count" so that the public sphere model is just one of many modes of publicness, rather than the reigning one that sets the standard for all the others.[5]

Open to all this, we saw a new covertness in Antigone's dirge for herself, in Chapter 5. As she sings her dirge for herself, she conspires with language (just as it may conspire with her). Her double entendre, pun, and parody speak over Creon's head and appeal to a public that may exist or may yet come into existence in response to her. This is not a "comprehensively public" speech act. *Adianoeta* is at work here and it is selective: some will pick up on Antigone's most radical meanings, others will not. Some will respond, others will not.

Finally, in Chapter 6, we looked in detail at Antigone's scenes with Ismene (which in the play precede the dirge that is the focus of Chapter 5) and here we saw conspiracy of a different sort. From the plotting of the play's first scene, the women have moved on to conspiring together. They air and settle their differences, they do not further aggravate them. Here there is double entendre, as there will be in her later dirge for herself, but in the scene with Ismene, Antigone's adianoetic words are uttered sotto voce. This may, ironically, read as Antigone getting more conventional – more feminine, less in-your-face, less radically public – but I argue that she is better seen, beyond this binary, as conspiring. It may sometimes be hard to tell the difference between these two, between conspiracy and the feminine, or between conspiracy and the weapons of the weak, but the fact that Antigone moves in the time of the play from her first conflict with her sister to this sotto voce conspiracy with her to an out loud conspiracy with language in the later dirge for herself suggests a trajectory from plotting to conspiracy to conspiracy with language that highlights the politicality of all three tactics. Through it all, Antigone, on this reading, learns persuasion – in her second scene with Ismene, Antigone succeeds in bringing her sister around to her own views – and she graduates, as it were, from plotting to sororal conspiracy to a more ambitious conspiracy to constitute new publics (or reconstitute old ones). If we recur to the chapters of Part I, thinking of them as a template of sorts for the later ones in Part II, we may see this graduation as emblematic of that other step called for here: from a politics of *lamentation* to a *politics* of lamentation, and more: from sentimental maternalism and mortalist humanism to agonistic humanism.[6]

About the Cover Image

Girl Sitting in the Attic Doorway (1995) is a Lucian Freud painting of Nicola Bateman around the time that her husband, Leigh Bowery, died of AIDS. The image on the cover of this book is a photograph of that painting sitting on Freud's easel, with the woman posing for the painting visible in the upper right corner of the photograph.

The photograph, by Bruce Bernard, is of the scene of painting. Depicting the painting *and* its subject, the picture highlights the differences between them, accenting the interpretative powers of the painter, and seeming to let the photograph speak for itself. (This is the conceit of photography.) The painter's easel, visible in the photo, calls attention to the painterliness of the lower painted image, by contrast with the photographed image of the painting's model in the upper corner. Enacting a reception of Freud's work, depicting a woman in mourning, reflecting on the powers of media and representation, trafficking in tropes of doubling and, ironically, instancing the legacies of father/son or intergenerational inheritance (Lucian Freud is a grandson of Sigmund Freud, the so-called "father" of psychoanalysis), Bernard's photograph connects, almost uncannily, with many of this book's central themes.

It also raises some questions. Bernard's depiction of the painted image and its model, one quite old, the other quite young, may well lead viewers to wonder what Freud was doing here. Is this how he saw the subject of his painting? How could his vision be at such a distance from ours? And from the reality of the photograph? Where is Freud's renowned realism?

Readers of this book, though, may recall Peter Brooks' claim that melodrama as a genre externalizes inner states of violence or feeling. His claim comes to my mind when I look at the Bernard photograph, and it helps make clear that Freud's *Girl Sitting in the Attic Doorway* is a painting not of the subject but of her grief. Much as his grandfather pressed past the surface of subjectivity to find the affective and moral truths of a person well beneath the surface, so Lucian Freud puts Bateman's bereavement onto the embodied surface of this still young woman, making her mournful loss visible, inviting us to see her suffering in its embodied form. The woman's grief is exhibited in the weight and age borne by her painted image, which appears to be twenty years or more older than the woman sitting for the portrait. The live model is young and vibrant, if somewhat sad. The painted woman, by contrast, is worn. This is what has become of her, what will become of her, as she bears life's sorrows, Freud seems to say. (Perhaps the attic here is the very one that once hid the portrait of Dorian Gray?)

But, making her an older woman, Freud does not only express her inner feeling. He also thereby corrects one aspect of the injustice she suffers. She is too young to be a widow. By aging her, we may say, Freud indulges in a kind of wish fulfillment: this is how old she should be before experiencing such loss. In afflicting the young, as it so often does, AIDS violates the proper order of life and death. If, as Douglas Crimp argues, art cannot redeem this, perhaps, Lucian Freud seems to say, it can correct it.

Freud's painting starts the book off where we begin, with its focus on the mourning woman and associated themes and imagery: the blackness of the attic doorway is cavelike, tomblike, and the woman can be seen, Antigone-like, to be retreating into that dark space, or – perhaps – emerging from it. Either way, the *mise en scène* is one of confinement, and this evokes tragedy, melodrama, the gender of mourning and its representation, the injustices of AIDS.

Bernard's photograph of Freud's painting and its model takes us in the direction we want to go. Bernard does not only contextualize the painting, he also restages Freud's work and creates an art object of his own, one that does not only mourn, but also interrupts and conspires with Freud's painting while suggesting further possibilities of interruption and conspiracy as well. Depicting two women, not one, synchronically young and old, the photograph hints at a possible alliance between them. Viewers of the photograph may see here a mother and daughter, or perhaps even two sisters, or a single woman in an artist's meditation on aging. In all of these, there is a suggestion of a rivalry or conspiracy between women depicted in the picture's several frames between past and future.

We may add to that sense by noting the rope that snakes alongside the young photographed woman, and disappears into the black recess behind her. The rope does not appear in the Freud painting. I want to say it cannot appear because it would give too much away; it is how the live woman climbed up to the doorway in which she poses. But it would also give too much away in another sense, for it hints at Antigonean suicide, by hanging. By depicting the rope, Bernard's photograph suggests something beyond Freud's frame: boxed in, cornered by the ceiling that hovers too close above her, surely tantalized by the rope and its promise of escape, the mourning woman, Bernard's photograph intimates, nonetheless chooses life.

This book takes seriously the reception studies claim, indebted to deconstruction, that the original is not betrayed or diminished by later receptions but, rather, wins a kind of overlife of new meanings from its new contexts. The painting by Freud when seen on its own simply does not have the same power as when it is viewed, through the photographic lens, as part of this complex composition by Bernard. Indeed, once one has seen the Bernard photograph, it is no longer possible to view the Freud painting without being haunted by the image of the young woman posing for it but absent from its frame. Bernard's photograph is no mere copy of Freud's work but a restaging of it, a comment on it, an appropriation of it, and an expression of reverence for it, all at the same time. Thus, it serves as a model of sorts for this book's aspirational relationship to Sophocles' *Antigone* and its reception history.

But the copy does not only inspirit the original and breathe new life into it. Sometimes, as I have argued here, the original fights back and traces of that resistance may distort and add to the scene of reception. Such agonism is discernible in Bernard's photograph. Its mix of photography and (photographed) painting enacts a rivalry or conspiracy between the artists (Freud and Bernard, who were also friends) and their media. Surely the painting better plumbs the emotional depths of the situation? Freud might protest. But which better reaches beyond it? I want to ask. Bernard's photograph interrupts the reception scene of Freud's art, and inaugurates a new one in which the two men comment on each other, just as the depicted women can be seen to comment on each other, interrupt each other, and perhaps even plot and conspire together. I imagine a scene in which the younger woman takes hold of that rope, throws it to the older woman, and both climb down out of their black holes.

Notes

Preface

1 "Buried in detail" aptly captures the situation of Borges' Ireneo Funes (1964: 59–66), whom Adriana Cavarero describes as "the most audacious empiricist" (2005: 49). In the words of the narrator of the Borges story: "In the overloaded world of Funes, there were only details, almost immediate . . . He was the solitary and lucid spectator of a multiform, instantaneous and almost intolerably precise world." For Funes, everything he experienced was so radically particular, that it was necessarily and inevitably betrayed by language: "it bothered him that the dog at three-fourteen (seen from the side) should have the same name as the dog at three-fifteen (seen from the front)" (cited in Cavarero 2005: 48–49).

2 In other words, with all due respect to Norman Jacobson (1978), political theory is not only or even primarily about solace: it is about disturbance.

3 On the Persian carpet as a mark of Persian exceptionalism, see my review of Kapuscinski's *Shah of Shahs* (Honig 2008c).

4 This detail, from the book not the film, is shadowed by a detail from the ancient world noted by Simon Goldhill: "the Hippocratic Corpus talks of the 'hysterical' diseases of young unmarried girls, for whom marriage and pregnancy are a suggested cure" (1986: 102, n. 41). Thanks to Christina Tarnopolsky on this point.

5 What shall we say of this felicitous therapeutic intervention, performed by an African American nurse, on behalf of a privileged white teenager? It is less a talking cure and more of a talking-to cure, less neurotic Jewish, I want to say, and more a pick yourself up by your bootstraps / get yourself together intervention. Here Whoopi Goldberg replays a role she has played elsewhere along with so many other African Americans in Hollywood movies, from Sam (Dooley Wilson), the man who provides the music for white heterosexual romance in *Casablanca* to Will Smith's starring roles in films such as *Independence Day* and *I Am Legend*. In twentieth-century mainstream film, those African Americans who do not represent danger or degradation serve as helpful black facilitators to flawed whites who cannot quite heal, empower, or love themselves. Among Goldberg's similarly structured films are: *Ghost* and *Corrina, Corrina*; Smith's include *The Legend of Bagger Vance* and *Men in Black*.

6 It is then left to her audience to wonder: does she fulfill her desires or has she betrayed them when she finds she can pursue them within the frame of what Lacan calls the "service of the goods" (1992: 302–303)?

7 Lacan is himself dismissive of Anouilh, and calls his protagonist the "little fascist Antigone" (1992: 250).

8 These modern Antigones may then put us in mind of Augustine's judgment of Lucretia whose guilt or innocence we cannot know, since these hinge upon intent, he said (1998: I.16–19). But if she was innocent, she did not deserve to die and thus, when she committed suicide, she showed herself to be, Catherine Belsey says, "motivated by the desire for fame" (2001: 315, n. 2).

9 I may well return her to the mirror, however, when I consider tragedy's relation to melodrama at the end of Part I and then in Part II develop readings of Sophocles' play that are, arguably, melodrama-inflected. On this point, I am indebted to Sunetra Gupta.

10 In this I have some company: Yannis Stavrakakis' anti-heroic social theory is developed in critical engagement with Lacan and Žižek. Stavrakakis says that nothing is gained, politically, from the central suicide that Žižek is drawn to in Sophocles' play: "What is 'gained' in terms of the purity of the act at the subjective level – now reduced to the solipsistic pursuit of death – is lost in terms of its socio-political efficacy" (2010: 5). So why is Žižek drawn to it? Why is he "insisting so much on Antigone"? Because he is concerned about "the danger of the re-absorption of an act, of its co-optation" (2010: 5). Stavrakakis counters that this strategy is not only "undesirably anti-political but also ultimately impossible [since] . . . even the purest of real acts is ultimately attached to certain symbolic conditions of possibility" (2010: 6). I too will make this case below, with reference to both Antigone's suicide, a virginal death co-opted for patriarchal order when her betrothed takes her, post mortem, in a marriage to death, and Haemon's suicide, by way of which he means to wed himself to his betrothed and leave the natal family of his birth for which, however, his live father reclaims the son post mortem. Thus, both are co-opted or subverted for purposes not their own. Stavrakakis' point about the unavoidability of reabsorption is also made, as we shall see in Chapter 2, by Lee Edelman in his critique of Judith Butler and the question hovers over the directors' *agon* in the film *Germany in Autumn*, as we shall see in Chapter 3. My aim throughout is to track what work this set of concerns does rather than try to resolve the issue. The concern to identify which acts are truly singular enough to break the tedium of the everyday may make us miss the power of/in the everyday which I here track throughout Part II, but especially in Chapter 6, and which I, along with James Martel, refer to as "conspiracy" (2011). On the contempt of some, in particular French, receptions of *Antigone* for the everyday, see Eagleton (2010).

Introduction

1 Notably, in recent years, there has been increased attention to the mourning of animals, laments of death by chimps and elephants, in an apparent attempt to "humanize" them. If they mourn, that is thought to be a more powerful argument than their mere sentience (already in play with little effect) to treat them with dignity. See, for example, Andy Soltis, "Monkeys in Mourning" (2009): "More than a dozen grief-stricken chimpanzees joined in an extraordinary expression of mourning as an elder in their family was laid to rest at a West African animal sanctuary ... everyone at the sanctuary was deeply moved by what they saw at the burial. [One said,] 'Even the employees, a lot of whom grew up as villagers potentially eating apes ... The human onlookers also were stunned by how human the chimps could be.'"

2 It is also to move beyond feminist theory's sometime embrace of the ordinary, revaluing it over the extraordinary, but maintaining an opposition between them. Relatedly, see Jodi Dean (2009) on neo-liberalism for a critique of left politics' embrace at century's turn of its own irrelevance as a politics.

3 There are many such *agons* of lamentation: in Part I of the book, I look at the politics of beautiful death (Chapter 1) and the AIDS quilt (Chapter 2) and the two funerals that bookend *Germany in Autumn*: those of Hans-Martin Schleyer (former Nazi and member of democratic West Germany's business elite) and three Red Army Faction (RAF) members, charged with terrorism, who commit suicide or are murdered in a West-German prison.

4 When in *The Graduate*, Dustin Hoffman's character, Benjamin, hijacks a wedding rather dramatically and unexpectedly, he makes clear the unique capacity of interruption to work as a speech act without taking speech action's formulaic forms and without respecting its conditions of felicity. J. L. Austin grants that speech acts can be felicitous even when they depart from the pure forms by way of which he analyzes them (I promise, I do). The power of speech acts is best seen via the formulaic form but is not restricted to formal utterance, he says. Still, interruption finds itself at greatest distance from Austin's rubric.

5 Taxidou notes that "Athens and Thebes in myth and tragedy have an interdependent relationship, Thebes usually standing in for the other of Athens, for all the things of which the democratic state wants to rid itself" (2004: 127). Louis Gernet suggests (in Michelle Gellrich's parsing) that tragedy's "orientation toward the social context is interrogative and even adversarial, for it holds us in the grip of conflicts that various mechanisms of the culture aim to neutralize and dissipate" (Gellrich 1988: 68).

6 See also Froma Zeitlin (1990) on this point.

7 Citations to the play indicate first the Greek lines and then, in square brackets, the lines from the Fagles translation (1984) which unless otherwise noted is the one used throughout.

8 Although since she calls her tomb her marriage bed, does she consent in advance to this conjugation?

9 Hegel's treatment of the play has become essential to any critical engagement with his own work on gender, death, modernity, state sovereignty, and more. Among the better readings of Hegel that work through his treatment of the play are: Seyla Benhabib (1996), Tina Chanter (1995), Luce Irigaray (1985), Patchen Markell (2003), Patricia Mills (1996), and Allen Speight (2001).

10 Among political theorists, Peter Euben (1997) is an exception: he stands out for his theater-sensitive readings of tragedy as a dramatic form. Judith Butler's *Antigone's Claim* (2000) does focus on speech acts, tracking the repetition, iteration, and circulation of words by sovereign and sovereignty-seeking characters in the play. She does not attend to interruption, per se, though she does in her reading of the play note the failure of some speech acts. Among classicists working on tragedy, all of whom are much more attentive to performance and staging of tragedy than are theorists and philosophers, Pat Easterling and Simon Goldhill stand out for their attention to dramaturgical elements, to voice, to who is on and off stage at certain moments, to the experience of spectatorship, and more: Goldhill (2009) argues that when – as in Sophocles – a character who observes on stage is observed observing by the audience, this puts the audience, as it were, on stage.

11 Treating the play this way is relatively easy to justify, but I would argue in favor of treating all texts of political theory this way, attending to tone, genre, emplotment, character, and examples as well as to the success or failure of the text's effort to interpellate the reader into the world imagined by the text. For more on this, see my "The Genres of Democracy" in *Democracy and the Foreigner* (2001) and James Martel, who also argues for treating literary texts politically and political texts literarily (2011).

12 That is, although the aspiration is to perform what Eve Sedgwick, drawing on Melanie Klein, calls recuperative reading – aspirational, complex, plural, futural – my argument is indebted in no small way to Sedgwick's other option, the paranoid reading style – focused, exposé-oriented – that Sedgwick seeks to overcome (2003: chapter 4).

13 I discuss Butler's "turn to Antigone" in detail in Chapter 2. The emphasis on equality, rather than singularity, is strong in her work in the last ten years, from *Precarious Life* (2004a) to *Frames of War* (2009).

14 See, for instance, Spencer (2012), Wilson (2009), and the *Frankfurter Allgemeine Zeitung*'s report, "*Antigone* westöstlich: erste Schauspielschule in Palästina" (2009). If Antigone is of interest in Ramallah, it is not only because the play is about righteous dissidence. It is also, surely, because of efforts like that of Israel's foreign minister, Avigdor Lieberman, to imprison Palestinians who mourn on Israel's Independence Day (Beinart 2010).

Fatima Festic comments on Antigone and the Palestinian situation in "*Antigone* in (Post-)Modern Palestine" and, like me, seeks an Antigone that is not only dissident but also combative in other ways. Antigone, she says, is "a case-history of a girl who, instead of hanging herself, 'rapes back' with her suicide and asks for a reader far advanced in reading the cross-cultural, political and gender knots and dead-ends … Perhaps in that way we should read anxiety in Žižek's claim against 'the overblown celebration of Antigone'" (2003: 96).

15 Following Eduard Devrient (1869), Jason Geary points out that, for Ludwig Tieck, who staged the play in the 1840s for Friedrich Wilhelm IV, *Antigone* "came closer than any other Greek drama to conveying a modern, Christian sentiment" (2006: 196). "Tieck," Geary explains, "was presumably referring to Antigone's willingness to give up her own life in exchange for granting her brother a proper burial – an act sometimes thought to indicate love in a Christian as opposed to a pagan sense," in which Antigone appears as the self-sacrificing Mary Magdalen taking Jesus down from the cross (2006: 196–197). If Friedrich Wilhelm wanted the play staged, that was because, on Tieck's account of it anyway, it would appeal to Friedrich Wilhelm's vision of a "Christian-German state" (2006: 197). Antigone's history of Christianization is the history of her character as a (certain kind of) martyr.

Introduction to Part I

1 This, Martel (2011) says, is the point of Benjamin's embrace of Baudelaire – a response to Marx's rejection of drunkenness as politically retrograde. I discuss the point in Chapter 3 when I turn to Fassbinder.

2 We might say that rather than focus on survival as mere life, Crimp calls attention to the importance of sur-vivance, as more life, a distinction inspired by Derrida, which I thematize in *Emergency Politics* (2009a).

3 Most recently, Elizabeth Freeman (2010) and Castiglia and Reed (2011). As I argue below, this forgetting is due not to the facticity of the disease but also to the active politics of forgetting pursued through the eighties and nineties. Castiglia and Reed track the amnesia-inducing moves in play.

4 Hence my discussion in *Democracy and the Foreigner* of the need in democratic theory to dispose of the lawgiver, often by way of violence, and of the importance of that textual rite of passage to the assumption of democratic maturity (2001).

1 Tragedy, maternalism, ethics: toward an agonistic humanism

1 This thought is always carefully put by Butler: see for example, *Undoing Gender* (2004b), where she says: "There is a certain departure from the human that takes place in order to start the process of remaking the human" (3–4). That this remaking always disappoints to become mere repetition is a critique of Butler leveled by Lee Edelman and discussed below (see 50ff.). As this book went to press, I found Inge Arteel's article, "Judith Butler and the Catachretic Human," in which she documents Butler's "growing concern with the human" (2011: 84), providing further details to support the claims made here. The catachretic human is an apt figure for agonistic humanism. But Butler's version of the catachresis comes with a sentimental reluctance to vie for sovereign power, a certain ethical hesitation about implication in (even a

reiterated) sovereignty, and is weighted, I think, more toward a lamentation of politics than a politics of lamentation. As these careful phrasings suggest, the differences here are sometimes mere matters of emphasis.

2 Tully is redeploying here a quote from Foucault (1984).

3 For further discussion, see Myers (2008), Davis and Womack (2001), Rancière (2006a), and Garber et al. (2000).

4 On agonism, see Honig (1993b), William Connolly (2005), Thomas Fossen (2008), and Alexander Hirsch (2013).

5 Vivasvan Soni (2010) argues, however, that this "blighting" helps constitute the practice of judgment whereby we decide on whether a man can indeed be called "happy." Thus, for Soni, tragedy is figured as a training ground (see in particular chapters 1, 3, and 8).

6 Eagleton dissents, however, noting (against Krook's *Elements of Tragedy* [1969]) that tragedy (in particular the Greek form) is about events, not characters: "Characters for Aristotle, in what not so long ago might have been dubbed "theoretical antihumanism," are a kind of ethical colouring on the action rather than its nub" (2003: 77). Michel would agree, presumably, given his own call to focus on form and plot, not character.

7 This is Euben's view. The tragic sensibility "enable(s) a redemptive moment by transforming suffering and loss into a story of human endurance" (2000: 68). Here he may be channeling Hannah Arendt's view, not restricted to tragedy, and indebted to Isak Dinesen: "All sorrows can be borne if you put them into a story or tell a story about them" (quoted in Arendt 1958: 175).

8 This may be the curiously attractive achievement of Giorgio Agamben's theorization of irredeemable bare life in *Homo Sacer: Sovereign Power and Bare Life* (1998). Here we have precisely the de-civilized human celebrated by humanism, recast in devalued form – as bare life, the abject product of biopolitics. The same may apply to Hobbes' observations about universal human vulnerability in the state of the nature, which however grounds not humanism but statist political order.

9 "A disturbingly large amount of theory seems explicitly to undertake the proliferation of one affect, or maybe two, of whatever kind ... " (2003: 146). When she gives mourning and militancy as an example of "two" positive affects, Sedgwick may be thinking critically of Douglas Crimp, whose work I discuss in Chapter 2.

10 Rancière's preference for Oedipus over Antigone is also a criticism of Lacan, who aestheticizes Antigone in order to enlist her for ethics. Against Lacan, Rancière marginalizes Antigone, seeking to insulate politics and also aesthetics from the ethical turn with which he identifies her. For further discussion, see Rancière (2006a).

11 Political interventions slide easily into ethical ones, however. Consider, for instance, this phrasing of Butler's: "Within the ethical frame of the Levinasian position, we begin by positing a dyad. But the sphere of politics, in his terms, is one in which there are always more than two subjects at play

in the scene ... what if there is an Other who does violence to an Other? [Butler poses this as a political question, but then immediately asks:] To which Other do I respond ethically?" (2004a: 139–140).

12 Butler does not ask the question in this way. We could note further that, her critique of Hegel notwithstanding, Butler's call for a new kinship does not upend, it extends Hegel's project. Hegel, after all, also saw the *Antigone* as evidence of the need for a shift in kinship forms. In Hegel's case that need was attributed to modern individuality, while in Butler it is tied to alternative forms of sexuality. For Hegel, the shift comes with Christianity's transition from inherited forms of guilt and curse, now expiated by Christ, to new, more voluntaristic and free forms of kin relation, emblematized in modernity by the marriage contract which is the instrumental expression of free individuality. But it is more than that, actually. For Hegel, the marriage contract is not just expressive; it is also productive. It helps constitute the forms of individuality it postulates, for it enhances voluntarism by displacing the passions that might otherwise ground marriage unstably with a contract that rationalizes and stabilizes this conjugal kinship form (on this see Hegel [1991], Mills [1996], and Derrida [1986a]). Thus, when Butler posits Antigone as a new site of kinship forms yet to come, she seems to extend rather than overcome Hegel's history; she may not follow Hegel in looking to conventional conjugal marriage to resolve the problem of Antigone (who is tragically and inadequately individuated, on his account). Instead, Butler looks to Antigone to resolve the problem of conjugal marriage kinship (which is normalizing and patriarchal). In sum, we could say that Butler extends the Hegelian adventure of (mutually implicated) individuation, which moved in Hegel from the device of brother–sister in the *Phenomenology* to that of husband–wife in the *Philosophy of Spirit*, and now in Butler to new aberrant kinship forms that are still Hegelian because those aberrant kinship forms are premised on and recognitive of the mutuality in every would-be individuality ("it is not as if an 'I' exists independently over here and then simply loses a 'you' over there, especially if the attachment to 'you' is part of what composes who 'I' am" Butler says in *Precarious Life* [2004a: 22]).

13 Vernant is here drawing on three episodes in the *Iliad* and elsewhere and "in all three cases the scenario is about the same" (1991: 74). Achilles' destruction of Hector is discussed later (see 26–29). The idea that decomposition begins in life, with aging, and is a source of anxiety (as it obviously is in our culture and as it was in the ancient world, a fact to which Priam, Hector's father, alerts us) suggests that in concerns about the decomposition of the dead there may be not only anxiety about mortality but also a certain displacement of this other concern.

14 As we shall see in Part II, Chapter 4, the Funeral Oration is itself already a replacement for a prior practice, and it houses in itself the contaminations of threat, intimidation, reconciliation that Derrida here seems to attribute to our replacements for the Oration, but not to the original.

15   The comparison is further warranted by the fact that, for Derrida, friendship is, as such, always premised on the death of the friend.

16   When Achilles sets the race for Patroclus' funeral games (*Iliad* 23.326–333), he takes as a race marker a stone that Homer describes as *maybe* a former grave marker; that is, in the context of a rite of memory, Homer tells us what we know: even grave markers are not forever, contra Vernant on steles, above. I discuss this further in n. 32 below.

17   As Derrida says in *Glas*: "The old humanist and metaphysical theme is familiar: (the) burial (place) is the proper(ty) of (the) man . . . This operation prevents the corpse from returning to nature . . . [and] raises the corpse to the universality of spirit" (1986a: 144). This testifies not only to the humanist resistance to nature but also to the "probably cannibal violence of the survivors' unconscious desires" (146).

18   Rancière agrees there is a shift from Oedipus to Antigone (or *Antigone*! He slips from the character to the play without notice) but he does not value it: "Under Oedipus' sign the trauma was the forgotten event whose reactivation could cure the wound. When Antigone replaces Oedipus in the Lacanian theorisation, a new form of secret is established [beyond] any saving knowledge. The trauma that is summarised in *Antigone* is without beginning or end" (2006a: 5).

19   As I noted above, it is unclear whether this is a statement about the universality of suffering or the universality of motherhood. In other words, what is doing the work here: the mother or the tears? Or do the tears make the mother (into a signifier of universality)? That is, isn't maternalism at work as the ground but also as the political effect of such humanist efforts to get beyond politics?

20   The wording here is Felski's, but she is drawing on the arguments of Dennis Schmidt.

21   Loraux finds in *The Birth of Tragedy* an invitation thus far unaccepted by the discipline formed around his expulsion: to follow the strain of language to music, the stretch of semantics to semiotics and song (2002b: 74).

22   Similarly, Martha Nussbaum says (citing Page duBois's essay in the same volume [2008]): by way of grief and mourning, spectators come to "a moment of recognition that exceeds the homogenous civic community, to an acknowledgement of his or her place among humankind, as mortal" (duBois 2008: 75; cited in Nussbaum 2008: 151). In her essay, "The Uses of Reception," Miriam Leonard (2006a) sees Loraux as fundamentally political, not ethical. Leonard may have in mind Loraux's main work prior to her embrace of lamentation for an extra-political humanism.

23   Loraux often defines her project in opposition to Aristotle, but she travels a similar path, offering Charles Segal a historical context for humanism. Segal says: "Aristotle shifts his emphasis from the civic solidarity expressed by Athenian tragedy as an intensely political and communal form to its universality as a dramatization of the sufferings and uncertainties in the lives of all of us as fellow-mortals who share a common humanity" because in his lifetime,

Aristotle saw "the large-scale export of Athenian drama from its intensely local setting in the Periclean theater in Athens to the rest of Greece." The fourth-century "expansion of the audience from Athens to the rest of the Greek *oikoumene* requires a new mode of interpretation for tragedy, a new horizon of expectation. Tragedy ceases to be Athenian tragedy and becomes Hellenic tragedy and eventually world tragedy" (Segal 1995b: 23–34).

24 For more detailed engagement with White's book, criticizing his weak ontology project from an agonistic perspective, see my review, "The Politics of Ethos" (2011c).

25 Although I do not discuss her work on this point, Arendt's (1990) critiques of pity and compassion as damaging to politics, and her preference for solidarity as the sort of joining together that *is* fit for politics and public life, are in the background of much of the work I am doing here.

26 On the historicity of death, see Dana Luciano, *Arranging Grief* (2007). Changes in perceptions of death meant that in the eighteenth century, "American sermons had begun to move away from the traditional disapproval of mournfulness as defiance of God's will, using Biblical texts to argue that sorrow on the death of a loved one was to be expected" (2007: 30). By the nineteenth century, Luciano argues, grief was natural, healthy, and embodied, but this was a new development.

27 It seems merely to be a difference of emphasis sometimes in Butler as, for example, when she says in *Frames of War*: "there can be no celebration [of birth] without an implicit understanding that the life is grievable, that it would be grieved if it were lost, and that this future anterior is installed as the condition of its life" (2009: 15). This is perhaps better seen as *a* condition, and not the essential one, however. The difference of emphasis reverberates throughout as Butler emphasizes fragility and precarity, more than resilience. The hegemony of mortalism, which enlists everything to its cause, is clearest in Butler's implication, which I discuss below, that she and Douglas Crimp are in agreement that the AIDS quilt admirably stands for grieving ungrievable life. Crimp is actually ambivalent about this, as we shall see, and prefers other less sentimental and more spontaneous mourning practices.

28 All *Iliad* citations are from the Lattimore translation.

29 This is not the Chorus' first such invitation. Notably, the first *parados* appeals to the city to forget the war and to shake the city in Dionysian revelry in a festival of forgetting. The mood here is one of elation – the city has survived attack – but forgetting is also necessary because the attack, while foreign, also came from within. The army was the Argives' but it was led by Thebes' native son: Polynices.

30 As Butler notes in *The Psychic Life of Power*, Freud comes to a different view in "The Ego and the Id," that melancholia makes mourning possible (1997: 179). This is the view depicted in Lars von Trier's *Melancholia*.

31 Also quoted in Staten (1995: 44).

32 Those games feature a moving, unsettling detail: before the chariot race, one of the games in honor of Patroclus, Nestor advises his son Antilochus about

how to win, though his horses are not the fastest: "He who has put all his confidence in his horses and his chariot and recklessly makes a turn that is loose one way or another finds his horses drifting out of the course and does not control them. But the man, though he drive the slower horses, who takes his advantage, keeps his eye always on the post and turns tight, ever watchful, pulled with the ox-hide reins on the course, as in the beginning, and holds his horses steady in hand, and watches the leader" (23.318–325). (Agamben discusses the scene in *Infancy and History* [1993], meaning to show the fundamental connection between games and burial, a connection one could also arrive at via Freud's discussion of fort-da, a game that provides small children with a controlled way to practice loss.) That turning point is, as Nestor says, "a clear mark, and you cannot fail to notice it" (23.326). But it is unclear what it is: "Either it is the grave-mark of someone who died long ago, or was set as a racing goal by men who lived before our time. You must drive your chariot and horses so as to hug this" (23.331–334). The grave marker/turning post marks mourning and its interruption, the internment of the dead, the festival by way of which people memorialize the dead, and the sheer passage of *time* that erases such efforts.

33 On the parsing of this right as a "right to taste," see Honig (2009a), on Slow Food and the politics of emergent rights.

34 When we neglect the natal Antigone to focus only on the precarious, mortal one, we contribute to the sentimental public sphere that Lauren Berlant (2008) and others have done so much to identify and criticize. The critique of sentimentalism might offer a language in which to develop or restate this book's interruption of many of the received Antigones. But Berlant's criticism of sentimentalism has also led her to criticize melodrama as anti-political; it is the contemporary genre most identified with the sentimentalism she rejects. I, by contrast, will explore in Chapter 3 the potential of this genre for a political rather than a sentimental Antigone. The example I focus on, certain segments of *Germany in Autumn* – chosen because they traffic in several Antigones to pose questions of law, violence, repetition, and innovation – are male melodrama and not, therefore, per se, an instance of what Berlant calls "the female complaint." On sentimentalism, see also Luciano's *Arranging Grief* (2007), where Luciano cites Mary Louise Kete (2000), who, Luciano says, "characterize[s] sentimentality as a type of mourning" (2007: 19).

35 I owe thanks to Miriam Leonard for pressing me to clarify the difference between classicism and classicization.

36 Porter refers to this definition as "the sheer *tautology* of classicism" (2006a: 8; emphasis original).

37 See Mee (2010) on the way in which repeated performances of the tragedies enhance our sense of their universalism.

38 If Moore does not classicize her that may be because he reserves for himself the voice of political opposition premised on the intrinsic worth of life. It is his own voice in the voiceover that closes the film pleading with sovereign powers to be more responsible in their use of troops.

39 In Part II, Chapter 5, we will encounter the story of Intaphrenes' wife who weeps outside the palace of Darius and seeks to save her family from his violence. Risking the charge of inappropriate classicization, I cannot help but suggest that the woman in Moore's film takes up that place.

40 Full script available at www.script-o-rama.com/movie_scripts/f/fahrenheit-911-script-transcript.html (accessed August 4, 2011).

41 *Fahrenheit 9/11* also has other details that may connect the film with Sophocles' text. Most important, I think, is the fact that the first third of the film sits uncomfortably with the rest. It performs the same function as what we might call the prequel to Sophocles' play: in both, the exploration of the politics of lamentation is preceded by the unjust usurpation of power in a struggle between two parties: the brothers' rivalry, undepicted but referred to in Sophocles' *Antigone*, and Bush's Supreme Court-legitimated claim to a contested electoral victory.

42 On Sheehan, see Amy and David Goodman (2006) and Pease (2009). On Sheehan as Antigone, see Jan Hartman (2005) and Nicholas Powers (2005).

43 Perhaps there is no avoiding the disappointment of finding that actual imperfect persons, who take up or are taken up by worthwhile causes, are then buffeted by giant media and turn out to be smaller than the hopes we invest in them, as when Sheehan embraces Hugo Chavez, seems to flirt with anti-Semitism in her criticisms of the second Iraq war, and leverages her personal pain into blunt criticism of US foreign policy.

44 Another example of this would be Hegel, who turns to Antigone to find a precursor for German Christianity that sidesteps Christianity's unfortunate (from his perspective) predecessor – Judaism. But his sources are not simply compliant. The Greeks, as it were, fight back, as interpreters from Luce Irigaray to Alan Speight have argued, noting that Hegel's project is undone, sometimes, by his literary examples. This possibility is also explored by Jacques Derrida who, in *Glas* (1986a), exposes the politicality of Hegel's deployment of Antigone for a Christian politics that sidesteps both its Judaic origins and its current Jewish minorities. For further discussion, see Miriam Leonard's "Uses of Reception" (2006a) as well as Luciano's *Arranging Grief* (2007).

2 *"Antigone versus Oedipus," I: feminist theory and the turn to Antigone*

1 This line is spoken by IRA hunger striker, Bobby Sands, to a republican priest, who asks whether the protesters have yet used all the Bible's pages to roll their cigarettes. For a reading of the film that emphasizes the non-instrumental character of the hunger strike, see Peter Bradshaw (2008).

2 Recently some turn to Ismene in place of the supposedly too masculine or heroic Antigone. On the turn to Ismene, see Chapter 6.

3 My reading of Antigone's lamentations in Chapter 4 as primarily political takes seriously the fifth-century context and seeks to put an obstacle in the way of the otherwise seemingly inevitable ethical slide.

4 That Elshtain and Butler each have two Antigones is apt, since the *Antigone* is all about doubling – the doubling of kinship roles in which Oedipus the incest is father/brother to his children/siblings, the doubling of two brothers fighting over the throne and two sisters, differently locked in struggle over how to survive in the aftermath of civil war in a city that mistrusts and admires their family. (This is one reason I was drawn to the Bruce Bernard image on this book's cover: because of its iterative doubling of Lucian Freud's mourning woman in *Girl Sitting in the Attic Doorway*.) I note below too: these two receptions map onto the split orientation toward tragedy: as a genre of conflict and a genre of suffering. The latter is eventually taken up by melodrama which, I will argue in Chapter 3, is, however, itself usefully seen as a conflict genre as well. On the move from tragedy to sentimentality, see Viv Soni's important book, *Mourning Happiness* (2010). I am indebted to Soni as well for conversation on this topic.

5 For further discussion, see Wendy Brown, "Resisting Left Melancholy" (1999). Responding in different ways to Brown, see James Martel (2011) and Jodi Dean (2009).

6 When she wonders why feminists had not yet turned to Antigone as a resource, Elshtain is focused perhaps on the American literature. Irigaray's reclamation of Antigone for feminism had appeared years earlier in the mid-70s in France and her work was included in an edited volume, *New French Feminisms* (Marks and de Courtivron 1980), cited by Elshtain in this very essay (1982: 311, n. 13). In *Antigone's Claim*, Butler wonders, for her part, whether Antigone might be a queer heroine. Peggy Phelan dismisses the possibility in *Mourning Sex* (1997).

7 Ruddick's maternal thinking, Elshtain said, focused on "the concrete reality of a single human child" in opposition to forms of public policy that tend to be "impersonal, calculating, and technocratic" and "amoral." An early critique of maternalist politics, and a sharp rejection of Elshtain, in particular, is Mary Dietz (1985).

8 The distinction between resistance and mourning is real but tenuous. Elshtain embraces the women's mourning that Hegel saw as a threat to state stability precisely because women's laments do threaten state stability, on her account. Still the difference is there: Elshtain's two essays map onto the two strands of tragedy which center, respectively, on conflict and suffering and which devolve into two distinct genres – tragedy and melodrama.

9 A recent illustration of death's specific power to equalize: an op-ed cartoon depicts three identical flag-draped coffins with the caption "Which is the gay one?" (*South Florida Sun Sentinel*, April 14, 2009).

10 See, for example, the documentary film, *Following Antigone: Forensic Anthropology and Human Rights Investigations* (2002), produced by EAAF and the American NGO, Witness. Thanks to Lindsey Smith for alerting me to this film.

11 On Antigone's calls to vengeance, see Chapter 4. Elshtain also, I can't help but note, discloses her own role in the contingent materiality of the

universality she claims to discover, when she mentions in her second essay that she shared her first one, "Antigone's Daughters," with one of the Madres, who read it and saw herself in its mirror: "'[W]e *are* your daughters of Antigone,'" the woman said to Elshtain in response: "'I did not get to bury my children, as Antigone buried her brother. But I have risked my life to make public their suffering'" (1989: 232). Such classicization is not, however, entirely Elshtain's doing. The identification with Antigone goes on in a larger context, a point made by Diana Taylor in her work on the Madres and noted by R. Clifton Spargo when he lists just a few of the prior Argentine and Latin American Antigones (2008: 130).

12 Or, more accurately, classicization introduces not an apolitics but a different politics. James Porter makes the point (2006b). Similarly, Marita Sturken notes in the context of the AIDS quilt that its apoliticality operates *as a politics* (1997: 195).

13 And they were making real and visible "a duality that," on Spargo's account, "haunts apolitics, as the sign both of excluded personhood and of voices decrying such exclusion, as the expression both of a true realm outside the polis and of claims exercised exorbitantly against it" (2008: 130). In a way, Butler's Antigonean turn is focused on the very trait named "apolitical" by Spargo: the duality of exclusion and exorbitancy produced by apolitical politicking in which we "effectively protest the procedures and binding force of the State by way of motives and principles purporting to be constituted elsewhere" (2008: 119). For Spargo, this paradoxical site of exclusion and exorbitance goes by the name "Antigone" in both its classical Sophoclean form and its more modern Kierkegaardian formation. And, as he puts it, "any invocation of universalist obligation so as to supersede the political ordering of the public realm necessarily exploits, by my account, a hypothesis of apolitical positionality I wish to associate with Antigone's gesture. At the same time, it is my working assumption that Antigone's gesture, even as it hypothesizes a possibility of standing beyond the sphere of the polis, depends crucially on its located political context" (2008: 119; cf. 130).

14 I suppose then the idea is to join Nietzsche in tracking what happens when people turn their ideals into norms for others.

15 Missing and marked by the first ellipsis is Taylor's universalizing qualifier: the Oedipal script "has problematized [and constructed] generational and family boundaries for thousands of years" (1997a: 203).

16 The Madres "accepted the Jocastian logo for their movement: 'Our sons [*hijos*] gave birth to us; they left us pregnant forever'" (Taylor 1997a: 220).

17 That is, if, as Gillian Rose (1996) suggests, "mourning becomes the law," it may not be a good law. See also Rajan, paralleling Taylor. Regarding the Mothers' Front in Sri Lanka, Rajan says "The mothers' cause and their idiom of spontaneous protest – in the form of tears and curses – had a sanction, even sanctity, because of their association with traditional femininity," but their strategy also "'reinscribed gender and class hierarchies'" and so eventually "the

participants returned to their marginalized roles little changed by their experience" (2010: 186). Rajan concludes that there is a space available to and created by maternal mourning but it is constrained to shaming and subduing the state, not transforming it. Women can here "constitute themselves as political antagonists of the state" but "the *very success* (in strategic terms) of political mourning becomes a measure of its limitations [as] . . . it exhausts the repertoire of women's antagonism toward the state; it attenuates their politics by situating it *in extremis*" (2010: 192).

18 This tension is in Sophocles' play, too: Antigone experiences a tension between life and death, belongs to neither, and marks her liminality when she calls herself a *metic* (852).

19 As Maria Florencia Nelli reports, Gambaro "was exiled to Spain in 1977 after a presidential decree banned one of her novels, *Ganarse la muerte*, 'To Earn One's Death'" (2010: 355). In the same volume, S. E. Wilmer notes that Gambaro, who writes to protest on behalf of the disappeared of Argentina, provides an adaptation of the play in which the body of the brother disappears, by contrast with the situation in Sophocles' play, where there is simply no getting rid of the body. Also, Gambaro's *Antígona* takes on masculine characteristics normally attributed to Haemon, who is, Diana Taylor says, "furious, heroic, individuated" (1997a: 221). *Antígona* is also more "loving and vulnerable" than Sophocles' heroine and less "inhuman" and onstage for the whole play (post-mortem) (1997a: 216).

20 For Schmitt, such Hamletization was an effect of history's intrusion into the world of the play, a point to which I return in Chapter 5.

21 One of my interests here is to explore the bifurcation of Antigone into a humanist extra-political lamenter versus political agent of resistance and to find ways to pull these back together or, given that Butler's project is not that different in this regard, to find other ways to pull these back together. This requires that we de-sentimentalize Antigone. I focus here on Butler's *Antigone's Claim* (2000) and *Precarious Life* (2004a) before turning finally to *Frames of War* (2009). *Undoing Gender* (2004b) has a chapter on Antigone, focused on her political action, and this may seem to put in question my claim of chronological shift from a sovereignty-seeking Antigone in 2000 to a later one given to lamentation in Butler's work (2004a). However, the Antigone in *Undoing Gender* is the very one from *Antigone's Claim*. The chapter, "Bodily Confessions," recasts the earlier material as part of an argument about confession and the chapter is indeed noted to have been given as a lecture in 1999, before what we may call Butler's ethical turn.

22 The conflict is driven by Antigone's singular devotion to her brother. The devotion to the brother stands for Antigone's identity as an incest, says Butler, whose observation works against Elshtain's celebration of the private as a resource for politics, itself untouched by politics: unlike Elshtain, Butler sees that the brother is actually a radically plural kin position in this incestuous family, available to be occupied by three distinct people: Oedipus, Eteocles, and Polynices. Beyond that, Butler might also have noted the

varieties of incest, the difference between cross-generational and same-generational desire (vertical and horizontal), for example, a point noted by Steiner and explored by John Seery (2006) in a critique of Butler. But Butler claims such distinctions are rendered ambiguous by incest itself which casts the same person as both horizontal and vertical, father and brother.

23 The argument about grievable life is prefigured most clearly in *The Psychic Life of Power* where Butler argues that "The ego becomes moralized on the condition of ungrieved loss" and then asks: "But what conditions make it possible to grieve, or not to grieve, loss?" (1997: 186). Butler is not yet here attending specifically to death practice but this formulation is later pressed into service in that context.

24 Elsewhere the third appears, briefly, when Butler mentions "mortality, vulnerability, agency" as all implied by the body (2004a: 26).

25 Arendt notes that labor, work, and action are *all* rooted in natality but action is closest (1958: 9).

26 These communities are not non-sovereign, for Arendt. They are constituted as limitedly sovereign (1958).

27 For further discussion see Arendt (1958). I note too that action is uniquely governed by the timelessness of immortality and postulates human (non-sensual) pleasure, individuation, vulnerability, and risk. In other words, Arendtian action may be seen as one way of countering mortalism. It is not, in the end, my way here.

28 Thanks to Moya Lloyd for reminding me of these exceptions to Butler's later focus on grievable life. For further discussion, see Lloyd (2005). Fiona Jenkins pressed me on the same point. I note here that Butler was criticized in the 1990s for being inadequately mournful of the transsexual Venus Xtravaganza, whose desire for a house in the suburbs with a washer and dryer Butler found less than inspiring. It is possible that Butler, who has been talking about mourning and melancholy throughout her writing career, may have turned to Antigone a few years later to deliver on the mourning demanded of her by critics like Jay Prosser (1998). If so, the great irony is that *Antigone's Claim* is surely less oriented to mourning and loss than any other reading of the play since Hegel. Thanks to Nick Davis for reminding me of the *contretemps* regarding Venus and for good conversation generally about mourning, melodrama, and film theory.

29 Loraux dubs Athens the "city of forgetting" in *The Divided City* (2002a).

30 I return in Chapter 3 briefly to reconsider *Precarious Life* in the context of a different genre. For now, I note that neither of Butler's two Antigones is oriented toward festival but it would not be correct to say that both are identically oriented toward death. Butler's first Antigone, the heroine of *Antigone's Claim*, is grabbed by grief but her grief is not solely about loss and finitude, as it will later come closer to being, in *Precarious Life*. Instead, Butler connects it to Antigone's liminal status; she is a forbidden daughter of incest, Oedipus' daughter, and his half-sister, born of the same mother. If Antigone seems excessive in her laments, this is only a sign of the

excessiveness of incest which always, from the perspective of the ban on it, seems to double and redouble. To be clear, melancholy plays a role through-out Butler's work (and in all her references to this play) and this is because melancholy, as she understands it, is a constitutive feature of the gendered subject whose formation in heternormative social orders requires, on Butler's account, the foreclosure of same-sex desire, and prohibits the treatment of that foreclosure as a loss to be mourned. Melancholy appears as a theme, major and minor, in virtually every book Butler has authored from *Subjects of Desire* (1987) to *Frames of War* (2009).

31 Notably the sovereignty claims made by Antigone are reiterations of Creon's, on Butler's account. I argue in Chapter 4 that the play is best seen as dramatizing a conflict between two orientations to democratic sovereignty, both aristocratic: one accommodates itself to the democratic polis, the other recalcitrantly refuses to do so.

32 Later, in *Frames of War*, Butler will describe the human as a category to criticize, assert, embrace (2009: 77) and as "the double or trace of what is human that confounds the norm of the human or, alternatively, seeks to escape its violence . . . when the 'human' tries to order its instances, a certain incommensurability emerges between the norm and the life it seeks to organize" (2009: 94–5). Working with other texts by Butler, Luciano notes Butler's care regarding humanism and the human: "Never simply given, the human, for Butler, 'comes into being, again and again, as that which we have yet to know'" (2007: 264; citing Butler 2004a: 30; 23). Still, for Luciano, even Butler's careful "humanism" shares traits with "sentimental mourning care," especially "a certain faith in the instructive value of grief" (2007: 264–265). Seeking to render contestable Butler's "embrace of grief as a political resource," Luciano turns to Emerson's 1844 essay, "Experience," in which he laments (the death of his son) otherwise: "'I grieve that grief can teach me nothing, nor carry me one step into real nature'" (Emerson 1880: 29; cited in Luciano 2007: 265). Emerson's account of grief is usefully balanced in my view by the call to lament – but not only to lament – and/as action in Douglas Crimp's work, which I discuss shortly.

33 Creon then calls her attention to the different criterion that grips him – not citizen-slave but friend-enemy: Polynices died, Creon says, "Ravaging our country! – but Eteocles died fighting in our behalf," to which Antigone responds by invoking her famous principle of equality for the dead: "No matter – Death longs for the same rites for all" (518–519 [582–584]). But we already know her "all" is not quite all for it does not include slaves. On the connections between the friend–enemy distinction and that between freed-man and slave, see Jacqueline Stevens' *Reproducing the State* (1999) and Nicole Loraux's *The Children of Athena* (1993).

34 There is a similar split in Holocaust studies, which distinguishes Jean Améry, cast as resentful and vengeful, from Primo Levi, cast (by Améry himself) as the "forgiver." Notably Butler has engaged Levi in detail but not Améry (2012). Nancy Wood (1999), in a nuanced reading of the two, focuses on this

way of dividing them, pointing out the more vengeful and resentful moments in Levi's writing and the world-building aspirations of Améry's. I note Levi's more resentful sentiments come out in the writings addressed to a German audience and that he hazards this addressee only later on.

35 Diana Taylor: "In speaking of the Madres' movement in terms of performance, then, I wish to make the connection between the public and ritualistic display of mourning and protest orchestrated by the Madres, and the notion of motherhood and womanhood as a product of a coercive system of representation that promoted certain roles as acceptable for females and eclipsed (and at times literally 'disappeared') other ways of being" (1997a: 186).

36 Livability is not grievability. In *The Psychic Life of Power*, the focus is on ungrievable love (1997: 140) and then in *Precarious Life* this has shifted to ungrievable life. If ungrievable love is constitutive of would-be straight subjectivity and its "culture of gender melancholy" (1997: 140), ungrievable life is less constitutive, more remediable through insistent institutions of equality (2009).

37 In short, for Butler, there is more promise in fusion than faction, contra Rancière who draws this contrast (as I noted in Chapter 1), and so when she embraces Antigone it is in principle the very same Antigone, rejected by him as an ethicization of politics, that Butler embraces as the most or best political figure we can turn to on behalf of those marginalized by current kinship forms. The Antigone that fits Rancière's epithet "ethical" in other respects, the great lamenter who witnesses catastrophe, *that* Antigone is not part of Butler's conceptual universe until *Precarious Life*, that is: after 9/11. Julia Lupton refuses this framing of fusion versus faction when she argues that Antigone represents not incest but its sublimation, not a contaminated mixture of natal and conjugal but the transformation of their conflict via "citizenship" (2005).

38 Just as Lacan in his reading of the play shifts attention from Oedipus to Jocasta as the bearer of incestuous desire.

39 Relevant here is Butler's response to Adam Phillips in *The Psychic Life of Power*, in which she says that it may be necessary to create "a typology of 'refusal' and 'exclusion' that might help us distinguish between what is rigorously repudiated and foreclosed and what happens to be less rigidly or permanently declined" (1997: 163). *Hasty* foreclosures – not yet mentioned by Butler at this point in her work – might find a place in such a typology.

40 As some classicists point out, the circumstances of Oedipus' body's disappearance suggest a hero cult.

41 Butler's aim here is to move beyond negative dialectics, which only gives us a (Creonic or Oedipal) law "*invested* in perversion" and does not go beyond that to make possible "other forms of social life" that may be inadvertently "produced by the prohibition" and may "come to undermine the conclusion" that the "social organization of sexuality follows of necessity from the

prohibitive law" (2000: 68). See also Butler, reading *Lana*, endorsing the "generative effects" of Lacan's law of desire, contra Foucault (1990b: 12).

42 Mere negation, she suggests in *Antigone's Claim*, is Irigaray's error, though in *Undoing Gender* Butler expresses greater appreciation of Irigaray's contribution here: "She derives a place for women where there was no place" (2004b: 201).

43 Where deliberativists and others charge that Butler is too negative and has nothing positive to offer a politics beyond critique, Lacanians like Lee Edelman argue that she is not negative or critical enough.

44 Butler notes that "[s]he [Antigone] is not of the human but speaks in its language . . . she upsets the vocabulary of kinship that is a precondition of the human," questioning "what those preconditions really must be . . . If she is human then the human has entered into catachresis; we no longer know its proper usage" (2000: 82). Antigone does indeed upset vocabularies, but it is interesting that on Butler's account, she does so monologically, as it were, to an audience perhaps but never also among conspirators. Moreover, as Butler reads Antigone, her citational and appropriative claims of sovereignty are not conspiratorial in another way too: they are done flagrantly in a way Creon and the audience cannot really miss. On my reading, by contrast, Antigone traffics in subtleties that Creon and audience members, and readers ever since, may well miss.

45 For example, Butler positions Antigone as a martyr for a cause but she does not ask after the politics of martyrdom and sacrifice. Heroes who die to make our future better are fundamental to humanism, which gives redemptive meaning to forms of suffering that might otherwise seem senseless. Humanism makes an exception of the human (only our suffering *means* something), at the cost of licensing the infliction of suffering on others (animals, and sometimes other races, are said not to feel pain like we do, or not in the same way, or not in a way that matters, and so on).

46 Edelman says: "Like the 'aberrant, unprecedented future' [Lacan's terms, appropriated by Butler] to which she stakes her political claim, Butler's Antigone, far from transforming Symbolic law, *repeats* it – and repeats it, in fact, as nothing less than the law of repetition by which our fate is bound to the fate of meaning through signification whose continued functioning has always relied on reproductive futurism" (2004: 105). For Edelman, Butler is drawn back into the mere repetition demanded by the Symbolic. For Butler, however, this is no mere repetition but rather a productive iteration. She denies (in Edelman's parsing) "the assertion that Symbolic law necessitates such repetition [of the logic of intelligibility], insisting, rather, that the law depends on the *appearance* of such necessity," thus reprising the theme of her *Gender Trouble* (1990a: 102; emphasis added).

47 I cannot follow this up here but it is worth noting that Edelman's rejection of the Child as a political figure is echoed by Arendt (with whom he would otherwise not much agree, given that she naturalizes mere repetition and excises it from politics), who condemned what she saw as the "use" of

children for political purposes at Little Rock. Arendt was not talking about the iconic Child but about children. But the comparison rewards some attention, nonetheless. Arendt was famously taken to task by Ralph Ellison, who schooled her in the politics of sacrifice all too familiar to African Americans. The episode between Ellison and Arendt is discussed by Danielle Allen in the *Oklahoma City Law Review* (2001). Jean Elshtain (1995), in what we may see as an extension of her social feminism argument, has opposed Arendt on this point to champion children's role in politics.

48 The common cultural motif – an expression of the maternalism endorsed by Elshtain – in which we are called to mourn in the way that a mother mourns her child is subjected also to withering critique by Edelman in his discussion of the Matthew Shepard murder (2004: 115–117).

49 There are two sorts of birds in Hitchcock, as well: one domesticated in the pet store and others that are wild and threatening. Edelman points this out, noting the several sorts of bird that appear in the film – the doves, love birds, mynah birds, and more.

50 Butler is not really vulnerable to this critique, however, since she notes that in the narrative Antigone "occupies, linguistically, every kin position except 'mother'" (2000: 72).

51 For a critique of Edelman as rejecting not just future but also past, see chapter 4 of Castiglia and Reed (2011), whose work tries to move past these debates.

52 As I argue elsewhere, that sacrificial logic is apparent in Kant's own faith in, or his call for us to have faith in, progressive history, a point to which Moses Mendelssohn was particularly sensitive. For further discussion, see Honig (2009a: chapter 2). Elizabeth Freeman, in the context of a critique of progressive history, says Edelman goes too far: generation should "not necessarily be tossed out with the bathwater of reproductive thinking . . . [Instead, what if we] thought less in the psychic time of the individual [and more] in the movement time of collective political fantasy" (2010: 65). Edelman might respond that this would be a future, not futurism (which is a reproductive ideology, not a temporality or a tense).

53 It may be the case that Antigone is simply resistant to all assimilations to (re)production and destruction. This possibility is invited by Butler, who notes that Antigone's name can be taken to mean both "in the place of the mother" and "anti-generation," the former connoting a promisingly different (re)production and the latter the destruction of conventional kinship forms (2000: 22). But see Goldhill (1986), particularly "The City of Words."

54 Butler's position is reminiscent of the line from Ellison's *Invisible Man*, when the dying grandfather bequeaths a final lesson to the boy: "Agree 'em to death and destruction" (1990: 16).

55 That said, this book's commitment to return again to Sophocles' play in quest of a different Antigone instances my agreement with Butler that how we inherit is the issue, not whether we do. If Antigone, "by obeying the curse upon her, stops the future operations of that chain" (2000: 52), then this

reading accepts that a certain "Antigone" is upon us, while seeking if not to stop then to divert or redirect (so as to exploit) its future operations.

56 The Antigone-effect is not uniform, as I note throughout, at least not in Butler's work. In *Who Sings the Nation-State?* she sides with undocumented immigrants who claim their place in the sovereign democratic state when they sing the US national anthem in Spanish. Arguably, the fairest reading of Butler here would point out that some of her work is addressed to relatively empowered subjects and some to those who are less so. To the former, she recommends lamentation and she issues a call to abjure sovereignty, to cross the lines of friend/enemy and to experience all life as grieveable. To the latter, who are less in need of such lessons, Butler addresses admiration for and encouragement of dissidence. Rarely, however, is sovereignty treated as a necessary part of politics (the first Antigone book stands out as an exception). (Notably, the term, Antigone-effect, is used also by Eric Kligerman [2011].)

57 I note, however, that at the end of *Frames of War*, Butler gestures beyond precarity (e.g. 2009: 150).

58 As I noted earlier, the differences I track here among her books have to do with the weight of emphasis, tone, and – as I shall argue in the next chapter – genre. Rage over loss is an important feature of the argument in *The Psychic Life of Power* (1997: 148), but in *Precarious Life* grief is less partisan and more humanistic.

59 Here the contrast with Derrida's treatment of eulogy in *The Work of Mourning* (2001), as always already contaminated and contested, is useful.

60 This problem – Antigone's lone and therefore inefficacious heroism – is occasionally noted by others as well. In a letter written as if from Antigone to Ismene, Jina Politi goes further to suggest such heroes are often enlisted by authorities seeking to defeat them: Politi has Antigone say: "what the Antigonids forget is the fact that Authority bases its power on the icons of heroes and saints" (2006: 134). Also promoting less heroic views of political agency and models of political action, see Martel (2011).

61 Casting Crimp's reflections on mourning as a "road not taken" risks seeming like a tragic emplotment, which is problematic, I argue here and in the next chapter, for democratic theory. The risk, in my view, is worth it. It helps to put Crimp's work in dialogue with democratic theory.

62 This comes out most clearly in his essay on the AIDS quilt, "Melancholia and Moralism," to which I refer below. I want to thank Stephanie Youngblood, as well as some other members of my 2010 Antigone seminar at the School of Criticism and Theory, for sharing with me their enthusiasm for Crimp's work just as I was turning finally to it. For further discussion of Crimp, I am grateful to Nick Davis.

63 Crimp responds to the idea that AIDS has a "positive value": "Kaufman quotes Michael Denneny of St. Martin's Press as saying, 'We're on the verge of getting a literature out of this that will be a renaissance'" (1987b: 4).

64 "Art," Crimp says, "does have the power to save lives, and it is this very power that must be recognized, fostered, and supported in every way possible. But if

we are to do this, we will have to abandon the idealist conception of art" (2002: 32–33). Daniel Harris, in a *Vanity Fair* article, shared Crimp's concerns about tragedy: he worried that the tragic emplotment of suffering "placed a higher burden on those who do not seek a higher meaning in their disease" and who refuse to occupy expected stock roles of brave heroes or innocent children (cited in Sturken 1997: 184). See also Rajan who says: "the figure of tragedy cannot be easily recuperated as a model for a transformational politics," adding that the genre of tragedy is "that uniquely ideological product of Western humanism." I have thus far looked at the reverse, the production of humanism by – a certain reception of – tragedy. Temporalizing, as past, arguments like Butler's, Rajan concludes that "earlier feminist efforts to 'confront and defy the state,' however admirable, appear to be something of a spent impulse now and the desire to honor Antigone's defiance as a model for feminism, while understandable, seems to me to have limited value for contemporary feminist struggles" (2010: 178).

65 Echoing, as we will see in Chapter 3, a eulogy in Kluge's film, *Germany in Autumn*: "If you are truly outraged, you won't shout but will consider what to do." The echo is unsurprising, since Hill's words are a rallying cry for activists of all sorts.

66 If we think of activism, as Hannah Arendt does, as a kind of natal aliveness, then we may see that rather than circumvent mourning, activism may help bring mourning to a good end. Notably, in Crimp, the return to life is not just a return to political action; it is also a return to non-normative sex. Publishing "How to have Promiscuity in an Epidemic" in 1987, Crimp countered securitarian responses to AIDS like that in "How to Have Sex in an Epidemic," and echoed Sophocles' call to pleasure's oblivion, refusing to give in to emergency politics. But the invitation was difficult in the context of a new, frightening, and fatal disease that is sexually (but not only sexually) transmitted and such calls are in any case barely heard amid the noise of the Creons and Antigones, the moralizers and the lamenters. As Adam Phillips says in his reply to Butler, "Mourning makes moralists of us all" (1997: 154).

67 Mourning is necessary to those suffering the loss and rage and abandonment of AIDS in the context of a US politics of neglect, Crimp concludes, but so is militancy, even though militancy may well be mourning in denial, a product of a certain refusal to deal with the psyche's death drive, rather than an acceptance of it or a working-through. (Although Crimp does not note it, Lacan allows that the death drive's "will to destruction" may be synonymous with the "will to make a fresh start," the "will to begin again" [Lacan 1992: 212].) That is, Crimp, who opens this essay with a critique of an early essay by Edelman, here proposes something like Edelman's later proposal in *No Future*: a resignification or queering of the death drive. Crimp himself acknowledges this proximity to Edelman in his later collection of essays, *Melancholia and Moralism*, which includes "Mourning and Militancy."

68 Might this be because this road not taken is Antigonizing but not, per se, Antigonean? This distinction is drawn by Thomas Elsaesser (2004), and

I discuss it in Chapter 3. I note here that Crimp's work and that of ACT UP more generally have, however, found traction in the area of trauma studies. See, for example, "The AIDS Crisis is Not Over," a conversation with Crimp, Gregg Bordowitz, and Laura Pinsky (Caruth and Keenan 1995). Recently, others have been turning to ACT UP as well. I should make clear that my own interest in Crimp and ACT UP is in their capacity to pluralize our understandings of lamentation and politics and also, by way of contrast, to highlight the political limitations of some turns to Antigone.

69 Endorsing a similar move in South African resistance politics and seeing in it the possibility of a new "health citizenship," see Jean Comaroff (2007). Arguably, the Madres took on a role more like that called for by Crimp, seeking to compel the state to act, after the end of the Dirty War. That is, once they were in the terrain of liberal democratic politics, their demands were no longer anti-statist as such: they sought to enlist the state, seeking its support for their cause, demanding trials, accountings, blood tests of adoptees who might have been kidnapped, and so on.

70 In this respect, ACT UP twenty years ago was working out of an agonism called for by Foucault to offset the too-easy anti-statism of the Left, or what he calls "state-phobia," which collapses the administrative welfare, bureaucratic, fascist, and totalitarian state as all part of "the same great tree of state control in its continuous and unified expansion." In a remarkable anticipation of Agamben, Foucault says: "And, in the move from social security to concentration camps the requisite specificity of analysis is diluted" (2008: 188 and *passim*; for calling my attention to these passages, thanks to Annie Menzel). Such an agonistic engagement with – rather than opposition to – the state is also what Rajan calls for (in the name of feminism): "a feminist agonism that has a 'transactional nature'" and "inhabits the production of critical oppositionality to *and* engagement with the state" (2010: 165). As my earlier references to this essay also indicate, there are uncanny similarities between my project here and Rajan's essay, which I found as this book went to press: her attention to the materiality of cultural texts, genre, gender, and the various vernaculars of political action, especially the limits of feminist anti-statism. I find especially congenial her observation that "contemporary Western feminists of all persuasions – Jean Bethke Elshtain, Patricia Mills, Luce Irigaray, Butler, prominently – despite their differences and disagreements, are united in this: they rescue Antigone from the Hegelian dialectic to deliver her over to Sophoclean tragedy" (2010: 167). Where we part: Rajan wants to decenter Antigone and draw on other non-Western models of female agency who may also offer more empowering narratives and tactics. I agree. But we must not only decenter Antigone in this way. It is also important to pluralize her and this is my own strategy, to show how the text supports also another Antigone and in so doing to highlight the insistences whereby we have received her until now.

71 As Steven Epstein notes, "[f]or a generation of relatively privileged, middle-class gay men, government had been something to restrict, to keep out of

their 'private' lives. As the boundary between private illness and public health exploded, these same men sought active governmental involvement to fund emergency AIDS research and to protect people with AIDS against discriminatory treatment" (1996: 187).

72 "I first became aware of ACT UP, like many other New Yorkers, when I saw a poster appear on lower Broadway with the equation: SILENCE=DEATH. Accompanying these words, sited on a black background, was a pink triangle ... For anyone conversant with this iconography, there was no question that this was a poster designed to provoke and heighten awareness of the AIDS crisis. To me, it was more than that: it was among the most significant works of art that had yet been done which was inspired and produced within the arms of the crisis" (Bill Olander, quoted in Crimp 2002: 32). Though it is also the case, as with breast cancer, argues S. Lochlann Jain in "Cancer Butch," that "ubiquity = death" (2007: 506).

73 "As anyone involved in the struggle against AIDS knows from horrendous experience, we cannot afford to leave anything up to the 'experts.' We must become our own experts," said Crimp (2002: 7). ACT UP used a combination of "insider and outsider tactics," as Steven Epstein explains, and "resisted the notion – found for example in the animal rights movement – that the scientific establishment was 'the enemy' in some absolutist sense" (1996: 226). Epstein quotes Mark Harrington, who says, "I wouldn't exaggerate how polite we were ... At the same time, I would just say that it was clear from the very beginning [that we recognized that], as Maggie Thatcher said when she met Gorbachev, 'We can do business'" (1996: 226).

74 One exemplary pathway to expertise was Mark Harrington's. A writer with a background in German Critical Theory, he "stayed up one night and made a list of all the words he needed to understand. That list evolved into a fifty page glossary that was distributed to ACT UP members" (Epstein 1996: 230). See also the documentary *How to Survive a Plague* (2012).

75 And not unlike Fassbinder, whose sequence in *Germany in Autumn* is all these things, cast in melodramatic terms. The body-too-much that, we will see in Chapter 3, Elsaesser describes as obese, unattractive, and vulnerable – *is* vulnerable – but not especially abject. Crimp calls for a body-too-much also, but not the one described by Elsaesser: Crimp sees militancy in the body-too-much of pleasure and promiscuity that was the product of communal gay forms of life before the crisis. Yet another option is presented by David Halperin (2012) who endorses gay responses to tragedy that are "inappropriate."

76 She had also been Christianized, as I noted above, by Hegel who positioned her as precursor to German Christianity in place of Christianity's Judaic predecessors (Leonard 2005).

77 As Jean Comaroff points out in the context of AIDS activism in South Africa twenty years later, South African activists follow ACT UP's lead when they constitute certain goods as public and assign responsibility for them to the state which otherwise is less and less poised to see itself as responsible for

(constituting) publics and more and more inclined simply to respond to neo-liberal demands.

78 This is part of Butler's argument that "Gay melancholia [which is consti-tutive] also contains anger that can be translated into political expression" (1997: 148) and this suggests that her turn to mourning harbours anger within it and is less sentimental than I've suggested. But the political expression she directs us to is the quilt, which many, including Crimp, have argued is not angry enough. The quilt exerts a maternal power that sanitizes the queerness on behalf of whose explosive power Butler seeks to write.

79 I find a similar sensibility in Elizabeth Freeman's effort to move queer theory to a focus on pleasure rather than pain: "Why is it that in queer theory, only pain seems so socially and theoretically generative?" She cites with approval the "simultaneously mourning and lusting spectator" of the film *K.I.P.*, who "seems to want to have sex with history" (2010: 12–13). In *Emergency Politics* (2009a), I discussed the attraction of Slow Food's politics of "virtuous globalization" as a politics of pleasure.

80 As I noted in Chapter 1, Rancière and Butler seem to converge on the politics of naming, about which, as we see here, Crimp expresses ambivalence. This politics of naming is worth more attention than I can give it here.

81 That is, the quilt may be as undecidable as the headstones discussed in Chapter 1. Comparing the Vietnam Memorial and the Names Project quilt, Sturken is especially good at tracking the sentimentalizing powers of the quilt. She also notes the importance of the sheer size of the quilt in conveying the huge loss of life, noting too the numbers: twice as many deaths from AIDS in ten years as US dead in the Vietnam war. On sentimentalism, which privileges pity (but not the fear that Aristotle said was also part of the affective response elicited by tragedy), as a mode of self-absorption that also absorbs other modes into itself, see Viv Soni (2010: chapter 8). Sentimentalism seeks to open the self to the other, Soni argues, but ultimately calls attention to the virtues of a self capable of imagining another's pain, and so ironically returns the focus to the self, whose boundaries sentimentalism wanted to attenuate. Opposed to sentimentalism, or alert to its inherent limitations, Soni posits Solon's wisdom and the Periclean Oration as sites of commemoration and political contestation.

82 Queer natality is also less assimilable to the sentimental public sphere than is grievability.

83 An analogous point is implied by Simon Stow who, citing Ronald K. Barrett, says that "African-Americans are more '*death-accepting*' than whites" (Stow 2010: 683; emphasis original). Stow looks at the politics of the death practices subtended by that acceptance, while Crimp seeks to forestall such acceptance and, more fundamentally, "acceptability" in the context of AIDS politics. On the place of transitional objects, though not the quilt, in a democratic politics of mourning, see David McIvor's (2010) Kleinian critique of Butler.

84 That is, if this mother does the laundry, she uses FAB: I refer here to Elizabeth Freeman's mention of the quilt. Neither sentimental nor angry,

the quilt, in her view, breaks through their partnership with waggish comedy: "among all the blocks of the AIDS Memorial Names Quilt, only one persists in my visual memory: It said 'I had a FABulous time,' the word 'fabulous' emerging from the label of a bright orange bottle of laundry detergent. Queers have, it is fair to say, fabricated, confabulated, told fables, and do so fabulously" (2010: xxi–xxii). Perhaps this is the right place to note the difference between my own critical engagement with maternalism developed throughout Part I and the critique of maternalism developed by Mary Dietz in response to Jean Elshtain. For Dietz, maternity is not an apt category for politics: citizenship is (1985: 31). The position developed here, however, is not either for (as with Elshtain) nor against (as with Dietz) political maternity. Instead, the idea is twofold: first, to politicize maternity. Second, once politicized, that is, once it is no longer treated as a natural or extra-political resource for politics, certain forms of maternal thinking or practice (not the ideology of maternalism) may well contribute to and find a place in democratic public life. The idea that democratic citizenship tolerates only relations of equality is akin to Arendt's, but for those of us working from more Foucauldian premises about the always already unequal situation of citizens and subjects, the aim is surely not to banish mothering from politics but rather to pluralize the identities and practices of mothering that may inform and shape public life. I agree with the critique of Elshtain that resists her privileging of maternalism as "the" right orientation for politics, but would not mirror her error by rejecting maternalism as such. That is, if Elshtain naturalizes maternity, as pre-political, those like Dietz, who would bar it from politics, also treat maternity as extra-political. Instead, following Wittgenstein's critique of referential theories of language, I would say that mothering is one thing we do in politics: not the one right thing, not the only thing, not the model for proper democratic relations. That Elshtain's maternalism tends to support a certain reflexive anti-statism in her work, is one more reason to resist rather than embrace it, in my view. When I close this book with some thoughts on sorority, it will be clear that the aim is not to promote a single kin relation as good for democratic politics but to pluralize the options. More to the point, the idea in any case is to highlight not the kin relation but the conspiratorial agency that in this instance is placed there.

85 See also Sturken on the photos that dehumanize "people with AIDS by emphasizing their death rather than their strength in living with AIDS" (1997: 155). I note that Crimp has been criticized for focusing too much on natality and refusing to concede the need to show how people stricken with AIDS suffer.

86 See also Crimp's discussion of British filmmaker Isaac Julien's *This is Not an AIDS Advertisement*: "Using footage shot in Venice and London, *This is Not an AIDS Advertisement* is divided into two parts, the first elegiac, lyrical; the second, building upon and repeating images from the first, paced to a Bronski Beat rock song. Images of gay male sexual desire are coupled with

the song's refrain, 'This is not an AIDS advertisement. Feel no guilt in your desire'" (2002: 81).

87 There is, in short, a politics around the quilt to which Butler is oddly inattentive. Jeff Weinstein dubs it "A map of preventable death" which has a more politicizing edge than Butler's treatment of it as an expression of grief for ungrievable life (*Village Voice*, cited in Sturken 1997: 188). It is charged, as already noted above, with being inadequately queer, sentimental, sanitizing (1997: 205). It is credited with reconfiguring relationships of males and masculinity to loss (1997: 206). And it is interestingly non-referential: *anyone* can make a panel and one person can have several panels devoted to them.

88 For a similar critique of Butler on this point, albeit not with reference to the quilt, see Lauren Berlant (2007: 293). Adjudicating other issues between them, see Fiona Jenkins (2009). For an argument, analogous to mine in many ways, about the power of sentimentalism to depoliticize, in his terms by serving as hinge in the turn from tragic to trial narratives in the eighteenth century, see Soni (2010). Where Berlant's critique of sentimentalism is focused on its displacement of politics into communities of affect, Soni is more focused on the self-absorption that is the hidden truth of the practice of proclaimed sympathy with others (chapter 8).

89 Marita Sturken points to hesitations larger than Crimp's regarding the mainstreaming and sentimentalizing politics of the Names Project quilt. These are unmentioned by Butler, whose frame of grievability makes it difficult to fasten on sentimentality as a problem or to specify what exactly that problem is (since grievability seems to be always already sentimental and yet irreducible to it).

90 Both Butler's grievable life and the beautiful death channeled by Crimp yoke together the natal and the mortal, but they are differently inflected and generate different political postures in response to devastation: for Butler, precarity, for Crimp – resilience.

91 See above, note 82.

92 I develop the argument about dignity and use in more detail in Honig (2013). Butler notes how after 9/11 the eulogies of US dead situate the lost in heteronormative family structures – all were said to be married, or about to be – and so doubled the humanizing power of the obituary (2004a: 32).

93 If, as Jean Comaroff (2007) argues, the respectful treatment of the dead by the living is part of a needful practice that connects present to future, then improper (non)burial, as it were, may at times be needed to connect present to a better future.

94 Thus, we may venture, he escapes the criticism implicit in Sedgwick, when she says that it is not enough to move from one affect to two, as in mourning *and* militancy. As I noted above, she does not name Crimp, but it seems she may have him and ACT UP in mind.

95 See my discussion in Chapter 1 of the beautiful death in Vernant.

96 See also Richard Rambuss (1994).

97 The context Crimp wants here is not an original one – it is the one we want for political purposes, for the pictures we want disseminated, as in Benjamin's "The Work of Art in the Age of Mechanical Reproduction" (1969), in which the reproducible image breaks with its context and institutes new ones. See also Butler using Benjamin to talk about frames in *Frames of War* (2009: 9). "No more pictures without context" could also be Butler's slogan when she contests the regulations governing photographs of war dead (2009: 65). Butler cites Sontag, who is exasperated by photos that make her feel outrage but don't show "how to transform that affect into effective political action" (echoing Berlant's critique of Butler, actually, and anticipating critics of melodrama, as we shall see in a moment). Without guidance to such transformation, our encounter with such photographs "excites our moral sentiments at the same time as it confirms our political paralysis," Sontag says (quoted in Butler 2009: 99).

98 Castiglia and Reed (2011) look at queer theory and television sitcoms as resources by way of which to reconnect past and future.

99 It is worth noting that Crimp too is aware of the politics of genre, by which he is clearly informed when he criticizes Larry Kramer's *The Normal Heart* and Randy Shilts' *And the Band Played On*. The former, Crimp says, "is a purely personal – not a political – drama, a drama of a few heroic individuals in the AIDS movement. From time to time, some of these characters talk 'politics.'" Crimp calls attention as well to "the choice of the bourgeois form of drama" which is a "political choice that will have necessary political consequences. Among these is the fact that the play's 'politics' sound very didactic [and] don't 'work'" (2002: 58). Another consequence is the promotion of a singular hero who is made to stand out by contrast with demonized enemies or antagonists. These concerns will return in Part II's reading of *Antigone*.

3 *"Antigone versus Oedipus," II: the directors'* agon *in* Germany in Autumn

1 Though I have argued elsewhere that Gothic romance may be the best genre for democratic theory . . . see "Does Democracy Have a Genre?" in *Democracy and the Foreigner* (2001).

2 The term "Antigone fever" appears in Eric Santner (1992) and may have been coined by George Steiner, in *Antigones* (1996: 107–108), who notes the two periods in the twentieth century in which Antigone's (re)production was particularly fecund: 1934–1944 and 1978–1979. Notably, *Germany in Autumn* was produced in 1978. For further discussion, see Spargo (2008).

3 Jacob Weisberg (2008) emplots Bush's presidency as tragedy. As Michiko Kakutani (2008) says in a *New York Times* review of the book, Weisberg casts George W. Bush as having "'been driven since childhood by a need to differentiate himself from his father, to challenge, surpass and overcome him'; and 'to challenge a thoughtful, moderate and pragmatic father, he

trained himself to be hasty, extreme and unbending,' traits that would ill serve him in his presidency and help lead him into the morass of the Iraq war."

4 Similarly, Max Frisch is seen in *Germany in Autumn* giving a speech in which he castigates the new liberal economy for providing no meaning for youth, but only empty consumerism.

5 In addition to Kluge, the other contributing directors are: Hans Peter Cloos, Rainer Werner Fassbinder, Maxmiliane Mainka, Edgar Reitz, Katja Rupé, Volker Schlöndorff, Peter Schubert, and Bernhard Sinkel.

6 See Jetter et al. (1997) for an essay by a former torture victim describing her experience seeing her torturer after the Dirty War, seated and sipping coffee in a Buenos Aires cafe.

7 Fassbinder's ejection of the stranger undoes the hospitality offered by his partner, Armin, and is duly noted by Douglas Crimp (1982) who, reading others' views of Fassbinder's inhospitality as calling attention to the politics of private property, objects that the more fundamental issue here is his relationship to his lover, Armin. Crimp sees continuities in this regard across three of Fassbinder's films. I would argue that in the context of *Germany in Autumn*, an omnibus film in which Fassbinder is dependent in a way on the hospitality of the film's master director, Kluge, the inhospitality may be seen as directed not (just) toward the hapless fellow ejected in the middle of the night, but at the director on whose (in)hospitality Fassbinder, the director, is (unaccustomedly) dependent. This is in opposition to Kluge's romanticization of German hospitality, presented in the film's other scenes. In short, we may see this as a critique of Kluge and not (just) as a depiction of personal shortcoming. And if it is a critique, it is no mere criticism, for it highlights the material conditions under which hospitality is (im)possible.

8 "Antigone is 'free' after she has become excommunicated from the community. In our time, such acts seem almost unthinkable: their pendants are usually disqualified as 'terrorism,' like the gesture of Gudrun Ensslin, leader of the Red Army Faction" (Žižek, 2001: 77).

9 In the end, the bodies are taken by a Stuttgart cemetery with a distinguished clientele that includes, rather tragically, members of both families – Ensslin's and Schleyer's. As Elsaesser points out, the social distinction of the cemetery's dead makes the larger point that Stuttgart was, like Thebes, home to both parties in conflict: the Ensslin family and the Daimler factory run by Schleyer.

10 Elsaesser writes, "halfway through *Germany in Autumn* a sketch directed by Volker Schlöndorff (and written by novelist Heinrich Böll) turns on a cancelled television production of Sophocles' play." With Antigone, we get "an entire post-romantic politics of interpretation, connoting rebellion and opposition to the State, as well as an order of refusal and resistance of such categorical negation that it challenges the foundations of any form of government, a subject of evident relevance in West Germany, since the Bonn government considered itself the sole legal representative of the German Reich, an ambiguous mandate given the Nazi legacy, and precisely the one contested by the RAF's violent protest" (2004).

11 A recent review of *Germany in Autumn* (Kindley: 2010) summarizes the decision of the television executives regarding the broadcast: "Ultimately they decide not to scrap the film but to 'put it on ice until quieter times' – the exact opposite strategy as that undertaken by the makers of *Germany in Autumn*."

12 Perhaps, then, this is a further "Hamletization" in which dead fathers speak and law's sovereignty dies. The term, Carl Schmitt's, is one I mentioned above and discuss in more detail below. Schleyer also laments his betrayal by the state, which failed to rescue or redeem him from his captors. That betrayal is backgrounded for those in the know by the open (if denied) secret of Schleyer's service in the SS during the war. The real betrayal, for Schleyer, is the regime change. For others, of course, it is the fact that regime change from German Reich to constitutional democracy was unaccompanied by elite change. As Elsaesser says, in his letter Schleyer "implicitly accus[es] the Government of having sacrificed him out of clearly political calculations." He adds in a note: "The sense of official hypocrisy – strongly felt by the members of the Schleyer family at the funeral itself – was also alluded to by the federal president, Walter Scheel, who in his funeral oration said: 'the face of terrorism makes us blanch. But we ourselves may have to look more often into the mirror.'" Schleyer denied his Nazi past, but as Elsaesser puts it, "behind [his] Biedermann appearance the RAF wanted to expose the fervent SS officer he strenuously denied ever having been" (2004). In captivity, Schleyer was apparently several times interrogated by his guards as to his Nazi past, and photos of him in SS uniform circulated in the left-wing press.

13 Rommel's nickname was of course – the Desert Fox. In a further doubling, as Miriam Hansen notes, the German rescuers of the hostages from Mogadishu were hailed in a British newspaper as "desert foxes" (1981: 52).

14 Rommel was suspected of plotting against Hitler so Rommel senior could be cast not just in the role of Nazi father to democratic, if decisive, mayor (son), but also as parricidal son who, Haemon-like, commits suicide when his attempted violence against his own father (Hitler) fails. Like Haemon who is mourned in elegiac terms by his father, Rommel is given the honorific state funeral promised by his.

15 Elsaesser continues: " . . . a feature from which the women's movement had to extricate itself, perhaps by countering this 'Hamletization' of German post-war history with its own (agonising) 'Antigonising'" (2004). I find Elsaesser's critique of the limits of the father–son frame very useful but see no reason why this problem should be cast as necessary just for the women's movement to work through. That said, Taylor did see it that way as well: as we saw in Chapter 2, she had a similar concern, though she worried less about the depoliticizing impact of the Oedipal frame and more about its political power as an instrument of patriarchal politics. Those who turned to it seeking narrative order sought also a route to emancipation but in the end they only found themselves trapped in the eternal return of the same (sons were killed by their fathers or grew up to take their place and women were returned to the home).

16 Fassbinder's "body too much" rendering of Antigone is echoed in more recent attention to Antigone's corporeality in a Deleuzean vein and by way of

melodramatic devices: for example, in a reading of Hertmans' Antigone, Christel Stalpaert says: "Hertmans looks for the tension between personal, corporeal memory, collective memory, and 'public' images of cruelty to actualize Greek tragedies. He does not look for catharsis within a classical dramatic aesthetic, but for a painful and embarrassing actualization 'without catharsis, so that in the end,' he says, 'you do not know which way to go with your emotions.' You are thrown out of kilter and are overwhelmed with images and voices of disgust and suffering" (2008: 149).

17 I return to Rancière's argument in a bit more detail in the Conclusion.

18 Elsaesser may be citing Kaja Silverman (1992) here, who uses this phrase in her book's very brief treatment of the film. We might see "Kluge's own anti-Antigone" as a sharp contrast: Kluge's is a tragic-comic character named Gabi Teichart, a history teacher who in a different sequence in the film professes dissatisfaction with the history curriculum in school, and says she wants to find the foundations of German history. "I'm trying to see things in their proper context," she says. She goes out with a shovel not to bury a body like Antigone does, but to unbury some. Trying to dig in the frozen ground, she finds nothing. Fassbinder, by contrast, puts before us not a no-body but a body-too-much. This is not the erotic body sought by Crimp – Fassbinder is not erect when he touches himself absentmindedly in one scene while talking (again) on the telephone with his ex-wife (or maybe it *is* the erotic body sought by Crimp, then . . .).

19 And this also recalls the tie between mother and child that undergirds, on Irigaray's account, the link between Antigone and Polynices, to whom Antigone repeatedly refers, in Sophocles' text, as son of the same mother.

20 At the end of this chapter, I raise some questions about what the idea of directorial agonism signifies in this context. I note here that when Elsaesser argues that Fassbinder makes clear that the "potential for resistance comes from [a certain] non-equivalence between son and mother, between male and female subjectivity" (2004), there is yet more to be said on this. Fassbinder's character in the film moves from feminine to masculine, abject to authoritarian many times, back and forth, and Elsaesser may rush too quickly to celebrate the mother–son pairing as non- or post-Oedipal. It is also important in this context to note, as Anna Parkinson suggests in a brilliant reading, that Fassbinder shows the son hunting the mother (he wears a safari shirt, she a leopard print top) and that the mother toys with the son, smiling indulgently when she finally confesses a longing for a kind, authoritarian ruler.

21 Is his collapse a defeatist resignation, a performance of impotence in the face of new sovereign state powers? Presumably that would be Marx's view, but we should recall in this context also Benjamin, who rejected as "deprecatory" Marx's "criticism of the professional conspirators as being overly fond of wine" (Martel 2011: 31). Drinking was part of the revolutionary apparatus, Benjamin argued, not a sign of its defeat. Where Marx saw *bambocheurs* or boozers, Benjamin tied the atmosphere of drinking in the taverns of nineteenth-century Paris not to a "miasma" that would undoubtedly have

been familiar to Baudelaire but to an insight given to us by his poetry. For Baudelaire, drunkenness and poetry had something deeply in common: in both a certain subject-decentering confusion attenuates our otherwise devoted relationship to the false promises of the everyday. I am indebted to Samuel Weber's *Benjamin's -abilities* (2008) and also, especially, to James Martel's *Textual Conspiracies* (2011) on which I draw explicitly here. See his discussion of Baudelaire's poem "The Ragpicker's Wine," in which Baudelaire analogizes the drunken ragpicker to the poet: both, "heedless of police informers," pour out their hearts "in glorious devisings" (2011: 32).

22 Miriam Hansen (1981), focusing on film technique rather than text, plot, or genre, sees Kluge's contribution as more radical than that. Hansen argues that Kluge uses marginal shots, voice-overs, and so on to generate a felt need in the spectator for alternative views and to move away from didacticism. Hansen, however, does not attend to the politics of classicization or emplotment.

23 Dissonant music that is either atonal or in some way at odds with the scene depicted is the only one of Brooks' listed traits *not* in Fassbinder's sequence. It is worth noting as well that this *mise en scène* of melodrama, the move from the small town to the big city then back to the now ever more alien small town, characterizes the lives of gay men reported by Crimp, including his own. As Sturken notes, too, in the context of the AIDS crisis, "many young men have returned to their families from the urban centers where they lived in order to be cared for at home, a reversal of the expected movement of children outward from home," a return to the natal rather than conjugal family form, we might say (1997: 192).

24 Does Elsaesser, author of a canonical essay on melodrama, miss this key point in his discussion thirty years later of Fassbinder's sequence in which the genre of melodrama is never mentioned? Why? It may well be because Elsaesser's aim here is different: to show how the tragic "clash between two rights under a system of domination" – preferred by Rancière (2006a) and arguably adopted by Kluge – is self-consuming (2004). Elsaesser makes this clear. The emplotment of political conflict as tragic Oedipal rivalries of fathers and sons yields not saving revelations (contra Rancière) but only unwelcome repetitions, one of which Elsaesser argues is the 1990s television drama, *Todesspiel*, about which more in n.30 below.

25 See Katie Fleming (2008) and Erika Fischer-Lichte (2010: 339): the Nazis "proclaimed a racial kinship between Greeks and Germans . . . Nazi Germany was to be regarded as the legitimate heir of and actual successor to ancient Greece." From 1940 until September 1944 when Goebbels shut down all the Reich theaters, there were 15 productions and 150 performances of *Antigone* recorded on the German stage, reports Fischer-Lichte (2010: 338). See also Suzanne Marchand: the Olympic flame was reintroduced in the 1928 Amsterdam Olympics but the relay from Olympia to the host city was done first in modern times in the 1936 Berlin Olympics. The 1936 Games were, for Hitler, a way to connect the Aryan ideal to classical Greece (1996: 343–368).

26 Focused on the limitations of the Oedipal script of fathers and sons, Elsaesser does not make his argument in genred terms. Indeed, he himself, years earlier, expressed doubts that the distinction I use here to organize his argument, that between tragedy and melodrama, can be sustained. In his 1972 article written about thirty years before his treatment of *Germany in Autumn*, Elsaesser assimilates melodrama to tragedy. Is melodrama simply "tragedy that doesn't quite come off," or is it tragedy in a new key, featuring "pocket-size tragic heroes and heroines" (2003: 392)?

27 Analogously, Adorno charged that Benjamin's inquiry into bohemianism is a sign of Benjamin's seduction "by the cult of futility, wine and magic." In Benjamin's defense, James Martel says something we could say as well of Fassbinder: Benjamin turns abject failure and depoliticization [of "drunken conspirators" of nineteenth-century France] into its opposite (2011: 37).

28 Some deleterious effects of melodrama (albeit not film) on US politics are outlined by Elizabeth Anker in her essay, "Villains, Victims and Heroes: Melodrama, Media and September 11" (2005). However, in a later essay (2011) she considers some of the more positive aspects of the genre.

29 And this scene offers something festive, not funereal. But, as I imagine Elsaesser might say, it may be too little too late, preceded by three hours of father–son clashes that script politics as an ineluctable generational trauma. Elsaesser never mentions this shot, nor responds to its invitation to think that Kluge is trying in some small way perhaps to interrupt and not just reperform conventional, classical tragic forms.

30 Elsaesser points in particular to the mid-1990s television film, *Todesspiel*, which recuperates the story of the hot autumn twenty years after Kluge's *Germany in Autumn*, this time depicting the official leaders of 1970s West Germany as well prepared for their role to defend the state from attack precisely by their experience as (denazified) *Wehrmacht* soldiers in the Second World War. The very traits that at midcentury were seen as evidence of the incipient authoritarianism of the would-be democratic state, are twenty years later co-opted, rescripted (in the way perhaps called for by Schleyer in his letter to his son) as the necessary and laudable ingredients of its success in defending itself against terrorist violence. "And so," Elsaesser sums up, with *Todesspiel*, "the past is mastered to the extent that we gain good fathers [and] it is de-oedipalized and it is de-antigonised as well" (2004). This 1990s version of Germany's hot autumn is a kinder gentler drama of sons and fathers, more romance than tragedy. Kluge invites this problematic *Aufhebung*, Elsaesser argues, by trying to master events with his Oedipal frame rather than aestheticize them in their sublime singularity.

31 Indeed, Fassbinder was annoyed that other directors took longer to produce their sequences and had more time to process events and deliver more sober, polished products.

32 This presses on us a question: is Agamben positioned in relation to political theory as Fassbinder is to Kluge? Disrupting in an apparently easily dismissed way the "serious" work of analysis by making reference in overheated prose

and exaggerated examples to a violence that is real and no one is talking about? LaCapra does not call him melodramatic but clearly casts him that way when he objects to "the shrill yet leveling logic in Agamben's exclamation" (2004: 178) that "if we do not succeed in understanding that match, in stopping it, there will never be hope" (Agamben, quoted in LaCapra 2004: 178). This, for Rancière, who otherwise has little in common with trauma theorists like LaCapra, is precisely the problem with Agamben: "all differences are erased [by him] in the global situation" whose law seems to be "the accomplishment of an ontological destiny that leaves no room for political dissension and expects salvation only from an improbably ontological revolution" (2006a, 10). The turn to catastrophe is, for Rancière, the turn to Antigone.

I am reminded here of J. M. Coetzee's melodramatic Elizabeth Costello, a catastrophic thinker who feels that the modern treatment and consumption of animals is comparable to the Holocaust, and who at one point is so astounded that no one else seems to share her perspective, that she says she feels like she is the only one in the world who sees that the lampshades others treat as ordinary are made of Jewish skin: no matter how many times she points it out, no one seems to see it or mind it.

33 Diana Taylor was drawn to the possibility that *Antigone* might be reiterated in more promising ways than those, like the Madres' lamentation politics, that are too easily co-opted by male-centered politics of fathers and sons. Although Taylor worried about the tendency of certain scripts, like the Oedipal one, to slide from tragedy into pornography, she did not put it in these terms and she never posed the question of genre as such. On the reactionary effects of pornographic protest against torture, see her first chapter in *Disappearing Acts* (1997a), which also conveys her felt inability as an American academic effectively to object to it. The quest to escape the father–son dyad by way of the daughter is complicated by the fact that Oedipus, in his play, refers to his daughters as sons, while feminizing and orientalizing his sons as daughter-like. This bit of gender trouble is not noted in political theory's reception of Oedipus, though Butler does note it in *Antigone's Claim* (2000: 62).

34 I think it is fair to ally genre-switching with what Martel calls, following Benjamin, the "deepening of intent," part of a Benjaminian conspiracy with language (2011).

35 In his essay, "Dramaturgy and Sentimentality in *Antigone*," O'Hanlon sees Anouilh as rendering Antigone melodramatic, but I want to say if this is true it is Anouilh intensifying something already in the play. For O'Hanlon, "Anouilh has let this sentimentality so overwhelm his play that he cannot expect any further complicity on our part in a scheme designed to exploit our shoddier emotional susceptibilities: he cannot expect to regain the cooperation of those still left in the auditorium until intelligence, distance and control reappear on stage to balance the uninterrupted gush of cheap feeling. This, I believe, does not happen until the central speech of the Chorus" (1990: 131). O'Hanlon continues: "The fact that Anouilh feels it necessary to induce in us the affective response to the action and suffering of tragedy *by external*

means; the fact that he gives us this lesson in such a self-conscious and distorted way; the fact that pathos and sentimentality break through the control exercised by the Chorus in the opening section of the great central speech – all point to the submersion of tragedy in [Anouilh's] *Antigone* by the melodramatic mode" (1990: 135).

36 On genre-switching, see my "The Event of Genre: From Rancière to Von Trier" (Forthcoming).

Introduction to Part II

1 Weber parsing Benjamin: "'Through a gesture of submission' to classical models and standards, the baroque in its novelty sought 'to secure for itself the most binding authority,' that of ancient Greece" (2008: 142). Arendt (1990, chapter 5) will later provide a similar critique of the American founders for seeking the authority of ancient Rome and failing to own their own invention. James Martel notes that for Benjamin there was something positive about how "in their stumbling and accidental way, playwright and characters alike are undermining and countering the very spectacle of state power that these plays formally set out to depict (and praise)" (2011: 6). Diego Rossello notes the same detail: the German mourning play is a space for the swaying about of its characters as "torn and flapping banners," imprisoned in the "emotional storm" of their "changing resolve" (2011: 71; 251).

2 We shall encounter in Chapter 5 a similar king, surrounded by plotters, in Cavarero's reading of the Calvino story, "A King Listens," but that king is not beyond redemption: he listens and so is available to be lured, beyond the world of court intrigue, by the sound of a woman singing.

3 This obviously calls into question the commitment of Mark Griffith to the idea that in "the surviving plays . . . the minor characters' attitudes and desires tend to be affected by, *but never to cause or determine*, the key crises and reversals of the plot" (1998: 20; emphasis added). It is worth noting now that this is one of the many places where I propose attributing greater agency to characters to counterbalance interpretations of the play that, until now, grant greater agency to language, to the gods, or to the tragic. This is not to deny the powers of the latter, nor to assume more sovereign subject-centered forms of agency. It is rather to use the possibility of intentionality, but not just that, to enable a certain redistribution of the weights of intention, language, and context throughout the play and to pluralize the possibilities of interpretation. Perhaps, then, this is a weak messianic reading of the play – in which small alterations, not always intended, may open up chasms of change.

4 That is, as I noted above in Part I, Chapter 2, what Butler says about the curse in tragedy and the norms by which we are constituted now: it is possible to turn them in new directions. We are not just constrained by them, we may inherit them otherwise. As I argued above, this should be the case as well with frames, which should be alterable, as sovereignty may be, and not just in need

of replacement, as Butler argues with reference to sovereignty – that it needs to be replaced by precariousness.

5 In Martel's parsing, "our own agency can 'survive' our turning away from what passes for our intentionality and toward a 'progressive deepening . . . of intention'" (2011: 9).

6 What is important here, as Martel also points out, is that louts are not just failures but potentially signs of revolutionary promise. After all they are failures when judged by the standards of the very system Benjamin thinks betrays us.

7 An example of how conspiracy and plot are debased from the liberal democratic perspective of transparency is Judith Fletcher's claim that "Public talk has become displaced in Thebes – squeezed into private conversations and secret debates – but it cannot be completely silenced." Here Fletcher implies that it is in the absence of the open modes of communication that gossip flourishes. The former is the proper political mode, the latter its abject other. Elsewhere, however, she grants to both modes of communication their importance and place: "Thebes is abuzz with talk of the interdiction and Antigone's defiance, but the informal yet conventional modes of communication [e.g. gossip] which had authority in the Athenian democracy, are occluded in the Theban tyranny" (2010: 176). She cites Ober on gossip and rumor "as one of several political forums of debate and communication, along with the courts, assembly, and theater," suggesting Ober does not distinguish high and low forms of communication, as most democratic theorists do (1989: 148–151).

8 The violation of chronology is an aspect of reception studies invited most by Charles Martindale. But the preference expressed here for the alien over the familiar violates what is left of context by Martindale's hermeneutics. Other contributors to reception studies ultimately replace one context with another. Treating classical tragedy, for example, in the context of nineteenth- or twentieth-century "receptions," they do not abandon contextualism, they re-locate it, and the "original" gets its meaning from its (now non-original) context.

9 That these three key scenes are those in which Antigone does not directly address Creon may help account for the possibility of a new way of interpreting the text. In most treatments, the *agon* with Creon takes center stage and everything else that happens in the play orbits this central event. Oriented toward plotting and conspiracy we are drawn rather to the several scenes that are not so confrontational and that are arguably more politically promising.

10 Contra Simon Goldhill's reading of my argument (charging that mine is a "drastic redrafting of Sophocles' play [that] offers a new image of sisters who despite their bitter arguments really love each other and would always be there for each other" [2012: 247]), and in anticipation of other such misconstruals, I underline one of the final lines of my essay, "Ismene's Forced Choice," amended and expanded into Chapter 6 here: "The move to mark the sororal agency in this play should not be mistaken for a normative effort to promote

sorority as a privileged site of agency ... That we find here an agonistic sorority is not reason to privilege sorority as a site of agency everywhere." That said, I see no reason why we should rule out as overly modern (Goldhill's charge) the possibility that the two sisters at the center of Sophocles' tragedy do love each other and act accordingly, which is to say when they act out (of) love they may do any of the thousands of ordinary to mad things that people do or have done in other times and places. I return to Goldhill in Chapter 6.

11 This is the move made by Jennet Kirkpatrick (2009) in a reading that otherwise has some affinities with mine in Chapter 6. I discuss this reading in more detail in the notes to Chapter 6.

12 But it risks introducing a host of questions and assumptions about story-patterns, plot-outcomes, character, and causation that are anachronistic. In the latter case, the move to genre is "too crude a tool, encouraging a view of genre that is too prescriptive and that oversimplifies the stemmatics of inter-generic affinities" (Mastronarde 2010: 61). Melodrama, Mastronarde says, originally (at the turn of the nineteenth century) referred to theater that incorporated musical numbers "but soon came to apply to a genre of play with a double plot, containing a mixed reversal for the persecuted virtuous characters and the villain ... Melodrama was stigmatized for its moralizing and for its strong emotional effects by the critics of a century ago," who preferred realism in drama (2010: 62). (Thanks to Demetra Kasimis for calling my attention to Mastronarde's discussion of melodrama.) Recalling melodrama's preference for members of the lower orders over elites, Euripides again fits well with the modern genre: as Mark Griffith notes, "late fifth-century critics do indeed complain on occasion that Euripides has debased tragedy by putting beggars, whores, and criminals on stage" (1998: 21, n. 7).

13 Notably, Mastronarde says: "an unprejudiced critic might note melodra-matic features even in *Oedipus Tyrannus,* taken by so many theorists as the paradigm of true tragedy" (2010: 61; citing Redmond 1992). Noting such prejudice, Mastronarde rightly says that Heilman's *Tragedy and Melodrama* (1968) discusses the contrast between the two genres in several ways and defends the place of melodrama in the dramatic tradition, but throughout his discussion "there is undeniably an undertone of his acceptance of the superiority not only of real tragedy but also of the audience that wants tragedy" (2010: 61).

14 Craik aims here to make clear the historical possibility that Sophocles was perhaps even influenced by Euripides. I am more focused on the interpretative possibilities opened up once we permit ourselves, for whatever (historical or interpretative) reason, to approach Sophocles (and not just the late Sophocles of the *Philoctetes*), through the genre expectations of melodrama. In this vein, Knox (1964), quoted by Craik, says that in some tragedies the hero suffers rather than acts. Here too Antigone seems to be a hybrid.

15 Aristotle himself defends tragedy over epic, but makes it clear that common opinion differs. I am indebted here to Christina Tarnopolsky.

16 He then goes on to say that the same person cannot be good at writing comedy and tragedy: "the same men aren't capable of producing good imitation in both at the same time" (395a). Plato here also prohibits his guardians from imitating anyone who abuses her husband or who is "caught in the grip of misfortune, mourning and wailing" (395e). He frames this material saying it is necessary to banish laughter and lamentation from the stories about heroes. In our own time, we can see this as a concern to contain not just tragedy, as we know it, but also melodrama – or to collapse them.

17 Melodrama is not only counterposed to tragedy. Carolyn Williams suggests a certain continuity between tragedy and melodrama (here echoing Elsaesser), especially with regard to themes of freedom and necessity when she notes that melodrama "insistently concentrates on the implacable force of social relations and the consequences of deviating from their conventions of normalization" (2004: 115). In Fassbinder, of course, the state and not society is the locus of implacability, though conventional social mores are also sources of pressure.

18 As Brooks says, melodrama "generally ends in resignation" with characters "emerg[ing] as lesser human beings for having become wise and acquiescent to the ways of the world" (1976: 77). Thus it seems to invert tragedy which, as we just saw, ennobles heroes who refuse to acquiesce, even when confronted by terrible obstacles.

19 I am indebted to conversation with James Martel on this point.

4 Mourning, membership, and the politics of exception: plotting Creon's conspiracy with democracy

1 An earlier version of this chapter appeared in *Political Theory* as "Antigone's Laments, Creon's Grief: Mourning, Membership, and the Politics of Exception" (2009b). I have in the Acknowledgments thanked Sage Press for permission to reuse the material here. But I would like to point out that this chapter significantly amends elements of the essay's argument I have come to think of as erroneous. For example, I do not argue here that Creon represents democracy but rather that he exemplifies one elite tactic for coming to terms with the new democratic order: that is, he conspires with democracy. And I moderate my earlier view of Creon's grief as explosive of all codes of mourning as such.

2 "The fixation articulated by Antigone with regard to her Oedipal family may also be seen as a reflexion of Sophocles' (or the Athenians') fantasy of elite family relations in particular as they are configured by – and reactive to – the (relatively newly) dominant structures and limitations of democratic Athenian society. For Antigone, a member of Thebes' most distinguished family, the 'honour' and 'glory' of Oedipus and his son can only be matched and perpetuated by philoi of equivalent social stature – that is, themselves . . . Creon, by contrast, seems to represent the newer breed of elites who are willing to work within the democratic system and to shape their own claims and choices to conform with what is 'good for the city'" (Griffith 2010: 123).

That is, the reading here looks at Creon's "democratic entanglements," to borrow the title phrase of Sara Monoson's book on Plato, though in Creon's case, as we shall see, there is also complicity.

3 I cite several sources for this contextualization, an argument that finds abundant support from Richard Seaford's *Reciprocity and Ritual* (1994) (see especially chapter 4, "Collective Death Ritual"), and more briefly from Boedeker and Raaflaub's essay in Bushnell (2005), "Tragedy and the City": "The conflict over Polynices' burial reminds us of the Athenian burial of war dead in a public cemetery, a custom introduced soon after the Persian Wars, in which the state clearly arrogated a family function: Thucydides, 2.34" (2005: 121).

4 In short, the play does what Jean-Pierre Vernant says all tragedy does: "The true subject matter of tragedy is social thought and most especially juridical thought in the very process of elaboration. Tragedy poses problems of law, and the question of what justice is" (1972: 278–279). David Roselli (2006) and H. A. Shapiro (2006) document the contestedness of new burial legislation that limited the size and appearance of grave markers. The forbidden markers are Homeric/heroic, the permitted markers feature citizens in their civic rather than martial roles and feature women, for the first time, perhaps because of the new domestic ideology of the polis or perhaps, Roselli argues, because new citizenship laws require citizen mothers as well as fathers, and grave markers are a way of marking (maternal) citizenship. I use the term Homeric here and throughout not to assume a specific reference to Homer in fifth-century elite practices of burial but rather to suggest that if, as I argue here, Sophocles sought, among other things, to explore the contestedness of fifth-century funerary practice, he may well have found resources for doing so in Homeric epic and the values expressed therein. (See Goldhill 2012: esp. 248 but throughout, contrasting the "Homeric household" and the "(democratic) city state.") I treat the Homeric as a rival world view or table of values, not (yet) confined to the household.

5 See my *Democracy and the Foreigner* (2001) on the analogous use of the foreigner or outsider to explore or displace domestic political problems.

6 This view of Antigone goes against the common claim that she is democratic. I suggest we distinguish between the claim that a "typically Athenian democratic ideology [runs] through the *Antigone*" (I agree that it does, but I do not see it as belonging to any one character, it is in circulation among Creon, Haemon, the Chorus, and more), and the idea (which Andreas Markantonatos calls "persuasive") that "Antigone should be treated as a praiseworthy guardian of democratic values and assurances." As evidence for this, Markantonatos points to precisely the evidence I argue here indicates the opposite: "By the standards of Attic ideology, Antigone espouses fundamental concepts of the democracy, so remarkably celebrated in the politically charged genre of the Funeral Oration in honour of the war dead." This argument seems to me to rest on a somewhat vague association of Antigone the lamenter, with the Oration, with the democracy. And the actual evidence then given for

Antigone's democratic character is thin – it is simply that she opposes someone who is not democratic. Moreover, here too the argument is associative: she opposes Creon's authoritarianism, his imperviousness to public recommendations, and his rejection of the better judgment of others. But these are merely procedural dimensions of democracy and notably, these flaws are shared by Antigone herself, who cares not a whit for the better judgments of others. As evidence of her democratic nature, Markantonatos offers, in the end, only her opposition to Creon's "authoritarian government" – but the democrats, as I argue here, looked authoritarian to aristocrats in the fifth century, as well, so the argument here seems to me to fall short (2007: 222).

7 For Derrida's reading of *Oedipus at Colonus*, see *Of Hospitality: Anne Dufourmantelle Invites Jacques Derrida to Respond* (2000). That Antigone is deprived of lamentation rites for both her father/brother and her brother calls attention to another pair of details: Oedipus' body mysteriously disappears (in Sophocles' *Oedipus at Colonus*) while that of Polynices refuses to disappear and repeatedly turns up as carrion in the city. Both circumstances make proper lament impossible.

8 Arlene Saxonhouse (2005) seeks to de-exceptionalize Antigone's dissidence too. She turns to Euripides' version because she finds in him but not in Sophocles an account of the "conditions" under which Antigone acquires political agency.

9 I discuss her self-location between the two extremes of marriage in Chapter 5, below.

10 On this point as on others, I differ from Christiane Sourvinou-Inwood (1989), one of the few to suggest Creon represents the democracy. She focuses in her reading not on the ban on lamentation but on the classical democracy's demand for unity and obedience. She seems to think these are represented in the play in a way that *endorses* the democratic ideology. I return to her argument in Chapter 5.

11 As Rush Rehm puts it, "[i]t seems to have been standard Athenian practice to refuse burial on Attic soil to traitors and those guilty of sacrilege . . . Against this practice however was the pan-Hellenic custom that the dead were owed burial *somewhere* . . . a compulsion that was magnified if the dead were kin" (1994: 181, n. 9). Cf. Burian (2010).

12 Thus, on this reading, we do not have to choose, as most classicists do, between Creon as democrat versus Creon as tyrant, nor need we say that the audience was divided between these two options. See Kathryn Morgan (2003).

13 For an argument that supports my view of Creon as reminiscent in some ways of Pericles, albeit made in a referential register, arguing that Creon *is* Pericles, see Michael Vickers's *Sophocles and Alcibiades*: "It has often been noted that Creon's insistence that the interests of the state should always come before those of family (182–90) resemble the views that Thucydides puts into Pericles' mouth (Thuc. 2.38–46 and 2.60). But there is more to say on this particular point, for just as Creon's first speech (162–210) contains obtrusive

references to himself and his personal opinions . . . the same is true of Pericles'
second Thucydidean speech" (2008: 16–17, and *passim*). Citing Plutarch,
Vickers notes that "'Pericles was overbearing and insolent in conversation
and his pride had in it a great deal of contempt for others.'" This, Vickers says,
"corresponds closely to the Creon of *Antigone*" (2008: 18).

14 Creon's focus is on Polynices' treason, as Rush Rehm points out, but Polynices confounds the effort to binarize: he is "both *philos* to Antigone and
echthros to Thebes" (1994: 12–13). Antigone makes the point clear when she
says to Ismene in the first scene of the play: "The doom reserved for enemies
marches on the ones we love the most" (9–10 [12–13]). The confusion is
unfortunate for Creon since (as Rehm says in the context of a discussion of
Medea) his "principle of doing 'harm to your enemies and good to your
friends' . . . demands a clear distinction between the two end-terms, 'friends'
and 'enemies'" (1994: 148). See also Foley on this issue: "Antigone and Creon
use the same vocabulary in subtly different ways – the words *philos* (friend)
and *echthros* (enemy), for example, develop different connotations in the
context in which each character deploys them" (2001: 173). That Antigone
and Creon share a vocabulary is a point fundamental to Butler's reading of the
play in *Antigone's Claim*.

Creon is sensitive to the flux of status and identity, more so than
Antigone who argues for Polynices' burial by reference to his status: "it
was . . . not some slave that died" (517 [581]). Her point is challenged *avant
la lettre*, when Creon subtly points to the flux of the identity "slave" saying
of Polynices: "he thirsted to drink his kinsmen's blood and sell the rest to
slavery." Those who are free citizens one day may be slaves the next, if their
city is conquered. Thus for Creon, action or deeds and not, contra Antigone,
status, are what matters most. Jill Frank's treatment of this idea in Aristotle
alerted me to it here. See Jill Frank (2005) and Saxonhouse (1996), in
particular chapter 5.

The flux of status argues against Roselli, who reads Creon and Antigone as
offering different views of Polynices' (static) class status. Notably, Roselli
quotes only the part of Creon's speech that says "he thirsted to drink his
kinsmen's blood" but not the part about selling the rest to slavery (2006: 144).
Roselli, however, is right to see that the mid-fifth-century regulation of
burial, specifically, is at issue in this play. He offers a wealth of material
evidence that supports the claims made here. I differ from him, however, in
emphasizing in my reading of the play specifically the ban on lamentation, the
several dirges sung in the play (not just the burial of Polynices), and in treating
the heroic/elite practices under pressure as not just an elite fashion statement
(2006: 168, n. 85) but a rival form of life under pressure from the democracy in
this period.

15 And, notes Charles Segal, "Plutarch adds that even [500 years after *Antigone*]
the *gunaikonomoi* could punish those who indulged in 'unmanly and
womanly expressions of emotion and grieving'" (1993: 63). For more on the
gunaikonomoi, see Nicole Loraux (1998: 23–24).

16 See also Garland (1985: 33 and *passim*); Douglas MacDowell (1978: 109ff.); Foley (2001: 22–27).

17 Garland, citing a study of surviving dirges, notes that the ritual was "intended at least partly to satisfy the soul of the deceased . . . The deceased's passage to the next world had yet to begin" (1985: 30–31).

18 Although, as Garland points out, drawing on Eberhard Friedrich Bruck's *Totenteil und Seelgerät im griechischen Recht* (1970 [1926]), the regulation of excess in funerary practice may cut both ways, as far as democracy is concerned: limiting "the amount which goes into a tomb increases the amount which can be inherited by the heirs" (Garland 1985: xxii). Aubrey Cannon suggests another counter-intuitive explanation, parsed by Foley: rather than democratize, rules against ostentatious funerals may have guarded a class distinction under pressure, protecting "symbolic distinctions in death rituals" from being blurred by lower-class imitations of the wealthy (2001: 23, n. 8).

19 See also Foley (2001: 22–27) and Loraux (1998). McClure says: "The association of laments with blood vendetta, as well as their extravagant feminine nature, perhaps contributed to the many reforms of excessive funerary displays in Athens and elsewhere" (1999: 45).

20 The shift is noted by Holst-Warhaft, most pointedly, but tracked as well by Foley and Taxidou. Vernant explicates the Homeric episteme in detail, but attends less to the shift. Testifying to the contestedness of this shift over a century or more, Plato in the *Republic* has Socrates argue for the erasure from Homer of all the passages that describe death or the dead in ways that arouse emotions: "We'll beg Homer and the other poets not to be harsh if we strike out these things and all similar things. It's not that they are not poetic and sweet for many to hear, but the more poetic they are, the less should they be heard by boys and men who must be free and accustomed to fearing slavery more than death" (387b). For a contrary view, see Jonathan Shay, *Achilles in Vietnam: Combat Trauma and the Undoing of Character* (1994). Shay finds in Homer inspiration for soldiers today. A differently contrary view is to be found in Adriana Cavarero, *For More Than One Voice* (2005), discussed in more detail in Chapter 5. Cavarero notes the importance of voice to Homer and says that for Plato, voice was a problem because of its materiality and instability. In the *Republic*, Plato has Socrates rewrite into indirect speech or narration a part of the *Iliad* that Homer presents as direct speech. The aim of the rewrite is to mute Agamemnon's rage and a priest's call for revenge. In Book X, 603c–606b, Socrates worries about the dangers of Homeric mourning as represented in tragedy. On the shift from vengeance to law in classical Athens, see Danielle Allen (2000).

21 The point is made by Kerri J. Hame (2008) as well in an essay arguing that the focus on female lamentation in classics is an overplayed hand, the unfortunate result of an admirable desire to find something to say about the virtually voiceless (given the few survivals left to scholars to work with) women of the

fifth century. There were both, Hame says, male and female roles in burial and lament and it is an error to treat this set of rituals as specifically belonging to a female domain (as, she argues, Alexious does). This does not address the issue presented here, which has to do with the feminization of aspects of the ritual, which is part of their abjection.

22 Perhaps they had become such; but apart from empirics, the point is that they were experienced as excessive.

23 The laments, especially the kinswomen's, "are not filled with praise of [the dead's] heroic feats but generally focus on the plight of the bereaved" (Holst-Warhaft 1992: 114). This fits the pattern of Antigone's *goos* for Polynices (his treason would make it difficult to praise his deeds, in any case). Historical evidence suggests that in the wake of Solon's ban on laments, a culture war may have followed: the mourning outlawed at home and gendered feminine is cast as excessive, barbaric, and "eastern." With the Persian War, more than a century later, the referent of these traits – excessive, barbaric, and eastern – becomes: "Persian." Depicted as prone to excess in mourning, Persia was figured as vulnerable to Greek power and this further secured the Greek resolve to mourn, by contrast, moderately and patriotically: "the longest and most intense lamentation by tragic males is to be found in Aeschylus' *Persians* [where] the mourners are defeated barbarians, and as Edith Hall has demonstrated, their lament clearly feminizes them, makes them from the Greek perspective the antitype of the idealized male. Unlike Greek men, Xerxes and the Persian elders tear their beards and their clothes (feminine *peploi*) and beat their flesh" (Foley 2001: 29). The lamentations, nearly equally the property of men and women in Homer, then cast as the domain of women in Greece, are rendered other in Aeschylus' *Persians*.

24 Some had in them names to be cursed: "[i]n certain cases as many as ten or fifteen persons are cursed on a single tablet. Other tablets are more explicit, containing formulae which curse the tongue, the eyes, the mouth, the psyche, the sanity, the arms and the legs of the named person, and invoke the assistance of the underworld deities, Persephone and Hermes." The same may be true of another innovation, a "form of cursing [that] set a small lead figure with bound hands inside a lead coffin with an inscription on the inside lid." Plato refers to the practice at 364c in the *Republic*, as Garland points out. "Often the reason for cursing appears to have been a lawcourt testimony" (1985: 6–7). The *katadesmoi* may have been an iteration of the earlier, now-forbidden, revenge-seeking laments.

25 But not just women's lamentations: "[m]ale lament in Homer does not carry the connotations of femininity and theatricality that are attached to it after Solon's laws are implemented" (Taxidou 2004: 176). Still, there may have been gendered differences in mourning: "the two main gestures of mourning on Geometric vases [were] the female attitude of holding both hands to the head and tearing the hair, and the male attitude of holding one hand to the head, apparently beating it but not actually tearing the hair" (Garland 1985: 29).

26 Also at issue, speculate some commentators, was a power struggle among women's clans, the aristocracy, Solon, and the new polis form. On this, see Foley (2001: 23–25) and Holst-Warhaft (1992: 114–119). Two centuries later, Plato identified women with loud mourning, while acknowledging that men so weep too. In Plato's *Phaedo*, when Socrates drinks the poison, the men who surround him begin to weep but he quickly calls them to order: "What is this strange outcry?" asks Socrates, "I sent away the women mainly in order that they might not offend in this way" (117d). Monicka Patterson-Tutschka (2007), taking a cue from Iris Young, comments on this as an instance of *logos* disciplining emotion. See also Loraux (1998: 10–11) on Plato's hostility to maternal mourning.

27 Students in Tina Chanter's Antigone seminar at DePaul alerted me to this passage.

28 On this, see Loraux (1986: especially 42–50) whose work is foundational for all the contemporary authors referred to here.

29 This distinction is hard to maintain, since we only know about the beauteous bodies because of Homer's beautiful words. Still Homer's words do not call attention to themselves as a source of solace in the way that the language of the Funeral Oration does. See also Saxonhouse on "the bodiless world of" Pericles' Funeral Oration where "death is unfelt" and whose "model of democracy," she says, "abstracts from history, from particularistic ties, and most especially from bodies" (1996: 64; 60). Pericles, she adds, "does not talk of training bodies or fashioning arms but instead discusses the Athenian policy of openness" (1996: 63–64). His underestimation of the importance of bodies is brought home with a vengeance, she notes, when Thucydides turns to discuss the plague and its effects on Athenian bodies.

30 "The women, having lamented before the public funeral, could no longer reenact the memory of their lost ones afterward, for the common war grave of the fallen soldiers buried tribe by tribe prohibited contact with individual dead" (Blok 2001: 106).

31 Taxidou adds that "Phrynicus himself, as a corrective gesture, wrote the *Phoenician Women* twenty years later" (2004: 97). Phrynicus' error, says Loraux, was to elicit a mourning with which Athenians, who *shared* an identity as Ions with the Miletans, identified too closely, and to replay events in which Athenians were implicated. Tragedy requires distance (in space and time) to be safe (1998: 85; 87). For Taxidou, *Persians*, also historically based, "needs to be read in the shadow of that extraordinary ban" (2004: 96–97).

32 On the active role of spectators in classical theater, see Sara Monoson (2000). Charles Segal (1995a), in his elegant chapter 5 of *Sophocles' Tragic World*, comes close to the reading I offer here. He too sees Creon as representing a broader Athenian effort to contain certain forms of mourning. We differ both on details I specify below, and also, more importantly, on the larger issue of what is at stake in the containment effort. For Segal the threat to polis order has not to do with a Homeric/heroic table of values but, more narrowly, with

women's mourning and loud grief that threatens the polis. Though he mentions vengeance in passing, his structuralism points him rather to a culture/nature divide, so he identifies Antigone with lamentation and nature, and Creon with civilization, as such. Thus, Segal misses the significance of Creon's lament, which I discuss below, and more broadly the politics of elite (non)accommodations to democracy. For further discussion, see Segal (1995a: 119–123; 135–136). Others who identify Antigone with elements of what I am calling a Homeric episteme include Simon Goldhill (1986) and Theodore Ziolkowski (1997). For Goldhill, Antigone's Homeric identity is represented by her individuality (a rather formal trait, as opposed to the more substantive markers identified here) and for Ziolkowski, as for Hegel, Antigone represents the chthonic effeminate accorded more respect in Homer than in democratic Athens.

33 "The fifth-century performance of *Antigone* could have raised important questions about the valuation of the individual as opposed to that of the collective citizen body, the legitimacy of the imposition (by *nomos* or otherwise) of democratic uniformity on individual tomb markers, and the right of the polis to bury – and to memorialize – its own fallen warriors outside of or above the claims of their families," says Sarah Brown Ferrario in an article that provides archaeological evidence for this claim and supports my reading of the play (2006: 104). Ferrario offers no reading of the play, but, in passing references to it, she assumes Creon is a tyrant. For her, then, the citation of Creon's Periclean speech by Demosthenes in the fourth century needs explanation (2006: 80). Ferrario suggests that by the fourth century Creon has been rehabilitated. On my reading, no such explanation is needed since Creon was in both centuries marked as democratic, even if hyperbolically so. Sourvinou-Inwood's "Assumptions and the Creation of Meaning" also cites Demosthenes' use of Creon's speech as evidence in favor of her view that Creon is democratic. Her reading rests on different details than mine, centrally on the issue of treason and burial, and positions a democratic Creon against Antigone's "bad girl" dissidence with no alertness to the complexities of lamentation politics.

34 If Antigone buries Polynices twice, she mirrors Creon, who upon hearing of Eurydice's death wails "I died once, you kill me again and again!" (1288 [1416]) or as in Gibbons and Segal's (2003) translation "Aiee! You have killed a destroyed man twice over!" (122). This may repay Creon for trying to kill Polynices twice. For the view that Creon's refusal to bury Polynices evidences rage and the desire to kill him again, see George Steiner (1996: esp. 50–51) on Goethe.

35 Achilles says, "There is a dead man who lies by the ships, unwept, unburied: Patroklos: and I will not forget him … " (22.386).

36 I note below another commonality with Achilles: Antigone tries herself to secure, before her death, the terms of her *kleos*.

37 Her first mourning, unrecorded, is unwitnessed but is performed out in the open, at night. This may be a way to suggest that under the ban on lamentation,

mourning occurs in secret, but out in the open; as an open secret. Or, Charles Segal may be right when he suggests brilliantly that if the first burial speech is unrecorded, unwitnessed, that may be because it is actually not performed by Antigone but rather, as the elders worriedly suggest, by the gods (1999a: 160). This possibility opens the play up and may explain why Antigone will not disavow the deed nor own up to it, a point made much of by Butler in *Antigone's Claim* and revisited by her in the context of a reading of confessions in *Undoing Gender* (2004b). This may seem to argue against my point that Antigone in burying Polynices twice buries to excess, but it is surely excessive to bury a second time, regardless of whose agency is responsible for the first burial. For Creon, in any case, the second burial is "excessive" since it indulges in the forbidden laments. I attend to the first burial in detail in Chapter 6.

38 Not quite all the forbidden elements of lament are in play here. Antigone does not self-lacerate. This may suggest she is less excessive than Creon (excessively) thinks. And/or it may suggest she is already domesticated by the polis' substitution of *logos* for embodiment. If she does not self-lacerate, does that mean her grief is somehow articulable or subject to expression in ways that can do without the fleshly expression common in Homer?

Notably, since the sentry *describes* what he heard, the report is witness testimony and therefore potentially suspect. Sophocles could have had Antigone perform the *goos* on stage; she is said to have done it openly, with the sun high in the sky. Yet we do not hear her directly (might this be a way of staging its prohibition?) and so the question arises – what did the sentry really hear? And how might his report itself be affected by the expectations he would have had of what Antigone *would* do, as an elite/Homeric figure? The report is his perception of what she did; it may be framed by their class difference, it may be the report of a plotter. We might say the same of Eurydice's laments, discussed below, which are also reported by a member of the lower orders. In this context, it is worth noting the play itself flags the possible unreliability of the sentry's testimony when the sentry says that he and his fellows watched Antigone pour libations but also says "soon as we saw her we rushed her" (432–433 [480–481]). This last line might garner quite a laugh from audiences: if he is a plotter, he is not a very good one.

39 Dewald and Kitzinger note that Antigone's doubts may be exacerbated by the fact that she has no idea anyone supports her. She does not witness Haemon's argument with Creon and has heard nothing positive from anyone (2006: 125). I will argue in Chapter 6 that Antigone has Ismene's support and this may matter. A more subtle indicator of popular support is also offered by the sentry. In a line whose significance no one notes, the sentry says as he brings Antigone to Creon, "it hurts a man to bring down his friends. But all that, I'm afraid, means less to me than my own skin" (438–440 [487–489]). If he, an ordinary man, an everyman, thinks of Antigone as a friend betrayed, that suggests the people are not against her. This is said in her presence, she hears it, and it opens the possibility I have tendered here: that this sentry is a plotter.

40 White cites Simone Weil, "*The Iliad*, or The Poem of Force" (1945). Of course, Antigone's refusal to distinguish between her brothers is also compatible with the idea that she simply privileges her natal family over all other considerations.

41 For this point I am indebted to conversation with Josh Ober.

42 Spectators may have included Athenians and foreigners. Still, I take it to be uncontroversial that tragic and comic theater in some way engaged issues of political or cultural import to Athens. This leaves open the question of whether theater supported or subverted Athenian civic ideology or anything else. For further discussion, see Simon Goldhill (1990).

43 Foley is just one of many to note the offensiveness of Creon's suggestion (2001: 184). Andrew Brown (1987) refers to it as "perhaps the coarsest line in Greek tragedy." In their focus on its offensiveness, critics may miss its irony and referent. Vickers agrees with Brown, though Page duBois has done a great deal to study the not uncommon use of the term "furrow" in Greek texts. For further discussion, see duBois's "Toppling the Hero" (2008), as well as her *Sowing the Body* (1988). Importantly, Loraux also discusses duBois's work in *Mothers in Mourning* (1998: 75–76). For Vickers, this line is simply more evidence that Creon is Pericles: the line draws "cruel and crude attention to the string of women whose company Pericles enjoyed" (2008: 21).

44 I discuss these lines in further detail in Chapter 5. For now, I note that, for Saxonhouse, Creon echoes "democracy's emphasis on interchangeability rather than particularity" (1992: 74). Euben, though, disagrees (1997: 157 and n. 51). In Chapter 5, reading Antigone's dirge in relation to Pericles' Funeral Oration, I connect Pericles' instruction to have more children to Antigone's refusal to do so; it will not work given the (biological) irreplaceability of her brother (but maybe also of anyone). The play may alert us to a problem with democracy as such, or specifically to this imperial democracy's perpetual hunger for more bodies and more people, as evidenced in the Funeral Oration. As Saxonhouse argues in *Athenian Democracy*, that hunger for more bodies is not self-avowed (1996: 62–71). Instead, Pericles tries to enable its satisfaction by replacing civic affective attachment to bodies or embodiment with speech, a more reliable imaginary around which to form a polis. This fits well with the argument developed here regarding the substitution of *logos* in Periclean democracy for the beauteous bodies of Homeric epic. Interestingly, the identification of the beauteous body with singularity and speech with interchangeability reverses the Arendtian assumption that as bodies we are all alike, while as speakers and actors we distinguish ourselves. For more on Arendt's melding of Homeric and Periclean motifs, see Ackerman and Honig (2011). The singular voice (embodied, material) may contribute to the singularity of speech, however, a point explored by Cavarero at length as an anti-metaphysics in *For More Than One Voice* (2005). On the politics of sound and voice see Chapter 1, via the work of Nicole Loraux, and Chapter 5, via Cavarero.

45 Anouilh's adaptation (1946) picks up on this when it has Creon confess that he is not sure which of the two brothers' bodies was buried and which was left out to rot. Having worked so hard to distinguish them in terms of friendship and enmity, it turns out he did not trouble himself to distinguish their actual bodies from each other. The fact that this revelation bothers us is one of the reasons the play continues to this day to grip us.

46 The idea that Antigone routs the line is countered by Julia Lupton who, in an incredible, creative reading, argues that Antigone, on the contrary, sutures the hoplite chain. Lupton insists more generally on Antigone's powerful act of sublimation – she desires to lie down with her brother but finds in Haemon an opportunity to replace the brother with a more acceptable object and thus is able to realize her aim of lying down with the brother in a way that transforms the object from forbidden lover to fellow soldier (2005: 134). Through Antigone, Lupton argues, "Polynices is the last hero and the first citizen" (2005: 136). Thus, in response to Lacan's "I just wonder what the reconciliation at the end of the Antigone might be," Lupton responds: "citizenship" (2005: 259). This is a true reconciliation, as well, since "Antigone's *act* is to transform [broken aristocratic citizenship] into the foundation of a *politeia*" that provides "normative equalizations" while keeping open a space for singularity (2005: 138). For a different but also appreciative take on Antigone's simultaneous commitment to equality and singularity, see below, Chapter 5. Notably, Lupton's reading leaves Creon out, however, and this matters, for if, as in my view, the clash between Antigone and Creon is a clash between two rival forms of citizenship, then citizenship is the problem not the solution.

47 It is not irrelevant to the fight with Haemon that, as Mark Howenstein points out: "In ancient Greece, the power of the father over his son was quite despotic, though it was limited. A father could expose his son on a distant mountaintop (as Laius had done to Oedipus), but he could not enslave him, and a son upon marriage was freed from his father's rule" (2000: 499, n. 16). Others (e.g. Griffith 1998) note that free adulthood is connected to reaching the age of maturity. If we attend to marriage as the trigger to adulthood, we may see Haemon's effort to save Antigone as part of an effort to free himself from his father, to whose will he is subject, something Creon would have known: once married, Haemon is free. Perhaps Creon toys with this notion when he claims, in one of the play's several references to slaves and slavery, that Haemon has allowed himself to be enslaved by Antigone.

48 "It is a trick and a victory of statist law and politics in liberal democracies to ascribe to individuals those significant actions that are actually (also) the products of a concerted politics. Rival sovereignties, oppositional movements, and political dissidence are thereby erased from view and we are left only with small individuals (three girls [in headscarves]) or large phantoms (Islam, radical particularism, etc.)" (Honig 2009a: 128). Hence, for instance, the American celebration of "Rosa Parks" but not of the movement that

prompted her to action. On the importance of the movement, see Aldon Morris, *The Origins of the Civil Rights Movement* (1984: 51–53).

49 Saxonhouse is citing here M. I. Finley's *Democracy Ancient and Modern* (1973: 19). Saxonhouse criticizes Finley, arguing there was more to ancient democracy than this. Her difference with him replays longstanding debates within political science: Finley here defines democracy in formal institutional terms and Saxonhouse argues for a more expansive approach attentive to political culture and practice.

50 Later, when the sentry returns to Creon a second time, having apprehended Antigone in the act, he says "no casting lots this time; this is *my* luck, my prize, no one else's" (396–397 [438–439]). In so saying, he refers to a different mechanism of distribution in which a man gets what he is known to be owed – the lot fell to the sentry who earlier took the risk, now without lottery he gets the real prize. Rather than by way of randomness, the quintessentially democratic distributive principle, the sentry now gets what is coming to *him*. Has he shifted from a democratic political economy to an aristocratic one? Peter Euben suggests (personal communication) this binary is too stark, since there is evidence that people felt the gods had a role in the lottery, that lot-based selections were not random. Still, this idea is not apparent when the sentry says "no casting lots this time; this is *my* luck, my prize, no one else's."

51 The same evidence suggests to Roselli that Creon was a tyrant: "Creon's frequent references to 'payment' and 'hiring' [use] such low vocabulary [that they] may also serve to highlight Creon's vulgar character and improper (tyrannical) behavior as ruler of Thebes" (2006: 166, n. 68). (Roselli cites Mark Griffith's [1999] translation of Sophocles' *Antigone*, 175 ad 302–303; 303 ad 1035–1039.) But a low vocabulary could also show Creon, a democratically identified elite, as he would appear from an elite perspective.

52 I say "further to explain" since the fact that she is a woman is already a reason for him to be bewildered since, as he makes clear, he does not expect women to act in this way.

53 "At Athens, the emphasis is on the banning of offerings at the grave and the limitation of the right to mourn to kinswomen" (Holst-Warhaft 1992: 115).

54 I think the details of the play when read in light of the regulation of lamentation suggest the play is a critical one, mostly because most of the humor appears on the side critical of democracy. Taxidou, however, argues for Sophocles' fundamental identification with the democracy. Underlining his friendship with Pericles, she positions Sophocles as too intimate with power and too rewarded with Athenian theater prizes to be unimplicated in the ideology of the "Greek miracle." By contrast with Sophocles, who sets up an organic relationship to the city state, Taxidou argues, Euripides "sets up a critical, combative relationship with the city state ... quite consciously sever[ing] the supposed organic link between tragedy and the city state" (2004: 12). She prefers Euripides, the exile, reportedly torn to death by dogs

at the order of his finally inhospitable host, Archelaos, the King of Macedon (2004: 12; 99).

55 This is the Tom Sawyer moment, the desire to attend or even stage one's own funeral. "Antigone sings for herself the very wedding hymn and funeral dirge that Kreon has denied her," says Rehm (1994: 64). In fact, Creon interrupts her and says to take her away. But she resumes her dirge and goes on until Creon threatens the soldiers again. Creon also denies her her rite in a different way unnoted by Rehm, not by silencing her – that Creon tries and fails the first time to do – but by mocking her as self-indulgent and implying also that she is cowardly, a point I detail below. Segal says Creon is "scornful" but does not read that scorn as conveying a classical perspective on Homeric/heroic lament (1995a: 249, n. 22). Antigone's self-sung dirge is not unique to her. Cassandra chants her own *threnos* as well, as does Electra. On this, see Loraux's conclusion to *The Mourning Voice* (2002b).

56 But the city may mourn her; Haemon has told Creon the people sympathize with her while Antigone is still alive (692–693 [775–778]). Sophocles does not show the city mourning her after her death, however. This elision of the question of whether she is mourned after death may be significant in a play that centers on the (im)permissibility of mourning as an indication of polis (dis)loyalty.

57 This highlights one side effect of discrediting this speech. If the speech is a later addition as Jebb (who called Creon's "delay" a "dramatic blemish"), Kitto, and Goethe hoped, then Creon is less impotent (Sophocles 1902: xviii–xix). Antigone would presumably, prior to the later addition, have been interred immediately, on Creon's first, direct orders. Thus, assumptions about the robustness of sovereign power may have subtly influenced the judgment of some incredulous readers of Antigone's dirge, about which more in Chapter 5.

58 For a more detailed look at the collectivization of lament in Athens, first by Solon, later on by Pericles, see Richard Seaford (1994). On the persistence of Creon's efforts in this regard, see Goldhill's "The City of Words" (1986). Goldhill notes Creon's effort to assimilate even Haemon's death to the city's purpose: Creon's language, Goldhill argues, evokes official funerary discourse but his effort fails when he hears of his wife's suicide. Eurydice's death is the final blow to the project of collectivization. If Hegel is right that in this play each character goes to the limit and then feels regret, then Creon's effort to appropriate Haemon, even after all that has happened, to the city's purpose marks the limit beyond which he cannot go. Eurydice pulls him back and it is in response to *her* acts (of lament, blame, and suicide) that he comes finally to guilt.

59 Though his alarm may not be sincere. If we read him as a plotter, as I suggested we may in the Introduction to Part II above, then having caused her distress he may have intended precisely to alarm her and to lure her to the suicide that will be Creon's undoing.

60 Eurydice's is a modified Homeric lament. She experiences her son's death as a physical searing pain and she laments it loudly *but* she does so indoors and few, other than the messenger who reports it and maybe her household

servants, seem to have heard her cries. It is unclear whether the audience may have. What should we make of the fact that her cries might have been unknown were it not for their transmission through the agency of the male soldier? Segal says Eurydice's mourning conforms to classical women's lamentation. He thereby generates a great reading of many of the play's details but he misses the scene's departure from those forms. He also argues that Antigone and Eurydice are perfectly parallel in their mourning, erring, in my view, by apparently focusing on Antigone's first recorded lamentation, not her second (for herself). Antigone's first lament for Polynices (at the second burial of his body) is, like Eurydice's, reported by a witness; but Antigone's second dirge, for herself, is heard directly by the audience. Both occur outside (Segal 1995: 134–137).

61 The etymology is noted in Matthew S. Santirocco (1980: 15 and n. 39).

62 See Segal (1995: 125–129 and 134–137, esp. 135). Something Segal does not attend to: in the Homeric paradigm, women and men mourn similarly. But Segal refers repeatedly, as do most commentators in the last fifteen or twenty years, to "women's lamentation."

63 Foley criticizes "unilateral and antidialogic" readings and calls for approaches that attend to plural voices in drama rather than "privilege one voice over another" as the carrier of a play's meaning (1995: 143). Ancient Greek tragedy confronts us "not only with a cultural system that prided itself on being open to public exchanges of ideas and differences of opinion but also with a literary form such as drama, which unfolds as a complex dialogue that refuses to be bound in any direct fashion by the discourses of the agora" (1995: 132).

64 Against the claim that the play suggests the "city can only continue its existence by sacrificing those who are its most respected representatives, and there is no end to this persistent self-sacrifice," quoting T. C. Wouter Oudemans and André P. M. H. Lardinois (1987), Seaford insists the play offers a clear message: "[W]hat is enacted is precisely an end [as opposed to a never-ending] from which the democratic polis may persistently benefit." The political undesirability of a powerful family's "introverted autonomy" is enacted and the play also interpellates the audience into an "emotional cohesion of collective pity for those destroyed" (1995: 207). Thus, polis unity is twice achieved: powerful threats are eliminated and shared pity for them elicited.

65 In a way, we may see the concern here to be the philosophical reception of tragedy in terms of "the tragic," versus the reception studies view of tragedy as performance, versus what Seaford prizes as the historical context of religious ritual. The politics of tragedy versus the tragic is a theme to which I return below.

66 Thus I differ from Roselli's conclusion that "*Antigone* may question some of the fault lines of Athenian society, but it also affirms an archaic and elitist practice of celebrating the elite citizen male, as archaic elites had done and as a few Athenian families continued to do" (2006: 158). The practice is referenced in the play but is also presented in politicizing and parodic terms.

67 This is Creon's view, but it is largely the conventional view as well. She may be admirable and principled, but empathic she is not. I argue in Chapter 6, however, that she is motivated throughout by consideration for Ismene and that our failure to see this until now is due to the dominance of Creon's perspective and also of the genre of tragedy itself, which trains our eyes on individual tragic heroes.

68 Another example of hyperbole in the play is given but not recognized in those terms by Foley, who treats it instead as evidence that Creon does not represent democracy: "[d]espite democratic ideology that privileges the interests of the state, Creon's blanket denial of the importance of kin ties may well have signaled an inadequacy in his attitude to leadership from the first speech on" (1995: 139). He overdoes it.

69 In this context, recall Creon's line to Antigone: "There is too much of you" (573). This is the Grene and Lattimore translation (1991a: 184), cited by Liz Appel (2010: 233).

70 This goes against the claim made by Vickers that the play is an indictment of Pericles, a criticism of his treatment of the Samians and also of his stewardship of Alcibiades (claims which depend on redating the play from 441–2 to 438): by way of the play, Vickers argues, "Pericles' inhuman activity on Samos had been held up to public scrutiny and was attacked for its cruelty. The results of his indifferent guardianship of Alcibiades (whose education was entrusted to a Thracian slave who was 'useless on account of old age' [Pl. *Alc.* 1.122b; cf. Plut. *Lyc.* 15]) are also laid at his door. We can only assume that some of this criticism was effective and that Pericles' policies were less harsh in the future" (2008: 33). But tragedy cannot be merely a critique of one side; as a tragedy it presupposes and requires a clash between what Bernard Williams would call, two "oughts." In short, there are enough criticisms in the play of both the democratic and the Homeric world views to go around.

71 For Roselli, "Creon's decision to construct a tomb *first* (and to release Antigone second) underscores the importance of the [Homeric burial] monument and its significance to the audience" (2006: 152). This reading of Creon's (in)action shows the limits of Roselli's otherwise valuable burial-focused interpretation of the play. His insistence that the play is about burial as a marker of status makes him miss other important elements of the play and leaves him vulnerable to Foley's criticism of narrowly historicist, referential readings. Patchen Markell imaginatively describes the events otherwise: Creon's deed, he says, outraces Creon's efforts to undo or control it, thus illustrating the contingency and finitude of the human world, in which our actions exceed our ability to contain or control them (see Markell's third chapter in *Bound by Recognition* [2003] for further discussion). But the text suggests another reading as well: as I suggest above, it is also true that Creon's failure to undo his deeds is partly due to his failure to listen to the Chorus' leader and may suggest he is still plotting and conspiring. Going to Polynices first and to Antigone only second, Creon chooses not only to try (and fail) to undo his deed, as Markell suggests, but also or instead to *permit* the deed to

continue to outrace his efforts to undo it – Antigone dies in the time it takes Creon to get there, having stopped first to bury Polynices. There may be more agency here and more power than Markell notes, both in Creon's choices and in Antigone's. Indeed, that is what tragedy may be said to require, a sense that until the last possible moment it could have been otherwise, and even then . . . (though this is not to suggest that a different course of action would have necessarily achieved its intended effect, merely that alternatives are available until the last moment, and that they might have had *an* effect). Moreover, there is agency here beyond that of the primary players. The messengers, sentry, soldiers accelerate the action by reporting the goings-on to the various players, even though the reactions to what is heard are predictably tragic (lament, suicide). There is something of an upstairs–downstairs class politics at work here, highlighted from the perspective of melodrama and *Trauerspiel*.

72 Shapiro compares Creon and Achilles (2006: 45), but as I suggested in the Introduction the better comparison may be of Antigone and Achilles. For Antigone/Achilles, Polynices is not Hector but rather Patroclus – brother or brother-like and an incestuous love.

73 D. A. Hester thinks Eurydice's death is that of a minor character, a price Sophocles thinks is worth paying in order to increase the suffering of Creon (1971: 40). Although I focus at this moment on the suffering of Creon, I think, as my reading in the last section suggests, that Eurydice's death serves another purpose as well: it is part of the play's exhibition of plural and diverse styles of lamentation. The spectrum of lamentation styles is the *mise en scène* for the antagonists' conflict, and its occasion.

74 Here I use not the Fagles translation but rather that of Gibbons and Segal (2003) because it better captures the sense of Creon's grief, perhaps because it is informed by Segal's sense that Creon mourns like a woman. For further discussion on this point, see Segal (1995a: 127–131). We may note that the theme of belatedness, privileged by Markell, is again in play here. Creon wishes someone would plunge a sword into him, shortly after he evaded Haemon's effort to do precisely this.

75 Segal sees that Creon mourns like a woman but does not note the significance of Creon's departure from the form of women's lamentation when he takes the guilt upon himself rather than call for revenge (1995a: 127; 130). In a wonderful essay on Hegel's *Antigone* (framed by Hegel's reading of the play as a dispute between public and private, but in powerful contention with that reading nonetheless), Patricia Mills focuses on this detail (without noting its character as a departure from lamentation codes) and asks if Creon's embrace of his guilt is evidence of his superiority to Antigone: "Creon's admission of guilt makes him the hero of the play [on Hegel's account] since it gives him a higher ethical consciousness" (1996: 70). Mills focuses, that is, on what the admission tells us about Creon. I focus on what the admission *does*: Creon's lament ends the cycle of violence. The dramatic counterpoint of Creon's lament is not just Antigone's but also Eurydice's. She called to avenge Creon's wrongs, and thereby staged his assumption of guilt (though he could still have

sensibly refused it and have called for revenge, blaming it all on Antigone or lashing out at Ismene, not yet sacrificed in all this). One thing is sure: at this point, *the play is not about Polynices any more, if it ever was.*

76 The Chorus shows its awareness of Creon's penchant to delegate when it says, earlier: "Do it now, go, don't leave it to others" (1107 [1231]). We can almost hear the echo of Achilles to Agamemnon: "Do it yourself." Of course, the Chorus also urges Creon in this last scene to live out his life rather than end it, i.e., *not* to act on his own but rather to leave his fate to the gods.

77 Whether or not the "concession" anticipates Hegel's "solution" to the problem posed by this tragedy is a separate and important question.

78 That tragedy permits the impermissible is by now a commonplace (though Loraux's early work treats tragedy more as an instrument of the city than a source of subversion, as I noted above). Vickers makes the contrary point: "The dramatic stage was very much part of Athenian political life, and once we recall that a dramatic festival was the occasion of pouring the libations by the generals, for the display of the annual tribute, for the praise of the civic benefactors, and the parade in armour of war orphans [citing Goldhill 1990] then we can understand how plays might have a political resonance, and how the stage – whether tragic or comic – might be the place where things could be said that were impossible to say in other contexts" (2008: 25). I agree with Vickers's last phrase but would support it in the context of a rather broader view of "politics" than that which informs his work.

79 When Luce Irigaray shifts the focus of her earlier reading of Antigone as representing a blood bond that civic kinship disavows (in *Speculum of the Other Woman* [1985b]) to Antigone as articulating a claim to political power (briefly, in *Thinking the Difference: For a Peaceful Revolution* [1994]), Irigaray moves out of the range of this critique.

80 Seaford's suggestion points beyond his argument to another. The lure of the appetites (which are later whetted by the feast) may in Homer and elsewhere provide a way out of otherwise infinite grief, a point I noted in Chapter 1. For further discussion, see Seaford (1995). That said, the fifth *stasimon* (1115–1154 [1238–1272]) precedes Creon's grief. Does the invitation to the feast remain or is it overcome and defeated by Creon's later encounter with loss?

81 See, for example, Arendt (1958: 215), insisting that political equality cannot mean equality before death.

5 From lamentation to logos*: Antigone's conspiracy with language*

1 On the impact of history's intrusion on theater, see Schmitt (2009), which I discuss in more detail at the end of this chapter.

2 On lamentation as a genre of speech, in effect supporting the direction I take here, see Laura McClure (1999: 40ff.), though McClure characterizes ritual lament as a "highly conservative genre," while I here and throughout see the genre's politics as more open.

3 As Simon Goldhill has since noted: the lines are a "node of opacity in the text"
   that need not "be either simply comprehensible nor simply incomprehen-
   sible" (2012: 245), a position in some ways closer to Lacan than to the position
   argued for here. Goldhill thinks the lines merely call attention to the question
   of "what kinship ties are worth dying for." That may be. And he contrasts his
   position with those who seek either to delete or to domesticate the lines.
   Without doing either, that is, seeking to explain without explaining away,
   I will argue here that the lines carry more meanings than Goldhill credits.

4 Burian, too, finds a way, a different way, to grant the authenticity of the
   second law but skirts or undoes their seeming contradiction, rather than
   deepening it, as I do here: "her attempt to find a second 'law' does not negate
   her first law. The unwritten law told Antigone, and should tell the world, that
   her brother must receive burial rites, whether the state allows it or not. The
   law she improvises under the pressure of her impending death attempts to
   answer with a clear argument a different question – not must Polynices be
   buried, but why did I decide to bury him at the cost of my own life and
   future" (2010: 281). That is to say, on Burian's account, the second law does
   not contradict the first because it is an answer to a different question.

5 Thanks to Brooke Holmes for calling to my attention this detail of the
   comparison with Achilles and for good discussion and guidance regarding
   Antigone's dirge more generally.

6 "It is not normal to sing one's own *kommos*," says Simon Goldhill, making
   what seems to be an unintentionally funny observation (2012: 110). Goldhill
   notes the unusual nature of the *kommos* as well, that it is not primarily
   consoling but rather swings back and forth between consolation and condem-
   nation. This agonism between Antigone and the Chorus mirrors the similar to
   and fro that I argue in the next chapter characterizes Antigone's exchanges
   with Ismene. Goldhill sees it in the *kommos*, but not in the scenes between the
   sisters, and he thinks I overreach in my reading. I respond in detail below.

7 As I noted in Chapter 4, the charge of self-indulgence may also be a political
   criticism. The elite insistence on ostentatious burial could well – from a
   democratic perspective – be lampooned as indulgence, well represented by
   the synecdoche of an endless dirge for oneself.

8 Butler credits Antigone with a bit less self-will than Loraux or understands it
   differently: Antigone "authors her own death" but "some legacy of acts is
   being worked through the instrument of her agency" (2000: 27). Fletcher
   notes this as well (2010: 181, n. 39).

9 If it is a dirge for herself, then she is partaking of the practice dubbed
   "automourning" by Henry Staten (1995) who identifies it specifically with
   Homer's heroes, like Achilles, and sees it as overtaken by transcendent death
   practices introduced by Christianity.

10 In the speech's combination of singularity and replaceability (Polynices is
   singular, husbands and children, replaceable), Tyrrell and Bennett see Antigone in transition from aristocratic loyalties to polis values – staging her death
   as a marriage integrates her into a social form which allows her to accept

substitution (valued in the democratic polis) of some family members (Lupton cites them on this point [2005: 132]).

11 See Miriam Leonard's *Athens in Paris* (2005) for the view that Antigone's final speech is offensive and difficult to account for. In "Lacan's Heroines" (1998), Alenka Zupančič argues that "Antigone's lamentation is absolutely essential to the text and it does not mean that she suddenly became 'soft' and 'human.'" When she cries that she will never marry or have children, says Zupančič, Antigone does not betray herself: "this is rather the whole point: it is through this lack of common measure [the common measure is what is forgone] that the incommensurable, infinite measure which is desire can be realized, i.e., 'measured'" (1998: 114). For further discussion, see also Zupančič (2000). I agree with Zupančič, but with two caveats. As I shall argue here, the speech carries more meaning than Zupančič credits; it is less self-directed and more part of a continuing political *agon* with Creon than a Lacanian perspective grants. And second, if Antigone does here show some softness and humanity, it may not evidence a sudden transformation. She has shown indications of such traits already, as I argue in Chapter 6.

12 In this last speech of hers, Antigone seems to manifest some of the self-consciousness of which Hegel will later say she is incapable. If until this point she has seemed to act intuitively or with a certain unreflective immediacy, she in her final scene gives a rather different impression: here she seems a more reflective and self-conscious political actor than Hegel credits. Hegel does not notice how this last speech might undermine his claim about Antigone's singularly intuitive, unconscious, ethical character. Neither do Lacan or Žižek, both of whom assume she does not act politically.

13 Griffith calls the speech "notorious" (2010: 115).

14 On Goethe as responding to Hegel, see Steiner, *Antigones* (1996).

15 See also Peter Burian: "By insisting, however, both on Antigone's exemplarity and on the conflict of antithetical principles, embodied in the two main characters, Lacan reintroduces Hegel in spite of himself" (2010: 262–263). Also, Burian adds: "Lacan, who objects to the pious vision of Antigone's saintliness that he finds in Hegel and many more recent critics, creates his own version of Antigone Virgin and martyr" (2010: 263). Of course, as Burian notes, Lacan also repeats "Hegel's repression of any hint of incest in Antigone's choice of her dead brother over her husband-to-be" (2010: 263–264).

16 See also my discussion in Chapter 6 of Bernard Williams (no Lacanian, he), who also assumes Antigone is death-driven.

17 For Lacan, later, as Stavrakakis points out, law and desire are not opposed but rather enmeshed. Their contrast is to *jouissance* (2007).

18 The same reading without the moralism is developed by Griffith (2001: 131). He in fact sees no conflict between Antigone's law of equality and singularity since both manifest "her absolute commitment to natal family" (a point made also by Richard Seaford). Griffith cites in support Murnaghan (1986), Neuburg (1990), and Cropp (1997), noting that Knox (1964) and Reinhardt (1979) argue for the speech's excision.

19 Indeed, Foley (1995) says this in the context of a critique of Sourvinou-Inwood for being too referential in her reading of *Antigone*. But this moment in Foley's reading, while not unimportant to consider, seems to me to suffer a bit from the same defect. Hame (2008) supports Sourvinou-Inwood's judgment.

20 I am tempted here by the thought that Creon rules by edict, while Antigone is governed by law; or by the thought that from an elite perspective, democratic law may appear to be mere edict.

21 By noting that Antigone both conspires with language and is possibly also its conspiratorial plaything I mean quite deliberately to sidestep the implication of intentionalism here. I will argue as if she is doing things with words but it may just as well be, of course, that Sophocles is doing things with words through her and it may also be that words are doing things with him, as when parody, mimicry, and citation take the stage – these can be intentional strategies, of playwright or protagonist, but they can also be effects of language that is always already in circulation and that exceeds the intention of anyone, while nonetheless being freighted with meaning-making and meaning-breaking power.

22 Or these mechanisms are *supposed to* return survivors to life. As Richard Seaford (1994) points out, in Homer and also in the tragedies, practices of reciprocity and ritual seem to be in crisis. They repeatedly fail to bring closure precisely where closure is to be expected whether by way of marriage or funeral.

23 See, for example, Deborah Boedeker and Kurt Raaflaub, who note the overlap between the play's Ode to Man and Pericles' Oration: in both, "peace, stability and the city's prosperity can be achieved only by respecting, reconciling, weaving together the two sets of values" – Antigone's and Creon's (2005: 121).

24 As Nicole Loraux points out, the proviso about passing childbearing age is relevant to mothers not fathers, so Pericles seems to have mothers in mind. But he never mentions mothers, only parents, in the Oration and when he turns immediately from the implied comfort of more children to their usefulness in securing good deliberation, he addresses only male citizens, for only they deliberate. In this way, Loraux suggests, Pericles ends up erasing the figure his Oration means to replace, the mother in mourning (which is also the figure referenced by the iconic bird at the empty nest to which the sentry compares Antigone keening over Polynices' body) (1998: 15–16).

25 For further discussion on this point, see Roselli (2006) and Shapiro (2006). The claim also finds abundant support from Seaford (1994: especially in chapter 4) and more briefly from Boedeker and Raaflaub: "The conflict over Polynices' burial reminds us of the Athenian burial of war dead in a public cemetery, a custom introduced soon after the Persian Wars, in which the state clearly arrogated a family function" (2005: 121).

26 On parody in ancient Athens, see Robert Hariman (2008).

27 This translation combines those of Fagles (1984: 569 [542]) and Lloyd-Jones (2002: 569 [569]).

28 If Judith Butler is right to point out that Antigone appropriates Creon's voice and mimes his sovereignty, this is one of the places where Antigone does just that. On this point, see also Burian (2010: 281) on this line as a reversal of Creon's, citing Ormand (1999: 96).

29 The possibility is contemplated as well by Griffith who, notwithstanding his canvassing of the politics of natal versus conjugal family loyalties, finds "uncomfortable" rather than symptomatic or interesting the idea that Antigone is perhaps in this scene "possessed (reclaimed) by her exogamous husband, Haemon, in a posthumous but in some sense effective act of sexual consummation (rape? marriage?) that seeks to reinstate her within the world of the 'normal' and socially acceptable" (2005: 121). (But see his [revised?] view in "Psychoanalyzing Antigone" [2010] where his discomfort is unapparent.) I note elsewhere the necrophilic rape is not only about reclaiming Antigone as a bride (whether for the purposes of normalizing her or marrying her) but is also about Haemon's always thwarted efforts to claim equality with his father, first by trying to reason with him, then by trying to kill him, and finally by trying to marry out from under him. Each time, the son fails: Creon is unmoved by his son's reasons, unwounded by his sword, and undeterred by his suicide. When he takes his dead son home to his mother, and leaves his corpse-bride behind in the cave, Creon reclaims Haemon for the natal family he was determined to marry out of. For further discussion, see Honig (2011b).

30 This is the second reception of her act, and the Chorus' emplotment of the scene as romance governs most critical readings to this day, according to which Haemon dies in an iconically tragic "marriage-to-death" scene, embracing Antigone's corpse. When his body dies ejaculating blood on her cheeks, it mimes the rather different intimacies that would have occurred in life had things not gone so horribly awry. But the romance of marriage-to-death obscures the appropriative dimension of Haemon's act. As her dirge and her suicide make clear, Antigone's loyalty is not first and foremost to Haemon. Butler and others admire Antigone for this, but Antigone's rejection of conventional marriage is undone by events that occur after her death, as I argue here.

31 "Can the Subaltern Speak?" (1988) ends with the death of Bhuvaneswari Bhaduri whose suicide is read as apolitical in spite of the fact that it is the consequence of failing to carry out an assassination. Similarly, in "Woman in Difference: Mahasweta Devi's 'Douloti the Bountiful'" (1989), the dramatic death of Douloti is analyzed. School children find her "tormented corpse" lying on a map of India. My account also draws on J. L. Austin's analysis of performatives, from *How to Do Things with Words* (1962). It is worth noting that Yannis Stavrakakis (2007) rightly challenges Žižek's Lacanian reading of Antigone on the grounds that the perfect act of suicide is not the best model for a left progressive politics. Rather than fall for the lure of Antigone, Stavrakakis says, radical democratic actors need to forsake "radical suicidal gestures à la Antigone" on behalf of political acts that may exceed the merely "momentary" success of unconditional acts in order to "effect a radical

re-foundation of the social in a progressive direction" (2007: 134–135). There are grounds for yet further challenge given that for Lacan, as Stavrakakis explains, "suicide is the only act that can succeed without misfiring; a totally successful, 'unconditional' act" (2007: 135). In some sense, of course, Lacan and Žižek secure suicide's success by way of this tautology: suicide is perfect because it is what it is – life-ending, suicide. But suicide, like all other acts, depends upon its reception to be (in)felicitous.

32 Lupton (2005) is sensitive to the importance of Haemon's suicide over Antigone's, but she reads it differently: she claims Antigone dies into citizenship, when her autonomous suicide is recast by Haemon's later suicide as a marriage-to-death. Of course we might say that Antigone marries death one way with her suicide, marrying Hades or her dead parents, and then is reclaimed for a different marriage to death by Haemon's suicide.

33 The play presents the two extremes of marriage in prescriptive terms: first, Antigone, as an incest, represents the extreme of endogamy (she has, as Helene Foley points out, "implicitly foregone marital bonds for those with blood relations" [2001: 175]) and its outcome – barrenness and death. Second, Polynices, who married a daughter of the Argive Adrastos and then raised an army there to attack his native Thebes, represents the extreme of exogamy, and its outcome – enmity or treason and barrenness and death.

34 This last claim fits her mother's marriage as well: it murders Antigone's marriage, though the marriage of her mother is more tragic since it – unlike Polynices' – is also a condition of Antigone's possibility.

35 The play's reference to the story has been used to discredit Antigone's speech. Critics who doubt its authenticity point out that Herodotus wrote his *Histories* a few years after Sophocles wrote *Antigone*. Lacan (1992: 255) may reject the citation to Herodotus to protect the dirge's originality to the text (not knowing it can be both). Castoriadis points out, "Herodotus has already visited Athens, where he probably read parts of his *Histories* in public; Sophocles will compose a poem about him in 441" (2007: 12). Others point out that Aristotle refers to it not many years later, the stories Herodotus compiled in his *Histories* were in wide circulation, and Sophocles and Herodotus were friends. Thus Antigone's use of the same reasoning may refer to the story retold by Herodotus yet still predate his writing. Most critics now treat the passage as authentic. Also, if Lewis (1988) and others are right to redate the *Antigone* to the early 430s rather than the late 440s, the play can be seen in relation to the conflict with Samos, and the distance between Sophocles' text and Herodotus' recording of the Intaphrenes' wife story is considerably diminished. The possibility then also arises that the brutal desecration of Polynices by Creon calls attention to Pericles' brutal treatment of the Samians.

36 For further discussion, see Foley (2001: 168). Carolyn Dewald and Rachel Kitzinger (2006) are among the very few to attend to the story in any detail. I engage with their reading below. Most readers focus on the question of the (in)effectiveness of the reasons given in the two stories rather than on the

critical question posed in each about the costs of a certain form of reasoning's emergence. See the small literature on the topic listed in Dewald and Kitzinger (2006).

37 John Comaroff first called my attention to the familiarity of the story's structure to anthropologists.

38 On the trope of camping out at the palace gates to seek sovereign intercession, see François Guesnet (2007) on the practice of *shtadlanut*, modeled for early modern European Jewry by the Biblical Mordecai in the book of Esther. I would note that the practice remains in modern times. One evocative example is the woman in Michael Moore's film, *Fahrenheit 9/11* (discussed in Chapter 1) whose tent is pitched in Lafayette Park and is stumbled upon by Lila Lipscomb when she goes to the White House. Another is Cindy Sheehan's peace camp, outside Bush's Crawford Ranch. Both are met by responses that evoke Creon more than Darius.

39 Thanks to Laura Slatkin on this point.

40 Thanks to Stephen Mulhall for calling my attention to this passage in Wittgenstein.

41 Although this is less surprising if we attend to Lacan, who says that it is precisely because the parental/social demand for articulation does violence to the need expressed that the goods taken to be the referent of the whine will only inaugurate a chain of wants/satisfactions that is endless and endlessly unsatisfying.

42 Thus the story works, in my reading, differently from how Dewald and Kitzinger (2006) see it, for they see the *agon* between the woman and Darius as internal to *logos* rather than between *phonê* (her wailing) and *logos* (his reasons).

43 Samuel Weber (2004a) has gone further than most to note the significance of the *a*symmetries in the two stories: Antigone's argument about irreplaceability is on behalf of burial while Intaphrenes' wife forwards her argument to save her brother. Weber also points out that Intaphrenes' wife's situation is contingent, her circumstance a product of externalities, while Antigone's situation is fated, overdetermined by her familial destiny. There are other asymmetries as well. Intaphrenes' wife succeeds – her brother is saved by her argument – while Antigone's argument, as it were, fails. Intaphrenes' wife laments prospectively, with a hope of influencing a sovereign's acts and decisions, while Antigone speaks retrospectively, justifying post hoc a course already pursued and dealing with consequences that cannot be undone (unless we think of her as seeking to save Ismene, not just to bury Polynices, a case I argue for in detail in Chapter 6). Indeed, Antigone speaks from beyond the grave, as it were, in a moment of overliving, after having been condemned, interrupted, and condemned again. We could go on, cataloguing the similarities and differences, but to see the story's fuller significance to the play, we have to move away from the "argument" and the traits of Herodotus' story and look instead at what the story accomplishes, what associations it conjures in its audience's minds. Indeed, I am suggesting here that critics' focus on the

argument is in fact the story's intended didactic lesson, as it were; but if we resist that lesson, alternative possibilities of understanding emerge.

44 The comparability of Darius' cat-and-mouse game with the woman and Freud's account of the fort-da game, as Lear and then Santner describe it, is striking: "the child's play creates a moment of disruption in an already disrupted life. The invention of the game [of fort-da or, in Herodotus, the to-and-fro with Darius] converts this rip in the fabric of experience [which is, in Lear's terms, the remainder of life] into an experience of loss. It creates a cultural space in which the child can play with loss: in this way he comes to be able to tolerate it and name it." In this way the possibility of a "mother's absence [and reappearance] emerges . . . Inventing the game, the child thereby creates the capacity *to think* about the mother's absence. It is precisely in the creation of these sorts of playful activities that a child enters into the space of reasons" (Santner 2011: 70–71, citing Lear 2000: 94). That is, we may think of Lear's project as charting the path from lamentation to *logos* incited by Creon and Darius. Lear continues this line of thinking in his later *Radical Hope* (2008).

45 Is it ironic that when Antigone refuses to give up on her desire (as Lacan says), she does so by speaking through – reiterating – the very words in which Intaphrenes' wife may have given up on hers? The contrast between the two women is noted by Dewald and Kitzinger, who rightly observe that "it is safe to say that Intaphrenes' wife is no Antigone, but rather a survivor, in her political astuteness" (2006: 128). There is more to be said, however, about Antigone's skills as survivor, as we shall see.

46 In this, his is not unlike the sovereignty of modern states. Citing James Scott, Felicia Kornbluh says twentieth-century states "see" the world in two-dimensional perspective and see "the living things under the suzerainty as fundamentally interchangeable; state action works to make them so in order to impose order and to manipulate them more effectively" (2011: 543). Perhaps this is an apt place to note as well that interchangeability was also a non-controversial feature of family relations in the sixteenth and seventeenth centuries, according to Lawrence Stone, who says: "Family relationships were characterized by interchangeability, so that substitution of another wife or another child was easy, and by conformity to external rules of conduct" (1977: 88).

47 Dewald and Kitzinger, also noting the relevance of this story to the Intaphrenes' wife episode, conflate the two: "Like the people from the plain needing water . . . Intaphrenes' wife comes to Darius' *thuras*, gates, weeping and wailing. In both passages, a weeping population demands access to resources that one would expect to be rightly theirs rather than the king's (the local water supply, one's male relatives)" (2006: 123). However, the men do not weep, they bellow and their payments suggest they differ from Intaphrenes' wife in that they do not need the education into sovereign reason that the lamenting woman does show herself to need, from Darius' perspective. Dewald and Kitzinger go on to note a difference between the stories: the

"exchange [Intaphrenes' wife] undertakes with Darius" is not a matter of mere money but rather of "subtle, verbal negotiation" (2006: 123). They are right but they skip over the reason for the difference – that the men are in the economy of wants, while the woman is in an aneconomy of infinite need. Once we see this, we can also see that the "subtle, verbal negotiation" is not just a mark of the woman's survivor's agency, but is also in fact the *price* exacted by Darius from her.

48 Another argument in favor of this reading would return to Butler's focus on Antigone's appropriation of the terms of Creon's sovereign speech. As we see here, however, Antigone's penchant for parody goes further. Creon is not Antigone's only source. She borrows from others as well; in particular, her final speech re-cites that of Intaphrenes' wife, a woman who is powerless but a survivor, nonetheless. Butler argues: "It seems to me that there is a moment where the person who's not a person, the family that is not a family, has to use the dominant language and use it in a way that misuses it and contaminates it in order to allow it to mean something else or something different" (Butler and Rabinow 2001: 48). This is precisely the effect of Antigone's citation of the story, though it is not clear that it is "dominant language" that she is citing.

It should be noted that the *Antigone*'s traffic in citationality poses a problem for Phillipe Nonet's harsh criticism of the citational history of the *Antigone* (2006). Nonet recalls here not only Heidegger but also (if likely less advertently) Schmitt, who, in *Hamlet or Hecuba*, expresses impatience with the "infinitely" many interpretations of *Hamlet*. For a fabulous critique of Nonet on this point, see Adam Sitze (2006).

49 Claiming kinship with this woman also has another welcome effect. It focuses attention on the crime of treason and away from that of incest. That is, it distracts attention from the fact that the natal family Antigone wants to prioritize is not just traitorous (like Intaphrenes) but also incestuous (unlike the family of Intaphrenes).

50 Dewald and Kitzinger (2006), by contrast, argue that Antigone is in over her head. When she cites for support a story that exposes her overreaching, forcing her beyond her own experience, comparing an actual brother to a husband and children she can only imagine having, she is forced into faulty reasoning and becomes so unpersuasive that critics doubt the authenticity of her speech. Thus, Dewald and Kitzinger claim, we see *logos* betrays her, and this highlights how frantic she has become by the end of the play as a result of her failure to win support for her cause. She is pushed to extremes as she seeks, wildly toward the end, for a way finally to persuade others to side with her. On my account, Antigone has chosen it to outfox Creon and charge him with inadequacy or injustice right to his face. Interestingly, this capacity to outfox is attributed by the co-authors to Intaphrenes' wife but not to Antigone. On my account, Intaphrenes' wife may be clever and effective, but her move from lamentation into *logos*, no matter how well crafted, shows she has always already lost out in the encounter with Darius. Antigone, by contrast, outwits

Creon with her citation (her accusations may register with the audience but they go over his head), as she will do again with her suicide and more. This is what she does: she outwits.

51 I note it fits well with John J. Winkler's proposal that we, in reading the *Odyssey*, "try out the possibility that both author and heroine are not simply victims of the performance rules within which they operate, and that both are capable of a strategically concealed cunning – Penelope to outwit her audience of suitors, Homer to outwit his listening audience" (1989: 145).

52 Although vengeance is an economy as well, as Richard Seaford and Henry Staten both point out, even while it is cast by its rivals as aneconomic, anarchic, and unstable. Seaford tracks its workings and its limits in the *Iliad* and elsewhere. Staten notes that, in effect, vengeance commensurates the incommensurable, as do all economies in a way (1995: 33). In other words, we might say that vengeance generates the rule "an eye for an eye" while taking its abundant force from the sentiment that "no single eye could compensate me for the loss of *my* eye."

53 Voice is attended to by Butler in a reading of Lévinas: the face "seems to be a kind of sound," she says, explaining that here sound is "the sound of language evacuating its sense, the sonorous substratum of vocalization that precedes and limits the delivery of any semantic sense" (2004a: 134). To Butler's "precedes and limits" I would add *enables*. I now return to that story focusing on the role of voice in it and treating the story as a recognition scene of the sort theorized by Butler with Lévinas. I add this fourth reading as a possibility that opens room for further thought on the themes presented here for reflection; not to triumph over the previous contextual, textual, and inter-textual readings of the story which, in my view, remain forceful.

54 On the significance of such non-communicative sound or announcement to Kant's account of the origins of language, see Honig (1993a, chapter 2).

55 See here Rancière: politics occurs in the space of "the double sense of logos, as speech and as account" (1999: 26).

56 See also Sarah Pomeroy, *Goddesses, Whores, Wives, and Slaves* (1975).

57 As I note above, one risk for Darius is that the saved son may one day explode the stable economy of reasoning that Darius seeks here to inaugurate. That may be the price of the gift. Or that may be Darius' plan: to sow the seeds of future discord into a family he seeks to destroy, while also ridding himself bloodlessly of the woman who ceaselessly laments outside the palace gates. Either way, Darius, in leaving alive the eldest son, surely consigns the two family forms – natal and conjugal – to further future contention. Similarly Ismene, the remnant, urged by Antigone to save rather than sacrifice herself, may also signal the possibility of future, recurrent conflict. This hint, that there is a remainder to the doomed natal family form, may be another of Antigone's covert messages (on this see Chapter 6). From this angle of vision, contra all those who identify her with Intaphrenes' wife, Antigone recalls not just the wife/mother of Herodotus' story, but also, just like Ismene, the improbably saved son. When she tends to the dead, in both her dirge for

Polynices and for herself, she airs the vengefulness that Intaphrenes' son might have borne and that democratic Athens sought to contain. On that containment effort, see Gabriel Herman (2006).

58 But there may yet be a gift, even in this: for by giving both brother and son to her, Darius provided Intaphrenes' wife with the ingredients of stasis, the bond of hostility, that Nicole Loraux argues is the glue of Athenian life. See Loraux (2002a).

59 Sheila Murnaghan notes: Darius' "reward is not only a reward but also a correction of her choice" (1986: 203). When he grants the life of her eldest son, Darius indicates this is the relative she should have chosen, the one she should have valued the most.

60 Thus, Foley is right but a bit misleading when she says that Antigone "uses lamentation to carry her point assertively in a public context that might otherwise have silenced her speech" (2001: 32–33). The binary of assertiveness versus silence here occludes the vast in-between of Antigone's conspiracy with language – from parody, mimicry, citation, double entendre, and, as we shall see in Chapter 6, sotto voce communication which has public effects but does not assertively seek out publicity (in fact, quite the opposite). Also noting this line from Foley, McClure in her book, *Spoken Like a Woman*, lights on some of that in-between when she goes on to analyze several plays, but not *Antigone*, and finds that "By assimilating fifth-century concerns about rhetoric and speech to an archaic prototype, that of women's treacherous verbal guile, the plays examined in the remainder of this book find a vehicle for meditating on the problems posed by persuasive speech of men in the democratic polis" (1999: 69). Antigone might be seen as offering, by way of *adianoeta*, an example of "women's treacherous verbal guile" but it is important, I would argue, to broaden the range of options between silence and open speech. Conspiracy, too, belongs on the spectrum, and contrasts with persuasion, represented in this play by the unsuccessful Haemon. Reservations about conspiracy – obscured by the binary of silence versus speech – tend to come out of the assumption that it is mere plotting, like gossip, and that it is lacking in seriousness or virility. This way of thinking about conspiracy – as nugatory – works only once we prise it apart from Benjamin's weak messianism.

61 Recall, in this context, Hannah Arendt's observation that one of the many evils of totalitarianism is that it makes martyrdom impossible. Martyrdom postulates the eventfulness of the death, that it will be known, that it can be talked about, that it has meaning, and so on (1973: 451).

62 With the move from Niobe to Intaphrenes' wife, Antigone also shifts from a figure who boasted about her fecund powers of maternity (she had numerous children) and was punished by the gods for boasting about it, to one who did not so define herself and was rewarded, not punished. There is surely some irony then in the fact that Antigone is in the play chastised for allying herself with hyper-maternity only to become in our time affiliated with an ideology of maternalism.

63 Among the notable exceptions are Irigaray, Derrida, and Jacobs.

64 Thanks to Diego Rossello for calling my attention to this line from Benjamin, and for his own very instructive work on melancholy and lycanthropy in Benjamin, Schmitt, and Hobbes. See Rossello (2012).

65 Cavarero's emphasis on voice seems to put us back into the metaphysics of presence criticized by Derrida. One response might be to attend to voice as *both* corporeal and extra-corporeal, as a marker of the remainders of both *logos* and lamentation, as I do here. Cavarero's is to locate her seeming move to presence on the register of intersubjectivity not ontology.

66 For Rancière on literarity, see (2004). See also Samuel Chambers (2005).

67 On the crux and the cross, see Jeffrey Masten (2009).

68 Rancière says this is repetition with a difference: e.g., the plebeians who seceded on the Aventine, faced with the refusal of the patricians to grant that the plebs could speak and had made claims, do "not set up a fortified camp in the manner of the Scythian slaves. They do what would have been unthinkable for the latter: they establish another order, another partition of the perceptible, by constituting themselves not as warriors equal to other warriors but as speaking beings sharing the same properties as those who deny them these. They thereby execute a series of speech acts that mimic those of the patricians; they pronounce imprecations and apotheoses; they delegate one of their number to go and consult *their* oracles; they give themselves representatives by rebaptizing them. In a word, they conduct themselves like beings with names" (1999: 24).

69 There are many tensions between the democratic theory of Rancière and Hannah Arendt, but Rancière's description of the plebs' action is strikingly resonant with and invites a new reading of Arendt's account of the frenzy of compact-making with which the original English colonists settled the New World. Could this be a mimicry by way of which the colonists tasted a freedom that had been reserved for others? Arendt would not call it mimicry, but it may be enlightening to rethink her example in Rancière's terms. For more on Rancière and Arendt, see Jason Frank (2010) and Andrew Schaap (2011).

70 On living otherwise as an enactment of freedom, see James Tully (2008).

71 Though, as I noted earlier, this is not the case on Griffith's and Seaford's readings, which insist she is always and only devoted to kin.

72 I am indebted to Eric Santner for first asking me about the possible comparisons between my reading of *Antigone* with the historical figure of Intaphrenes' wife and Schmitt's reading of *Hamlet* with James I.

73 A similar though not quite the same point is made by Burian, who says of his own reading of the play, "I am claiming transhistorical importance, then, for a reading that corresponds to our own interests and needs, but seems at least implicit in Sophocles' tragedy" (2010: 287).

74 An excess of theatricality is also a good way to describe the sort of performative political theory reading performed here, though it may, with its overtones of melodrama, be a risky way to do so. Still, recuperating melodrama and reading performatively and dramaturgically, opens Sophocles' *Antigone* to renewed interpretation and theoretical reflection.

6 Sacrifice, sorority, integrity: Antigone's conspiracy with Ismene

1 For further discussion, see Loraux (1986, 1998), Edith Hall (1991), John Winkler and Froma Zeitlin (1992), Miriam Leonard (2005), and Simon Goldhill (2006).

2 On this point, see Euben (1997: chapter 6), and Elshtain (1982).

3 For further discussion, see Taylor (2003). For an appreciative performance-centered response to Taylor, see Worthen (2008).

4 In an imagined dialogue with Ismene, Jina Politi says: "Come to think of it, not even Aristotle noticed that you were a real scandal, an inexplicable 'gap' in Sophocles' well-made play, being the only character in familial tragedy, even in myth for that matter, to escape τo τετελεσμένον" (2006: 134).

5 Bennett and Tyrrell note the tendency to treat Ismene as a "foil," citing Bernard Knox as an example (2008–2009: 2). Griffith says Ismene's "role has been to articulate 'normal' conventional female attitudes and expectations, in order to throw into even sharper relief Antigone's extreme and unconventional views" (2001: 129). Burian (2010), in an important article whose project is similar to mine – to read Antigone as a political actor – but whose reading of the play differs from mine on almost every detail, echoes the view expressed by Griffith: "Ismene is an 'ordinary' woman" (2010: 275). In my view, however, Antigone is not so extreme and Ismene is not quite so conventional. More important, Ismene may, if approached less conventionally (perhaps, that is, it is we who are conventional not she), illustrate the possibility of traveling from the starting point of convention to other agentic possibilities.

6 Žižek's criticism of the idea that Antigone is a "gentle protectress of her family and household" (the guardian role to which Antigone is often consigned) is echoed by Alenka Zupančič. I think Antigone can be protective without necessarily being "gentle."

7 In a recent article, Bennett and Tyrrell (2008–2009) also try to undo the splitting by insisting on the connection between the two sisters. Their creative, Girardian reading of them as "Enemy Sisters" could not be more different from mine.

8 Jennet Kirkpatrick's recent reading (2011), in which Ismene admirably acts in stealth also fits this pattern of interpretation.

9 I am struck here by similarities, again, between this project and James Martel's: he tracks "how a subject can go from being a deeply complicit colluder with the phantasmagoria to a conspirator with language" (2011: 151). This in my view is Ismene's trajectory, thus far undetected, though I would add that she takes a step into the role of plotter en route, as we shall see.

10 Butler says that "when [Antigone] breaks with Ismene, it mirrors the break that Polynices has made with Eteocles, thus acting, we might say, as brothers do" (2000: 62). I note that to get sorority for Antigone, as it were, Lupton has to go to Shakespeare's Isabella. See her discussion of adopted sisterhood (2005: 127).

11   This is not to suggest that others have not turned to Ismene. Many have, and
     I note some efforts below. They include, for example, Lot Vekemans, a
     Flemish author, who wrote a theatre text (entitled *Zus Van*, or *Sister Of*) from
     Ismene's perspective (thanks to Katharina Pewny for calling this to my
     attention). My point in this chapter is that there is every reason to take
     seriously Ismene's role in Sophocles' text itself, without rewriting it; and there
     are good reasons not to move to Ismene in Antigone's place, but to allow the
     focus on Ismene to open up the question of sorority which pulls Antigone
     back a bit from the radical heroic agency model that she has heretofore been
     taken to exemplify.

12   Goldhill sees how tragedy has been taken over by Romantic individuality and
     returns our attention to linguistic structure and reception (2012). On demo-
     cratic theory's misplaced preference for rupture over maintenance, see my
     Emergency Politics (2009a), in particular chapters 1 and 4. For a similar
     concern about the Left's captivation by revolution, its neglect of weak
     messianism, and its preference to mourn the loss of great politics, see Martel
     (2011). Notably for Martel, mourning harbors another alternative. Regarding
     Assie Djebar's *White Nights*, he says: "A book that looks on the surface like a
     mournful elegy . . . can instead be reread as a conspiracy with the dead. As
     with the ghosts she encounters throughout the book, the declarations of loss
     and mourning permit the unexpected" (2011: 222).

13   That the different burials accomplish something necessary but inadequate for
     the dead and for survivors is an idea that first came to me in viewing the
     powerful film *The Three Burials of Melquiades Estrada* (Jones 2006), which
     also has many other points of contact with the play discussed here. It is a point
     obscured by readings like Hame's which may, however, be in some way
     correct with reference to the play: Hame says "While Antigone does succeed
     in burying Polyneikes, it is the last burial by Kreon, the proper male authority
     and relative, that finally lays Polyneikes' body to rest (Ant. 1196–1205) and
     stops the pollution inflicted on Thebes by the gods" (2008: 11). The idea that
     the play performs a sort of restoration is interesting. For Hame, the transgres-
     sive intervention of the women is necessitated by the tyrannos' abdication of
     his responsibility, and ends when he returns to perform his proper duty. But
     Hame does not attend to the larger fifth-century politics of burial that may
     serve as the play's context (as noted in Chapter 4, above). Read as a depiction
     of the various contenders for legitimacy in the fifth century, the play may
     present Creon's burial of Polynices not as a restoration, but as one contending
     model of proper burial among others. Moreover, seeing the burial of Polynices
     as a restoration calls attention away from the two burials yet left to be
     performed at the end of the play – those of Creon's immediate family
     members.

14   For further discussion on this point, see also Rose (1952). More recently,
     Hame argues that "Antigone on her own can provide only a limited number
     of funeral procedures for her brother in two separate visits to his body:
     sprinkling of dust on the body (Ant. 245–47, 255–56, 429) and pouring

libations (Ant. 430–31). The rites Antigone is able to perform for Polyneikes are interpreted in the play as equivalent to burial. Antigone thus assumed responsibility for her brother's funeral rites and, although she was unable to perform preparatory rites, she did complete the main act of burial" (2008: 11). Hame is right to point to the difference between the first and second "burials," but she does not comment on why dust and libations would be performed in two separate visits to the corpse. That is the very problem Jebb sought to solve. On Jebb's and other solutions to the problem of the second burial, see Rose (1952: 219–223 and 245–251). For further sources, see Hame (2008: n. 37 and n. 38).

15 Or she may seek to hide her conspiratorial thoughts. Somehow or other, other critics explain it, as Alan L. Boegehold (1999) shows, but they resort to claims that she is ashamed of her action or scared of Creon. That is, they try to make sense of the Greek term for lowered head at the expense of what we know to be the case about Antigone, who is neither ashamed nor frightened. Boege-hold argues that her eyes on the ground signifies a gesture of nodding – in this instance in agreement with the sentry's charges as he makes them upon entering – her resistance to Creon in his presence, wordless, begins immedi-ately. Boegehold thus distinguishes, as I do, between the cowardly downward glances of the sentries and the nodding of Antigone. Some alternative explan-ation (perhaps mine) might be called for, however, by the vase noted by Boegehold in the final footnote of his paper, which depicts Antigone with head lowered as two guards bring her before Creon: "she is nodding, saying Yes" Boegehold says. "If she were showing shame or guilt or confusion, she would be covering her face with her himation." (Surely, though, this is more clearly the case for shame or guilt than for confusion.) Boegehold goes on: "This should be clear enough, but a convention of the times was for a painter to represent honorable women as looking downward. And so the illustration is ambivalent" (1999: 23, n. 15).

16 Butler calls attention to this denial as well, in *Antigone's Claim*, there focusing on the power of language as Antigone calls on it, and on the importance of the fact that the crime is as much (or more) the speech, the saying "I did it" (which Creon refers to as her insolence) as it is the purported act of burial (2000: 34). I offer two other not incompatible readings of this speech act here.

17 As I noted in Chapter 4, Charles Segal is one of few to consider it seriously, in both *Sophocles' Tragic World* (1995) and *Tragedy and Civilization* (1981). Carol Jacobs, in "Dusting Antigone" (1996), notes with interest efforts to establish the non-overlap between Antigone's agency and the gods' (Benardete 1999), or the contiguity of their actions (Steiner 1996).

18 When Creon accuses Antigone of "insolence, twice over," he does not intend to address the two burials question (482 [539]). He explains that the burials are the first insolence, and the publicity of her actions the second insolence. But his term "twice over" could also refer to the two burials.

19 Their exchange is typically sororal in that sisters fight like cats and dogs and soon again are best friends. Thus, it is not difficult to make sense of the fact

that Antigone "moves from a passionate appeal to the normativity of sister-hood to an equally total rejection of her sister. From intense recognition to no recognition at all, from common blood to refusing the claim of the common" (Goldhill 2006: 157–158). Goldhill, whom I quote here, says this is a symptom of fifth-century shifts in family form, a claim I decenter below.

20 If so, then Antigone's words have had some impact, albeit unbeknownst to her. This is consistent with a point noted by Dewald and Kitzinger (2006), who notice that Antigone is under the wrong impression that she has no support. She is not present when Haemon makes the case for her to his father. There is more evidence of support than noted by Dewald and Kitzinger, however, as in lines (438–440 [487–489]), when the sentry describes his mixed emotions at catching Antigone: "it hurts a man to bring down his friends," he says, "But all that, I'm afraid, means less to me than my own skin." So the sentry, an ordinary everyman sort of character, thinks of Antigone as a friend betrayed and says so to Creon. This line may help account as well for Creon's continued impatience with the sentry though he has caught the culprit. The sentry has let show where his loyalties lie. In my view, taking into account this scene which Antigone does witness, Antigone's sense of isolation is a central part of her tragedy; that she has more support than she realizes is truer still, as we shall see, on the reading tendered here.

21 There are three exceptions. Jennet Kirkpatrick (2011) whose paper appeared at the same time as mine, and two sources to which she points: a research note and a reference to it, both from 1911: Rouse (1911: 40–42) and Harry (1911: 3–46). Rouse's reading lights on some of the same details as mine (uncannily, he even borrows, as I do below, Shakespeare's "methinks she doth protest too much") – but he does not treat the first burial in connec-tion with the play's later development of the sororal relationship on which I focus here. That is, he sees the plot (failed) and Ismene's agency, but not the conspiracy between the sisters and not their conspiracy with language, which I will argue for, further, here. Still, the existence of this research note poses the question of why this reading has failed to penetrate *Antigone* scholarship. This goes to the power of critics' investments in Ismene's passivity. Kirkpatrick lights on the same possibility as I do here regarding the first burial, but she allies Ismene with the "weapons of the weak" literature, which leads her to underline, in the end, the contrast between the sisters, one powerful, the other weak. Moreover, as I note below, Kirkpatrick also treats the sisters' second scene in conventional terms. By contrast, for me, the possibility of Ismene's transgressive action invites a new consideration of sororal action in concert, largely elided or dismissed by critics in spite of the text's hospitality to it. Moreover, without the second scene's transformation, we get the plotting of the sisters but not their conspiracy. Women plotting in secret is a bit of an old story (though Kirkpatrick's reading is certainly new – I refer to the frame, not to her reading), one that falls too readily, in my view, into conventional views of female agency, or the lack thereof.

22 Thanks to Maria Panezi, who pointed out that Ismene, as I read her here, is close to the poetic meditation on her written by Yannis Ritsos (1993).

23 In other words, Ismene's confession, which depends on another's, is a speech act that combines constative and performative features. If such speech acts work it is not in spite but rather because of that category-breaking commingling, as Derrida argues in "Declarations of Independence" (1986b).

24 Garry Wills (2004) articulates the conventional view: Antigone "says it is the highest duty to be true to 'one's own' (philoi, not 'friends' merely, but family and allies – the adjective refers as well to one's own property or one's limbs); yet she turns with enmity on her sister, Ismene, when the latter says the burial cannot succeed (it doesn't), and then generously tries to join her in taking credit for the failed attempt at burial."

25 Including Kirkpatrick's, which claims Ismene performed the first burial, but then reverts to the conventional reading. Although, citing my own earlier essay on this (Honig 2011a), she acknowledges the possibility that Antigone makes an effort to preserve Ismene (acting cruelly "in the name of kindness" [420]), Kirkpatrick returns to her more fundamental claim that the sisters are "fiercely at odds and seemingly unable to act in concert" (411) and that Ismene is "cunning" (described as "unmanly") while Antigone wants "no part in subterfuge" (408). Kirkpatrick then underlines again her focus on division rather than unity between the sisters, splitting them again. Arguing that Antigone demands "oneness," that she has a "vision of an undivided sisterhood," Kirkpatrick suggests that what result, therefore, are "harsh words, heated clashes and an inability to act in concert" (420). All this has the "effect of tearing Ismene and Antigone apart" (420). "By their final exchange, Ismene's and Antigone's relationship is in tatters, destroyed by hurled insults, charges of mockery, and declarations of hatred. Though they are similarly situated, the sisters do not act in concert or accomplish anything *together* throughout the play because divergent tactics, principles, values, and worldviews are wedged between them. While the invocation of *koinon autadelphon kara* at the beginning of the play raises the hope that they will act in concert, this optimism is dashed over the course of the play" (422).

26 Antigone need not suspect Ismene's secret support regarding the first burial in order to be motivated to treat her sister in this last scene with the kindness and self-sacrifice I attribute to her here. That is, my reading of this second scene as one of conspiratorial sororal action in concert does not depend upon my reading of Ismene as having performed the first burial, though dramaturgically, establishing the possibility of Ismene's earlier action renders this later scene especially powerful. This point needs underlining in response to Simon Goldhill's critique of the article version of this chapter (2011a) in his *Sophocles and the Language of Tragedy* (2012), which appeared just as this book went to press.

    Goldhill says my focus on sorority presupposes that "the first burial of Polyneices is actually completed by Ismene" (2012: 247). But that is not the case. The second sororal scene's conspiracy is the key one, and my reading of that scene in no way depends upon Ismene having performed the first burial. At most, the suggestion is, as noted above and in the earlier article, as well, that the mere contemplation of the possibility that Ismene did it helps to unsettle long held assumptions about female agency in this tragedy and thus helps open the sisters' second scene to be read otherwise too. But this help is not needed. Simpson and Millar, as I note below, consider a reading of the sisters' second quarrel that is quite close to mine, without ever reconsidering the conventional assumptions regarding the first burial. (This is not Goldhill's only criticism. There are others and I discuss them below.)

27 The paradox is analogous to the one that plagued words, as well, noted in Chapter 4, when we saw that the Chorus called Eurydice's laments "empty outcries" but also worried they were potentially dangerous. The puzzle can be solved, they are empty insofar as they cannot bring the dead back, but they are not at all empty insofar as they can restart a cycle of vengeance and destabilize the city. Still, the sense that words are both nothing and everything recurs.

28 Butler rejects the idea of female solidarity between Antigone and her sister, saying: "She owns the deed that she did which is in itself a somewhat awesome thing; she's asserting that she is a sovereign subject who performs an act [i.e., she was not put up to it] and that it is her act and hers alone. And she won't let anyone else take credit for the act. Ismene tries to come in, claim solidarity, says: 'I'll say I did it too.' Antigone says: 'No, no you didn't do it.' So it is not a notion of feminist solidarity that one derives from Antigone! I think that's one of the misappropriations one sees in Luce Irigaray and others" (Butler and Rabinow 2001: 39). In response to Butler, I would note that Antigone's protest, "Never share my dying, don't lay claim to what you never touched," does not end there but rather with "My death will be enough," which suggests she has made a calculation and is thinking not (just) about the rightness or justice of the claims of who did what but also about the consequences of owning the act. Also, Butler seems to share what she takes to be Antigone's perspective when she suggests Ismene's words are empty, or unearned, unconnected as they are to real actions. But we can read the charge made by Antigone as intentionally false. All of this suggests, contra Butler, that the text allows for the possibility of solidarity, though of what sort remains an open question.

29 She does not also say, though she might have: "earn this." The gift is unconditional. "Earn this" are the last words of the Tom Hanks character who, in *Saving Private Ryan* (Spielberg 1998), dies on a mission to save Private Ryan, the last of a single family's three sons serving in the US military during the Second World War. Private Ryan goes on to live an ordinary life, amply reproductive (at the film's end, he is surrounded by many grown children and grandchildren) but not distinguished by any particular extraordinariness. The final words uttered by the lieutenant who sacrifices himself for Ryan seem to be uttered as a gift but they are surely a curse. What could Ryan possibly do to earn his savior's death? And how can he go on to live a life

under the shadow of this instruction or command? In a way, however, as these last two formulations already suggest, these words also summarize the human condition, especially in a Christian context: how to live a life that is worthy of the sacrifices of those – or the one – who came before us. For a more detailed discussion of the film in the context of its politics of patriotism as sacrifice, see Steven Johnston (2007).

30 D. A. Hester (1971) cites Simpson and Millar (1948) for the view that Antigone's harshness is a device meant to save Ismene. Hester says critics are overly subtle in making this case, but Simpson and Millar's arguments, which I discovered only after developing the reading offered here, are compelling, and Hester in his otherwise fine article offers few reasons for dismissing them. As Simpson and Millar themselves note, their reading is supported also by Jebb, who says that Antigone's "taunt in 549 was made from Antigone's wish to save Ismene's life" (Simpson and Millar 1948: 79). Simpson and Millar go on, rightly, to ask: "Is it not possible that the whole scene may be interpreted in this way? Might not Antigone throughout the whole scene be acting the part of harshness, to mislead Creon as to Ismene's part in the affair?" (1948: 79). In support of their reading, they cite as well J. T. Sheppard's wonderful little book, *The Wisdom of Sophocles* (1947). They do not however connect the innovative reading of this scene with any re-exploration of the question of the first burial, as I do here. That is, they do not look into what they refer to as Ismene's "part in the affair." And my reading differs from theirs on several points. The largest point is this: for them, what motivates Antigone is familial love for her sister. They make Antigone consistent – she bears both Ismene and Polynices a sisterly love. In my view, things are somewhat more complicated, as Antigone's change of tone with her sister suggests. Love for a dead brother is different from love for a live sister. Also, there is in the sororal relation a politics of equality and conspiracy.

31 Some critics, notably Winkler, have argued that the coy exchanges between Odysseus and Penelope toward the end of the *Odyssey*, before he fully reveals his identity, are due in part to the presence of slaves, before whom they have to speak cautiously; this corresponds well to the suggestion here that Antigone and Ismene are speaking in code, as it were, in the presence of Creon and the Chorus – it offers a precedent that Greek audiences would have recognized. (Thanks to David Konstan on this.) Another, closer comparison would be the deception speech in Sophocles' *Ajax*, whose closing lines R. L. H. Fowler describes as "perfect double-entendres" (personal communication). This may be an apt place to note that although others see Sophocles as the tragedian of failed or inadvertent communication, the play as I read it features excessive communication: conspiracy and *adianoeta*. For another example in classical context, see McClure on "Clytemnestra's duplicitous bilingualism" (1999: 99) which is a kind of covert or conspiratorial speech (also described by McClure as "androgynous").

32 Thus, Sophocles' play, like Machiavelli's *Mandragola* on James Martel's reading of it, shows "how to commit conspiracy in plain sight" (Martel 2011: 174), though, as Martel points out in the context of his book's later

reading of Lorca, the risk – and promise – of this is that "[t]he manipulations and deceptions of conspiracy do not produce a brand new reality ... they simply rescramble, rejuxtapose the existing materials of the characters' lives" (2011: 178). Such rescramblings, however, can have powerful, transformative impacts.

33 Antigone's treatment of Ismene here is seen as brutal: Simpson and Millar (1948: 78) cite Gilbert Norwood (1928): "'That tenderness and womanly affection which we attribute to (her) are ... inventions of our own, except the love she bears Polyneices. This love ... is simply an instinct ... to which she will ... sacrifice all else,'" and "'Antigone has no reasons; she has only an instinct.'" He also calls her conduct "'brutality,'" in a reading that complements the anti-humanist reception of Antigone by Lacan and his followers.

34 Simpson and Millar (1948) do not make this connection, though it fits with their reading as well as mine. It is also possible that Antigone imagines herself unmourned because she not unreasonably expects Ismene will be prevented by Creon from mourning her, just as she herself was prevented from mourning Polynices. Jina Politi gives new poetic voice to the forgetting of Ismene, as just desert for her choices: "Ironically, my fury was roused by the fact that you dared defy the time-honoured role allotted to us women as the appointed guardians of subterranean jouissance, keepers of the sacred obligation towards the insoluble bonds of blood. Hence, by refusing to obey and, as expected, turn yourself into a magnificent spectacle as 'Bride of Hades,' you, my Ismene, were punished by History and forgotten by all. Indeed, even I forgot you and spoke of myself in my lament as 'the last daughter of the house of [our] kings'!" (2006: 134). In my view, this "forgetting" can be seen as quite deliberate.

35 Thus she is different from the protagonist of Butler's imagining in her chapter, "Promiscuous Obedience," in *Antigone's Claim* (2000). For Butler, the issue is Antigone's failed efforts to restrict her meaning, by contrast with my reading, in which she exploits double entendres. In support of the latter emphasis, I note Froma Zeitlin's point that central to tragic theater's peda-gogical function "was the notion of 'discrepant awareness': what one character sees and knows and what another does not; or what the audience knows and the characters do not" (1985: 75). For Zeitlin, this is a pedagogical tool: "Employing this mechanism, tragedy sought to train its democratic audience by demonstrating that any viewpoint is necessarily partial and illustrating the disastrous consequences of blindness (literal and figurative)" (1985: 75). Discrepant awareness is also a postulate of the conspiracy with language I explore here, a constitutive feature of *adianoeta*.

36 Dewald and Kitzinger (2006) argue that Antigone never masters *logos*, but is rather mastered by it. On my reading, however, Antigone does outwit Creon, more than once, precisely by mastering *logos* and *phonê* both.

37 Anna Mudde (2009) is just the most recent in a long line to charge Antigone with needless cruelty to her sister and with wrongly privileging her brother. Notably, the reading that I give here and that developed by Simpson and

Millar (and Jebb, more limitedly) all grant to Antigone a victory over Creon and assume she has a subtlety that eludes him. Might it be that this is among the reasons for the ongoing resistance to the idea that Antigone's lines be read in the double entendre way I sketch out here, or, in Simpson and Millar's words, as an "aside"? That is, do most of the play's readers have trouble envisioning Antigone outdoing Creon? But, as I just noted above, Antigone outwits Creon with her suicide, so the idea that her character can outwit him is established by the play. Might it be that there is resistance in particular to the idea that this woman can outwit him with *logos*, as she does in my reading of this scene (contra Dewald and Kitzinger)? Griffith says "that a likely or inevitable consequence of whole-hearted dedication to the Name of the Father (and brother) is the destruction of the close bonds that should tie sister to 'self-wombed' sister" (2010: 131–2). On the reading developed here that sororal tie is not destroyed but is rather deepened, elevated, intensified.

38 This reading only becomes conceivable if we give up our commitment to Antigone as always and necessarily flagrant. That is, we need to set aside the idea that "Like Creon ... Antigone wants her speech act to be radically and comprehensively public" (Butler 2000: 28). This is true for the burial of Polynices and perhaps even for her confession (though even there there may be care in language, as we have seen), but it is not apt for a reading of Antigone's dirge, which works at several registers, public, semi-public, and private, nor for her scene with Ismene, which conspires and uses *adianoeta* for conspiratorial purposes.

39 The view is voiced as well by the Chorus who call her "autonomos" and compare her in this regard to her father/brother Oedipus. But they have some admiration for her as well, and do not seem to judge this trait in the same narrow way as Creon.

40 This is from Elizabeth Wickoff's translation (39–40), cited by Kirkpatrick (2011: 407).

41 On this, see Paul Allen Miller (2007), who criticizes classicists who fuss with the text, supposedly philologically, in order to position Antigone's stated willingness to die as an effect of Creon's edict. That makes Antigone's death-wish less disorienting but also allows them to avoid not confront her monstrosity.

42 In Miller's words: "Creon, then, does not so much represent the tyrant who forces Antigone to make an impossible choice between life and freedom, but rather he is the inflexible embodiment of the civic norms that her pursuit of a desire beyond the bounds of those articulated within the realms of common life both requires and transcends" (2007: 83). Miller adds: "Creon's dictates make possible Antigone's desire to transgress them, and Antigone's affirm-ation of her desire can only point beyond the law by recognizing that it is defined and bounded by the law. If Antigone were an innocent, blithely unaware of Creon's edict, when she buried her brother, there would be no tragedy, no transcendence. In more orthodox Freudian terms, the death drive is necessarily implicated in the pleasure and reality principles even as it points

beyond them" (2007: 84). Truly, if Antigone were that innocent, she would be more like Billy Budd, the hero of the Melville story in which the only really tragic character is, as Hannah Arendt said, not the innocent Billy, but rather the knowing and conflicted Captain Vere (1990: 82–86).

43 Her choice to act and die "is shaped," Paul Allen Miller says, "neither by the banality of a self-interested selection among communally recognized goods nor the self-loathing of conforming to a code that is both recognized and despised" (2007: 83, citing Julien 1990: 112 and Žižek 2001: 77).

44 There are two other key differences between Williams and Lacan: Lacan is drawn to the beauty of such situations, while Williams focuses more forcefully on the suffering that attends them. As Miller says: "for Lacan, it is the beauty of Antigone's choice of a good beyond all recognized goods, beyond the pleasure principle, that gives her character its monumental status and makes her a model for an ethics of creation as opposed to conformity" (83, citing Lacan 1991: 13). Second, Lacan is focused on being-toward-death while Williams is focused on survival.

45 Žižek emphasizes the inaugural quality of the ethical act in Lacan (2000: see especially 672–673), but when he does so he also channels Hannah Arendt and ironically so, since this very essay – which offers a pointed critique of left melancholy (pre 9/11) – also features at the outset a rather gratuitous dismissal of this important and influential thinker (2000: 658).

46 That I enlist Lacan, as Zupančič reads him, on behalf of a reading of *Antigone*, should not be taken as an endorsement of Lacan nor a commitment to what he calls "ethics." I think Terry Eagleton (2003) is right to point us to Lacan's apparent disdain for the everyday on behalf of the singular heroic act (and I note that Bernard Williams does the reverse). My move to Ismene as the bearer of the Lacanian forced choice forces us beyond Lacan, and beyond ethics, I would argue, to an agonistic politics.

47 The subject is able to makes the impossible choice because (s)he identifies with something beyond life – this is why we say that he or she is "larger than life," Zupančič points out (1998: 110).

48 Thus, although there is warrant for reading Haemon in terms of the Lacanian forced choice as well – as Griffith notes in his edited version of *Antigone*, at 632–634, Haemon is asked to choose, to declare allegiance to one side or the other (1999: 233) – it is not clear that Haemon's situation meets the strict requirements of the Lacanian forced choice.

49 From this angle of vision, as Zupančič notes, Antigone moves out of the traditional position to which she is relegated (first, by Hegel) as guardian of divine law or family honor, and into the position of creator.

50 Žižek cites both Zupančič's book and conversations with her (2000: 672, n. 14), but his references to Antigone in this essay are peculiarly Hegelian rather than like Zupančič's Lacanian treatment of the play. Žižek insists repeatedly that Antigone is committed to "just the blind insistence on her right" (2000: 667). And where he seems better opposed to Hegel, as when he says that "Antigone does not merely relate to the Other-Thing, she – for a brief passing

moment of, precisely, decision – directly is the Thing, thus excluding herself from the community regulated by the intermediate agency of symbolic regulations" (2000: 669), he seems to me to get Antigone wrong (as I argued in Chapter 4, she represents not the rupture of the Symbolic but a rival – the aristocratic form of life under pressure in the new democratic polis). This is not to suggest that all elements of the recalcitrant Real can be remediated by the right symbolic order. It is simply to say, rather, that Ismene rather than Antigone may perform this ruptural function, depicting a kind of tear in the fabric obscured by the monstrous and to that extent also familiar creature: Antigone.

51 Similarly, the beautiful death analyzed by Vernant in Homer is not simply the death of the actor but the whole trajectory of action from the oiling of the body in preparation for battle to the burning of the body on the pyre after death.

52 In *Antigone's Claim* (2000), Butler sees rivalry in this aspiration for glory, not the reformatting celebrated by Žižek and Zupančič but, specifically, an ambition to win the hero's glory that eluded Polynices. Arguably, the scene of the sisters' first fight, in which these bold claims are made, frames Butler's reading as a whole.

53 Recall, Ismene does a similar thing: asked if she would confess or not to implication in the crime, she responded creatively, not with a yes or no as demanded but with a hybrid conditional, yes I did it – if she consents. This is a combination, illicit and productive, of constative and performative utterance.

54 On this second law, long thought to be inauthentic and still discomfiting to many, see Chapter 5.

55 Another reading is possible. What if Antigone merely mimics Creon when she presents Ismene with a forced choice? Rather than repackage the terms, doesn't Antigone merely pass them along? (So it seems in Žižek's reading.) On such a reading, she re-enacts against her sister the violence enacted by Creon against her. Even in this mimicry, however, might something open up (especially if we think of mimicry in Butler's terms)? I have argued throughout for the non-privacy of Antigone's act, but here we see a new dimension of its public nature. It solicits others, enlists them into the performative ethico-political frame of action, challenging them as well to alter the frame and find in the forced choice some other, possibly orthogonal way to act. Something like this is what Carol Jacobs (2008) seems to have in mind when she talks of "skirting the ethical" in her book by that name.

56 On the displacement of subtlety by stridency see Lars Tønder (2011).

57 For further discussion, see also Zupančič's *Ethics of the Real* (2000, esp. 21ff.).

58 Williams imagines the hero of his example, Jim, faced with a similarly mortifying tragic situation, having the same initial reaction before coming to his senses. Jim wildly thinks about grabbing a gun from his tormentors and shooting them all, but quickly realizes this is impractical and will only make matters worse. Jim is not counseled by Williams to live without the

thing most precious to him. For Jim, Williams argues, such sacrifice is super-erogatory at best, and certainly not morally required (Smart and Williams 1973: 93–107).

59 Notwithstanding my comparison of Lacan and Williams, it is important to note that this self-sacrifice is not the same as – it is only similar to – the utilitarian self-sacrifice or self-instrumentalization decried by Williams. In "Melancholy and the Act," Žižek makes clear the triangulation of Kantianism, utilitarianism, and the (Lacanian) Act. Similarly, Williams inserts "integrity" as the third term to highlight the limitations of Kantianism and utilitarianism, both rule-applying moralities, in his estimation.

60 She dies protecting Turelure. Does she sacrifice herself for the husband who forced her into marriage? Or does she find a way, in keeping with her sacrifice, to free herself from the hostage situation? Or both?

61 For Lacan, it is only in modernity that other definitive features of tragedy emerge, for example: the status of the sign, for which Sygne's name is said to stand, but this is not germane to Zupančič's largely formal reading.

62 As Rajan describes Kamaki, the Tamil heroine of *Song of the Anklet*, her "choice" is similar to Sygne's. Faced with Kovolan's [her husband's] corpse, Kamaki reviews her only two options: to die with him or to live (a while) beyond his death. It is in her decision to postpone her death until she has avenged her husband that she exercises a significant choice (2010: 170).

63 Although there are vast differences among those influenced by Lacan – from Žižek to Lupton – engaged in this project of reading Antigone for politics.

64 Strikingly, this very formulation, "the subject is asked to accept with enjoyment the very injustice at which he is horrified," parses Bernard Williams's own rather horrified criticism of utilitarianism (Smart and Williams 1973).

65 For this phrasing, I am indebted to Kris Trujillo.

66 See Jacques Rancière: "[I]n order to constitute a moment in thinking, a moment that gives itself to thought, it is perhaps always necessary for there to be two temporalities at work," and "[t]o conceptualize the 'contemporaneity' of thought requires the reliance on a certain anachronism or untimeliness" (Rancière and Panagia 2000: 125; 123).

67 On classics texts' role in constituting post-colonial modernity, see Barbara Goff and Michael Simpson (2007). On their perpetual recirculation, see Adam Sitze (2006).

68 This phrase is translated by Charles Segal as "common self-sistered head of Ismene" (Sophocles 2003). Comparing translations of this most "monstrously untranslatable line in Greek tragedy," see Deborah H. Roberts (2010: 286–290).

69 For an extended reading of efforts to translate it, see Paul Allen Miller (2007) who, as I noted above, also criticizes philological domestications of its alienness.

70 This may hold, by implication, for sister cities as well, another resource often belittled as non-serious. Politics, it is said, belongs to states, and to transnational institutions with serious power. What can sister cities do? Exchange

books? Send postcards? Hang flags? But the work of sister city movements can be differently powerful. Like Ismene and Antigone, sister cities may speak their own language, act in violation of sovereign power and pluralize lines of political identification.

71 On agonism so understood, see Nietzsche, "Homer's Contest" (1994); Connolly, *Pluralism* (2005); Honig, "The Politics of Agonism" (1993b); Honig, "An Agonist's Reply" (2008b).

72 On this point, I am especially misconstrued by Goldhill; see below.

73 I am grateful to Anna Rosensweig for calling Phelan's book to my attention.

74 I have not attended to the *atê* that Lacan thinks is central to Antigone's importance to ethics. I have been trying to reclaim Antigone for a kind of politics that is not one of the two dominant modes prominent now: resistance and lamentation. The result is a reading that is in some ways secular and humanist, ironically, in the absence of the excess that troubles the Imaginary and the Symbolic (see Griffith 2010). But its humanism is, as I argue throughout, an agonistic humanism.

75 Here, I note, Goldhill moves from the idea that "Sisterhood has proved a grounding metaphor of modern feminism" to the concern that "black feminists or feminists from the Third World have questioned whether they are or want to be included in appeals to a universal sisterhood . . . " (248). Although I do not promote sisterhood as a norm, it is nonetheless important here to note that, for those who do, there are forms of sisterhood that are not universal, but rather agonistic, or coalitional.

76 "The move to mark the sororal agency in this play should not be mistaken for a normative effort to promote sorority as a privileged site of agency" (cf. 152 above; Honig 2011a: 31).

77 It seems ironic to me that Goldhill, who was so sensitive to the impositional nature of collective pronouns, such as "universal sisterhood" (248), in the context of contemporary feminism, here assumes that an avoidance of such a pronoun bespeaks a failure of collective imagination rather than an active imagination of an alternative collectivity.

78 Thanks to Christina Tarnopolsky on this point and many others. We might also note that the idea broached here that Creon's perception of Antigone as wild, anarchic, and solitary frames receptions of Antigone for centuries to come is dismissed by Goldhill who goes on, however, to broach the idea that Plato's hostility to the crowd frames receptions of the Chorus for centuries to come.

Conclusion

1 Here we get support again from Benjamin (1969). Butler, too, avails herself of it when she says in *Frames of War* that when a circulating image (or text!) "lands in new contexts . . . it also creates new contexts by virtue of that landing." The frame, she says, reiterating her account of the Symbolic from her earlier work, is vulnerable "to reversal, to subversion, even to critical instrumentalization" (2009: 9–10). Further on, what Butler says about the

body can be said as well about the text: it is not "a mere surface upon which social meanings are inscribed" but rather "that which suffers, enjoys, and responds to the exteriority of the world, an exteriority that defines its disposition and activity" (2009: 33–34).

2 Another paradox of classicization: classical texts are often turned to as resources of resistance, sometimes because they are a way to evade censors. But, as classical texts, they also have a more conservative effect: they may reabsorb dissent and dissipate it, or they may universalize and harden the political formations we mean to break out of. If our resistance is in the tradition of Antigone, if her mourning speaks to mourning mothers everywhere, if Creon is a universal tyrant, and Antigone a universal heroine of conscience, then we may just remobilize rather than really decenter Oedipal politics in which the law of the father invariably wins. Or tragedy may serve as a Trojan horse bearing within it otherwise contestable universalisms, such as nature, gender or sexual difference, rationalism, sovereignty, or kinship. Page duBois also uses the term "Trojan horse" to describe the workings of classical texts in cultural politics.

3 Rancière identifies Antigone fundamentally with mourning, Hegel identifies her with conflict, one side of which is her thoughtless impulse to lament, presaging Lacan's identification of her with desire that will not be denied.

4 I discuss Rancière's argument in detail elsewhere. See Honig, "The Event of Genre" (Forthcoming).

5 This adjustment is, since Nancy Fraser's (1993) critique of Habermas on alternative public spheres, to some extent old news and yet still necessary to make.

6 Mortalist and agonistic humanism could be added to the useful list of humanism's types in Mousley and Halliwell (2004).

Bibliography

Ackerman, J. Wolfe, and Bonnie Honig. 2011. "Agonality: Conceptions of Agonism in Arendt and Arendt Scholarship," in *Arendt Handbuch: Leben – Werk – Wirkung*, ed. Wolfgang Heuer, Bernd Heiter and Stefanie Rosenmuller. Stuttgart: J. B. Metzler, 341–347.

Agamben, Giorgio. 1993. *Infancy and History: the Destruction of Experience*. London: Verso.

1998. *Homo Sacer: Sovereign Power and Bare Life*. Stanford University Press.

2000. *Remnants of Auschwitz: the Witness and the Archive*. New York: Zone Books.

2005. *State of Exception*. University of Chicago Press.

Ahmed, Sara. 2010. "Feminist Killjoys (and Other Willful Subjects)," *S&F Online* 8 (3) (Summer).

Allen, Danielle S. 2000. *The World of Prometheus: the Politics of Punishing in Democratic Athens*. Princeton University Press.

2001. "Law's Forcefulness: Hannah Arendt vs Ralph Ellison on the Battle of Little Rock," *Oklahoma City Law Review* (October): 857.

Améry, Jean. 1980. "Resentments," in *At the Mind's Limits: Contemplations by a Survivor on Auschwitz and Its Realities*. Bloomington: Indiana University Press, 62–81.

Anker, Elisabeth. 2005. "Villains, Victims and Heroes: Melodrama, Media and September 11," *Journal of Communication* 55 (1): 22–37.

2011. "Left Melodrama," *Contemporary Political Theory* 11 (2): 1–23.

Forthcoming. *Orgies of Feeling: Melodramatic Politics and the Pursuit of Freedom*. Durham, NC: Duke University Press.

Anouilh, Jean. 1946. *Antigone*. Paris: La Table Ronde.

"*Antigone* westöstlich: erste Schauspielschule in Palästina." 2009. *Frankfurter Allgemeine Zeitung*.

Appel, Liz. 2010. "Autochthonous Antigone: Breaking Ground," in *Interrogating Antigone in Postmodern Philosophy and Criticism*, ed. S. E. Wilmer and Audrone Žukauskaitė. Oxford; New York: Oxford University Press, 229–239.

Arendt, Hannah. 1958. *The Human Condition*. University of Chicago Press.

1973. *The Origins of Totalitarianism*. New York: Harcourt Brace Javanovich.

1990. *On Revolution*. New York: Penguin Books.

Aristotle. 1986. *Poetics*, trans. Stephen Halliwell. Chapel Hill: University of North Carolina Press.

Arteel, Inge. 2011. "Judith Butler and the Catachretic Human," in *Towards a New Literary Humanism*, ed. Andrew Mousley. London: Palgrave Macmillan, 77–92.

Augustine. 1998. *The City of God Against the Pagans*, ed. R. W. Dyson. Cambridge University Press.

Austin, J. L. 1962. *How to Do Things with Words*. Cambridge, Mass.: Harvard University Press.

Babich, Babette E. 2006. *Words in Blood, Like Flowers: Philosophy and Poetry, Music and Eros in Hölderlin, Nietzsche, and Heidegger*. Albany: State University of New York Press.

Barker, Derek W. M. 2009. *Tragedy and Citizenship: Conflict, Reconciliation and Democracy from Haemon to Hegel*. Albany: State University of New York Press.

Barnett, Stuart. 1998. *Hegel after Derrida*. London; New York: Routledge.

Basterra, Gabriela. 2004. *Seductions of Fate: Tragic Subjectivity, Ethics, Politics*. New York: Palgrave Macmillan.

Beiser, Frederick C. 1993. *The Cambridge Companion to Hegel*. Cambridge; New York: Cambridge University Press.

Belsey, Catherine. 2001. "Tarquin Dispossessed: Expropriation and Consent in *The Rape of Lucrece*," *Shakespeare Quarterly* 52 (3): 315–335.

2003. "Reading and Critical Practice," *Critical Quarterly* 45 (3): 22–31.

2005. *Culture and the Real: Theorizing Cultural Criticism*. London; New York: Routledge.

Benardete, Seth. 1975. "A Reading of Sophocles' *Antigone*: II," *Interpretation: A Journal of Political Philosophy* 5 (1): 1–55.

1999. *Sacred Transgressions: a Reading of Sophocles' Antigone*. South Bend, Ind.: St. Augustine's Press.

Benhabib, Seyla. 1996. "On Hegel, Women and Irony," in *Feminist Interpretations of G. W. F. Hegel*, ed. Patricia Jagentowicz Mills. University Park: Pennsylvania State University Press, 25–44.

Benjamin, Walter. 2000. "On Language as Such and on the Language of Man," in *Walter Benjamin: Selected Writings, 1913–1926*, ed. Marcus Bullock and Michael W. Jennings. Cambridge, Mass.: Belknap Press, 62–74.

2003. *The Origin of German Tragic Drama*. New York: Verso.

Benjamin, Walter, and Hannah Arendt. 1969. "The Work of Art in the Age of Mechanical Reproduction," in *Illuminations*. New York: Schocken Books.

Bennett, Jane. 2004. "The Force of Things," *Political Theory* 32 (3): 347–372.

Bennett, Larry J., and William Blake Tyrrell. 1990. "Sophocles' *Antigone* and Funeral Oratory," *American Journal of Philology* 111 (4): 441–456.

2008–2009. "Sophocles's Enemy Sisters: Antigone and Ismene," *Contagion: Journal of Violence, Mimesis, and Culture* 15: 1–18.

Berlant, Lauren. 2007. "Nearly Utopian, Nearly Normal: Post-Fordist Affect in *La Promesse* and *Rosetta*," *Public Culture* 19 (2): 273–301.

2008. *The Female Complaint: the Unfinished Business of Sentimentality in American Culture*. Durham, NC: Duke University Press.

Berlin, Isaiah. 2000. *The Proper Study of Mankind: an Anthology of Essays*. New York: Farrar, Straus and Giroux.

Biro, David. 2010. *The Language of Pain: Finding Words, Compassion, and Relief*. New York: W. W. Norton.

Blok, Josine H. 2001. "Virtual Voices: Toward a Choreography of Women's Speech in Classical Athens," in *Making Silence Speak: Women's Voices in Greek Literature and Society*, ed. A. P. M. H. Lardinois and Laura McClure. Princeton University Press, 95–116.

Blondell, Ruby. 1989. *Helping Friends and Harming Enemies: a Study in Sophocles and Greek Ethics*. Cambridge; New York: Cambridge University Press.

Blumenthal-Barby, Martin. 2007. "*Germany in Autumn*: the Return of the Human," *Discourse: Journal for Theoretical Studies in Media and Culture* 29 (1): 140–168.

Boedeker, Deborah, and Kurt Raaflaub. 2005. "Tragedy and City," in *A Companion to Tragedy*, ed. Rebecca W. Bushnell. Malden, Mass.: Blackwell, 109–127.

Boegehold, Alan L. 1999. "Antigone Nodding, Unbowed," in *The Eye Expanded: Life and the Arts in Greco-Roman Antiquity*, ed. Frances B. Titchener and Richard F. Moorton. Berkeley: University of California Press, 19–23.

Bordowitz, Gregg. 2002. *Drive: the AIDS Crisis is Still Beginning: a Collection of Essays, Dialogues, and Texts Surrounding Gregg Bordowitz's Films* Fast Trip, Long Drop, *and* Habit, *and His Exhibition* Drive, *Held at the Museum of Contemporary Art, Chicago, April 6–July 7, 2003*. Chicago, Ill.: Whitewalls.

Borges, Jorge Luis, Donald A. Yates, and James East Irby. 1964. *Labyrinths; Selected Stories and Other Writings*. New York: New Directions.

Bosteels, Bruno. 2008. "Force of Nonlaw: Alain Badiou's Theory of Justice," *Cardozo Law Review* 29 (5): 1905–1926.

2011. "Reviewing Rancière. Or, the persistence of discrepancies," *Radical Philosophy* 170 (November/December).

Bradley, A. C. 1929. *Shakespearean Tragedy: Lectures on* Hamlet, Othello, King Lear, Macbeth. London: Macmillan.

Bradshaw, Peter. 2008. "Hunger," *The Guardian*, Thursday October 30.

Bronfen, Elisabeth. 2008. "Femme Fatale: Negotiations of Tragic Desire," in *Rethinking Tragedy*, ed. Rita Felski. Baltimore, Md.: Johns Hopkins University Press, 287–301.

Brooks, Peter. 1976. *The Melodramatic Imagination: Balzac, Henry James, Melodrama, and the Mode of Excess*. New Haven, Conn.: Yale University Press.

Brown, Wendy. 1999. "Resisting Left Melancholy," *boundary 2* 26 (3): 19–27.

Bruck, Eberhard Friedrich. 1970. *Totenteil und Seelgerät im griechischen Recht. Eine entwicklungsgeschichtliche Untersuchung zum Verhältnis von Recht und Religion mit Beiträgen zur Geschichte des Eigentums und des Erbrechts*. Munich: Beck.

Burckhardt, Jacob, and Oswyn Murray. 1998. *The Greeks and Greek Civilization*. New York: St. Martin's Press.

Burian, Peter. 2010. "Gender and the City: *Antigone* from Hegel to Butler and Back," in *When Worlds Elide*, ed. J. Peter Euben and Karen Bassi. Lanham, Md.: Lexington Books, 255–299.

Burke, Victoria I. 2010. "Hegel, Antigone, and First-Person Authority," *Philosophy & Literature* 34 (2): 373–380.

Burns, Tony. 2002. "Sophocles' *Antigone* and the History of the Concept of Natural Law," *Political Studies* 50: 545–557.

Bushnell, Rebecca W. 2005. *A Companion to Tragedy*. Malden, Mass.: Blackwell.

Butler, Judith. 1987. *Subjects of Desire: Hegelian Reflections in Twentieth-Century France*. New York: Columbia University Press.

　1990a. *Gender Trouble: Feminism and the Subversion of Identity*. New York: Routledge.

　1990b. "Lana's 'Imitation': Melodramatic Repetition and the Gender Performative," *Genders* 1 (9): 1–18.

　1993. *Bodies that Matter: on the Discursive Limits of "Sex."* New York: Routledge.

　1997. *The Psychic Life of Power: Theories in Subjection*. Stanford University Press.

　1999. "Revisiting Bodies and Pleasures," *Theory Culture Society* 16: 11–20.

　2000. *Antigone's Claim: Kinship Between Life and Death*. New York: Columbia University Press.

　2004a. *Precarious Life: the Powers of Mourning and Violence*. London: Verso.

　2004b. *Undoing Gender*. New York: Routledge.

　2004c. "Bracha's Eurydice," *Theory, Culture & Society* 21: 95–100.

　2005. *Giving an Account of Oneself*. New York: Fordham University Press.

　2009. *Frames of War: When is Life Grievable?* London: Verso.

　2010. "Performative Agency," *Journal of Cultural Economy* 3 (2): 147–161.

Butler, Judith, and Paul Rabinow. 2001. "Dialogue: *Antigone*, Speech, Performance, and Power," in *Talk Talk Talk: the Cultural Life of Everyday Conversation*, ed. S. I. Salamensky. New York: Routledge, 37–48.

Calvino, Italo. 1999. *Why Read the Classics?* New York: Pantheon Books.

　2009. "A King Listens," in *Under the Jaguar Sun*. London: Penguin.

Carlson, Lisa. 1987. *Caring for Your Own Dead*. Hinesburg, Vt.: Upper Access Publishers.

Carroll, Noël. 1999. "Film, Emotion, and Genre," in *Passionate Views: Film, Cognition, and Emotion*, ed. Carl R. Plantinga and Greg M. Smith. Baltimore, Md.: Johns Hopkins University Press, 21–47.

Carson, Anne. 1995. *Glass, Irony, and God*. New York: New Directions.

　1999. *Economy of the Unlost: Reading Simonides of Keos with Paul Celan*. Princeton University Press.

　2005. *Decreation: Poetry, Essays, Opera*. New York: Knopf: Distributed by Random House.

Caruth, Cathy. 1996. *Unclaimed Experience: Trauma, Narrative, and History*. Baltimore, Md.: Johns Hopkins University Press.

Caruth, Cathy, and Thomas Keenan. 1995. "'The AIDS Crisis is Not Over': A Conversation with Gregg Bordowitz, Douglas Crimp, and Laura Pinsky," in *Trauma: Explorations in Memory*, ed. Cathy Caruth. Baltimore, Md.: Johns Hopkins University Press, 256–272.

Castiglia, Christopher, and Christopher Reed. 2011. *If Memory Serves: Gay Men, AIDS, and the Promise of the Queer Past*. Minneapolis: University of Minnesota Press.

Castoriadis, Cornelius. 2007. *Figures of the Thinkable*, trans. Helen Arnold. Stanford University Press.

Cavarero, Adriana. 1995. *In Spite of Plato: a Feminist Rewriting of Ancient Philosophy*. Cambridge: Polity Press.

2002. *Stately Bodies: Literature, Philosophy, and the Question of Gender*. Ann Arbor: University of Michigan Press.

2005. *For More Than One Voice: Toward a Philosophy of Vocal Expression*. Stanford University Press.

2009. *Horrorism: Naming Contemporary Violence*. New York: Columbia University Press.

Cavell, Stanley. 1976. "The Avoidance of Love: a Reading of *King Lear*," in *Must We Mean What We Say? A Book of Essays*, ed. Stanley Cavell. Cambridge University Press, 267–356.

1979. *The Claim of Reason: Wittgenstein, Skepticism, Morality and Tragedy*. Oxford; New York: Clarendon Press; Oxford University Press.

1994. *A Pitch of Philosophy: Autobiographical Exercises*. Cambridge, Mass.: Harvard University Press.

1995. *Philosophical Passages: Wittgenstein, Emerson, Austin, Derrida*. Oxford; Cambridge, Mass.: Blackwell.

1997. *Contesting Tears: the Hollywood Melodrama of the Unknown Woman*. University of Chicago Press.

Chambers, Samuel Allen. 2005. "The Politics of Literarity," *Theory and Event* (3).

2012. *The Lessons of Rancière*. New York: Oxford University Press.

Chanter, Tina. 1995. *Ethics of Eros: Irigaray's Re-writing of the Philosophers*. New York: Routledge.

2008. *The Picture of Abjection: Film, Fetish, and the Nature of Difference*. Bloomington: Indiana University Press.

Cheng, Sinkwan. 2004. *Law, Justice, and Power: Between Reason and Will*. Stanford University Press.

Claudel, Paul. 1911. *L'otage: drame en trois actes*. Paris: Gallimard.

Coetzee, J. M. 2007. *Diary of a Bad Year*. London: Harvill Secker.

Cohen, David. 1995. *Law, Violence, and Community in Classical Athens*. Cambridge; New York: Cambridge University Press.

Comaroff, Jean. 2007. "Beyond the Politics of Bare Life: AIDS and the Global Order," *Public Culture* 19 (1): 197–219.

Comaroff, John L., and Jean Comaroff. 2009. *Ethnicity, Inc.* University of Chicago Press.

Connolly, William E. 1984. *Legitimacy and the State*. New York University Press.
   1995. *The Ethos of Pluralization*. Minneapolis: University of Minnesota Press.
   1999. *Why I Am Not a Secularist*. Minneapolis: University of Minnesota Press.
   2005. *Pluralism*. Durham, NC: Duke University Press.
   2008. *Capitalism and Christianity, American Style*. Durham, NC: Duke University Press.
Copjec, Joan. 2002. *Imagine There's No Woman: Ethics and Sublimation*. Cambridge, Mass.: MIT Press.
Cornell, Drucilla, Michel Rosenfeld, and David Carlson, eds. 1991. *Hegel and Legal Theory*. New York: Routledge.
Cornwell, Rupert. 2005. "Bush: God Told Me to Invade Iraq: President 'revealed reasons for war in private meeting,'" *The Independent*. www.commondreams.org/headlines05/1007–13.htm.
Cover, Robert M. 1975. *Justice Accused: Antislavery and the Judicial Process*. New Haven, Conn.: Yale University Press.
Cowell-Meyers, Kimberly. 2006. "Teaching Politics Using *Antigone*," *PS: Political Science and Politics* 39 (2): 347–349.
Craik, E. M. 1979. "*Philoktetes*: Sophoclean Melodrama," *L'Antiquité Classique* 48: 15–29.
Crépon, Marc. 2001. *Les Promesses du langage: Benjamin, Rosenzweig, Heidegger*. Paris: Vrin.
Crimp, Douglas. 1982. "Fassbinder, Franz, Fox, Elvira, Erwin, Armin, and All the Others," *October* 21 (supplement): 63–81.
   1987a. "How to Have Promiscuity in an Epidemic," *October* 43 (Winter) (special issue, *AIDS: Cultural Analysis, Cultural Activism*): 237–271.
   1987b. "Introduction," *October* 43 (Winter) (special issue, *AIDS: Cultural Analysis, Cultural Activism*): 3–16.
   2002. *Melancholia and Moralism: Essays on AIDS and Queer Politics*. Cambridge, Mass.: MIT Press.
Critchley, Simon. 1999. *Ethics, Politics, Subjectivity: Essays on Derrida, Levinas and Contemporary French Thought*. London: Verso.
   2001. *Continental Philosophy: a Very Short Introduction*. Oxford; New York: Oxford University Press.
   2005. "On the Ethics of Alain Badiou," in *Alain Badiou: Philosophy and Its Conditions*, ed. Gabriel Riera. Albany: State University of New York Press, 215–236.
   2007. *Infinitely Demanding: Ethics of Commitment, Politics of Resistance*. New York: Verso.
Critchley, Simon, and Robert Bernasconi. 2002. *The Cambridge Companion to Levinas*. Cambridge University Press.
Cropp, Martin. 1997. "Antigone's final speech (Sophocles, *Antigone* 891–928)," *Greece and Rome* 44: 137–160.
Culler, Jonathan D. 1981. *The Pursuit of Signs – Semiotics, Literature, Deconstruction*. Ithaca, NY: Cornell University Press.
   1988. *On Puns: the Foundation of Letters*. Oxford; New York: Blackwell.

Cvetkovich, Ann. 2003a. *An Archive of Feelings: Trauma, Sexuality, and Lesbian Public Cultures*. Durham, NC: Duke University Press.

— 2003b. "Legacies of Trauma, Legacies of Activism: ACT UP's Lesbians," in *Loss: the Politics of Mourning*, ed. David L. Eng and David Kazanjian. Berkeley: University of California Press, 427–457.

— 2007. "Public Feelings," *South Atlantic Quarterly* 106 (3): 459–468.

Dauenhauer, Bernard P. 1998. *Paul Ricoeur: the Promise and Risk of Politics*. Lanham, Md.: Rowman & Littlefield.

Davis, Creston, John Milbank, and Slavoj Žižek. 2005. *Theology and the Political: the New Debate*. Durham, NC: Duke University Press.

Davis, Todd F., and Kenneth Womack. 2001. *Mapping the Ethical Turn: a Reader in Ethics, Culture, and Literary Theory*. Charlottesville: University Press of Virginia.

Dean, Jodi. 2009. *Democracy and Other Neoliberal Fantasies: Communicative Capitalism and Left Politics*. Durham, NC: Duke University Press.

Derrida, Jacques. 1986a. *Glas*. Lincoln: University of Nebraska Press.

— 1986b. "Declarations of Independence," *New Political Science* 15: 3–19.

— 1988. *Limited Inc.*, ed. Gerald Graff, trans. Jeffrey Mehlman and Samuel Weber. Evanston, Ill.: Northwestern University Press.

— 1997. *Politics of Friendship*. London: Verso.

— 1998. *Monolingualism of the Other; or, the Prosthesis Of Origin*, trans. Patrick Mensah. Stanford University Press.

— 2007. *Psyche: Inventions of the Other*. Stanford University Press.

— 2011. *The Beast and the Sovereign*. Vol. II, ed. Michel Lisse, Marie-Louise Mallet, and Ginette Michaud, trans. Geoffrey Bennington. University of Chicago Press.

Derrida, Jacques, and Anne Dufourmantelle. 2000. *Of Hospitality: Anne Dufourmantelle Invites Jacques Derrida to Respond*. Stanford University Press.

Derrida, Jacques, and Elisabeth Roudinesco. 2004. *For What Tomorrow … : A Dialogue*. Stanford University Press.

Derrida, Jacques, and Jean Birnbaum. 2007. *Learning to Live Finally: an Interview with Jean Birnbaum*. Hoboken, NJ: Melville House.

Derrida, Jacques, Pascale-Anne Brault, and Michael Naas. 2001. *The Work of Mourning*. University of Chicago Press.

Detienne, Marcel, and Jean-Pierre Vernant. 1978. *Cunning Intelligence in Greek Culture and Society*. Hassocks, UK; Atlantic Highlands, NJ: Harvester Press; Humanities Press.

Detloff, Madelyn. 2009. *The Persistence of Modernism: Loss and Mourning in the Twentieth Century*. Cambridge; New York: Cambridge University Press.

Dewald, Carolyn, and Rachel Kitzinger. 2006. "Herodotus, Sophocles and the Woman Who Wanted Her Brother Saved," in *The Cambridge Companion to Herodotus*, ed. Carolyn Dewald and John Marincola. Cambridge; New York: Cambridge University Press, 122–129.

Dewald, Carolyn, and John Marincola, eds. 2006. *The Cambridge Companion to Herodotus*. Cambridge; New York: Cambridge University Press.

Dietz, Mary G. 1985. "Citizenship with a Feminist Face: the Problem with Maternal Thinking," *Political Theory* 13 (1): 19–37.

Dolar, Mladen. 2006. *A Voice and Nothing More*. Cambridge, Mass.: MIT Press.

Dollimore, Jonathan. 1998. *Death, Desire, and Loss in Western Culture*. New York: Routledge.

Dougherty, Carol, and Leslie Kurke. 1998. *Cultural Poetics in Archaic Greece: Cult, Performance, Politics*. New York: Oxford University Press.

Douglas, Lawrence. 2001. *The Memory of Judgment: Making Law and History in the Trials of the Holocaust*. New Haven, Conn.: Yale University Press.

Douzinas, Costas. 1995. "Law's Birth and Antigone's Death," *Cardozo Law Review* 16: 3–4.

Douzinas, Costas, and Ronnie Warrington. 1994. "Antigone's Law: a Geneaology of Jurisprudence," in *Politics, Postmodernity, and Critical Legal Studies: the Legality of the Contingent*, ed. Costas Douzinas, Peter Goodrich and Yifat Hachamovitch. London: Routledge, 187–225.

duBois, Page. 1988. *Sowing the Body: Psychoanalysis and Ancient Representations of Women*. University of Chicago Press.

———. 2008. "Toppling the Hero: Polyphony in the Tragic City," in *Rethinking Tragedy*, ed. Rita Felski. Baltimore, Md.: Johns Hopkins University Press, 127–147.

———. 2010. *Out of Athens: the New Ancient Greeks*. Cambridge, Mass.: Harvard University Press.

EAAF (Equipo Argentino de Anthropología Forense), and Witness. 2002. "Following Antigone: Forensic Anthropology and Human Rights Investigations." Documentary; 37 minutes.

Eagleton, Terry. 2003. *Sweet Violence: the Idea of the Tragic*. Malden, Mass.: Blackwell.

———. 2010. "Lacan's *Antigone*," in *Interrogating Antigone in Postmodern Philosophy and Criticism*, ed. S. E. Wilmer and Audronė Žukauskaitė. Oxford; New York: Oxford University Press, 101–109.

Easterling, P. E. 1997. *The Cambridge Companion to Greek Tragedy*. Cambridge; New York: Cambridge University Press.

Edelman, Lee. 1994. *Homographesis: Essays in Gay Literary and Cultural Theory*. New York: Routledge.

———. 2004. *No Future: Queer Theory and the Death Drive*. Durham, NC: Duke University Press.

Edkins, Jenny. 2003. *Trauma and the Memory of Politics*. Cambridge; New York: Cambridge University Press.

Eliot, George. 2000. *Middlemarch: an Authoritative Text, Backgrounds, Criticism*, ed. Bert G. Hornback. New York: W. W. Norton.

Ellison, Ralph. 1990. *Invisible Man*. New York: Vintage Books.

Elsaesser, Thomas. 2003. "Tales of Sound and Fury: Observations on the Family Melodrama," in *Film Genre Reader III*, ed. Barry Keith Grant. Austin: University of Texas Press, 366–395.

———. 2004. "Antigone Agonistes: Urban Guerrilla or Guerrilla Urbanism?" *Rouge* 4.

Elshtain, Jean Bethke. 1982. "Antigone's Daughters," *Democracy* 2 (2): 39–45.

    1989. "Antigone's Daughters Reconsidered: Continuing Reflections of Women, Politics and Power," in *Life-World and Politics: Between Modernity and Postmodernity: Essays in Honor of Fred R. Dallmayr*, ed. Stephen K. White. West Bend, Ind.: University of Notre Dame Press, 222–236.

    1995. "Political Children," in *Feminist Interpretations of Hannah Arendt*, ed. Bonnie Honig. University Park: Pennsylvania State University Press, 263–284.

    1996. "The Mothers of the Disappeared: an Encounter with Antigone's Daughters," in *Finding a New Feminism: Rethinking the Woman Question for Liberal Democracy*, ed. Pamela Grande Jensen. Lanham, Md.: Rowman & Littlefield, 129–148.

    1997. *Real Politics: at the Center of Everyday Life*. Baltimore, Md.: Johns Hopkins University Press.

Emden, Christian. 2008. *Friedrich Nietzsche and the Politics of History*. Cambridge; New York: Cambridge University Press.

Emerson, Ralph Waldo. 1880. *Works of Ralph Waldo Emerson*. Boston: Houghton Osgood.

Epstein, Steven. 1996. *Impure Science: AIDS, Activism, and the Politics of Knowledge*. Berkeley: University of California Press.

    2007. *Inclusion: the Politics of Difference in Medical Research*. University of Chicago Press.

Euben, J. Peter, ed. 1986. *Greek Tragedy and Political Theory*. Berkeley: University of California Press.

    1990. *The Tragedy of Political Theory: the Road Not Taken*. Princeton University Press.

    1997. *Corrupting Youth: Political Education, Democratic Culture, and Political Theory*. Princeton University Press.

    2000. "The Politics of Nostalgia and Theories of Loss," in *Vocations of Political Theory*, ed. Jason A. Frank and John Tambornino. Minneapolis: University of Minnesota Press, 59–92.

    2003. *Platonic Noise*. Princeton University Press.

Euripides. 2006. *Grief Lessons: Four Plays by Euripides*, ed. Anne Carson. New York Review of Books.

"*Fahrenheit 9/11*: script; dialogue transcript." www.script-o-rama.com/movie_scripts/f/fahrenheit-911-script-transcript.html (accessed August 4, 2011).

Fassin, Didier, and Richard Rechtman. 2009. *The Empire of Trauma: an Inquiry into the Condition of Victimhood*. Princeton University Press.

Faust, Drew Gilpin. 2008. *This Republic of Suffering: Death and the American Civil War*. New York: Alfred A. Knopf.

Felski, Rita. 2008. "Introduction," in *Rethinking Tragedy*, ed. Rita Felski. Baltimore, Md.: Johns Hopkins University Press, 1–28.

Ferrario, Sarah Brown. 2006. "Replaying *Antigone*: Changing Patterns of Public and Private Commemoration at Athens, *c.* 440–350," *Helios* 33 (supplement): 79–117.

Festic, Fatima. 2003. *"Antigone* in (Post-)Modern Palestine," *Hecate* 29 (2): 86–96.

Fink, Bruce. 1995. *The Lacanian Subject: Between Language and Jouissance.* Princeton University Press.

　　2004. *Lacan to the Letter: Reading Écrits Closely.* Minneapolis: University of Minnesota Press.

Finley, M. I. 1972. *The World of Odysseus.* Harmondsworth; New York: Penguin Books.

　　1973. *Democracy Ancient and Modern.* New Brunswick, NJ: Rutgers University Press.

Fischer-Lichte, Erika. 2010. "Politicizing *Antigone,*" in *Interrogating* Antigone *in Postmodern Philosophy and Criticism,* ed. S. E. Wilmer and Audronė Žukauskaitė. Oxford; New York: Oxford University Press, 329–352.

Fisk, Gloria. 2008. "Putting Tragedy to Work for the Polis: The Rhetoric of Pity and Terror, Before and After Modernity," *New Literary History* 39 (4): 891–902.

Fleming, Katie. 2006. "Fascism on Stage: Jean Anouilh's *Antigone,*" in *Laughing with Medusa: Classical Myth and Feminist Thought,* ed. Vanda Zajko and Miriam Leonard. Oxford; New York: Oxford University Press, 163–186.

Fletcher, Judith. 2010. "Sophocles' *Antigone* and the Democratic Voice," in *Interrogating* Antigone *in Postmodern Philosophy and Criticism,* ed. S. E. Wilmer and Audronė Žukauskaitė. Oxford; New York: Oxford University Press, 168–184.

Foley, Helene P. 1995. "Tragedy and Democratic Ideology: the Case of Sophocles' *Antigone,*" in *History, Tragedy, Theory: Dialogues on Athenian Drama,* ed. Barbara E. Goff. Austin: University of Texas Press, 131–150.

　　2001. *Female Acts in Greek Tragedy.* Princeton University Press.

Fossen, Thomas. 2008. "Agonistic Critiques of Liberalism: Perfection and Emancipation," *Contemporary Political Theory* 7: 376–394.

Fóti, Véronique Marion. 2006. *Epochal Discordance: Hölderlin's Philosophy of Tragedy.* Albany: State University of New York Press.

Foucault, Michel, and Paul Rabinow. 1984. *The Foucault Reader.* New York: Pantheon Books.

Foucault, Michel, and Michel Senellart. 2008. *The Birth of Biopolitics: Lectures at the Collège De France, 1978–1979.* Basingstoke; New York: Palgrave Macmillan.

Foucault, Michel, Michel Senellart, François Ewald, and Alessandro Fontana. 2007. *Security, Territory, Population: Lectures at the Collège de France, 1977–1978.* Basingstoke; New York: Palgrave Macmillan.

Foust, Mathew A. 2009. "Grief and Mourning in Confucius's *Analects,*" *Journal of Chinese Philosophy* 36 (2): 348–358.

Franco, Jean. 1989. *Plotting Women: Gender and Representation in Mexico.* New York: Columbia University Press.

Frank, Jason A. 2010. *Constituent Moments: Enacting the People in Postrevolutionary America.* Durham, NC: Duke University Press.

Frank, Jill. 2005. *A Democracy of Distinction: Aristotle and the Work of Politics*. University of Chicago Press.

    2006. "The *Antigone's* Law," *Law, Culture and the Humanities* 2 (3): 336–340.

    2007. "Wages of War: on Judgment in Plato's *Republic*," *Political Theory* 35 (4): 443–467.

Fraser, Nancy. 1993. "Rethinking the Public Sphere: a Contribution to the Critique of Actually Existing Democracy," in *Habermas and the Public Sphere*, ed. Craig Calhoun. Cambridge, Mass.: MIT Press, 109–142.

Freeman, Elizabeth. 2010. *Time Binds: Queer Temporalities, Queer Histories*. Durham, NC: Duke University Press.

Freud, Sigmund. 1963. "Mourning and Melancholia," in *The Standard Edition of the Complete Psychological Works of Sigmund Freud*, ed. James Strachey and Anna Freud. London: Hogarth Press, 237–260.

    1989. *Beyond the Pleasure Principle*, ed. James Strachey. New York: Norton.

Fustel de Coulanges. 2006. *The Ancient City: a Study of the Religion, Laws, and Institutions of Greece and Rome*. Mineola, NY: Dover Publications.

Garber, Marjorie B., Beatrice Hanssen, and Rebecca L. Walkowitz. 2000. *The Turn to Ethics*. New York: Routledge.

Garland, Robert. 1985. *The Greek Way of Death*. London: Duckworth.

Gearhart, Suzanne. 1992. *The Interrupted Dialectic: Philosophy, Psychoanalysis, and Their Tragic Other*. Baltimore, Md.: Johns Hopkins University Press.

Geary, Jason. 2006. "Reinventing the Past: Mendelssohn's *Antigone* and the Creation of an Ancient Greek Musical Language," *The Journal of Musicology* 23 (2): 187–226.

Gellrich, Michelle. 1988. *Tragedy and Theory: the Problem of Conflict Since Aristotle*. Princeton University Press.

Gernet, Louis. 1955. *Droit et société dans la Grèce ancienne*. Paris: Recueil Sirey.

Geroulanos, Stefanos. 2010. *An Atheism that Is not Humanist Emerges in French Thought*. Stanford University Press.

Gillman, Susan Kay. 2003. *Blood Talk: American Race Melodrama and the Culture of the Occult*. University of Chicago Press.

Gilman, Sander L. 1998. *Love+Marriage=Death: and Other Essays on Representing Difference*. Stanford University Press.

Goethe, Johann Wolfgang von. 2005. *Conversations of Goethe with Eckermann and Soret*, trans. John Oxenford. Whitefish, Mont.: Kessinger Publishing.

Goff, Barbara E., ed. 1995. *History, Tragedy, Theory: Dialogues on Athenian Drama*. Austin: University of Texas Press.

Goff, Barbara E., and Michael Simpson. 2007. *Crossroads in the Black Aegean: Oedipus, Antigone, and Dramas of the African Diaspora*. Oxford University Press.

Goldhill, Simon. 1986. *Reading Greek Tragedy*. Cambridge University Press.

    1990. "The Great Dionysia and Civic Ideology," in *Nothing to Do with Dionysos? Athenian Drama in Its Social Context*, ed. John J. Winkler and Froma I. Zeitlin. Princeton University Press, 97–129.

2004. *Love, Sex and Tragedy: How the Ancient World Shapes Our Lives*. London: John Murray.

2006. "Antigone and the Politics of Sisterhood," in *Laughing with Medusa: Classical Myth and Feminist Thought*, ed. Vanda Zajko and Miriam Leonard. Oxford University Press, 141–162.

2008. *Jerusalem: City of Longing*. Cambridge, Mass.: Belknap Press of Harvard University Press.

2009. "The Audience on Stage: Rhetoric, Emotion, and Judgement in Sophoclean Theatre," in *Sophocles and the Greek Tragic Tradition*, ed. Simon Goldhill and Edith Hall. Cambridge; New York: Cambridge University Press, 27–47.

2012. *Sophocles and the Language of Tragedy*. Oxford; New York: Oxford University Press.

Goldhill, Simon, and Robin Osborne. 1999. *Performance Culture and Athenian Democracy*. Cambridge; New York: Cambridge University Press.

Goldhill, Simon, and Edith Hall, eds. 2009. *Sophocles and the Greek Tragic Tradition*. Cambridge; New York: Cambridge University Press.

Goodman, Amy, and David Goodman. 2006. *Static: Government Liars, Media Cheerleaders, and the People who Fight Back*. New York: Hyperion.

Goodwin, Jeff, James M. Jasper, and Francesca Polletta. 2001. *Passionate Politics: Emotions and Social Movements*. University of Chicago Press.

Goodwin, Sarah McKim Webster, and Elisabeth Bronfen. 1993. *Death and Representation*. Baltimore, Md.: Johns Hopkins University Press.

Gourgouris, Stathis. 2003. *Does Literature Think? Literature as Theory for an Antimythical Era*. Stanford University Press.

Greengard, Carola. 1987. *Theatre in Crisis: Sophocles' Reconstruction Of Genre and Politics in Philoctetes*. Amsterdam: Hakkert.

Gregory, Justina. 2005. *A Companion to Greek Tragedy*. Malden, Mass.: Blackwell.

Griffin, Jasper. 1980. *Homer on Life and Death*. Oxford: Clarendon Press.

Griffith, Mark. 1998. "The King and the Eye: the Rule of the Father in Greek Tragedy," *Proceedings of the Cambridge Philological Society* 44: 62–129.

1999. *Introduction to Sophocles: Antigone*. Cambridge University Press.

2001. "Antigone and Her Sister(s): Embodying Women in Greek Tragedy," in *Making Silence Speak: Women's Voices in Greek Literature and Society*, ed. A. P. M. H. Lardinois and Laura McClure. Princeton University Press, 117–136.

2005. "The Subject of Desire in Sophocles' *Antigone*," in *The Soul of Tragedy: Essays on Athenian Drama*, ed. Victoria Pedrick and Steven M. Oberhelman. University of Chicago Press, 91–136.

2010. "Psychoanalysing Antigone," in *Interrogating* Antigone *in Postmodern Philosophy and Criticism*, ed. S. E. Wilmer and Audronė Žukauskaitė. Oxford; New York: Oxford University Press, 110–134.

Grosz, E. A. 1989. *Sexual Subversions: Three French Feminists*. Sydney; Boston: Allen & Unwin.

Guenoun, Solange, James H. Kavanagh, and Roxanne Lapidus. 2000. "Jacques Rancière: Literature, Politics, Aesthetics: Approaches to Democratic Disagreement," *SubStance* 29 (2): 3–24.

Guesnet, François. 2007. "The Turkish Cavalry in Swarzedz, or: Jewish Political Culture at the Borderlines of Modern History," in *Jahrbuch des Simon-Dubnow-Instituts*, ed. Dan Diner. Göttingen: Vandenhoek and Ruprecht, 227–248.

Habermas, Jürgen, Jacques Derrida, and Giovanna Borradori. 2003. *Philosophy in a Time of Terror: Dialogues with Jürgen Habermas and Jacques Derrida*. University of Chicago Press.

Haenni, Sabine. 2006. "Book Review. Susan Gillman, *Blood Talk: American Race Melodrama and the Culture of the Occult*," *Modern Philology* 103 (4) (May): 577–581.

Hall, Edith. 1991. *Inventing the Barbarian: Greek Self-Definition Through Tragedy*. Oxford University Press.

Halperin, David. 2012. *How to Be Gay*. Cambridge, Mass.: Belknap Press of Harvard University Press.

Hame, Kerri J. 2008. "Female Control of Funeral Rites in Greek Tragedy: Klytaimestra, Medea, and Antigone," *Classical Philology* 103 (1): 1–15.

Hansen, Miriam. 1981. "Cooperative Auteur Cinema and Oppositional Public Sphere: Alexander Kluge's Contribution to Germany in Autumn," *New German Critique* (24/25): 36–56.

Hariman, Robert. 2008. "Political Parody and Public Culture," *Quarterly Journal of Speech* 94 (3): 247–272.

Harris, Edward Monroe. 2004. "Antigone the Lawyer, or the Ambiguities of Nomos," in *The Law and the Courts in Ancient Greece*. London: Duckworth, 19–56.

2006. *Democracy and the Rule of Law in Classical Athens: Essays on Law, Society, and Politics*. Cambridge; New York: Cambridge University Press.

Harris, Stefanie. 2009. *Mediating Modernity: German Literature and the "New" Media, 1895–1930*. University Park: Pennsylvania State University Press.

Harry, J. E. 1911. "Studies in Sophocles," *University of Cincinnati Studies* 27: 3–46.

Hartman, Jan. 2005. "Cindy Sheehan: American Antigone." 18 August. www.commondreams.org/views05/0818–21.htm (accessed June 12, 2011).

Hartouni, Valerie A. 1986. "Antigone's Dilemma: A Problem in Political Membership," *Hypatia* 1 (1) (Spring): 3–20.

Hawley, Thomas M. 2005. *The Remains of War: Bodies, Politics, and the Search for American Soldiers Unaccounted for in Southeast Asia*. Durham, NC: Duke University Press.

Hazan, Pierre. 2010. *Judging War, Judging History: Behind Truth and Reconciliation*. Stanford University Press.

Hegel, Georg Wilhelm Friedrich. 1975. *Aesthetics: Lectures on Fine Art*. Oxford: Clarendon Press.

1977. *Phenomenology of Spirit*, ed. J. N. Findlay. Oxford: Clarendon Press.

1991. *Elements of the Philosophy of Right*, ed. Allen W. Wood, trans. H. B. Nisbet. Cambridge University Press.

1993. *Introductory Lectures on Aesthetics*, ed. Bernard Bosanquet and M. J. Inwood. London; New York: Penguin Books.

Heidegger, Martin. 2000. *Introduction to Metaphysics*, new translation by Gregory Fried and Richard Polt. New Haven, Conn.: Yale University Press.

Heilman, Robert Bechtold. 1968. *Tragedy and Melodrama: Versions of Experience.* Seattle: University of Washington Press.

Herman, Gabriel. 2006. *Morality and Behaviour in Democratic Athens: A Social History.* Cambridge University Press.

Herodotus. 1996. *The Histories*, trans. Aubrey de Sélincourt, rev. John Marincola. London: Penguin Books.

Herodotus, Xenophon, Thucydides, and Arrian. 1942. *The Greek Historians: the Complete and Unabridged Historical Works*, trans. Benjamin Jowett, Henry G. Dakyns, and Edward J. Chinnock; introduction, revisions, and additional notes by F. R. B. Godolphin. New York: Random House.

Hester, D. A. 1971. "Sophocles the Unphilosophical: A Study in the *Antigone*," *Mnemosyne* 24 (1): 11–59.

Hirsch, Alexander Keller. 2012. *Theorizing Post-Conflict Reconciliation: Agonism, Restitution and Repair.* Milton Park, Abingdon, Oxfordshire; New York: Routledge.

2013. "The Promise of the Unforgiven: Violence, Power, and Paradox in Arendt," *Philosophy & Social Criticism* 39 (1): 45–61.

Holmes, Brooke. *Antigone at Colonus and the End(s) of Tragedy.* Unpublished manuscript.

2012. *Gender: Antiquity and its Legacy.* New York: Oxford University Press.

Holmes, Brooke, and W. H. Shearin. 2012. "Introduction: Swerves, Events, and Unexpected Effects," in *Dynamic Reading: Studies in the Reception of Epicureanism.* New York: Oxford University Press, 3–29.

Holst-Warhaft, Gail. 1992. *Dangerous Voices: Women's Laments and Greek Literature.* London: Routledge.

Homer. 1961. *The Iliad of Homer*, trans. Richmond Lattimore. University of Chicago Press.

Honig, Bonnie. 1993a. *Political Theory and the Displacement of Politics.* Ithaca, NY: Cornell University Press.

1993b. "The Politics of Agonism: a Critical Response to *Beyond Good and Evil: Arendt, Nietzsche, and the Aestheticization of Political Action* by Dana R. Villa," *Political Theory* 21 (3): 528–533.

ed. 1995. *Feminist Interpretations of Hannah Arendt.* University Park: Pennsylvania State University Press.

1996. "Difference, Dilemmas, and the Politics of Home," in *Democracy and Difference: Contesting the Boundaries of the Political*, ed. Seyla Benhabib. Princeton University Press, 257–277.

2001. *Democracy and the Foreigner.* Princeton University Press.

2006. "Another Cosmopolitanism? Law and Politics in the New Europe," in *Another Cosmopolitanism*, ed. Seyla Benhabib. New York: Oxford University Press, 102–127.

2008a. "The Other is Dead: Mourning, Justice and the Politics of Burial," *Triquarterly Review* 131: 89–111.

2008b. "An Agonist's Reply," *Rechtsfilosofie & Rechtstheorie* 2: 186–199.

2008c. "Review Essay: What Foucault Saw at the Revolution," *Political Theory* 36 (2): 301–312.

2009a. *Emergency Politics: Paradox, Law, Democracy.* Princeton University Press.

2009b. "Antigone's Laments, Creon's Grief: Mourning, Membership, and the Politics of Exception," *Political Theory* 37 (1): 5–43.

2010. "Antigone's Two Laws: Greek Tragedy and the Politics of Humanism," *New Literary History* 41 (1): 1–38.

2011a. "Ismene's Forced Choice: Sacrifice and Sorority in Sophocles' *Antigone*," *Arethusa* 44 (1): 29–68.

2011b. "'[Un]Dazzled by the Ideal?': James Tully's Politics and Humanism in Tragic Perspective," *Political Theory* 39 (1): 138–144.

2011c. "Review Article: the Politics of Ethos," *European Journal of Political Theory* 10 (3): 422–429.

2013. "Corpses for Kilowatts?" in *Second Nature: Rethinking the Natural Through Politics*, ed. Crina Archer, Laura Ephraim, and Lida Maxwell. New York: Fordham University Press.

Forthcoming. "The Event of Genre: from Rancière to Von Trier."

How to Survive a Plague. 2012. Sundance Selects.

Howenstein, Mark S. 2000. "The Tragedy of Law and the Law of Tragedy in Sophocles' *Antigone*," *Legal Studies Forum* 24: 493–526.

Hutchings, Kimberly. 2003. *Hegel and Feminist Philosophy.* Oxford: Polity.

Hutchings, Kimberly, and Tuija Pulkkinen, eds. 2010. *Hegel's Philosophy and Feminist Thought: Beyond Antigone?* New York: Palgrave Macmillan.

Irigaray, Luce. 1985a. "The Eternal Irony of the Community," in *Speculum of the Other Woman.* Ithaca, NY: Cornell University Press, 214–227.

1985b. *Speculum of the Other Woman.* Ithaca, NY: Cornell University Press.

1994. *Thinking the Difference: for a Peaceful Revolution.* New York: Routledge.

2008. *Sharing the World.* London; New York: Continuum.

Irwin, Robert. 2006. *Dangerous Knowledge: Orientalism and Its Discontents.* Woodstock, NY: Overlook Press.

Jacobs, Carol. 1996. "Dusting Antigone," *MLN* 111 (5): 889–917.

2008. *Skirting the Ethical.* Stanford University Press.

Jacobson, Norman. 1978. *Pride and Solace: the Functions and Limits of Political Theory.* Berkeley: University of California Press.

Jagodzinski, Jan. 2011. *Misreading Postmodern Antigone: Marco Bellocchio's Devil in the Flesh (Diavolo in Corpo).* Bristol: Intellect.

Jain, S. Lochlann. 2007. "Cancer Butch," *Cultural Anthropology* 22 (4): 501–538.

James, Ian. 2005. "On Interrupted Myth," *Journal for Cultural Research* 9 (4): 331–349.

Jebb, Richard. 1900. *Sophocles:* Antigone. Cambridge University Press.

1966. *The Antigone of Sophocles.* Cambridge University Press.

Jenkins, Fiona. 2009a. "Humorous Commitments and Non-Violent Politics," *Critical Horizons* 19 (2) (special issue): 257–271.

2009b. "Queering Foetal Life: Between Butler and Berlant," *The Australian Feminist Law Journal* 30 (June): 63–85.

2010. "Judith Butler: Disturbance, Provocation and the Ethics of Non-Violence," *Humanities Research* 16 (2).

Jetter, Alexis, Annelise Orleck, and Diana Taylor, eds. 1997. *The Politics of Motherhood: Activist Voices from Left to Right.* Hanover, NH: Darmouth.

Johnson, Barbara. 2008. *Persons and Things.* Cambridge, Mass.: Harvard University Press.

Johnston, Sarah Iles. 1999. *Restless Dead: Encounters Between the Living and the Dead in Ancient Greece.* Berkeley: University of California Press.

Johnston, Steven. 2007. *The Truth about Patriotism.* Durham, NC: Duke University Press.

Jones, Tommy Lee. 2006. *The Three Burials of Melquiades Estrada.* Culver City, Calif.: Sony Pictures Home Entertainment.

Julien, Phillipe. 1990. *Pour lire Jacques Lacan.* Paris: Seuil.

Kakutani, Michiko. 2008. "Who's Your Daddy?" *The New York Times.* www.nytimes.com/2008/02/01/books/01book.html.

Kalimtzis, Kostas. 2000. *Aristotle on Political Enmity and Disease: an Inquiry into Stasis.* Albany: State University of New York Press.

Kaysen, Susanna. 1993. *Girl, Interrupted.* New York: Random House.

Keenan, Dennis King. 2005. *The Question of Sacrifice.* Bloomington: Indiana University Press.

Kellogg, Catherine M. 2010. *Law's Trace: from Hegel to Derrida.* New York: Routledge.

Kennedy, Barbara M. 2003. *Deleuze and Cinema: the Aesthetics of Sensation.* Edinburgh University Press.

Kete, Mary Louise. 2000. *Sentimental Collaborations: Mourning and Middle-Class Identity in Nineteenth-Century America.* Durham, NC: Duke University Press.

Kindley, Evan. 2010. "Germany in Autumn." www.notcoming.com/reviews/germanyinautumn/.

Kirkpatrick, Jennet. 2009. "The Safeguard of Silence: Un-Heroic Resistance in Sophocles' *Antigone*." SSRN eLibrary.

2011. "The Prudent Dissident: Unheroic Resistance in Sophocles' Antigone." *The Review of Politics* 73 (3): 401–424.

Kitto, H. D. F. 1966. *Greek Tragedy: a Literary Study.* London: Methuen.

Kitzinger, Carolyn Dewald, and Rachel Kitzinger. 2006. "Herodotus, Sophocles and the Woman Who Wanted Her Brother Saved," in *The Cambridge Companion to Herodotus,* ed. Carolyn Dewald and John Marincola. Cambridge; New York: Cambridge University Press.

Kligerman, Eric. 2011. "The Antigone Effect: Reinterring the Dead of Night and Fog in the German Autumn," *New German Critique* 38 (1 112) (Winter): 9–38.

Kluge, Alexander. 2010. *Deutschland im Herbst*. The Alexander Kluge Collection. Facets Multimedia.

Knox, Bernard. 1964. *The Heroic Temper: Studies in Sophoclean Tragedy*. Berkeley: University of California Press.

Konstan, David. 2001. *Pity Transformed*. London: Duckworth.

Kornbluh, Felicia. 2011. "Queer Legal History: a Field Grows Up and Comes Out," *Law & Social Inquiry* 36 (2) (Spring), 537–559.

Kottman, Paul A. 2008. *A Politics of the Scene*. Stanford University Press.

Krook, Dorothea. 1969. *Elements of Tragedy*. New Haven, Conn.: Yale University Press.

Kurke, Leslie. 1999. *Coins, Bodies, Games, and Gold: the Politics of Meaning in Archaic Greece*. Princeton University Press.

Lacan, Jacques. 1986. *Le séminaire livre vii: l'éthique de la psychanalyse*. Paris: Seuil.
   1988. *The Seminar of Jacques Lacan*. London: Routledge.
   1991. *Le séminaire livre viii: le transfert*. Paris: Seuil.
   1992. *The Ethics of Psychoanalysis, 1959–1960*. New York: Norton.

LaCapra, Dominick. 2001. *Writing History, Writing Trauma*. Baltimore, Md.: Johns Hopkins University Press.
   2004. *History in Transit: Experience, Identity, Critical Theory*. Ithaca, NY: Cornell University Press.

Laclau, Ernesto. 2005. *On Populist Reason*. London: Verso.

Lane, Warren J., and Ann M. Lane. 1986. "The Politics of Antigone," in *Greek Tragedy and Political Theory*, ed. J. Peter Euben. Berkeley: University of California Press.

Lape, Susan. 2003. "Racializing Democracy: The Politics of Sexual Reproduction in Classical Athens," *Parallax* 9 (4): 52.

Laqueur, Thomas. 2002. "The Dead Body and Human Rights," in *The Body*, ed. Sean T. Sweeney and Ian Hodder. Cambridge University Press, 75–93.

Lardinois, A. P. M. H., and Laura McClure. 2001a. "Virtual Voices: Toward a Choreography of Women's Speech in Classical Athens," in *Making Silence Speak: Women's Voices in Greek Literature and Society*. Princeton University Press.
   eds. 2001b. *Making Silence Speak: Women's Voices in Greek Literature and Society*. Princeton University Press.

Lear, Jonathan. 2000. *Happiness, Death, and the Remainder of Life*. Cambridge, Mass.: Harvard University Press.
   2008. *Radical Hope: Ethics in the Face of Cultural Devastation*. Cambridge, Mass.: Harvard University Press.

Leonard, Miriam. 2005. *Athens in Paris: Ancient Greece and the Political in Post-War French Thought*. Oxford University Press.
   2006a. "The Uses of Reception: Derrida and the Historical Imperative," in *Classics and the Uses of Reception*, ed. Charles Martindale and Richard F. Thomas. Malden, Mass.: Blackwell, 116–126.
   2006b. "Lacan, Irigaray, and Beyond: Antigones and the Politics of Psychoanalysis," in *Laughing with Medusa: Classical Myth and Feminist Thought*, ed. Vanda Zajko and Miriam Leonard. Oxford University Press, 121–140.

2009. *How to Read Ancient Philosophy*. London: Granta.

Levi, Primo. 1988. *The Drowned and the Saved*. New York: Summit Books.

Lewis, R. G. 1988. "An Alternative Date for Sophocles' *Antigone*," *Greek, Roman and Byzantine Studies* 29 (1): 35–50.

Lezra, Jacques. 2010. *Wild Materialism: the Ethic of Terror and the Modern Republic*. New York: Fordham University Press.

Lison, Andrew. 2012. "Love's Unlimited Orchestra: Overcoming Left Melancholy via Dubstep and Microhouse," *New Formations* 75 (Spring): 122–139.

Lloyd, Moya. 1998–1999. "Politics and Melancholia," *Women's Philosophy Review* 20: 25–43.

2005. "Butler, Antigone and the State," *Contemporary Political Theory* 4 (4): 451–468.

Loraux, Nicole. 1986. *The Invention of Athens: the Funeral Oration in the Classical City*. Cambridge, Mass.: Harvard University Press.

1987. *Tragic Ways of Killing a Woman*. Cambridge, Mass.: Harvard University Press.

1993. *The Children of Athena: Athenian Ideas About Citizenship and the Division Between the Sexes*. Princeton University Press.

1998. *Mothers in Mourning: with the Essay of Amnesty and Its Opposite*. Ithaca, NY: Cornell University Press.

2000. *Born of the Earth: Myth and Politics in Athens*. Ithaca, NY: Cornell University Press.

2002a. *The Divided City: on Memory and Forgetting in Ancient Athens*. New York: Zone Books.

2002b. *The Mourning Voice: an Essay on Greek Tragedy*. Ithaca, NY: Cornell University Press.

Luciano, Dana. 2007. *Arranging Grief: Sacred Time and the Body in Nineteenth-Century America*. New York University Press.

Lupton, Julia Reinhard. 2005. *Citizen-Saints: Shakespeare and Political Theology*. University of Chicago Press.

Lupton, Julia Reinhard, and Kenneth Reinhard. 1993. *After Oedipus: Shakespeare in Psychoanalysis*. Ithaca, NY: Cornell University Press.

MacCannell, Juliet Flower. 1991. *The Regime of the Brother: After the Patriarchy*. London; New York: Routledge.

MacDowell, Douglas M. 1978. *The Law in Classical Athens*. Ithaca, NY: Cornell University Press.

Macksey, Richard, Eugenio Donato, and Johns Hopkins University Humanities Center. 2007. *The Structuralist Controversy: the Languages of Criticism and the Sciences of Man*. Baltimore, Md.: Johns Hopkins University Press.

Maier, Charles S. 1988. *The Unmasterable Past: History, Holocaust, and German National Identity*. Cambridge, Mass.: Harvard University Press.

Man Ling Lee, Theresa. 2007. "Rethinking the Personal and the Political: Feminist Activism and Civic Engagement," *Hypatia* 22 (4): 163–179.

Mangold, James. 1999. *Girl, Interrupted*. Culver City, Calif.: Columbia Tristar Home Video.

Marchand, Suzanne L. 1996. *Down from Olympus: Archaeology and Philhellenism in Germany, 1750–1970.* Princeton University Press.

Markantonatos, Andreas. 2007. *Oedipus at Colonus: Sophocles, Athens, and the World.* Berlin: Walter de Gruyter.

Markell, Patchen. 2003. *Bound by Recognition.* Princeton University Press.

Marks, Elaine, and Isabelle de Courtivron, eds. 1980. *New French Feminisms: An Anthology.* Amherst: University of Massachusetts Press.

Martel, James R. 2011. *Textual Conspiracies: Walter Benjamin, Idolatry, and Political Theory.* Ann Arbor: University of Michigan Press.

Martindale, Charles, and Richard F. Thomas, eds. 2006. *Classics and the Uses of Reception.* Malden, Mass.; Oxford: Blackwell.

Masten, Jeffrey. 2009. "The Passion of the Crux: Rhetorics of Shakespearean Editing," Paper presented at the Conference of the Shakespeare Association of America, Washington, DC, April 11.

Mastronarde, Donald J. 1993. *Introduction to Attic Greek.* Berkeley: University of California Press.

    2010. *The Art of Euripides: Dramatic Technique and Social Context.* Cambridge; New York: Cambridge University Press.

May, Todd. 2008. *The Political Thought of Jacques Rancière: Creating Equality.* Edinburgh University Press.

McClure, Laura. 1999. *Spoken Like a Woman: Speech and Gender in Athenian Drama.* Princeton University Press.

McCoskey, Denise Eileen, and Emily Zakin. 2009. *Bound by the City: Greek Tragedy, Sexual Difference, and the Formation of the Polis.* Albany: State University of New York Press.

McIvor, David. 2010. "Mourning in America: Racial Trauma and the Democratic Work of Mourning." Ph.D. thesis: Duke University.

McLaughlin, Kevin. 2003. "Benjamin Now: Afterthoughts on The Arcades Project," *boundary* 2 (30): 191–197.

    2006. "Benjamin's Barbarism," *The Germanic Review* 81 (1): 4–20.

    2007. "On Poetic Reason of State: Benjamin, Baudelaire, and the Multitudes," *Partial Answers: Journal of Literature and the History of Ideas* 5 (2): 247–265.

McQueen, Steve. 2009. *Hunger.* The Criterion Collection; 504. Irvington: Criterion Collection.

Mee, Erin B. 2010. "Classics, Cultural Politics, and the Role of Antigone in Manipur, NE India," in *India, Greece and Rome, 1757 to 2007*, ed. Edith Hall and Phiroze Vasunia. London: Institute of Classical Studies.

Menekseoglu, Jeremy. 2008. "Antigone." On file with author.

Michel, Laurence. 1961. "Shakespearean Tragedy: Critique of Humanism from the Inside," *Massachusetts Review: a Quarterly of Literature, the Arts and Public Affairs* 2: 633–650.

Michelakis, Pantelis. 2002. *Achilles in Greek Tragedy.* Cambridge; New York: Cambridge University Press.

Miller, Paul Allen. 2007. *Postmodern Spiritual Practices: the Construction of the Subject and the Reception of Plato in Lacan, Derrida, and Foucault.* Columbus: Ohio State University Press.

Mills, Patricia Jagentowicz. 1996a. "Hegel's *Antigone*," in *Feminist Interpretations of G. W. F. Hegel: Re-reading the Canon*, ed. Patricia Jagentowicz Mills. University Park: Pennsylvania State University Press, 59–88.

ed. 1996b. *Feminist Interpretations of G. W. F. Hegel*. University Park: Pennsylvania State University Press.

Mitchell, Greg. 2009. "US Soldier Killed Herself – After Refusing to Take Part in Torture," The Huffington Post. www.huffington post.com/greg-mitchell/ us-soldier-killed-herself_b_190517.html (accessed April 24, 2009).

Monoson, Susan Sara. 2000. *Plato's Democratic Entanglements: Athenian Politics and the Practice of Philosophy*. Princeton University Press.

Montague, Sarah, and Edward Stourton. 2009. "Former Church of Ireland Primate Lord Eames Discusses Proposals to Offer £12,000 to Families of Those Killed in the Troubles." *Today* program. BBC Radio 4.

Moore, Michael. 2004. *Fahrenheit 9/11*. Culver City, Calif.: Columbia TriStar Home Entertainment.

Morgan, Kathryn A. 2003. *Popular Tyranny: Sovereignty and Its Discontents in Ancient Greece*. Austin: University of Texas Press.

Morris, Aldon D. 1984. *The Origins of the Civil Rights Movement: Black Communities Organizing for Change*. New York: Free Press.

Morris, Ian. 1992. *Death-Ritual and Social Structure in Classical Antiquity*. Cambridge; New York: Cambridge University Press.

Mousley, Andy. 2011. *Towards a New Literary Humanism*. London: Palgrave Macmillan.

Mousley, Andy, and Martin Halliwell. 2004. *Critical Humanisms: Humanist/ Anti-Humanist Dialogues*. Edinburgh University Press.

Mudde, Anna. 2009. "Risky Subjectivity: Antigone, Action, and Universal Trespass," *Human Studies* 32 (2): 183–200.

Mulhall, Stephen. 2009. *The Wounded Animal: J. M. Coetzee and the Difficulty of Reality in Literature and Philosophy*. Princeton University Press.

Mulvey, Laura. 1996. *Fetishism and Curiosity*. Bloomington; London: Indiana University Press; British Film Institute.

Murnaghan, Sheila. 1986. "Antigone 904–920 and the Institution of Marriage," *The American Journal of Philology* 107 (2): 192–207.

Murray, Oswyn. 1993. *Early Greece*. Cambridge, Mass.: Harvard University Press.

Myers, Ella. 2008. "Resisting Foucauldian Ethics: Associative Politics and the Limits of the Care of the Self," *Contemporary Political Theory* 7 (2): 125–146.

Naas, Michael. 2003. "History's Remains: of Memory, Mourning, and the Event," *Research in Phenomenology* 33 (1): 75–96.

Naddaff, Ramona. 2002. *Exiling the Poets: the Production of Censorship in Plato's Republic*. University of Chicago Press.

Nelli, Maria Florencia. 2010. "From Ancient Greek Drama to Argentina's 'Dirty War'; Antigona Furiosa: On Bodies and the State," in *Interrogating* Antigone *in Postmodern Philosophy and Criticism*, ed. S. E. Wilmer and Audronė Žukauskaitė. Oxford; New York: Oxford University Press, 353–365.

Nelson, Cary, and Lawrence Grossberg. 1988. *Marxism and the Interpretation of Culture*. Urbana: University of Illinois Press.

Neuburg, Matt. 1990. "How Like a Woman: Antigone's 'Inconsistency'," *The Classical Quarterly* 40 (1): 54–76.

Nietzsche, Friedrich Wilhelm. 1967. *The Birth of Tragedy* and *The Case of Wagner*. New York: Vintage Books.

——— 1994. "Homer's Contest," in *On the Genealogy of Morality*, ed. Keith Ansell-Pearson and Carol Diethe. Cambridge University Press, 174–182.

Nonet, Phillipe. 2006. "Antigone's Law," *Law, Culture and the Humanities* 2 (3): 314–335.

Norwood, Gilbert. 1928. *Greek Tragedy*. London: Methuen.

Nowell-Smith, Geoffrey. 1977. "Dossier on Melodrama: Minnelli and Melodrama," *Screen* 18 (2): 113–118.

Nussbaum, Martha. 1986. *The Fragility of Goodness: Luck and Ethics in Greek Tragedy and Philosophy*. Cambridge University Press.

——— 2008. "The 'Morality of Pity': Sophocles' *Philoctetes*," in *Rethinking Tragedy*, ed. Rita Felski. Baltimore, Md.: Johns Hopkins University Press, 148–169.

Nuttall, A. D. 1996. *Why Does Tragedy Give Pleasure?* Oxford; New York: Clarendon Press; Oxford University Press.

O'Hanlon, Redmond. 1990. "Dramaturgy and Sentimentality in *Antigone*," *Journal of Dramatic Theory and Criticism* 4 (2): 125–137.

Oakeshott, Michael. 1991. *On Human Conduct*. New York: Oxford University Press.

Ober, Josiah. 1989. *Mass and Elite in Democratic Athens: Rhetoric, Ideology, and the Power of the People*. Princeton University Press.

——— 1996. *The Athenian Revolution: Essays on Ancient Greek Democracy and Political Theory*. Princeton University Press.

——— 1998. *Political Dissent in Democratic Athens: Intellectual Critics of Popular Rule*. Princeton University Press.

——— 2005. *Athenian Legacies: Essays on the Politics of Going on Together*. Princeton University Press.

Olick, Jeffrey K. 2007. *The Politics of Regret: on Collective Memory and Historical Responsibility*. New York: Routledge.

Ong, Walter J. 1988. *Orality and Literacy: the Technologizing of the Word*. London; New York: Routledge.

Ormand, Kirk. 1999. *Exchange and the Maiden: Marriage in Sophoclean Tragedy*. Austin: University of Texas Press.

Osiel, Mark J. 2001. "Constructing Subversion in Argentina's Dirty War," *Representations* 75 (1): 119–158.

Ostwald, Martin. 1986. *From Popular Sovereignty to the Sovereignty of Law: Law, Society, and Politics in Fifth-Century Athens*. Berkeley: University of California Press.

Oudemans, Th. C. W., and A. P. M. H. Lardinois. 1987. *Tragic Ambiguity: Anthropology, Philosophy and Sophocles' Antigone*. Leiden; New York: E. J. Brill.

Pastore, Judith Laurence. 1993. *Confronting AIDS Through Literature: the Responsibilities of Representation*. Urbana: University of Illinois Press.

300   *Bibliography*

Patterson-Tutschka, Monicka. 2007. "Silencing Xanthippe," *Review of Politics*
    69 (3): 466–468.
Paul, Joanna. 2010. "Cinematic Receptions of Antiquity: the Current State of
    Play," *Classical Receptions Journal* 2 (1): 136–155.
Pearl, Monica B. 2003. "Eve Sedgwick's Melancholic 'White Glasses'," *Textual
    Practice* 17 (1): 61–80.
Pease, Donald E. 2009. *The New American Exceptionalism*. Minneapolis: University
    of Minnesota Press.
Pettit, Philip. 1975. *The Concept of Structuralism: a Critical Analysis*. Berkeley:
    University of California Press.
Phelan, Peggy. 1997. *Mourning Sex: Performing Public Memories*. London: Routledge.
Phillips, Adam. 1997. "Commentary on Judith Butler," in Judith Butler, *The
    Psychic Life of Power: Theories in Subjection*. Stanford University Press.
Phillips, Kendall R. 2004. *Framing Public Memory*. Tuscaloosa: University of
    Alabama Press.
Philp, Mark. 2012. "Realism without Illusions," *Political Theory* 40 (5): 629–649.
Picard, Ken. 2007. "Dead Wrong: Are Vermonters Getting Stiffed on the Facts
    About Home Funerals?" *Seven Days*, January 30.
Pinkard, Terry P. 1994. *Hegel's Phenomenology: the Sociality of Reason*. Cambridge;
    New York: Cambridge University Press.
Pirro, Robert Carl. 2011. *The Politics of Tragedy and Democratic Citizenship*. New
    York: Continuum.
Plato. 2000. *The Republic*. Cambridge University Press.
    2011. *Meno and Phaedo*, ed. D. N. Sedley and Alex Long. Cambridge University Press.
Plutarch. 1960. *The Rise and Fall of Athens: Nine Greek Lives*, ed. Ian Scott-Kilvert.
    Baltimore, Md.: Penguin Books.
Politi, Jina. 2006. "Antigone's Letter," *Gramma: Journal of Theory and Criticism*
    14 (special issue, *Objects: Material, Psychic, Aesthetic*, ed. Sean Homer, Ruth
    Parkin-Gounelas, and Yannis Stavrakakis): 131–140.
Pomeroy, Sarah B. 1975. *Goddesses, Whores, Wives, and Slaves: Women in Classical
    Antiquity*. New York: Schocken Books.
Porter, James I. 1986. "Saussure and Derrida on the Figure of the Voice," French
    Centennial Issue of *Modern Language Notes* 101 (4): 871–894.
    2000. *Nietzsche and the Philology of the Future*. Stanford University Press.
    2006a. "What is 'Classical' About Classical Antiquity?" in *Classical Pasts: the
    Classical Traditions of Greece and Rome*, ed. James I. Porter. Princeton
    University Press, 1–68.
    2006b. "Feeling Classical: Classicism and Ancient Literary Criticism," in
    Classical Pasts: the Classical Traditions of Greece and Rome, ed. James I.
    Porter. Princeton University Press, 301–352.
Power, Paul F. 1970. "On Civil Disobedience in Recent American Democratic
    Thought," *The American Political Science Review* 64 (1): 35–47.
Powers, Nicholas. 2005. "Antigone Now." www.independent.org/2005/12/08/
    antigone-now.

Prosser, Jay. 1998. *Second Skins: the Body Narratives of Transsexuality*. New York: Columbia University Press.

Pucci, Pietro. 1987. *Odysseus Polutropos: Intertextual Readings in the* Odyssey *and the* Iliad. Ithaca, NY: Cornell University Press.

Raaflaub, Kurt A., Josiah Ober, and Robert W. Wallace. 2007. *Origins of Democracy in Ancient Greece*. Berkeley: University of California Press.

Rabaté, Jean-Michel. 2001. *Jacques Lacan: Psychoanalysis and the Subject of Literature*. Houndmills, Basingstoke, Hampshire; New York: Palgrave.

ed. 2003. *The Cambridge Companion to Lacan*. Cambridge; New York: Cambridge University Press.

Rabinowitz, Nancy Sorkin. 1993. *Anxiety Veiled: Euripides and the Traffic in Women*. Ithaca, NY: Cornell University Press.

Rader, Richard. 2008. "Review: *Guilt by Descent: Moral Inheritance and Decision Making in Greek Tragedy*, by N. J. Sewell-Rutter," *Classical Journal Online*, November 2.

2009a. "'And Whatever it Is, it Is You': the Autochthonous Self in Aeschylus's Seven Against Thebes," *Arethusa* 42: 1–44.

2009b. "The Fate of Humanism in Greek Tragedy," *Philosophy and Literature* 33 (2): 442–454.

2009c. "Review: Simon Goldhill and Edith Hall, eds., *Sophocles and the Greek Tragic Tradition*," *Bryn Mawr Classical Review* 17 (December).

Rajan, Rajeswari Sunder. 2010. "From Antagonism to Agonism: Shifting Paradigms of Women's Opposition to the State," *Comparative Studies of South Asia, Africa and the Middle East* 30 (2): 164–178.

Rambuss, Richard. 1994. "Sero Positive Conversion: New AIDS Photography," *Lesbian and Gay Studies Newsletter* 21: 38–40.

Rancière, Jacques. 1999. *Dis-Agreement: Politics and Philosophy*. Minneapolis: University of Minnesota Press.

2000. "Literature, Politics, Aesthetics: Approaches to Democratic Disagreement." Interview with Solange Guénoun and James H. Kavanagh. *SubStance* 92, 3–24.

2004. *The Flesh of Words: the Politics of Writing*. Stanford University Press.

2006a. "The Ethical Turn of Aesthetics and Politics," *Critical Horizons* 7 (1): 1–20.

2006b. *The Politics of Aesthetics: the Distribution of the Sensible*. New York: Continuum.

2006c. *Film Fables*. New York: Berg.

2007. *Hatred of Democracy*. London; New York: Verso.

2008. "Jacques Rancière and Interdisciplinarity," *Art and Research: a Journal of Ideas, Contexts and Methods* 2 (1): 1–10.

2010. *Dissensus: on Politics and Aesthetics*. London: Continuum.

2011. *Mute Speech: Literature, Critical Theory, and Politics*. New York: Columbia University Press.

Rancière, Jacques, and Davide Panagia. 2000. "Dissenting Words: A Conversation with Jacques Rancière," *Diacritics: A Review of Contemporary Criticism* 30 (2): 113–126.

Rawlinson, Mary. "Antigone, Agent of Fraternity: How Feminism Misreads Hegel's Misreading of Antigone, or Let the Other Sister Speak." Paper delivered at the Graduate Center, City University of New York, November 2.

Rawls, John, and Barbara Herman. 2000. *Lectures on the History of Moral Philosophy*. Cambridge, Mass.: Harvard University Press.

Redmond, James. 1992. *Melodrama*. Themes in Drama; 14. Cambridge University Press.

Rehm, Rush. 1994. *Marriage to Death: the Conflation of Wedding and Funeral Rituals in Greek Tragedy*. Princeton University Press.

Reinhardt, K. 1979. *Sophocles*, trans. H. and D. Harvey. Oxford University Press.

Renteln, Alison Dundes. 2004. *The Cultural Defense*. Oxford University Press.

Resnais, Alain. 1986. *Mélo*. MK2 Productions and A2.

Ricoeur, Paul. 1994. *Oneself as Another*. University of Chicago Press.

Ritsos, Yannis. 1993. "Ismene," in *The Fourth Dimension*, ed. Yannis Ritsos. Princeton University Press, 191–214.

Roach, Joseph R. 1996. *Cities of the Dead: Circum-Atlantic Performance*. New York: Columbia University Press.

Robert, William. 2010. "Antigone's Nature," *Hypatia* 25 (2): 412–436.

Roberts, Deborah. 1993. "The Frustrated Mourner: Strategies of Closure in Greek Tragedy," in *Nomodeiktes: Greek Studies in Honor of Martin Ostwald*, ed. Ralph Mark Rosen and Joseph Farrell. Ann Arbor: University of Michigan Press, 573–589.

———. 2010. "Reading *Antigone* in Translation: Text, Paratext, Intertext," in *Interrogating Antigone in Postmodern Philosophy and Criticism*, ed. S. E. Wilmer and Audronė Žukauskaitė. Oxford; New York: Oxford University Press, 283–313.

Robson, Ruthann. 2009. "Demokratia and Antigone: Before and After Sappho," *Stetson Law Review* 39 (3): 3–46.

Roisman, Hanna M. 2002. "Women's Free Speech in Greek Tragedy," in *Free Speech in Classical Antiquity*, ed. Ineke Sluiter and Ralph M. Rosen. Boston: Brill, 91–114.

Rooney, Caroline. 2000. *African Literature, Animism and Politics*. London; New York: Routledge.

Rose, Gillian. 1996. *Mourning Becomes the Law: Philosophy and Representation*. Cambridge; New York: Cambridge University Press.

Rose, J. L. 1952. "The Problem of the Second Burial in Sophocles' *Antigone*," *The Classical Journal* 47 (6): 219–251.

Roselli, David Kawalko. 2006. "Polyneices' Body and His Monument: Class, Social Status, and Funerary Commemoration in Sophocles' *Antigone*," *Helios* 33 (Supplement): 135–177.

Rossello, Diego. 2011. "The Melancholic Sovereign: The Politics of Human-Animal (In)distinction in Modern Sovereignty." Ph.D. Dissertation, Northwestern University.

———. 2012. "Hobbes and the Wolf-Man: Melancholy and Animality in Modern Sovereignty," *New Literary History* 43 (2) (Spring): 255–279.

Rouse, W. H. D. 1911. "The Two Burials in *Antigone*," *The Classical Review* 25 (2): 40–42.

Rousseau, Jean-Jacques. 1997. "Essay on the Origin of Languages," in *Rousseau: the Discourses and Other Early Political Writings*, ed. Victor Gourevitch. Cambridge University Press, 247–399.

Rubin, Leslie G., Paul Bullen, Brian Calvert, and Tim Collins. 1997. *Justice v. Law in Greek Political Thought*. Lanham, Md.: Rowman & Littlefield.

Ruddick, Sara. 1980. "Maternal Thinking," *Feminist Studies* 6 (2): 342–367.

— 1989. *Maternal Thinking: Toward a Politics of Peace*. Boston: Beacon Press.

Rudnytsky, Peter L. 1987. *Freud and Oedipus*. New York: Columbia University Press.

Sallis, John. 1991. *Crossings: Nietzsche and the Space of Tragedy*. University of Chicago Press.

Santirocco, M. S. 1980. "Justice in Sophocles' *Antigone*," *Philosophy and Literature* 4 (2): 180–198.

Santner, Eric L. 1990. *Stranded Objects: Mourning, Memory, and Film in Postwar Germany*. Ithaca, NY: Cornell University Press.

— 1992. "The Trouble with Hitler: Postwar German Aesthetics and the Legacy of Fascism," *New German Critique* (57): 5–24.

— 2011. *The Royal Remains: the People's Two Bodies and the Endgames of Sovereignty*. University of Chicago Press.

Saxonhouse, Arlene W. 1992. *Fear of Diversity: the Birth of Political Science in Ancient Greek Thought*. University of Chicago Press.

— 1996. *Athenian Democracy: Modern Mythmakers and Ancient Theorists*. University of Notre Dame Press.

— 2005. "Another Antigone: the Emergence of the Female Political Actor in Euripides' Phoenician Women," *Political Theory* 33 (4): 472–494.

— 2006. *Free Speech and Democracy in Ancient Athens*. Cambridge University Press.

Schaap, Andrew. 2011. "Enacting the Right to Have Rights: Jacques Rancière's Critique of Hannah Arendt," *European Journal of Political Theory* 10 (1): 22–45.

Schivelbusch, Wolfgang. 2003. *The Culture of Defeat: on National Trauma, Mourning, and Recovery*. New York: Metropolitan Books.

Schlesinger, Alfred C. 1963. *Boundaries of Dionysus: Athenian Foundations for the Theory of Tragedy*. Cambridge, Mass.: Harvard University Press.

Schmidt, Dennis J. 2001. *On Germans and Other Greeks: Tragedy and Ethical Life*. Bloomington: Indiana University Press.

Schmitt, Carl. 2009. *Hamlet or Hecuba: the Intrusion of the Time into the Play*. New York: Telos Press.

Schoeman, Ferdinand. 1984. "Privacy: Philosophical Dimensions," *American Philosophical Quarterly* 21 (3): 199–213.

Schott, Robin May, and Sara Heinämaa. 2010. *Birth, Death, and Femininity: Philosophies of Embodiment*. Bloomington: Indiana University Press.

Schrift, Alan D. 1997. *The Logic of the Gift: Toward an Ethic of Generosity*. New York: Routledge.

Scott, David. 2004. *Conscripts of Modernity: The Tragedy of Colonial Enlightenment.* Durham, NC: Duke University Press.

2008. "Tragedy's Time," in *Rethinking Tragedy*, ed. Rita Felski. Baltimore, Md.: Johns Hopkins University Press, 199–217.

Scott, James C. 1985. *Weapons of the Weak: Everyday Forms of Peasant Resistance.* New Haven, Conn.: Yale University Press.

Seaford, Richard. 1987. "Tragic Wedding," *Journal of Hellenic Studies* 107: 106–130.

1994. *Reciprocity and Ritual: Homer and Tragedy in the Developing City-State.* Oxford: Clarendon Press.

1995. "Historicizing Tragic Ambivalence: the Vote of Athena," in *History, Tragedy, Theory: Dialogues on Athenian Drama*, ed. Barbara E. Goff. Austin: University of Texas Press, 202–222.

2004. *Money and the Early Greek Mind: Homer, Philosophy, Tragedy.* Cambridge; New York: Cambridge University Press.

Sedgwick, Eve Kosofsky, and Adam Frank. 2003. *Touching Feeling: Affect, Pedagogy, Performativity.* Durham, NC: Duke University Press.

Seery, John Evan. 1996. *Political Theory for Mortals: Shades of Justice, Images of Death.* Ithaca, NY: Cornell University Press.

2006. "Acclaim for Antigone's Claim Reclaimed (or, Steiner, contra Butler)," *Theory & Event* 9 (1).

Segal, Alan F. 2004. *Life after Death: a History of the Afterlife in the Religions of the West.* New York: Doubleday.

Segal, Charles. 1981. *Tragedy and Civilization: an Interpretation of Sophocles.* Cambridge, Mass.: Published for Oberlin College by Harvard University Press.

1993. *Euripides and the Poetics of Sorrow: Art, Gender, and Commemoration in Alcestis, Hippolytus, and Hecuba.* Durham, NC: Duke University Press.

1995a. *Sophocles' Tragic World: Divinity, Nature, Society.* Cambridge, Mass.: Harvard University Press.

1995b. "Classics, Ecumenicism, and Greek Tragedy," *Transactions of the American Philological Association* 125: 1–26.

1999. *Tragedy and Civilization: an Interpretation of Sophocles.* Norman: University of Oklahoma Press.

Segal, Robert Alan. 2004. *Myth: a Very Short Introduction.* Oxford University Press.

Selick, Henry. 2009. *Coraline.* Universal City: Universal Studios Home Entertainment.

Shapiro, H. A. 2006. "The Wrath of Creon: Withholding Burial in Homer and Sophocles," *Helios*: 119–134.

2007. *The Cambridge Companion to Archaic Greece.* Cambridge; New York: Cambridge University Press.

Shay, Jonathan. 1994. *Achilles in Vietnam: Combat Trauma and the Undoing of Character.* New York: Atheneum.

Sheehan, Cindy. 2006. "A Capitol Offense," *Los Angeles Times*, February 3.

2010. *Peace Mom: a Mother's Journey through Heartache to Activism*. New York: Atria Books.

Shell, Marc. 1982. *Money, Language, and Thought: Literary and Philosophical Economies from the Medieval to the Modern Era*. Berkeley: University of California Press.

Sheppard, John Tresidder. 1947. *The Wisdom of Sophocles: an Essay*. London: George Allen & Unwin.

Silk, M. S., and J. P. Stern. 1981. *Nietzsche on Tragedy*. Cambridge; New York: Cambridge University Press.

Silverman, Kaja. 1992. *Male Subjectivity at the Margins*. New York: Routledge.

Simpson, A. W., and C. M. H. Millar. 1948. "A Note on Sophocles' *Antigone*, Lines 531–81," *Greece & Rome* 17 (50): 78–81.

Simpson, David. 2006. *9/11: the Culture of Commemoration*. University of Chicago Press.

Sitze, Adam. 2006. "What is a Citation?" *Law, Culture and the Humanities* 2 (3): 349–372.

Sjöholm, Cecilia. 2004. *The Antigone Complex: Ethics and the Invention of Feminine Desire*. Stanford University Press.

Smart, J. J. C., and Bernard Arthur Owen Williams. 1973. *Utilitarianism; for and Against*. Cambridge University Press.

Smith, Steven B. 1989. *Hegel's Critique of Liberalism: Rights in Context*. University of Chicago Press.

Söderbäck, Fanny. 2010. *Feminist Readings of* Antigone. Albany: State University of New York Press.

Soltis, Andy. 2009. "Monkeys in Mourning," *New York Post*. October 28.

Sommerstein, Alan H. 2010. *The Tangled Ways of Zeus and Other Studies in and around Greek Tragedy*. Oxford; New York: Oxford University Press.

Soni, Vivasvan. 2010. *Mourning Happiness: Narrative and the Politics of Modernity*. Ithaca, NY: Cornell University Press.

Sophocles. 1891. *The Plays and Fragments*, ed. R. C. Jebb. Cambridge University Press.

1902. *The Antigone of Sophocles, with a Commentary,* abridged from the large edition of Sir Richard C. Jebb by Evelyn Shirley Shuckburgh. Cambridge University Press.

1918. *Trauerspiele des Sophokles: Ödipus der Tyrann, Antigonä*, trans. Friedrich Hölderlin. Weimar: Gustav Kiepenheuer.

1984. *The Three Theban Plays*, trans. Robert Fagles and Bernard Knox. New York: Penguin Books.

1987. *Antigone*, ed. Andrew Brown. Warminster: Aris & Phillips.

1991. "Antigone," in *Greek Tragedies*, vol. I, trans. David Grene and Richmond Alexander Lattimore. 2nd edn. University of Chicago Press. Original edn: 1968.

1999. *Antigone*. Cambridge; New York: Cambridge University Press.

2003. *Antigone*, trans. Reginald Gibbons and Charles Segal. Oxford University Press.

2007. "Antigone," in *Sophocles*, vol. II, trans. Hugh Lloyd-Jones. Cambridge, Mass.: Harvard University Press.

Sourvinou-Inwood, Christiane. 1989. "Assumptions and the Creation of Meaning: Reading Sophocles' *Antigone*," *Journal of Hellenic Studies* 109: 134–148.

Spargo, R. Clifton. 2004. *The Ethics of Mourning: Grief and Responsibility in Elegiac Literature*. Baltimore, Md.: Johns Hopkins University Press.

2008. "The Apolitics of Antigone's Lament (From Sophocles to Ariel Dorfman)," *Mosaic: A Journal for the Interdisciplinary Study of Literature* 41 (3): 117–135.

Speight, Allen. 2001. *Hegel, Literature, and the Problem of Agency*. Cambridge; New York: Cambridge University Press.

Spencer, Charles. 2012. "*Antigone*, National Theatre, Review," *The Telegraph*. www.telegraph.co.uk/culture/theatre/theatre-reviews/9303336/Antigone-National-Theatre-review.html.

Spielberg, Steven. 1998. *Saving Private Ryan*. Universal City: DreamWorks LLC / Paramount Pictures / Amblin Entertainment.

Spivak, Gayatri Chakravorty. 1988. "Can the Subaltern Speak?" in *Marxism and the Interpretation of Culture*, ed. Cary Nelson and Lawrence Grossberg. Urbana: University of Illinois Press, 271–313.

1989. "Woman in Difference: Mahasweta Devi's 'Douloti the Bountiful,'" *Cultural Critique* 14: 105–128.

Stalpaert, Christel. 2008. "The Mind Taken Hostage: Antigone's Corporeal Memory in Mind the Gap," *Mosaic* 41 (3): 137–152.

Staten, Henry. 1995. *Eros in Mourning: Homer to Lacan*. Baltimore, Md.: Johns Hopkins University Press.

Stavrakakis, Yannis. 1999. *Lacan and the Political*. London; New York: Routledge.

2007. *The Lacanian Left: Psychoanalysis, Theory, Politics*. Edinburgh University Press.

2010. "On Acts, Pure and Impure," *International Journal of Žižek Studies* 4 (2): 1–35.

Stears, Marc. 2010. *Demanding Democracy: American Radicals in Search of a New Politics*. Princeton University Press.

Steiner, George. 1996. *Antigones*. New Haven, Conn.: Yale University Press.

Stevens, Jacqueline. 1999. *Reproducing the State*. Princeton University Press.

2010. *States Without Nations: Citizenship for Mortals*. New York: Columbia University Press.

Stone, Lawrence. 1977. *The Family, Sex and Marriage in England, 1500–1800*. New York: Harper & Row.

Stow, Simon. 2010. "Agonistic Homegoing: Frederick Douglass, Joseph Lowery, and the Democratic Value of African American Public Mourning," *The American Political Science Review* 104 (4): 681–697.

Strong, Thomas. 2002. "Kinship Between Judith Butler and Anthropology? A Review Essay," *Ethnos* 67 (3): 401–418.

Strong, Tracy B. 1990. *The Idea of Political Theory: Reflections on the Self in Political Time and Space*. University of Notre Dame Press.

Sturken, Marita. 1997. *Tangled Memories: the Vietnam War, the AIDS Epidemic, and the Politics of Remembering*. Berkeley: University of California Press.

Sullivan, Andrew. 2009. "As the Pieces Fall Into Place II," *The Dish*. http://andrewsullivan.thedailybeast.com/2009/04/as-the-pieces-fall-into-place-ii.html.

Szondi, Peter. 2002. *An Essay on the Tragic*. Stanford University Press.

Taplin, Oliver. 1977. *The Stagecraft of Aeschylus: the Dramatic Use of Exits and Entrances in Greek Tragedy*. Oxford; New York: Clarendon Press.

2007. *Pots and Plays: Interactions between Tragedy and Greek Vase-Painting of the Fourth Century BC*. Los Angeles: J. Paul Getty Museum.

Tarnopolsky, Christina. 2010. *Prudes, Perverts, and Tyrants: Plato's Gorgias and the Politics of Shame*. Princeton University Press.

Taxidou, Olga. 2004. *Tragedy, Modernity and Mourning*. Edinburgh University Press.

Taylor, Charles. 1977. *Hegel*. Cambridge; New York: Cambridge University Press.

2007. *A Secular Age*. Cambridge, Mass.: Belknap Press of Harvard University Press.

Taylor, Diana. 1997a. *Disappearing Acts: Spectacles of Gender and Nationalism in Argentina's "Dirty War"*. Durham, NC: Duke University Press.

1997b. "Making a Spectacle: the Mothers of the Plaza De Mayo," in *The Politics of Motherhood: Activist Voices from Left to Right*, ed. Alexis Jetter, Annelise Orleck, and Diana Taylor. Hanover, NH: Dartmouth.

2003. *The Archive and the Repertoire: Performing Cultural Memory in the Americas*. Durham, NC: Duke University Press.

Taylor, Gary. 2000. *Castration: an Abbreviated History of Western Manhood*. New York: Routledge.

Thucydides. 1881. *Thucydides Translated into English*, trans. Benjamin Jowett. Oxford: Clarendon Press.

Tiefenbrun, Susan W. 1999. "On Civil Disobedience, Jurisprudence, Feminism and the Law in the *Antigones* of Sophocles and Anouilh," *Cardozo Studies in Law and Literature* 11 (35): 35–51.

Tomain, Joseph P. 2009. *Creon's Ghost: Law, Justice, and the Humanities*. New York: Oxford University Press.

Tønder, Lars. 2011. "Freedom of Expression in an Age of Cartoon Wars," *Contemporary Political Theory* 10 (2): 255–272.

Tralau, Johan. 2005. "Tragedy as Political Theory: The Self-Destruction of Antigone's Laws," *History of Political Thought* 26: 377–396.

Tuhkanen, Mikko. 2003. Review of *Antigone's Claim*, by Judith Butler, *Umbr(a)*: 140–144.

Tully, James. 1995. *Strange Multiplicity: Constitutionalism in an Age of Diversity*. Cambridge University Press.

2008. *Public Philosophy in a New Key*. Cambridge University Press.

Valakas, Kostas. 2009. "Theoretical Views of Athenian Tragedy in the Fifth Century BC," in *Sophocles and the Greek Tragic Tradition*, ed. Simon Goldhill and Edith Hall. Cambridge; New York: Cambridge University Press, 179–207.

Verdery, Katherine. 1999. *The Political Lives of Dead Bodies: Reburial and Postsocialist Change*. New York: Columbia University Press.

Vernant, Jean-Pierre. 1972. *Greek Tragedy: Problems of Interpretation*. Baltimore, Md.: Johns Hopkins University Press.

1982. *The Origins of Greek Thought*. Ithaca, NY: Cornell University Press.

1991. *Mortals and Immortals: Collected Essays*, ed. Froma I. Zeitlin. Princeton University Press.

Vernant, Jean-Pierre, and Pierre Vidal-Naquet. 1988. *Myth and Tragedy in Ancient Greece*. New York: Zone Books.

Vetter, Lisa Pace. 2005. *"Women's Work" as Political Art: Weaving and Dialectical Politics in Homer, Aristophanes, and Plato*. Lanham, Md.: Lexington Books.

Vickers, Michael J. 2008. *Sophocles and Alcibiades: Athenian Politics in Ancient Greek Literature*. Ithaca, NY: Cornell University Press.

Vidal-Naquet, Pierre, and David Ames Curtis. 1996. *The Jews: History, Memory, and the Present*. New York: Columbia University Press.

Walzer, Michael. 1967. "The Obligation to Disobey," *Ethics* 77 (3) (April): 163–175.

1970. *Obligations: Essays on Disobedience, War, and Citizenship*. Cambridge, Mass.: Harvard University Press.

Warner, Michael. 2002. "Publics and Counterpublics," *Public Culture* 14 (1) (Winter): 49–90.

Watson, Wallace Steadman. 1996. *Understanding Rainer Werner Fassbinder: Film as Private and Public Art*. Columbia: University of South Carolina Press.

Weber, Samuel. 1991. "Le polynôme," in *Lacan avec les philosophes*, ed. Michel Albin. Paris: Bibliothèque du Collège international de philosophie, 50–60.

2004a. "Antigone's Nomos," in *Theatricality as Medium*. New York: Fordham University Press, 121–140.

2004b. *Theatricality as Medium*. New York: Fordham University Press.

2008. *Benjamin's -abilities*. Cambridge, Mass.: Harvard University Press.

Weil, Simone. 1945. *"The Iliad*, or The Poem of Force," *Politics* 2: 321–331.

Weisberg, Jacob. 2008. *The Bush Tragedy*. New York: Random House.

White, Hayden V. 1978. *Tropics of Discourse: Essays in Cultural Criticism*. Baltimore, Md.: Johns Hopkins University Press.

White, James Boyd. 1984. *When Words Lose their Meaning: Constitutions and Reconstitutions of Language, Character, and Community*. University of Chicago Press.

White, Stephen K. 2009. *The Ethos of a Late-Modern Citizen*. Cambridge, Mass.: Harvard University Press.

Whitman, Walt. 1990. *Leaves of Grass*, ed. Jerome Loving. Oxford University Press.

Whitman, Walt, and Peter Coviello. 2004. *Memoranda During the War*. New York: Oxford University Press.

Williams, Bernard Arthur Owen. 1993. *Shame and Necessity*. Berkeley: University of California Press.

Williams, Carolyn. 2004. "Moving Pictures: George Eliot and Melodrama," in *Compassion: The Culture and Politics of an Emotion*, ed. Lauren Gail Berlant. New York: Routledge, 105–144.

Williams, Raymond. 2001 [1966]. "Tragedy and Revolution," in *The Raymond Williams Reader*. Oxford: Blackwell.

Wills, Garry. 2004. "Red Thebes, Blue Thebes," *New York Times* (December 5).

Wilmer, S. E., and Audronė Žukauskaitė, eds. 2010. *Interrogating Antigone in Postmodern Philosophy and Criticism*. New York: Oxford University Press.

Wilson, Emily R. 2004. *Mocked with Death: Tragic Overliving from Sophocles to Milton*. Baltimore, Md.: Johns Hopkins University Press.

Wilson, Josephine. 2009. "Thinice's *Antigone*, Perth Festival," *Real Time Arts*. www.realtimearts.net/article/90/9426.

Winkler, John J. 1989. *The Constraints of Desire: The Anthropology of Sex and Gender in Ancient Greece*. New York: Routledge.

Winkler, John J., and Froma I. Zeitlin, eds. 1990. *Nothing to Do with Dionysos? Athenian Drama in Its Social Context*. Princeton University Press.

Winnington-Ingram, R. P. 1980. *Sophocles: an Interpretation*. Cambridge; New York: Cambridge University Press.

Wise, Jennifer. 2000. Review of *After Dionysus: A Theory of the Tragic* by William Storm, *Comparative Literature*, 52 (3) (Summer), 257–259.

Wittgenstein, Ludwig. 1953. *Philosophical Investigations*. New York: Macmillan.

  2007. *Zettel*, ed. G. E. M. Anscombe and G. H. von Wright. Berkeley: University of California Press.

Wohl, Victoria. 2005. "Tragedy and Feminism," in *A Companion to Tragedy*, ed. Rebecca W. Bushnell. Malden, Mass.: Blackwell, 145–160.

Wolfe, Cary. 2010. *What is Posthumanism?* Minneapolis: University of Minnesota Press.

Wood, Nancy. 1999. *Vectors of Memory: Legacies of Trauma in Postwar Europe*. Oxford: Berg.

Worthen, W. B. 2008. "Antigone's Bones," *TDR: The Drama Review* 52 (3): 10–33.

Wyatt-Brown, Bertram. 2001. "William Styron's *Sophie's Choice*: Poland, the South, and the Tragedy of Suicide," *The Southern Literary Journal* 34 (1): 56–67.

Wyndham, John. 1955. *The Chrysalids*. London: Michael Joseph.

Youngblood, Stephanie. 2011. "Self-Involved Subjects: The Rhetoric of Testimony in Contemporary American Literature." Ph.D. Dissertation, University of Wisconsin-Madison.

Zajko, Vanda, and Miriam Leonard, eds. 2006. *Laughing with Medusa: Classical Myth and Feminist Thought*. Oxford; New York: Oxford University Press.

Zeitlin, Froma I. 1985. "Playing the Other: Theater, Theatricality, and the Feminine in Greek Drama," *Representations* 11: 63–94.

  1990. "Introduction," in *Nothing to Do with Dionysos? Athenian Drama in Its Social Context*, ed. John J. Winkler and Froma I. Zeitlin. Princeton University Press, 3–11.

  1996. *Playing the Other: Gender and Society in Classical Greek Literature*. University of Chicago Press.

Ziolkowski, Theodore. 1997. *The Mirror of Justice: Literary Reflections of Legal Crises*. Princeton University Press.

Žižek, Slavoj. 1989. *The Sublime Object of Ideology*. London: Verso.

1993. *Tarrying with the Negative: Kant, Hegel, and the Critique of Ideology.* Durham, NC: Duke University Press.

2000. "Melancholy and the Act," *Critical Inquiry* 26 (4): 657–681.

2001. *Enjoy Your Symptom! Jacques Lacan in Hollywood and out.* New York: Routledge.

2004. "From Antigone to Joan of Arc," *Helios* 31 (1–2): 51–62.

Zupančič, Alenka. 1998. "Lacan's Heroines: Antigone and Sygne de Coufontaine," *New Formations: A Journal of Culture/Theory/Politics* 35: 109–121.

2000. *Ethics of the Real: Kant, Lacan.* London: Verso.

2003. *The Shortest Shadow: Nietzsche's Philosophy of the Two.* Cambridge, Mass.: MIT Press.

Index

Index